The New International Economic Order

MIT Bicentennial Studies

The Social Impact of the Telephone
Ithiel de Sola Pool, editor

The New International Economic Order: The North-South Debate
Jagdish N. Bhagwati, editor

The New International Economic Order:
The North-South Debate
Jagdish N. Bhagwati, Editor

The MIT Press
Cambridge, Massachusetts, and London, England

This book was set in IBM Composer Press Roman by Techdata Associates
Incorporated, printed on R & E Book and bound in GSB Style 535-34 Deep
Navy by Halliday Lithograph Corporation in the United States of America.

First printing, November 1977
Second printing, January 1978
Third printing, October 1978

Library of Congress Cataloging in Publication Data

Main entry under title:
     The New international economic order.

     (MIT Bicentennial studies ; 2)
     Based largely on a workshop held at MIT in May 1976.
     Includes index.
     1. International economic relations—Congresses. 2. Underdeveloped
areas—Foreign economic relations—Congresses. I. Bhagwati, Jagdish N.,
1934-
HF 1411.N435   382.1   77-7062
ISBN 0-262-02126-9 (hardcover)
ISBN 0-262-52042-7 (paperback)

Contents

MIT Bicentennial Studies Series

As part of its contribution to the celebration of the U.S. Bicentennial, MIT has carried out studies of several social and intellectual aspects of the world we inhabit at the beginning of our third century. Our objective has been to inquire how human beings might deal more intelligently and humanely with these factors, most of which are closely linked to developments in science and technology.

The papers prepared for these inquiries are being published in a MIT Bicentennial Studies Series of which this volume is a part. Other studies in the series deal with the future of computing and information processing, linguistics and cognitive psychology, the social impact of the telephone, administrative and economic factors in air pollution, and world change and world security.

It is our hope that these volumes will be of interest and value to those concerned now with these questions and, additionally, might provide useful historical perspective to those concerned with the same or similar questions on occasion of the U.S. Tricentennial.

Jerome B. Wiesner

Preface

This volume grew out of a workshop held at MIT in May 1976 on specific proposals and desirable response by developed countries to the demands of the less developed countries for a new international economic order.

The objective was to bring together the most distinguished international and developmental economists from the developed countries to examine the specifics of several specific proposals, some novel and others already in the mill, which could form the concrete content of a reformed world economy. To improve the meaningfulness of the discussions, some eminent economists from the less developed countries, as also noted political scientists with interest in the area, were invited.

The volume contains nearly all of the papers presented at the workshop, and a substantial fraction of the discussants' comments. The majority of the papers deal with specific proposals, often in a manner that should be accessible to nonprofessional readers as well. The editorial introduction (Chapter 1) and the panel discussion at the end of the volume, however, are far more general treatments of the underlying political economy of the North-South debate that has grown up around the issue of the new international economic order and provide the general context into which the discussions of the specific proposals must be set and assessed.

Thanks are due to the Ford Foundation for having provided generous financial support which made the workshop possible; to Peter Ruof of the Ford Foundation for substantial help in making the workshop successful; to Norman Dahl who helped to make this into an MIT bicentennial event; to him and Merry Bouscaren for assistance with the organization of the Workshop; and to Katherine Eisenhaure and Suzana Barros for secretarial assistance over a protracted period before, during, and after the Workshop. Mark Machina and Robert Dohner have assisted greatly with the editing of the volume and with research underlying the editorial introduction. It should also be mentioned that the papers by Gale Johnson, Sarris and Taylor, and Bhagwati appeared in a Special Symposium issue of the Oxford journal, *World Development*, December 1976; and that the editorial introduction will appear, with minor changes, in Japanese as part of the proceedings of the Nihon Keizai Shimbun Centennial Conference, held in October 1976.

J.N.B.

Contributors

C. Fred Bergsten is Assistant Secretary for International Affairs, U.S. Treasury, and Assistant for International Economic Affairs to the National Security Council. Dr. Bergsten's latest books include *American Multi-Nationals and American Interests* (1977, with Thomas Horst and Theodore Moran), *The Dilemmas of the Dollar: The Economics and Politics of United States International Monetary Policy* (1976), and *Toward a New International Economic Order: Selected Papers of C. Fred Bergsten, 1972-1974* (1975). He is a member of the editorial boards of *Foreign Affairs, International Organization*, and the *Journal of International Economics*.

Jagdish N. Bhagwati is Ford International Professor of Economics at the Massachusetts Institute of Technology.

Hollis Chenery is a vice president (Economics Department) of the World Bank and Professor of Economics at Harvard University. His many, influential publications are principally in the field of development and planning.

Richard N. Cooper is Under Secretary of State for Economic Affairs, U.S. State Department. He has worked for the President's Council of Economic Advisers, the United States State Department, and the National Security Council. He has written *The Economics of Interdependence, Economic Mobility and National Economic Policy*, and numerous other works.

John Edelman is an economist with the World Bank.

Isaiah Frank has been, since 1963, the William L. Clayton Professor of International Economics at The Johns Hopkins University School of Advanced International Studies. Previously he held various senior economic posts in the U.S. Department of State including that of Deputy Assistant Secretary for Economic Affairs. A recipient of the Rockefeller Public Service Award, he has also been a consultant to the U.S. Treasury, the World Bank, UNCTAD, and the Committee for Economic Development. His writings include books and articles in the field of international economic policy.

Koichi Hamada is Associate Professor of Economics at the University of Tokyo, Japan. His extensive theoretical contributions include research on international trade and finance. He is an associate editor of the *Journal of International Economics*.

Gerry Helleiner is Professor of Economics at the University of Toronto. He has been Director, Economic Research Bureau, Dar es Salaam, Tanzania, and Visiting Research Fellow, Nigerian Institute of Social and Economic Research and Institute of Development Studies, Sussex. He has recently edited *A World Divided: The Less Developed Countries in the International Economy* (Cambridge, 1976).

Nurul Islam was Professor of Economics at Dacca between 1955 and 1963, Director of the Institute of Development Economics in Pakistan between 1964 and 1971, and Deputy Chairman of the Bangladesh Planning Commission between 1972 and 1975. Since 1975 he has been a Visiting Fellow at Queen Elizabeth House, as well as at St. Antony's College, Oxford University. He is the author of numerous books and articles on economic development, planning, and international economic policies and problems.

D. Gale Johnson is the Eliakim Hastings Moore Distinguished Service Professor of Economics and Provost of the University of Chicago. He has written extensively on national and world agricultural policies and on world food problems and has served on committees of the National Academy of Sciences dealing with agricultural productivity and world food and nutrition problems.

Harry G. Johnson, F.B.A., F.R.S.C., has been Professor of Economics at the University of Manchester, the University of Chicago, the London School of Economics, and the Graduate Institute of International Studies. He is the author of eighteen books, including *Economic Policies toward Less Developed Countries*, and has written over 500 articles in economics.

Alexandre Kafka represents Brazil, Colombia, the Dominican Republic, Guyana, Haiti, Panama, Peru, as well as Trinidad and Tobago in the International Monetary Fund and was a vice-chairman of the Deputies of Committee (of Twenty) for the Reform of the International Monetary System from 1972 to 1974.

Peter B. Kenen is the Walker Professor of International Finance at Princeton University and was Professor of Economics and Provost at Columbia University. He has published extensively on the theory and econometrics of international trade and finance.

Charles P. Kindleberger is Emeritus Ford International Professor of Economics and Senior Lecturer, Massachusetts Institute of Technology. His research and publications are in international economics, particularly international financial relations, and in European economic history. His most recent books are *The World in Depression, 1929-1939* and, as joint editor with Tamir Agmon, *Multinationals from Small Countries* (MIT Press, 1977).

I. M. D. Little's major publications have included *A Critique of Welfare Economics*, 1950; *International Aid* (with J. M. Clifford), 1965; *Industry and*

Trade in Some Developing Countries (with M. FG. Scott and T. Scitovsky), 1970; and *Project Appraisal and Planning for Developing Countries* (with J. A. Mirrlees), 1974. He has been a Fellow of Nuffield College, Oxford, since 1952, was Deputy Director of the Economic Section, HM Treasury, 1953-1955, Vice President of the OECD Development Centre, 1965-1967, and Professor of the Economics of Underdeveloped Countries, Oxford, 1971-1975. He is currently a special adviser at the World Bank.

Erik Lundberg is Professor of Economics at the Stockholm School of Economics and is also Director of the Institute for International Economic Studies, Stockholm. Among his contributions are works on business cycles and fluctuations.

Stephen Magee is Professor of Economics at the University of Texas, Austin. He has contributed extensively to the theory and econometrics of international trade and finance and has recently published *International Trade and Distortions in Factor Markets*. He is an associate editor of the *Journal of International Economics*.

Harald Malmgren is Professor of Business and Public Administration, George Washington University, and at present associated with The Hudson Institute. Formerly, he was Ambassador, and the U.S. Deputy Special Representative for Trade Negotiations. In this latter capacity he served as chief trade negotiator for the U.S. government.

Ali Mazrui is a noted African political scientist, formerly teaching at Kampala and now Professor at the University of Michigan. Recently, he has written extensively on world order problems.

Gardner Patterson is Deputy Director-General, Trade Policy, at the General Agreement on Tariffs and Trade in Geneva. Before joining the GATT in 1969, Patterson was for many years Professor of Economics and International Affairs at Princeton University.

Alexander Sarris is Assistant Professor of Economics in the Department of Agricultural Economics at the University of California, Berkeley.

Robert M. Solow is an Institute Professor at the Massachusetts Institute of Technology and an internationally renowned economic theorist, with contributions chiefly in the theory of growth, capital, and technical change.

Paul Streeten is Warden of Queen Elizabeth House, Director of the Institute of Commonwealth Studies, and a Fellow of Balliol College, Oxford. He is on leave, working with the Development Policy Staff of the World Bank. He was a director of the Commonwealth Development Corporation and a member of the Royal Commission on Environmental Pollution.

Lance Taylor is Professor of Economics and Nutrition at the Massachusetts

Institute of Technology. He is the editor of the *Journal of Development Economics* and the author of numerous articles in professional journals on development and planning theory and policy.

John Williamson has been a Professor at the University of Warwick since 1970. From 1968-1970 he worked in the UK Treasury on a range of external economic questions, and from 1972-1974 he held a temporary appointment at the International Monetary Fund that involved work on international monetary reform in the Committee of Twenty. His articles include a survey on "International Liquidity" in the *Economic Journal*, September 1973, and a book arising from his period in the IMF, entitled *The Failure of World Monetary Reform, 1971-74*, is soon to be published.

The New International Economic Order

Introduction
Jagdish N. Bhagwati

North-South economic relations, three decades after the decline of colonial empires and the emergence of new developing countries on the international scene, have come to the forefront of international economics and politics. The concerted demands of the South for a new international economic order (NIEO), and the problems they raise for the North in setting the stage for negotiations on concrete proposals related to the NIEO, now define the agenda, as well as the political climate, of the numerous conferences and intergovernmental negotiating groups on international economic matters.[1]

In assessing North-South relations and their prospects and in suggesting the optimal reforms NIEO demands should and can sensibly (in terms of political feasibility) be directed to, a historical perspective is essential. It is necessary to trace the evolution of the economic and political philosophy of the developing countries that currently animates and conditions their views of the current international economic order and prompts their demands for changes therein.

Developing Countries: Shifting Postures

In fact, the present postures of the developing countries can be traced to three factors.

1. A substantial shift has occurred in the developing countries' perception of the gains to be had from economic relations with the developed countries under the existing rules of the game; the shift has been toward the gloomier side.

2. At the same time, the developing countries now perceive their own economic and hence political power vis-à-vis the developed countries to be sufficiently substantial to warrant a strategy of effective "trade unionism" to change the rules of the game and thereby to wrest a greater share of the world's wealth and income.

3. Finally, a straightforward political desire to participate more effectively in decision making on international economic matters is now evident: this is the "populist" aspect of the current situation.[2] Participation is thus demanded, not merely to ensure that the developing countries' interests are safeguarded but equally as an assertion of their rights as members of an international community and as a desired feature of a just international order.

A correct appreciation of each of these striking new aspects of the Southern postures is critical for a proper evaluation of the prospects for improved South-North collaboration on international economic issues.

Shifts in Perception of Existing International Economic Order[3]

The developing countries are linked to the developed countries through trade, aid, investment, and migration. The central issue for them is whether these links work to their detriment or advantage. Several ideologies compete for attention on this question; the influential policymakers in a number of developing countries have moved from more cheerful to gloomier ideologies as they have progressively made more forceful demands for changes in the world economic order.

The ideology that has traditionally been dominant is aptly characterized as that of "benign neglect"—links with the rich nations create benefits for the poor nations. This view of the world economy parallels the utilitarian economists' view that the invisible hand works to promote universal well-being. In this model, the laissez-faire view that private greed will produce public good translates on the international scene into the notion that, while the different actors in the world economy pursue their own interests, the result will nonetheless be to benefit the developing countries. Thus, while multinational corporations invest in these countries to make profits, they will increase these countries' incomes, diffuse technology, and harness their domestic savings.[4] The exchange of commodities and services in trade will reflect the principle of division of labor and hence bring gains from trade to these countries.[5] The migration of skilled labor, instead of constituting a troublesome brain drain, will help to remove impediments to progress such as inadequate remuneration of the educated elite.[6]

In direct contrast to this classical economic viewpoint, there is the doctrine of "malign neglect" which views the impact of these links between the rich and the poor nations as primarily detrimental to the latter group. In the apt description of Osvaldo Sunkel, integration of the developing countries in the international economy leads to their domestic disintegration. This doctrine also supports the economic notion, used extensively by the Swedish economists Knut Wicksell and Gunnar Myrdal, of growing disequilibrium and exploding sequences, rather than the classical notions of equilibrium. Thus, multinational corporations disrupt domestic salary structures by introducing islands of high-income jobs that cause exorbitant wage demands by others seeking to keep up with the Joneses in the multinationals. International trade leads to the perpetuation of the role of developing countries as producers of primary, unsophisticated products that relegate them to a secondary and inferior position in the international division of labor. Furthermore, in the classic Prebisch thesis, the terms of trade of the primary-product-exporting developing countries have declined and will continue to do so, conferring gains on the developed and inflicting losses on the developing countries.[7] The brain drain to the developed countries deprives the developing countries of scarce skills and the talents that make economic progress possible.[8] The attractions of Western standards of living make domestic setting of priorities and raising of savings difficult if not impossible.

These "malign neglect" views are merely the logical extension of the disenchantment with the "benign neglect" model. This disenchantment initially took the form of complaints that, instead of diffusing development, the links with the international economy were of no consequence to the developing countries. Thus, the early revisionist critics of foreign investment argued that these investments led to enclaves and had little genuine impact on the developing countries: the latter remained in consequence at the periphery of the world economy.[9] As Naipaul remarks wryly in his *Guerrillas*, "Tax holidays had been offered to foreign investors; many had come for the holidays and had then moved on elsewhere."[10] The "malign neglect" school takes this revisionism to its logical extreme and turns the argument on its head by claiming that the trouble with foreign investment is not that it makes no impact on the national economies of the developing countries because of its enclave nature but rather that it does and that this impact is adverse.

Also contrasting with these models are the two major ideological positions that focus not on the impact of the links but rather their intended objectives. Thus, the "benign intent" school of thought, to which the "white man's burden" philosophy belongs, considers the international links and institutions to be designed so as to transmit benefits to the poor nations. Private investment is regarded as motivated by the desire to spread the fruits of modern technology and enterprise to the developing countries. In particular, the foreign aid programs are conceived as humanitarian in origin, reflecting the Western ideals of liberalism and the enlightened objective of sharing the world's resources with the poor countries.

The polar opposite of this model is the "malign intent" view of the world, typically favored by the Marxist and New Left writings on the international economy. Foreign aid is seen as a natural extension of the imperialist designs on the poor nations aimed at creating dependence.[11] Private investments, following the flag in past models, are seen now as precursors of the flag, with brazen colonialism replaced by devious neocolonialism.[12]

Clearly, none of these models in their pure form capture the full complexity of the effects that the links with the outside world have on the developing countries' prospects for economic progress. However, it is clear that policy makers in several developing countries have moved over the three postwar decades from a world view based primarily on the benign neglect and intent models to one characterized more by varying shades of the malign neglect and intent models.

Thus, the early posturing of these countries was based on the view that the existing mechanisms governing trade and investment flows were primarily beneficial. Furthermore, aside from utilizing and expanding trade opportunities and attracting foreign investment funds, the developing countries could appeal to the developed countries on a purely moral plane for the provision of technical assistance and foreign aid for developmental programs. These premises were the basis for the first UNCTAD conference in Geneva in 1964, which led to a permanent creation of the UNCTAD secretariat and its eventual emergence as the principal forum for airing the problems of the developing countries.

UNCTAD I at Geneva and UNCTAD II at New Delhi thus concentrated primarily on defining and underlining aid targets for the developed countries, while laying principal stress on two aspects of trade policy: preferential access by developing countries into the markets of the developed countries, and the principle of nonreciprocity.

The trade efforts were to bear fruit, yielding to the developing countries the satisfaction of having utilized collective action at UNCTAD to some advantage. This advantage, however, was rather small; in retrospect, it is evident that the grant of preferential entry by the EEC and by other developed countries, including the United States in 1975, has been of limited value because of numerous exceptions and because of the importance of nontariff barriers to which it did not extend.[13] As for the principle of nonreciprocity, it is now increasingly obvious that the developing countries probably threw away the main instrument that governments have at their command to lower their own trade barriers—the ability to tell their protected industries that the protection must be reduced as part of the reciprocal bargaining process. Recent studies on the·foreign trade regimes of the developing countries have shown[14] that the degree and dispersion of the protection enjoyed by the industries of these countries have been disturbing; a continuation of reciprocity would have been most useful if effectively used by willing governments in the developing countries.[15]

The principal disappointments were to be in the field of international aid flows. The developing countries were faced with the incongruous contrast between the UNCTAD targets on foreign aid and the declining overall flows from the leading aid donors, particularly the United States, once the leader of the enlightened donors. Not merely were nominal aid flows decelerating, but their real worth was falling with inflation. It was increasingly clear that their worth was seriously reduced by practices such as aid-tying, which compelled the aid recipients to buy from the donor countries at artificially high prices. Their worth was further reduced because few of the aid funds were anything but loans to be repaid and hence were substantially less by way of genuine aid transfers than the publicized figures implied.[16]

Aside from the failure to meet the obligations which the developed countries appeared to have endorsed, however reluctantly, at international forums such as the UNCTAD, there was also an emerging sense that the declining efforts at international assistance were a reflection of the steady thaw in superpower relations. Thus, it became increasingly difficult to maintain that humanitarian motives, rather than the political necessities of the Cold War, were the major motivating factors behind the aid programs of the 1950s. These cynical perceptions of the aid efforts of the developed world were only to be reinforced by the misguided attempts at enforcing performance criteria in aid distribution. Typically, the aid donors, following economically wise but politically foolish precepts, insisted on examining and endorsing the entire set of economic policies of the recipient nations to ensure that their meager aid assistance was being utilized to advantage,[17] thereby generating resentments and charges of calculated attempts at imposing ideological solutions in the guise of "scientific" economic prescriptions.[18]

The confirmation of covert political interventions in the developing countries, euphemistically described as destabilization operations, engineered by developed countries from which one expected better behavior, often prompted and encouraged by multinational corporations (such as the ITT in Chile), must have helped in strengthening the radical theses regarding the Northern designs and impact on the South.

The growing sense that the benign intent and impact of the developed countries on the well-being of the developing countries could not be taken as the natural order of things under the existing international arrangements was finally to be accentuated and reinforced from yet another direction. The focus during the 1950s on the "gap" in the incomes, living standards, and wealth of the developing and the developed countries and on the gearing of international targets to narrowing and eventually eliminating such differences, was probably helpful in lending animation to the development decades and the attendant programs for developing countries. But it was also to lead inevitably to frustration—such gaps cannot possibly be narrowed in any significant manner in the foreseeable future despite any optimism as to the prospects of the developing countries' growth rates.[19] Thus, despite the fact that the developing countries, as a group, grew at the historically remarkable rate of 5.5 percent per annum during the first development decade of the 1960s, the awareness grew that these rates of growth could neither help measurably in "catching up" with the developed countries nor could they adequately diffuse the fruits of growth to the poor in the developing countries.[20] Poverty, both absolute at home and relative vis-à-vis the developed countries, thus seemed to be inescapable under the existing economic regimes. As a result, as far as domestic policies are concerned the intellectuals have turned increasingly to distributive implications of their developmental programs: the faith in the "trickle-down" process has been badly shattered. At the international level the implication is again for distribution: it is felt now that the growth rates of the poor countries, no matter how rapid, have to be supplemented by increasing transfers of resources on a simple, progressive argument. It is a question of a *moral* imperative that the world's limited wealth and incomes be shared more equitably. This is only the international counterpart of the sociological fact that as access to affluence diminishes, the resentment of success increases and the stress on redistribution is keener. For example, the greater American mobility surely explains the lack of success of socialist doctrines there whereas the social and economic rigidity of the British society explains the stresses on the social contract that are quite evident in their macroeconomic failures. The erosion of faith since the 1950s in the ability of the developing countries to catch up with the developed countries has surely contributed to their present "trade unionist" demands for greater shares in world income through the creation of a new international economic order.[21]

Post-OPEC Emphasis on Collective Action: The Rise of "Trade Unionism"

It was against the backdrop of this slow but inevitable shift in many developing countries' world view that the dramatic event of the successful cartelization of oil producers, nearly all members of the Third World, was to materialize. The OPEC had existed for a number of years prior to its dramatic success since 1973, but practically no serious analyst had considered its success probable. Indeed, my colleague Morris Adelman had the singular misfortune of writing a superb analysis of the oil industry, predicated entirely on the assumption that OPEC would not succeed, and having it published just as this basic assumption was being falsified![22]

The Third World's reaction to the nearly sevenfold rise in oil prices and the accentuation of the resource and foreign exchange difficulties of many of the poorer nations among the Third World, was to baffle the rich nations that sought to mobilize the poor against the OPEC. The developing countries refused to condemn, and indeed seemed to take great delight in, the oil price increases. This reaction can only be understood in light of the shifts in their views about the rich nations. Clearly there was a need for prudence vis-à-vis the nouveaux riches to whom the developing countries would have to turn for aid. But, far more than that, the developing countries seemed to feel that finally there was one dramatic instance of a set of primary producers in the Third World who were able to get a "fair share" of the world incomes by their own actions rather than by the unproductive route of morally persuading the rich nations for fairer shares. Even while many of them suffered from the fallout of the oil price increases, many developing countries therefore felt a sense of solidarity, a corps d'esprit with the OPEC countries and the exhilarating sense that they could finally take their economic destiny in their own hands. Thus, the stage was to be set psychologically and politically for the present phase of "trade unionist" militancy. The nascent sense that collective action, as crystallized in the developing countries' Group of 77 and the activities at UNCTAD, could yield some results (such as the schemes for preferential entry), was now to be transformed into an act of faith: solidarity in international bargaining, alternatively termed "collective self-reliance," on a variety of fronts would yield much more than had ever been thought possible.

The OPEC success crystallized the concepts of strength through collective action and "solidarity rather than charity." The developing countries also seemed to infer from the OPEC experience that their commodity exports, which had traditionally been viewed as a sign of weakness, could be turned instead into weapons of collective action. Thus, the notion of "commodity power" emerged and has shaped not merely the politics but also the economics of the demands for NIEO (as typified by the Corea plan for commodities at the UNCTAD).

Populism
The OPEC example was also to hold the further attraction that, contrary to aid flows (whether bilateral or multilateral), the earning of the new resources through improved terms of trade implied that the OPEC countries retained their national sovereignty in deciding how to spend these resources and also began to qualify as nations that commanded some voice in the management of international monetary affairs and therefore in other deliberations on the world economic regime as well.

Many developing countries, seeking both the assertion of fuller national sovereignty over their economic programs and increased participation in international deliberations on trade, aid, and monetary rules, thus saw the OPEC as an ideal case which they would hope to emulate.

The foregoing analysis underlines the complex nature of the current attitudes and demands of the developing countries while defining the limits within which the amicable evolution of a new international economic order will have to be defined. Several major points must be stressed.

1. Our analysis shows that the developing countries' objectives are economic and political. The economic objective is principally to increase their share of the world's income and wealth. The political objectives are that they should have better control over the use of these and their own resources and that they should also be allowed to participate actively in devising the new rules for managing world trade, aid, and monetary and other matters of global concern. Needless to say all of these objectives may not be in harmony; it may be possible to get more resources transferred if their use is not entirely within the prerogative of the recipient country—a conflict that is quite important in practice. However, these objectives do exist manifestly; the twin political objectives are the new elements on the scene, as compared with the 1950s and 1960s.

2. The developing countries' assessment of their capacity to achieve these objectives is grounded in their assessment of their capacity for collective action. There is some evidence that the early optimism about the use of commodity power has receded: except for bauxite, the results of collective cartelization seem to have borne little fruit. This should, in fact, have been expected from a realistic assessment of commodity markets since oil is a very special case with exceedingly low elasticities, considerable macro effects, and

no real parallel for other commodities. The "commodity power" that exists, outside of oil, is therefore only a short run, disruptive power; it may be currently exercised to some advantage[23] but is certainly self-destructing through high elasticities of substitution and through the use of augmented inventory policies by the developed countries (such as those proposed recently in the United States for certain raw materials).

Interestingly therefore the emphasis has shifted from the proposed use of weak and essentially short run "commodity power" to improve prices to pressuring the consuming developed countries to collaborate in the raising of the prices of these commodities to "fair" levels; this "indexing" idea parallels the domestic U.S. parity program for agriculture.[24] As Kindleberger has remarked, this is tantamount to asking the chicken to help in plucking its own feathers! And yet, the idea is not quite absurd; the developing countries now see their power not as accruing from commodities per se but rather from their capacity to create confrontations and impede agreements on a variety of global concerns such as the Law of the Sea. Thus, commodities today have become a chief vehicle through which the developing countries want resources transferred via increased prices, this increase being forced by the use of political power rather than the use of admittedly small commodity power.

3. It should finally be noted that the new affluence of the OPEC countries has already split the Third World into the Third and Fourth Worlds, the former being almost wholly the OPEC developing countries and the latter the rest. The two worlds have managed to collaborate effectively. Thus, the OPEC nations have extended credits and aid on a massive scale to the developing countries while also championing their cause politically.[25] As Fred Bergsten has noted, the OPEC countries managed to get developmental NIEOtype issues included on the agenda by withdrawing from the first ministerial session of the "energy dialogue" in Paris in April 1975. They also successfully pushed for further liberalization of IMF credits at Kingston in January 1976 by linking the usability of their currencies directly to liberalization of the credit tranches and by prompting the liberalization of the compensatory finance facility through their negotiating strategy in Paris.[26] Thus, far from compromising the collective action potential of the developing countries, the emergence of the more powerful OPEC countries has only served to increase the political potential for collective action by the developing countries.

4. In fact, the specific demands of the developing countries for institutional reform in the international economic order clearly reflect both the new objectives and the new political and economic realities that the oil price increases have imposed on the poor countries. Few of the current demands for specific reforms are entirely novel, but the choice of those that have been highlighted at UNCTAD IV and propagated at other forums is revealing. Two principal proposals have been the *Integrated Programme for Commodities*, christened the Corea Plan after the UNCTAD Secretary-General, and the demand for general *debt relief*.

The debt relief proposal would eliminate the accumulated debt burden, which many of the poorer developing countries find particularly onerous after the terms of trade losses from the increased oil prices. The elimination of this burden would provide for a transfer of resources (measurable as the present discounted value of the repayments canceled) in a form that is free of strings and high on the sovereignty scale. Generalized debt relief would also be politically and psychologically reinforcing to the developing countries because bilateral debt reliefs have usually been accompanied by extensive scrutiny and provisions by the creditor nations. Similarly the Integrated Programme for Commodities would also appear to do extremely well in light of the three objectives that were distinguished. Indexing of commodity prices (implied by the phrase "establishment and maintenance of commodity prices at levels which, in real terms, are . . . remunerative to producers"[27]) would yield transfer of resources by suitably raising them and maintaining them there. Indexing would mean that the developing countries had earned these increased incomes and therefore their national sovereignty over them would have been guaranteed. By participating in the arrangements designed to run these schemes, the developing countries would have earned the right to deliberate in international policy making in this sphere of international economic management.

Developed Countries: Factors Affecting Response

While these two proposals do not constitute the totality of the demands made by the developing countries nor have they been pushed with continuing vigor by the developing countries since UNCTAD IV—in fact, the demand for a generalized debt relief or moratorium has, if anything, lost ground within the Group of 77 itself and the Group of 24 at the Fund/Bank Manila meetings in the fall of 1976 avoided or even repudiated the subject altogether—they do illustrate the problems that the present aspirations and postures of the developing countries pose for the developed countries as the latter contemplate the nature of their response to the demands for the NIEO.

In particular, there are two dimensions to these proposals that are guaranteed to make the response to them lukewarm, if not hostile, in the United States: the developed country whose consent is critical to orderly adoption of such proposals, as it clearly constitutes a *force majeure* on the international economic scene. These dimensions relate to sovereignty and efficiency, both of which can add up to an ideological confrontation that will have to be cooled, if not circumvented, to usher in reforms in the international economic system.

Sovereignty

While the developing countries have come to stress the sovereignty over the use of their (and the transferred) resources, the rise of intellectual neoconservatism in the United States has tended to move the aid philosophy precisely in the opposite direction. To the exaggerated complaints about the misuse and inefficiency of aid programs, one must now add the moral concern that the developing countries suppress civil liberties and oppress their populations and that therefore aid cannot be justified any longer on "humanitarian" or progressive principles; the latter should apply to transfers between individuals, not governments.

Indeed, in the year of Adam Smith's bicentennial, it must be sadly admitted that the invisible hand has yielded to the iron fist in a number of developing countries. However, the neoconservative inference that therefore resources should not be provided to developing countries' governments on progressive principles is a nonsequitur.

The nation state, as an entity that transposes itself between individuals in the developing and the developed countries, cannot be wished away; world order therefore must surely be defined in terms of morality as between nations. Moreover, the freewheeling description of developing countries as dictatorships and tyrannies is an exaggeration and self-righteously ignores the moral lapses of the developed countries themselves.[28] In defining the new international economic order, it would therefore seem perfectly legitimate to apply the progressive tax principles to nation states, none of which is characterized by moral perfection and few of which can ever share a common perception of morality in all its dimensions.

However, the neoconservative arguments do have a superficial appeal, especially in the United States where Vietnam and Watergate have crystallized a psychological need for assertion of moral values in policy making. Thus the argument that "we cannot allow ourselves to be pushed around and lectured into giving aid to an undeserving, corrupt Third World" has several adherents in fashionable intellectual circles in the United States.[29] This attitude of hostility to the developing countries has been reinforced by the subtle but propagandistic caricaturing of the positions of developing countries in regard to the New International Economic Order by conservatives and neoconservatives alike in the United States. *Ignoratio elenchi* is a favorite fallacy of intellectuals who are prominent, rather than eminent; it works very well in its intended purpose, but it must be exposed. In particular, it has been argued that the developing countries wish to establish "Western guilt" for their own underdevelopment; thus developing countries seek transfers of resources as reparations for past and present damage to their economic success. On the other hand, no such guilt can be established since internal institutional changes are critical for development and account for the growth of countries; hence the demands for the NIEO are ill founded and must be rejected. This argument would be laughable were it not so superficially plausible, effective, and pernicious.[30] The argument for progressive redistribution of income and wealth does not rest on whether the rich have hurt the poor in the past or are currently doing so. Nor are the majority of the intellectuals in the developing countries so naive as to assume that the colonial rule was necessarily harmful economically; what many do challenge is the opposite thesis of the imperialist historical school that the colonial rule was necessarily beneficial. Moreover, the critical nature of internal reform for rapid economic advance is logically compatible with the importance of external factors in shaping both the nature and the momentum of domestic development. Moreover, the many developing countries that launched five-year plans designed to direct principally domestic efforts at development and many of their left wing intellectuals (who ridiculed Western economists' naivete about the ease with which foreign aid programs would take the developing countries to "self sustained" growth without radical internal reforms) would both (for different reasons) find the present lecturing by these Western intellectuals on the role of domestic reforms to be astonishing, and the inference that the external environment needs no fundamental changes to be a self-serving nonsequitur.

Turning from the conservative and neoconservative arguments, we must note next that the few remaining liberals who favor resource transfers to the developing countries on an increased scale remain untutored by the two important historical lessons of aid giving. First, economics rarely gives unique solutions *ex ante*—when you had six economists including Keynes, a witticism went, you had seven opinions—so that imposing donor-country economic solutions on recipient countries must often require an act of missionary zeal and faith. And second, local constraints on political action, much like in the donor countries, will often require the adoption of nth-best policies, contrary to the desires of the unconstrained policy advisers. They continue to see the application of strict, overall, economywide performance criteria as essential to a foreign aid policy. Experience points to the infeasibility of having such criteria scientifically and to the general inability to find such criteria. Assuming that consensus could be reached on what was the optimal policy to adopt in the first place, it would be impossible to apply such criteria meaningfully in light of local constraints. Thus, witness the following argument by Richard Cooper, an influential international economist of liberal persuasion and now at the center of U.S. policy making:[31]

If we are to justify resource transfers on ethical grounds, then, it must be on the basis of knowledge that via one mechanism or another the transferred resources will benefit those residents of the recipient countries that are clearly worse off than the worst-off "taxed" (including taxes levied implicitly through commodity prices) residents of the donor countries. That is, general transfers must be based on some kind of performance criterion satisfied by the recipient country, or else transfers should be made only in a form that benefits directly those who the ethical arguments suggest should be benefited. But this proposition has profound implications, . . . for it implies that no completely general transfer of resources from country to country can be supported on ethical grounds. This restriction would encompass the organic SDR link, general debt relief, actions to improve (not merely stabilize) the terms of trade of developing countries, and a brain drain tax that automatically remit the revenues to developing countries. Ethically based transfers should discriminate among recipient countries on the basis of performance in improving, directly or indirectly, the well-being of their general population, and/or they should discriminate among uses of the transfers to maximize the flow of benefits to those who are the intended beneficiaries, which generally means concentration on general nutrition, health care, and education in the recipient countries.

While this quote speaks for itself, one might note particularly that emphasis on nutrition, education, and health care leaves open important issues of the type that have traditionally created friction between recipients and donors on the utilization of aid and hence problems regarding national sovereignty. What should be the balance between these three areas? How much in total, by way of current and investment expenditures, should be allocated to the three sectors together? What should be the time profile of benefits provided in these sectors, given the limited volume of resources? Within education, what should be the allocation to education at different levels and in different geographical areas? All of these questions raise both economic and political issues and involve issues of intertemporal allocations of costs and benefits; in none of these cases does an analyst have any ability to proceed without making several value judgments and not simply economic behavioral assumptions. No wonder that the overly sensitive developing countries have occasionally felt that the zeal of the donor-country economist and his value-unfree (in Nobel laureate Gunnar Myrdal's sense) recommendations, which are to be imposed by arm twisting at the aid-consortia meetings, disguise not just economic naivete but also ideological intentions.

Whether one takes the neoconservative or the liberal position, the fact remains that the developing countries' growing insistence on sovereignty in the use of resources conflicts increasingly with the preferred stress of the intellectuals in the United States on evaluation of economic performance, on monitoring, and on the morality of their internal and even international conduct. The dilemma therefore is that, while the developing countries by and large have centralized political regimes and are able to formulate and coordinate their demands for resource transfers, the developed countries generally have democratic, decentralized regimes where resource transfers must be justified to the electorates. These transfers cannot be defended when the neoconservative position assiduously tries to undercut the moral case for such actions and the liberal case is undermined by the insistence on performance criteria that are now sought to be rejected by the developing countries seeking sovereignty. If only the developing countries had the democratic political regimes and the developed countries the centralized ones, the dilemma would disappear!

This dilemma obtains chiefly in the United States, and far less so in the European countries and in Japan. In fact, Erik Lundberg has observed that in Sweden, uneasiness over the political conditions in several developing countries has not, as in the United States, been taken to rationalize a neoconservative position of opting out of aid; rather the Swedish political parties have unanimously agreed that the aid transfers are a moral obligation and the

The interesting issues from an economist's viewpoint concern the desirable dimensions, in the form of concrete reform proposals, that the ongoing North-South negotiations should impart to the new international economic order. The record of the developing countries in finding and backing imaginative proposals, as is evident in the foregoing analysis, is not exactly exciting, nor have the developed countries put sufficient energy and initiative into developing a coherent and imaginative response to the specific demands of the developed countries.[37] In short, an overall categorization of desirable targets for the architects of the new international economic order is still to be evolved.

In my view, such a delineation must rest on a judicious combination of two major principles of reform: (1) the developing countries must receive an increased share of resources under the NIEO; and (2) bargains must be struck which are mutually profitable and which therefore appeal also to the developed countries' interests in areas of trade policy, regulation of multi-nationals, transfer of technology, migration, and food policy. By focusing on the transfer-of-resources proposals that can raise substantial resources *while circumventing the objections in the developed countries to the autonomous use of such resources by the developing countries*, (as can be done), and by appealing to the interests of all concerned parties through the mutual gain proposals (that can indeed be developed) in several different areas of international economic policy, the NIEO can be made a reality that accommodates the major political preferences and economic objectives of the developing and the developed countries. These two principles may now be developed briefly by spelling out the major reform proposals that might be entertained under them.

Resource Transfers

There are two proposals that can qualify as raising fairly substantial revenues for developing countries that are least likely to be perfect substitutes for normal aid flows because of the nature of the rationales on which they are justified and also because of the incidence of the revenues within the developed countries; these proposals are also least likely to raise the moral questions that are attached to uncontrolled transfers of resources from the developed to the developing countries.

The first and major proposal relates to the grant of a share in the profits of seabed mining to the developing countries and extending the arrangement further to oceans generally thereby bringing into the net the possible revenues from regulation of "overfishing" as well. Politically, such proposals are less likely to give rise to objections and therefore be more acceptable to developed countries because rights over these resources are still the subject of international negotiation; thus it is difficult to conceive of the allocation of some of the profits or revenues from seabed mining and licensing of overfished fisheries to the developing countries as a simple grant *from* the developed *to* the developing countries. Furthermore, since the regulation of overfishing is an efficiency-improving business (whereas the taxing of seabed mining would be tantamount to taxing rents unless the returns to innovation and risk were also taxed away), the gut reaction of neoclassical economists is to welcome such methods of yielding resources to the developing countries; in such a case one has that rare example of transfers that may even improve welfare (for fishing) and, at worst, not hurt it (for seabed mining).

The Law of the Sea Conference, which has just terminated its fifth session without reaching any agreement, is the forum for transacting such a resource transfer to the developing countries. The developing countries have, to date, held out for far more substantial control of the ocean resources while resisting lucrative offers of revenues as proposed here.[38] In the end, since the major developed countries are poised to mine the seabeds and will probably effectively threaten to continue unilaterally to do so, it is certain that a bargain will be struck and a substantial source of revenues for the developing countries will emerge. Richard Cooper has put together estimates of the sums that could be raised from the oceans and, while they are necessarily rough and ready, they do indicate the orders of magnitude that one is dealing with: by 1985 a full capture of rents on fish at 1974 levels of output could yield $2.2 billion, a 50 percent profits tax on offshore oil coming from waters more than 200 meters deep would yield $2.2 billion, and a 50 percent profits tax on manganese nodules would yield $0.1 billion. This is a total of $4.5 billion in revenues from the oceans.[39] Thus, even if a half of this revenue was allocated to the developing countries in an international oceans bargain, the developing countries would receive over $2 billion worth of revenues as of 1985. These would be characterized by autonomy in use; because they would be untied grants, they would be worth at least twice as much in grant-equivalent terms as an equal aid flow under the average terms would generally imply.

Yet another example of a proposal that would raise resources/revenues for the developing countries is the suggestion of a brain drain tax. The proposal is to levy a supplementary tax on the incomes earned in the developed countries by skilled migrants from the developing countries. The tax would be levied by the developing countries (for legal-constitutional reasons), collected by the developed countries (for administrative reasons), and the revenues would be transferred *en bloc* to the developing countries via the United Nations (the UNDP) for developmental spending.[40] Given the entry restrictions of the developed countries, the tax may be seen as essentially a tax on the rents generated by such quantitative interferences with the international mobility of labor; it would again be consistent with human rights for the identical reason that the countries that create such interferences on human mobility are the developed countries with their immigration quotas. A moral rationale for taxing the immigrants exists, quite aside from the case for taxing rents, and has been spelled out by me elsewhere:[41]

The rationale behind the tax implementation would consist of two arguments; in order of their importance: (1) Firstly, one would assert the moral principle that, in a world of imperfect mobility, those few who manage to get from LDCs into DCs to practice their professions at substantially-improved incomes ought to be asked to contribute a fraction of their gains for the improved welfare of those left behind in the LDCs; this would effectively be extending the usual principle of progressive taxation across national borders. (2) Moreover, since there is a widely-held presumption, based on several sound arguments and embodied in numerous international resolutions, that the brain drain creates difficulties for the LDCs, it would also constitute a simple and rough-and-ready way for the emigrating professionals to compensate the LDCs for these losses. In fact, the moral obligation to share one's gains with those who are unable to share in these gains would be reinforced if these others were also hurt by one's emigration.

The revenues from imposing the brain drain tax have been estimated with some thoroughness and are to be found in Koichi Hamada's contribution to this volume. They add up to half a billion U.S. dollars for 1976. Allowing for inflation at 5 percent to arrive at a figure comparable to Cooper's 1985 oceans-revenue estimate of over $2 billion (at half of the $4.5 billion overall revenue figure, as that allotted to the developing countries), the brain drain tax revenues would exceed a significant sum of $1 billion.

The brain drain tax proposal is based on well-defined moral principles and ought also to appeal to the developed country populations which often feel that the skilled immigrants from the developing countries also ought to make their contribution to their part of the world;[42] the human-rights objections to it are easily dismissed once the proposal is examined in any depth. In addition, the developed country policy makers should realize that the contributions will come from the skilled immigrants as a supplementary tax; hence the revenue is hardly a matter of significant concern for the overall fiscal policy of the developed countries any more than voluntary contributions to foreign countries under the existing U.S. laws are for example. Given the great concern expressed over the brain drain in many developing countries, and Mr. Kissinger's declaration of willingness to do something in the area at UNCTAD IV[43] ("Finally, the United States proposes that appropriate incentives and measures be devised to curb the emigration of highly trained manpower from developing countries."), it seems logical to place a measure such as the brain drain tax on the agenda for the new international economic order.[44]

Mutual-Gain Bargains
While these two examples of significant resource-flow proposals appeal primarily to the gains for the developing countries in a manner that does not hurt the economic interests of the developed countries or offend their political sensibilities on the issue of the sovereignty of the developing countries in the use of these resources, there are several possibilities of mutual-gain bargains in other areas of international economic reform. These

possibilities should prove to be more readily negotiable and are discussed in the concluding remarks of this paper.

In the field of trade policy it is clear that mutual gains can be had in two major spheres of policymaking. First, The Corea Plan needs to be explicitly modified to remove any traces of indexing: it should be clearly focused on stabilization. Further, the latter should explicitly distinguish among commodities that have supply problems and those that suffer from demand fluctuations if there is to be any clarity in the kinds of objectives such a stabilization is going to address itself meaningfully to; this also implies that the catch phrase "Integrated Programme" may be fetching but is certainly poor economics. Second, the developing countries have a clear interest in market access for the *sale* of manufactured exports that have run into nontariff barriers and often interrupted entry on the pretext of market disruption. At the same time, the developed countries (since the flourishing of commodity power by the OPEC countries) have become concerned with assuring market access for their *purchases* of raw materials. Here again therefore there is a prospect for a mutual-gain joint deal whereby the developed countries agree to new rules for regulating the use of trade barriers to handle market disruption problems in exchange for an agreement from developing countries (as well as the developed ones) to a new set of rules for regulating their use of export restrictions. Detailed proposals for such new rules, aimed at reforming the GATT on both counts, have been proposed recently and await policy makers' attention.[45] There is a clear case here for a joint bargain as against the piecemeal, issue-by-issue negotiating strategy that the developing countries seem to be following to little advantage, with little overall vision, in their current efforts at GATT and elsewhere.[46]

In the area of food policy the situation again seems to call for mutual-gain deals. The events of 1972-1974, leading up to the crisis-ridden Rome Conference of November 1974, are probably too unique to be repeated. The combined failures of the Soviet, Chinese, and Indian harvests, the depletion of the food surpluses in the United States, the unwillingness of the food exporting countries to part with grain because of inflation fed by the dramatic oil price increases, the foreign exchange difficulties that combined with high prices of fertilizers (related to the high oil price increases) to produce shortages of fertilizer availability in the developing countries where the Green Revolution had been important and could not be sustained without the fertilizers, the additional factor of the tragic drought in Suheil and Saharan Africa—all of these were to produce unprecedented panic in the grain-importing developing countries and confuse thinking on three separate issues that the world food problem raises for solution on a long-term basis.[47] These issues include (1) the need to have buffer stocks, exactly as with other commodities in the Corea Plan, to stabilize wild swings in prices such as happened most dramatically in 1972-1974; (2) the need to insulate the drought-affected developing countries from fearsome consequences by providing them with the assistance, not necessarily but most conveniently, in the form of food; and (3) the need to have an aid program for transferring food to the needy developing countries whose developmental programs cannot be sustained without such aid inflows and attendant food imports (which serve as the wage-goods, in the classical sense, supporting the needed investments for growth).

There is clearly nothing to be gained by the developed countries from having unplanned calls upon their food stocks for emergency relief in situations of drought; nor is it possible for them, on a long-term basis, to deny food aid to needy countries—after all, food has that special quality where conscience does hurt! For both these objectives, therefore, systematic planning ahead will be necessary. As for buffer stocks to handle stabilization, there are now sensible plans afloat that show both the relatively low levels of stocks that such an international operation will have to carry, as well as the feasibility of building up such stocks. The developing countries (such as India) are currently holding very substantial stocks of grain, largely because of successive good harvests but in part because of the immediacy of the lessons learned from the crisis of 1972-1974. Thus, the need for international stockholding seems to be correspondingly reduced; and this is also partly because the possibility of entering the grain market seems much more feasible now that the oil-price-hike-induced inflation has decelerated and harvests in the West, especially the United States, have been good.[48] Clearly, therefore, the time has come for an initiative on a world buffer stock for food program, or a substitute that also sounds like an excellent scheme: the grain insurance scheme of Gale Johnson who has proposed that the United States (and any other interested developed countries) join in a scheme under which they would assure, and build stocks to deliver on such an assurance, the developing countries that join such an insurance scheme that any shortfalls in their trend production larger than a prespecified percentage would be made up by the scheme.[49]

Finally, there is now clearly scope for a code on multinationals (MNCs) and their activities in the developing countries. Until now the developing countries that worried about the MNCs were considered to be somewhat bizarre, if not depraved and corrupted by socialist doctrines. Nothing works to cure one of illusions faster than to be proved naive by unpleasant revelations. The evidence of destabilization efforts directed against foreign regimes, the conviction that the oil companies collaborated in enforcing the Arab oil boycott, the exposé about the corporate bribing of foreign officials that has already ruined a prince and a prime minister,[50] are developments that have come just as the developing countries realized that they do need the technology and management expertise that MNCs can bring. Thus the awareness seems to have grown in influential circles in both the developing and the developed countries that MNCs are a good thing but need to have their international conduct regulated by explicit codes and legal sanctions, including the extension of trust-busting legislation to external operations in the social interest.

In trade, food, MNCs, brain drain, oceans, and a host of other smaller impact areas of international policy making, there seems to be scope for acceptable resource transfers and for mutual-gain bargains. Whether these initiatives will be taken constructively and the current momentum for creating a new international economic order will be directed toward these constructive channels will depend critically on the imaginativeness, empathy, and tolerance that the developed nations show toward the sentiments of the developing nations. For, it is only then that it will be possible to shift the developing countries toward the preferred reforms, as opposed to the ill-conceived proposals now current, and to collaborate with them in constructing a desirable and desired international economic order.

In conclusion, I might address my fellow economists who worry, quite naturally, about efficiency in international economic arrangements, and note explicitly that the only feasible way of guaranteeing such an outcome to the present debate on the new international economic order is to have the world system respond, in some significant manner, to the demands for distributive justice; the alternative politically is disorder from disenchanted developing countries, and that can hardly be expected to lead to conditions for international efficiency. Moreover, the program of reforms set out here fully meets these requirements, while ensuring a sense of fair play and justice to the developing countries and while moving substantially in the direction of assuring them of their sovereignty—newly discovered and therefore much valued. Thus, the brain drain tax, preferably matched by equal contribution from general taxation, would provide some sense of recompense to the developing countries for their present sense of loss of skills thereby making it easier for them to maintain freer flow of such skilled people. The evolution of new rules at the GATT to regulate the use of trade barriers and export controls for so-called market disruption and the holding back of supplies would guarantee freer trade. Commodity price stabilization, aimed at eliminating wild fluctuations in prices of the type that Keynes noted and that were acutely observed in 1972-1975, would supplement, not supplant, the market and would make it more efficient. And, by assuring that resources were transferred through the taxation of disexternalities (such as overfishing) and of rents (such as those from seabed mining and others from skilled migration from developing countries into highly-restricted developed countries), the developing countries would be assured of substantial, automatic, and continuing claims on revenues.

Such a program for the new international economic order can be judiciously embedded in an overall program of aid flows, restored to the higher (aid to GNP) levels enjoyed during the late 1950s and early 1960s, refocused on the poorer Fourth World, and disbursed with diplomatic surveillance, performance criteria, and scrutiny that would make these more substantial flows acceptable to the public opinion and parliamentary institutions of the donor countries.

The full agenda for the new international economic order, as developed and proposed here, is surely fully deserving of economists' support—support that is critical for its adoption by the developed countries.[51]

Notes

1 Among the major, recent conferences, UNCTAD IV at Nairobi in May 1976 and the ongoing Paris Conference on International Economic Cooperation (CIEC) are the principal ones. The 1976 ILO World Employment Conference and the earlier, 1975 UNIDO Lima Conference should also be mentioned.

2 The characterization as "populist" comes from C. P. Kindleberger, "World Populism," *Atlantic Economic Journal*, 3:2 (November 1975).

3 The alternative ideologies noted in this subsection were distinguished earlier in J. Bhagwati, "The Developing Countries," in *The Great Ideas Today*, (Chicago: Encyclopedia Britannica, Inc., 1976).

4 For a lucid statement of this viewpoint, see Raymond Vernon, *Sovereignty at Bay* (New York: Basic Books), 1972.

5 This is, of course, the central conclusion of the conventional theory of international trade and welfare.

6 Harry Johnson, among others, has noted several positive effects of the brain drain on developing countries. For a review, see J. Bhagwati and M. Partington (eds.), *Taxing the Brain Drain: A Proposal* (Amsterdam: North-Holland Publishing Company, 1976), Chapter 1, Appendix.

7 This view appears to be factually erroneous, though one could construct theoretical models to explain it. Ian Little has argued:

UNCTAD was founded on the mistaken view, which it has enshrined by constant repetition into the myth, that there is a trend in the terms of trade against developing countries as a result of an adverse trend in the terms of trade between manufactures and commodities. The mistake was originated by a League of Nations publication in 1945, and repeated by an early U.N. publication. Some more recent work suggests an *improvement* in the manufactures/commodities terms of trade for nearly a century before 1952-5, when there was a highly favourable and unsustainable peak in developing countries terms of trade associated with the Korean War boom. Thereafter for at least seven years they worsened, but then improved for a decade, even excluding oil. Any reasonably objective observer would have been saying for many years now that the evidence cannot possibly be held to give grounds for maintaining that there is a trend in the terms of trade against developing countries. Theories have been invented to explain this non-existent trend: they are treated with respect even though they explain what does not exist.

Cf. Little, "Economic Relations with the Third World—Old Myths and New Prospects," *Scottish Journal of Political Economy*, November 1975, p. 227.

8 For several models of such adverse impact, see J. Bhagwati (ed.), *The Brain Drain and Taxation: Theory and Empirical Analysis* (Amsterdam: North-Holland Publishing Company, 1976); note the contributions of Koichi Hamada and J. Bhagwati.

9 The writings of Hans Singer developed this theme; see, for example, *The Strategy of International Development* (New York: International Arts and Sciences Press, 1975).

10 V. S. Naipaul, *Guerrillas* (New York: Alfred S. Knopf, 1975), p. 5.

11 An excellent statement of this type of viewpoint can be found in Thomas Weisskopf, "Capitalism, Underdevelopment and the Future of the Poor Countries," in Bhagwati (ed.), *Economics and World Order* (New York: Macmillan, 1972).

12 See Kwame Nkrumah, *Neocolonialism: The Last Stage of Imperialism* (New York: International Publishers, 1965).

13 See the paper by Harald Malmgren in this volume.

14 For a review of the principal findings on this and other related issues in research by Little-Scitovsky-Scott for the OECD, Bhagwati-Krueger for the NBER, and Balassa for the IBRD, see J. Bhagwati, "Protection, Industrialization, Export Performance and Economic Development," paper prepared for the UNCTAD IV conference in Nairobi, May 1976.

15 One must concede, however, that for the 1950s and most of the 1960s, many of these governments were of the view that their protectionist policies were desirable.

16 See J. Bhagwati, *Amount and Sharing of Aid*, (Washington, D.C.: Overseas Development Council, 1970), Chapters I and II. Several different estimates are reviewed here and it is reported that the net worth of foreign aid to recipients was reduced to less than half of the alleged amounts and, in some cases, to little more than a third.

17 That aid may be misused unless the whole economic program of the recipient country is examined is a lesson that was learned by economists during the Marshall Plan. Needless to say, politically it seems outrageous to sovereign nations receiving such assistance to have their entire economic process be subjected to scrutiny and control by donors who contribute, in general, no more than 1-2 percent of the overall resources in the recipient countries.

18 Such resentments are inevitable as economic policies inevitably reflect ideological preferences and value judgments. An articulate expression of these resentments from a frustrated aid-recipient negotiator can be found in I. G. Patel's contribution in Barbara Ward (ed.), *The Widening Gap: Development in the 1970's* (New York: Columbia University Press, 1971).

19 The consequent need to redefine the goals of international efforts at development in the developing countries has been stressed by several writers. See, for example, the contributions by Pitambar Pant, Göran Ohlin, and J. Bhagwati (ed.) in *Economics and World Order*.

20 One can only agree with Little, however, in the judgment that the so-called statistics on income distribution for developing countries, which suggest *absolute* impoverishment of millions during the 1960s, are totally unreliable. See his critique of the Adelman-Morris claims to this effect in the *Journal of Development Economics*, Vol. 2 (1975).

21 An alternative view is that the demands for the NIEO have resulted from the "revolution of rising expectations" following the high rates of growth in the developing countries. However, this explanation is hardly plausible except for perhaps Brazil.

22 See M. A. Adelman, *The World Petroleum Market* (Baltimore: Johns Hopkins University Press, 1972).

23 For example, Japan as well as Western Europe (as noted by Bergsten in his paper for this volume) have raw material "dependence"—ratios that are of concern to their govern-

ments: the short run disruption to their economies from interruptions of supplies could be quite substantial.

24 For example, the 1972 Algiers demands and the resolutions of the special 1975 United Nations Conference on Raw Materials seem far more optimistic in regard to unilateral initiatives on commodities than does the February 1976 Manila Charter of the Group of 77 which sought to define the concerted position of these countries at the May 1976 Nairobi Conference of the UNCTAD. The Manila Charter demands the indexing of prices of exports of primary commodities by the developing countries to the prices of manufactured goods imported from the developed countries; this indexing is clearly to be achieved by cooperation toward that goal by both producing and consuming nations.

25 See Table 2.2 in the Edelman-Chenery paper in this volume, for the statistics on this.

26 See Bergsten, *Panel Discussion*, this volume.

27 Secretary-General of UNCTAD, 1975, *An Integrated Programme for Commodities: Specific Proposals for Decision and Action by Governments*, Report TD/B/C.1/193, 28 October 1975. For further details on the Integrated Programme, see the paper by Harry Johnson in this volume.

28 Indeed, it is arguable that some of these lapses (for example, the Vietnam war) were a greater affront to one's moral sense than the lapses that the developing countries are accused of.

29 The *locus classicus* of the neoconservative philosophical attitudes and their application to social policy issues is the magazine *The Public Interest*.

30 Variations on this basic theme have appeared in articles by Daniel Moynihan, Peter Bauer, and others, in American magazines such as *Commentary*. Even the *New York Times Sunday Magazine* (November 7, 1976) carried an article on the theme of Western guilt and its untenability written by two staffers of the Hudson Institute.

31 R. N. Cooper, *Panel Discussion*, this volume.

32 See Kenen's paper in this volume for the magnitudes involved.

33 This would be equally true for the not-so-poor developing countries (such as Brazil and Mexico) which fear being tainted by a generalized debt write-off or moratorium.

34 It is worth noting that Mr. Corea, the Secretary-General of UNCTAD, obtained a First in the Economics Tripos at Cambridge University, and that the UNCTAD draws in many consultants with considerable professional expertise and of much distinction. Unfortunately, it has become customary in certain professional circles (in this connection, read Harry Johnson in this volume and elsewhere) to equate the UNCTAD Secretariat with economic illiteracy—a charge that cannot be sustained, certainly relative to other international secretariats (such as the GATT) that also operate under governmental control rather than as autonomous university departments of economics!

35 Keynes' memorandum on the subject was discovered by Dr. Lal Jayawardene, then on the Committee of Twenty; I hastened to publish it in the *Journal of International Economics*, Vol. 4, no. 3 (August 1974).

36 One might add with regard to the subset of dictators, that lack of absolute power corrupts absolutely as well!

37 Thus, the *Tinbergen Report on Reshaping the International Order* (New York: E. P. Dutton & Co., 1976), concludes (p. 54):

It became apparent at the Seventh Special Session that, with few exceptions, the *Western European* Market economy countries and *Japan* although they have potentially more to lose than the U.S. from a failure to forge new international structures, were not only reluctant to take the initiative in redirecting the process of change, but were quite prepared to take refuge behind the United States' position when discussions became serious. That they are unwilling or unable to take serious initiatives is witnessed by the results of the first meeting of EEC Ministers for Development Cooperation held after the Seventh Special Session (3). It ended in complete failure; no agreement was reached on any important agenda point. *Despite a considerable effort, the 'nine' also failed to formulate a common position for UNCTAD IV* (italics added for emphasis).

38 It appears that the desire for full control stems again from residual notions of commodity power: it is feared that the access to seabeds would enable developed countries to reduce the potency of the developing countries' major weapon. Note that manganese is among the commodities that are included in the developing countries' list of commodities for exercise of commodity power!

39 R. N. Cooper, "Oceans as a Source of Revenue," in this volume.

40 For details, see Bhagwati and Partington (ed.), *Taxing the Brain Drain: A Proposal*, Amsterdam: North-Holland Publishing Co., 1976.

41 Bhagwati and Partington, p. 22. Also quoted in Koichi Hamada, "Taxing the Brain Drain: A Global Point of View," in this volume.

42 See the sociological evidence on this point in Partington's contribution in Bhagwati and Partington, *Taxing the Brain Drain.*

43 Note the speech delivered on May 5, 1976, in Nairobi; text available from Department of State, Press Release No. 224, p. 14.

44 While these two proposals do generate substantial magnitudes of resource flows to the developing countries in a manner that is consistent with the new political objectives and constraints spelled out earlier, they are to be regarded as supplements to the traditional aid programs. Indeed, aid flows need to be raised to more substantial levels; this is particularly the case for the poorest countries, many of which have been most seriously affected by the oil price increases. This group of "most affected countries" in the Fourth World is badly in need of substantially augmented resource transfers to maintain preOPEC growth performance, as is evident in the Edelman-Chenery paper in this volume. Furthermore, Edelman and Chenery underline the need to focus on these countries in deciding on the allocation of any given aid funds: the distribution of aid could be improved by giving more weight to poverty and need criteria than to bilateral, strategic and political criteria. Whether the overall aid flows and their distribution could be substantially moved in the directions that are so required is a matter about which one might be skeptical.

45 Proposals related to market disruption (addressed to developed countries but now awaiting the initiative of the developing countries) have been delineated in my paper in this volume. On the other hand, Bergsten's paper develops, at equal length, the proposals for GATT reform to regulate the use of export controls.

46 On the latter point, see Gardner Patterson's observations in this volume.

47 These issues have been distinguished, and their consequences for policy neatly analyzed, in the Sarris-Taylor paper in this volume.

48 Calculations of buffer stock requirements on alternative assumptions have been made recently by Lance Taylor, Alexander Sarris and Philip Abbot at MIT; others no doubt are in progress.

49 See Gale Johnson's paper in this volume.

50 Here, as elsewhere, one should distinguish between demand-determined and supply-determined bribes, however.

51 Thanks are due to Fred Bergsten, Joe Nye, and Hans Singer for helpful comments.

I
Resource Transfers

1

Aid and Income Distribution
John A. Edelman and Hollis B. Chenery

Political and economic events of the past few years have greatly affected both the need for capital transfers to developing countries and the conditions under which they are supplied. The economic crisis of 1973/1974—the main features of which were the rise in oil prices, recession in the OECD countries, and worsened terms of trade for oil importers—has greatly increased the demand for capital flows to cushion the adjustment of the developing countries to new trading conditions. Although there has also been a substantial increase in the supply of official capital since 1972, that increase has been by no means adequate to offset the terms of trade losses suffered by the developing countries from 1972 to 1975.

The impact of these events has fallen particularly heavily on the poorer countries. Terms of trade losses represent a larger proportion of imports for the poorer countries than for the middle-income group.[1] Moreover, the substantial increase in private capital flows has gone almost exclusively to the middle-income group. Private capital (and public capital on conventional terms) will continue to be available mainly to this group because of creditworthiness considerations. As a result the middle-income countries are likely to be able to return to a sustainable growth rate of more than 6 percent for the rest of the decade. However, unless there is a substantial increase in the flow of aid to the poorer countries—as well as changes in policies that will permit more efficient use of this aid—their per capita incomes are likely to be little higher by 1985 than they were in 1970.[2]

Political prospects for concessional assistance are uncertain. The steady decline in aid from member countries of the OECD was reversed in 1974 and 1975, and there is reason to hope that political obstacles to increased aid will diminish as these countries recover from the recession. Nevertheless, it hardly seems prudent to count on a rapid increase, especially since an important part of the recent increases was associated with the "emergency" situation created by the oil price increases. The most that can realistically be expected over the next several years is a modest expansion in real flows from recent levels. This outlook underscores the need to make more effective use of available external resources.

In this paper, we give an empirical analysis of the factors affecting the allocation of aid in the recent past. Our analysis provides a basis for judging the possibilities for improving aid allocation in the future.

Objectives and Criteria

Concern with the effects of development on the internal distribution of income has become an accepted part of the philosophy of most aid donors and is increasingly reflected in the criteria used for selecting projects and sectors for assistance. In applying these criteria, greater weight is often given to increases in the income of lower-income groups.[3] This can be done crudely by identifying a specific target group, such as poor farmers, or more systematically by using a welfare function that gives increasing weight to consumption or income in proportion to the poverty of the recipient.

In applying this principle, Ahluwalia and Chenery (1974) proposed for the evaluation of domestic poverty programs a simple welfare function that can be extended to cover international allocations as well. It replaces the income weights implicit in the use of the increase in total GNP as a measure of welfare by a more egalitarian measure such as population. As adapted to the evaluation of international programs this welfare measure would be:

$$W = \Sigma(\frac{n_i g_i}{N}) \tag{1}$$

where n_i is the population of country i, g_i the rate of GNP growth in country i due to receipts of aid and $N = \Sigma n_i$. In contrast, the conventional measure of growth of total GNP is equal to:

$$G = \frac{\Sigma(y_i g_i)}{Y} = \frac{\Delta Y}{Y} \tag{2}$$

where y_i is GNP in country i and $Y = \Sigma y_i$. In equation (2) an allocation of aid that produces a given increase in aggregate GNP will have the same impact on total GNP growth regardless of how it is distributed among countries, while in equation (1) a 1 percent increase in an income of \$100 is weighed equally with a 1 percent increase in an income of \$1,000. If there is no change of income distribution within countries, equation (1) can also be interpreted as the average growth of income for each person in the developing world.[4]

To judge the existing allocation of aid, it is also necessary to make allowance for variations in its marginal productivity. Although this cannot be determined with any accuracy, it will often be higher in richer countries. However, the effects of moderate productivity differences are not likely to offset the effects of large differences in income level.[5]

Allowance should also be made in intercountry comparisons for the effectiveness of different countries in reaching the poorer sections of their population. In principle, this can also be done by replacing the growth of GNP in country i in equation (1) by a population-weighted average.

The actual allocation of aid among countries is made by a number of individual agencies—bilateral and multilateral—with some form of consultation concerning the larger aid recipients. Although each agency has its own mixture of motives and criteria, there are some common elements in the approaches taken to aid allocation, which combine notions of equity and efficiency with aspects of national interest. In recent years, most of these agencies have moved in the direction of criteria that are more consistent with those suggested above.

There are, of course, many practical limitations to applying such criteria systematically. For one thing, it is not possible to obtain very satisfactory measures of the overall productivity of foreign aid, or of the effectiveness of domestic programs for improving income distribution. Considerations of national economic or political interest of the donors will inevitably modify considerations of global equity in the allocation of bilateral aid. For multilateral lenders, the bulk of whose funds must be raised from capital markets, important constraints are imposed on increasing allocations to poor countries by their limited capacity to service debt. Nevertheless, we believe there is significant scope for further progress in the application of equity criteria in aid allocation, particularly if the total supply of concessional assistance can be expanded at least moderately in the future.

Supply of External Capital

In response to the large increase in demand for external capital in the past three years, there has been a more limited increase in supply and a greater need to ration concessional public funds. The major part of this increased demand was met by expanded private flows. Of a $19.4 billion increase in the total capital inflow to oil-importing developing countries between 1970 to 1972 and 1974, some $12 billion was from private sources, while another $1.3 billion was provided by the IMF. Nevertheless, the increase in official long-term capital flows to this group of countries was impressive: in nominal terms, it rose from a net flow of $5.8 billion in 1970 to 1972 to $11.8 billion in 1974, and about $14.0 in 1975. The increase in net flows of official development assistance (ODA) from OECD countries in 1974 reversed—at least temporarily—the steady decline in its share of OECD GNP, from a low of .30 percent reached in 1973 to .33 percent in 1974, and .36 percent in 1975.[6]

Commitments of official assistance—which constitute the main focus of this paper—also doubled during the recent past from $11.5 billion in 1970 to 1972 to $24 billion in 1975 (see Table 1.1). At constant (1970-1972) prices, the 1975 increase over 1970 to 1972 is nearly 50 percent. More than half of this increase was provided by the OECD countries, primarily through the multilateral institutions. Nearly half was provided by OPEC member countries. While the distribution of the increase in the OECD and multilateral aid was quite wide, the distribution of OPEC commitments was much more concentrated, with over half the total going to three countries: Egypt, Pakistan, and Syria.

Despite these large increases in external flows (and future commitments),

Table 1.1 Commitments of Official Concessional Assistance (OCA) to Identified Countries, 1969-75 (billion $)

A. Current Prices	1969	1970	1971	1972	1973	1974	1975 est.
Bilateral ODA	5.6	5.9	7.2	8.2	8.5	10.2	(10.8)
Multilateral[a]	3.1	3.4	4.0	5.0	6.3	8.0	(9.4)
Subtotal	8.7	9.3	11.2	13.2	14.8	18.2	(20.2)
OPEC	(0.2)	(0.2)	(0.2)	0.3	0.7	3.8	(3.8)
Total OCA	8.9	9.5	11.4	13.5	15.5	22.0	(24.0)
B. 1970-72 Prices							
Bilateral ODA	7.4	6.9	7.1	7.3	6.9	7.7	(7.7)
Multilateral[a]	4.1	4.0	3.9	4.4	5.1	6.0	(6.6)
Subtotal	11.5	10.9	11.0	11.7	12.0	13.7	(14.3)
OPEC	(0.3)	(0.2)	(0.2)	0.3	0.6	2.9	(2.7)
Total OCA	11.8	11.1	11.2	12.0	12.6	16.6	(17.0)
IBRD Commitment Deflator: (1970-72 = 100)	76.1	85.8	101.4	112.8	123.4	132.8	141.4

Source: OECD, supplemented by Bank staff estimates. The commitment deflator takes account of projected inflation rates during the disbursement period.

[a]Includes IBRD commitments which strictly speaking do not meet the OECD definition of concessional assistance. The latter requires a grant element of 25 percent (calculated at a 10 percent opportunity cost) where IBRD commitments on this assumption had a grant element of only 19.5 percent during the 1969-73 period and a 12 percent grant element during the 1974-75 period after the interest rate was raised. However, at a 12 percent official concessional assumption, the grant element of IBRD was 22.5 percent in this period.

many developing countries have had to reduce their growth rates because of shortages of foreign exchange. For the low-income countries as a whole, the increase in total flows between 1972 and 1975 was only two thirds of the losses they suffered from the deterioration in their terms of trade in that period. For the middle-income group, the increase in total capital flows was moderately greater than the terms of trade loss, but they also suffered a substantial reduction in export volumes during 1975 as a consequence of the recession in the developed countries. Moreover, their medium-term debt outlook has become somewhat worse as a result of heavy private borrowing. The future growth of both groups of countries, but particularly of the low-income group, will depend in substantial measure on the volume of concessional assistance made available over the next several years, and on the way in which these funds are allocated.

Trends in Aid Allocation

Since even the most optimistic estimates of aid supplies fall substantially short of the requirements of the poorer countries, we will concentrate our analysis on the possibilities for making more effective use of the amounts that may be available. Our starting point is an analysis of recent trends in aid allocation in which we compare the allocation patterns since the economic crisis of 1973/1974 to earlier periods. We then discuss the possibility of further reallocation to the poorer countries.

Methodology

In order to analyze the net relationship between aid allocation and poverty, it is necessary to allow for country size and other factors that have been shown to affect the allocation of aid. This is done by means of multiple regression analysis, taking advantage of the earlier findings of Strout (1966), Henderson (1971), and Isenman (1975). In its 1974 Review (OECD, 1974), the Development Assistance Committee of the OECD also analyzed overall allocation patterns for the period from 1969 to 1974, but it did not separate the effects of individual factors. The principal innovations in the present study are:

1. the use of commitment data—which are indicative of donors' reactions to changing needs—instead of disbursements;

2. the extension of donors to include the OPEC countries, which have accounted for nearly half of the recent increase in commitments;[7] and

3. the use of grant equivalent, as well as nominal, values, which provides a more valid basis for comparing the value to the recipients of different forms of aid.

Our sample consists of eighty-nine aid recipients that cover 85 percent of the commitments included in the more complete OECD tabulation for 140 countries.[8] Separate regressions have been computed for three time periods: 1967-1969, 1970-1972, and 1973-1974.

The low absorptive capacity and limited creditworthiness of many poor countries limits the aid they receive, so that per capita aid receipts first rise and then fall as per capita income rises. To capture this effect statistically, we have used a regression equation that is nonlinear in income.[9] The form of the equation is adapted from the basic equation used by Chenery and Syrquin (1975) to analyze a variety of development patterns. The principal equation used is:

$$\log X = a + b \log N + c \log y + d (\log y)^2 + e(E/Y)$$

where

X = average per capita commitments for the relevant time period
N = population,   (3)
Y = per capita income,
E/Y = the ratio of exports to GNP for 1972.[10]

Six groups of per capita commitments were tested for each time period: bilateral, multilateral, and total, both in nominal values and grant equivalents. In addition, tests of the strength of the results were carried out by using total

rather than per capita commitments and on per capita commitments for a
reduced sample, which eliminates seven countries with extremely high per
capita commitments. (Regression results are available from the authors.)

Effects of Population Size

Although our main interest is in the relation between aid allocation and
income levels, it is necessary to allow first for the effects of size. A number of
earlier studies have remarked on the apparent bias in per capita aid allocations
in favor of small countries and against large countries.[11] Table 1.2 shows
these relationships for the three time periods we are considering.

Between 1967 to 1969 and 1973 to 1974, average commitments to
countries over 10 million population increased by significantly more than
those to smaller countries, thereby reducing the population bias somewhat.[12]
Nevertheless, the differences remained striking; in 1973 to 1974, countries
under 2 million population received more than twice the average for all other
groups, while countries over 25 million received only one quarter to one third
the average for smaller countries. The regression results for total commitments indicate that in 1973-74 a country with twice the population of
another had on average a commitment level 35 percent lower in nominal
terms and 44 percent lower on a grant equivalent basis.[13] The separate
regressions on bilateral and multilateral commitments in Table 1.2 show a

Table 1.2 Per Capita Commitments by Country Size (unweighted averages,
based on 1970 population for all periods)

1970 Population (million)	Number of Countries in Group		Nominal Values (US$)		
	1967-69	1970-74	1967-69	1970-72	1973-74
Less than 2.1	18	21	23.7	25.1	42.3
2.1-5.0	26	26	13.8	16.1	31.0
5.1-10.0	11	11	10.2	9.3	20.1
10.1-25.0	16	16	5.3	7.4	12.8
Over 25	14	15	3.1	5.4	9.7
Total/Average	85	89	12.0	14.0	25.5

	Grant Equivalents (US$)		
	1967-69	1970-72	1973-74
Less than 2.1	16.7	18.2	31.6
2.1-5.0	10.4	11.7	23.8
5.1-10.0	7.3	6.8	16.3
10.1-25.0	3.5	4.2	8.2
Over 25	2.1	2.9	5.6
Average	8.7	9.8	18.8

RELATIONSHIP BETWEEN PER CAPITA COMMITMENTS (GRANT EQUIVALENT)
AND COUNTRY SIZE (COMMITMENTS DEFLATED TO 1970–72 PRICES)

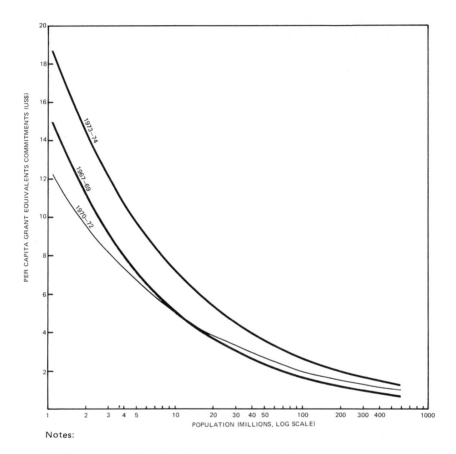

Notes:

1. These curves are based on the regression results given
   in Annex Table 1. Per Capita income and the ratio of
   exports to GNP have been fixed at their mean values,
   Vis.

Mean of Income/Capita	1967–69:		185.49 (US$)
	1970–72:		234.39
	1973–74:		262.96
Mean of Exp/GNP	1967–69:		.271
	1970–72 & 73–74:		.267

2. Commitment Deflators in both Fig. I & Fig. 2 are: 1967–69: .76
                                                      1973–74: 1.28

World Bank—16511

Figure 1.1 Relationship between per capita commitments (grant equivalent) and
country size (commitments deflated to 1970-72 prices)

very similar pattern. Figure 1.1 shows these relationships in graphic form for total grant equivalents.

There are a number of explanations for this strong negative relationship between per capita commitments and population size. The most important single determinant is probably the fact that all the nation-states included have independent foreign policies that can sometimes be influenced by foreign aid. Thus, these states tend to attract funds from a number of donors who may wish to exert such influence. In addition, relatively more of the small countries than the large tend to have close political, cultural, and economic ties with one or more donor.[14] These countries are also all members of one or more multilateral lending agencies. Multilateral lenders are virtually obliged to do some lending to all members, and constraints of minimum project size often lead to relatively large per capita commitments in small countries. Another important factor is the relatively large import component of GNP (and investment) in these countries. The large country extreme in this respect is India, whose imports account for only 5 percent of GNP. Thus, although concessional commitments are only some 1.7 percent of GNP, they correspond to 35 percent of imports, a relatively large share.

A substantial reduction of the small country bias could free a significant amount of resources for reallocation to larger poor countries. The forty-seven countries with populations under 5 million accounted in 1973/1974 for some $2.6 billion in grant equivalents or 20 percent of the total but only 7 percent of the population covered by this sample. A reduction by one third in these commitments would have permitted an increase in the averages for the fifteen largest countries by nearly $0.9 per capita which, in the case of India, would correspond to a 40 percent increase in the average 1973/1974 commitment level. Clearly, it is unrealistic to expect that such a large transfer could be achieved, although some reduction in the bias in favor of very small countries did take place between 1967 to 1969 and 1973/1974. The allocation criteria outlined above would argue for efforts to achieve at least a moderate further reduction in the future.

Effects of Income
In recent years, some 35 to 40 percent of total concessional commitments in nominal terms has gone to oil-importing countries under $200 per capita. As shown in Table 1.3, there was little change in this share between 1967 to 1969 and 1973/1974.[15] However, the grant equivalents for this group increased slightly from 44 percent in 1967 to 1969 to 46 percent in 1973/1974. This was the result of an increase in the grant element of commitments from OECD and multilateral donors from 77 percent to 80 percent. By contrast, the grant element of commitments to countries over $300 per capita dropped from 56 to 47 percent over the period.

The major beneficiaries of recent increases in commitments were in the $200-300 group (mainly Egypt and Syria). Between 1967 to 1969 and

1973/1974 the share of this group rose from 16 percent to 24 percent of the grant equivalents. The share of all oil-importing countries under $300 in total grant equivalents had risen in 1973/1974 to 72 percent, compared with 61 percent in 1967 to 1969.

Table 1.4 shows the grant equivalents of commitments on a per capita basis and as a percentage of GNP for the main income groups. During the period from 1967 to 1973 the average for the poorest countries (under $200) was consistently below that for all the other income groups except the highest.

The main reason for the low average of the poorest group is, of course, the great weight of India, which in 1973/1974 received only $2.2 per capita of grant equivalent commitments, compared to an average for all other countries of $9.5 per capita. Between 1967 to 1969 and 1974, commitments to India rose only moderately at current prices, and declined in real terms. Commitments to all other countries in this group showed a rise in real terms of over 80 percent between 1970 to 1972 and 1974, partly in response to the oil crisis. The ratio of grant equivalent commitments to GNP rose from 2.6 to 4.0 percent for the poorest group of countries between 1970 to 1972 and 1973/1974. However, ratios for India were only 1.5 and 1.7 percent, respectively, while for the other poorest countries, the average ratio went up from 4.0 percent to 7.0 percent.

In the regression analysis, the observations are unweighted, so that the Gambia has the same weight as India. The unweighted commitment average for all countries in 1973/1974 was $19 per capita for grant equivalents, compared with the weighted average of $6.4 shown in Table 1.4. This difference, of course, reflects the fact that so many small countries receive relatively high per capita commitments. Even correcting for this small country effect, the allocation pattern shows a rise with income up to the $200-400 range and then a decline, albeit a rather erratic one.

The quadratic term for income used in the regression analysis is designed to capture this tendency for per capita allocations to rise and then fall. The curves reflecting the shape of the regression results for total grant equivalent commitments in the three time periods are given in Figure 1.2.[16] The relationship between per capita allocation and income is significantly different as between bilateral and multilateral commitments. The regression curves for multilateral peak at a substantially higher income level than for bilateral, reflecting the fact that the largest component of multilateral lending consists of relatively hard funds from the IBRD, the IDB, and the ADB, which have to take account of creditworthiness considerations.

The peak income levels for per capita commitments implied by the separate regressions on bilateral and multilateral commitments, together with those for the totals, are shown on p. 38.

The main reason that per capita lending in nominal terms tends to rise with income is that creditworthiness and absorptive capacity also rise with income. These considerations affect the pattern of grant equivalent commitments with

Table 1.3 Distribution of Official Concessional Assistance by Income Group, 1967-74

	No. of Countries (70-74)	1970 Population (Million)	A. Concessional Commitments ($ billions)			
			1967-69	1970-72	1973	1974
A. Non-Oil Exporters[a]						
Under $200	38	932	2.82	3.30	4.99	7.80
India	1	538	1.10	1.10	1.46	1.77
Other	37	394	1.72	2.20	3.53	6.03
$201-$300	14	148	1.13	1.61	2.72	4.78
Over $300	28	367	2.25	3.01	3.80	4.47
$300-$500	13	204	1.40	1.79	2.60	2.27
Over $500	15	163	0.85	1.22	1.20	2.20
Total of A	80	1448	6.20	7.92	11.51	17.05
B. Oil Exporters[a]	9	232	0.96	1.51	1.69	2.07
Indonesia	1	116	0.43	0.82	0.96	1.01
Other	8	116	0.53	0.69	0.73	1.06
Total of A + B[a]	89	1630	7.16	9.42	13.20	19.12
Total of A + B in 1970-72 Prices			9.40	9.42	10.70	14.40

	B. Percent of Total Commitments			
	1967-69	1970-72	1973	1974
A. Non-Oil Exporters				
Under $200	39.4	35.0	37.8	40.8
India	15.4	11.7	11.1	9.3
Other	24.0	23.4	26.7	31.5
$201-$300	15.8	17.1	20.6	25.0
Over $300	31.4	32.0	28.8	23.4
$300-$500	19.6	19.0	19.7	11.9
Over $500	11.7	13.0	9.1	11.5
Total of A	86.6	84.1	87.2	89.2
B. Oil Exporters	13.4	16.0	12.8	10.8
Indonesia	6.0	8.7	7.3	5.3
Others	7.4	7.3	5.5	5.5
Total of A + B	100.0	100.0	100.0	100.0

[a]Current prices.

Table 1.3 (continued)

C. Grant Equivalent ($ billions)			
1967-69	1970-72	1973	1974
2.17	2.54	3.98	5.93
0.86	.84	1.12	1.27
1.31	1.70	2.86	4.66
0.85	1.08	1.90	3.34
1.27	1.27	1.72	2.19
0.87	0.83	1.23	1.06
0.40	0.44	0.49	1.13
4.29	4.89	7.60	11.46
0.62	0.95	1.14	1.39
0.27	0.58	0.73	0.77
0.35	0.37	0.41	0.62
4.91	5.84	8.74	12.85
6.46	5.83	7.08	9.68

D. Percent of Grant Equivalents			
1967-69	1970-72	1973	1974
44.2	43.5	45.5	46.2
17.5	14.4	12.8	9.9
26.7	29.1	32.7	36.3
17.3	18.5	21.7	26.0
25.9	21.8	19.7	17.0
17.7	14.2	14.1	8.3
8.1	7.5	5.6	8.8
87.4	83.7	87.0	89.2
12.6	16.3	13.0	10.8
5.5	9.9	8.3	6.0
7.1	6.3	4.7	4.8
100.0	100.0	100.0	100.0

Table 1.4 Commitments of Official Concessional Assistance: Grant Equivalent per Capita and as Ratio to GNP by Income Group, 1967-74

	Per Capita Grant Equivalents[a] (US$, current prices)				Ratio to GNP (percent)	
	1967-69 Average	1970-72 Average	1973	1974	1970-72 Av.[b]	1973/74 Av.[c]
A. Oil Importers						
Under $200	2.3	2.7	4.3	6.4	2.6	4.0
India	1.6	1.6	2.1	2.4	1.5	1.7
Other	3.3	4.3	7.3	11.8	4.0	7.0
$201-$300	5.7	7.3	12.8	22.6	3.2	5.2
Over $300	3.5	3.5	4.7	6.0	0.6	0.5
$300-500	4.3	4.1	6.0	5.2	1.1	0.8
Over 500	2.5	2.7	3.0	6.9	0.3	0.4
Total of A	3.0	3.4	5.2	7.9	1.4	1.8
B. Oil Exporters	2.7	4.1	4.9	6.0	2.1	1.5
Indonesia	2.3	5.0	6.3	6.6	6.5	4.7
Other	3.0	3.2	3.5	5.3	1.0	0.7
Total of A + B	2.9	3.5	5.2	7.6	1.5	1.7

[a]All based on 1970 population; this, of course, overstates the upward trend— by about 2.5 percent a year.
[b]Based on 1970 GNP.
[c]Based on 1973 GNP.

Income Turning Points for Per Capita Commitments (per capita income, 1970 prices)[a]

	For Nominal Commitments			For Grant Equivalents		
	Bilateral	Multilateral	Total	Bilateral	Multilateral	Total
1967-69	259	675	396	225	439	275
1970-72	*	*	(392)	*	*	(193)
1973-74	153	406	278	*	174	154

[a]The underlying income data used in the regressions are at current prices, converted into U.S. dollars at average exchange rates. The estimates given here have been deflated to 1970 dollars using the GNP deflator for the United States.

*The income coefficients for these time periods are not statistically significant. 1970-72 data in brackets are derived from regressions for the reduced sample. For 1973/74, the reduced sample gives turning points of 262 (total nominal) and 169 (total grant equivalent).

RELATIONSHIP BETWEEN PER CAPITA COMMITMENTS (GRANT EQUIVALENTS)
AND PER CAPITA INCOME
(COMMITMENTS DEFLATED TO 1970–72 PRICES)

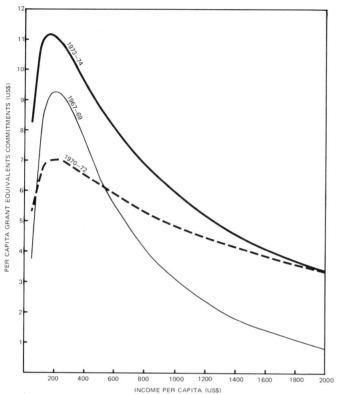

Notes:

1. These results are derived from the regression results
   given in Annex Table 1. Population and the Ratio of
   exports to GNP are fixed at their mean values. vis.

   Pop. 1967–69:   5.18 m.
         1970–72:   5.47 m.
         1973–74:   5.69 m.
   Exports: GNP   1967–69: .271
                     1970–72: .267
                     1973–74:

2. The dotted line for 1970–72 indicates the co-efficients
   underlying this curve are not statistically significant.

World Bank—16512

Figure 1.2 Relationship between per capita commitments (grant equivalents) and
per capita income (commitments deflated to 1970-72 prices)

less force, since grants and grant-like commitments tend to dominate in that pattern. However, an awareness of the greater needs of middle- and lower-income countries has led both multilateral and bilateral donors to reduce lending to a number of higher-income countries in recent years, despite their high creditworthiness. The grant equivalent of multilateral commitments to countries over $300 per capita income declined from 40 percent to 26 percent of the multilateral total between 1967 to 1969 and 1973/1974. At the same time, the share going to countries under $200 (including Indonesia and Nigeria) rose from 44 to 56 percent. A third of the latter increase was accounted for by Indonesia, whose share rose from 2 to 6 percent of the multilateral total. Countries in the $200-300 income range had an increase in their share of the multilateral grant equivalent from 16 to 18 percent.

The share of the bilateral ODA grant equivalent commitments allocated by OECD countries to countries over $300 per capita dropped from 24 percent to 17 percent between 1967 to 1969 and 1973/1974; while that going to the group under $200 per capita increased from 53 percent to 57 percent, despite a drop in bilateral allocations to India from 20 percent to 10 percent of the total. Bilateral ODA allocations to the $200-300 group rose from 23 percent to 26 percent over this period. OPEC assistance is also heavily concentrated in the latter category because Egypt, Syria, and Jordan are all in this group.

Undoubtedly, something of a bandwagon effect has developed in lending to a number of countries in the $200-300 group. While some of these were hard hit by losses from the terms of trade in 1973-74, others are net oil-exporters and have benefited substantially from the recent increase in oil prices: e.g., Algeria, Congo, Syria, and Tunisia. In spite of a decline in the share of total concessional assistance going to countries over the $300 level, a number of these were also still receiving relatively large per capita commitments in 1973-74. However, most of these were countries under 5 million population.[17]

Conclusions: The Potential for Reallocation

The total welfare of developing countries can be increased by allocating a larger share of aid to poorer countries so long as the productivity of aid at the margin is not so low as to offset differences in income levels. Other things being equal, there is also a presumption that the marginal productivity of aid will be higher in countries receiving relatively low levels than in those receiving very high levels. However, "other things" seldom are equal. Table 1.5 identifies fifteen oil-importing countries with per capita incomes under $201 in 1970 that received less than $10 per capita per annum in concessional aid (grant equivalents) during 1973 and 1974. Ten of these had receipts below $6.5 per capita—the weighted average for all countries covered by our sample in this period.

On grounds of per capita income and aid levels alone, it would appear that these ten would be the prime candidates for receiving higher allocations if aid were to be redistributed more equitably. However, one of the largest of these—Thailand—did not in fact have a pressing need for resource transfers in this period because of rising export earnings and comfortable foreign exchange reserves. Most of the others share two common characteristics—low absorptive capacity (a low marginal productivity of aid), and relatively weak political and economic ties with the major aid donors. The second factor is undoubtedly at least as important as the first in accounting for the large differences between the level of per capita aid for this group and that of the twenty-three small countries, grouped under "all other" in Table 1.5, that obtained average per capita commitments of $17.2 in this period.[18] In the latter group, there are a number of countries where the productivity of aid appears to be quite high; however, there are some in which it seems to be as low as in those receiving low per capita aid allocations. The relatively high allocations made to these countries may be explained in part by an expectation that productivity will rise because of a willingness on the part of the recipients to make changes in domestic economic policies and adminis-

Table 1.5 Grant Equivalent of Commitments of Concessional Assistance to Oil-Importing Countries Under $201 Per Capita Income, 1973/74

			Average 1973/74 Grant Equivalent Commitments		
A. Commitments under $10 Per Capita	1970 Per Capita (US$)	1970 Population (million)	Per Capita (US$)	Total ($ million)	Percent of 1973 GNP
India	110	538.1	2.2	1,193.4	1.7
Guinea	120	3.9	3.1	12.0	2.1
Burma	80	27.6	3.1	86.1	3.6
Sierra Leone	190	2.6	4.0	10.3	2.2
Nepal	80	11.1	4.3	47.9	4.4
Afghanistan	80	14.3	5.2	74.7	5.3
Thailand	200	36.2	5.2	186.9	1.8
Ethiopia	80	24.6	6.4	156.4	6.8
Sri Lanka	110	12.5	6.4	80.2	5.1
Haiti	110	4.5	6.4	29.0	5.1
Sudan	120	15.7	8.1	127.1	5.6
Bangladesh	70	67.8	8.5	574.0	9.7
Pakistan	100	62.4	8.9	556.8	7.2
Madagascar	130	7.3	9.1	66.6	5.3
Burundi	60	3.5	9.4	32.9	12.2
Subtotal	110	832.1	3.9	3,234.3	2.9
B. All Other Under $201	100	100.2	17.2	1,720.3	11.3
C. All Countries Under $201	110	932.3	5.3	4,954.6	3.7

trative practices perceived by the donors to be important requirements for ensuring efficient use of aid. Even if it takes a long time for such changes to produce tangible results, donors are more likely to maintain relatively high commitments in countries where they see such a willingness than in countries they believe to be unwilling or unable to make changes of this type. In these terms, a high degree of receptivity to aid may be said to "explain" relatively high commitments even if measured productivity remains low.

In principle, of course, a reallocation in favor of the poor countries with low aid receipts could be made by the donors without evidence of greater receptivity or of increases in marginal productivity. In practice, however, it is unlikely that this will be done, if only because donor agencies need to justify their aid allocations to their legislatures or boards of directors in terms of some sort of positive response (actual or expected) to the allocations they provide.

India is, of course, overwhelmingly the most important of the countries in this group. It is the lowest recipient of aid on a per capita basis, and the share of concessional aid going to India has declined steadily over the past decade. To some extent this is a reflection of competition from other countries for the available resources, resulting from the creation of newly independent states in Africa and Asia and increased receptivity to aid in some countries (for instance, Indonesia). However, the decline in India's share is also a function of India's own policies directed at reducing dependence on imports and on foreign assistance over the past decade. Although plausible at the start—given the size of the Indian economy—these policies have proved to be a disappointment in that in recent years they have produced very slow growth of real income (about 1 percent per capita since the early 1960s), food shortages, low productivity of capital, and severe foreign exchange constraints. Moreover, receptivity to policy changes recommended by donors has generally been low.

Recently, there have been signs of change. In addition to an excellent harvest in 1975, encouraging progress has been made in long-term agricultural development programs. Efforts to increase Indian exports have started to produce results, and some major import substitution investments in energy, steel, and fertilizers are finally becoming productive. This has been accompanied by significant increases in foreign aid commitments and flows in 1975 and 1976. If the recent improvements in India's economic performance can be sustained over the next five to ten years, it seems likely that aid agencies will be able to justify a further increase in India's share in the total of available aid resources.

If there is to be a reallocation of aid in favor of the poorer countries with very low per capita aid receipts, the most obvious candidates for reduced shares would be higher-income countries with relatively high per capita aid receipts. Table 1.6 lists by three income groups the countries over $200 per capita with commitments that are substantially above the average for countries under $200 per capita. It will be seen that a rough notion of progressivity is introduced by selecting lower commitment cutoff points to represent "substantial," as incomes rise, that is, for the $200-300 groups, fourteen dollars is used, while for the over $500 group, a level of seven dollars is used. The small country bias is clearly evident in this table. Of the thirty countries identified (in Group A) as being substantially above average, only six have populations over 5 million, and only two are over 20 million. Their total 1970 population was only 136 million, while commitments to them averaged $3.2 billion or twenty-three dollars per capita in the two years from 1973 to 1974. The remaining nineteen countries in our sample with incomes over $200 per capita had a total population of 441 million and received average per capita commitments of only $4.2 in this period.

Special political and economic relationships with major donors undoubtedly played an important role in determining the high levels of assistance to many of these countries. There is no reason to believe that these considerations will diminish greatly in importance for the main donors over the next few years. However, if the total supply of aid can be held at least constant in real terms, a gradual reallocation in favor of poorer countries might be achieved without unduly disturbing these special relationships. For example, if nominal commitments to these favored countries were, on average, maintained approximately constant, while inflation continued at about 6 percent a year, the result after six years would be to free about $1 billion in grant equivalents (at 1973/1974 prices) for transfer to the poorer countries. If this were devoted entirely to the fifteen poorer countries identified separately in Table 1.5, it would correspond to a 30 percent increase in their total commitment levels, raising per capita receipts from $3.9 to $5.0 in 1973/1974 prices. The corresponding reduction in real per capita allocations implied for the thirty countries identified in Table 1.6 (under group A) would be from $23 to $16.3.

One important qualification to the potential for reallocation needs to be noted here—namely, the limited scope for multilateral agencies that raise their funds on the capital markets to increase lending to poorer countries with very limited creditworthiness. About one quarter of the receipts of the countries shown separately in Table 1.6 are from multilateral agencies, and the great part of these derive from funds raised on capital markets. As this implies, not all the commitments we have lumped together as "grant equivalents" are in fact fungible as among countries. At present, none of the poor countries listed separately in Table 1.5, except Thailand, can afford any substantial increase in their borrowings on conventional terms because of prospective debt servicing problems. Of course, this outlook could change for some of them if recent improvements in economic policies can be reinforced and sustained over the next several years. But, in the meantime, this consideration means that any substantial reallocation to countries under $200 per capita will have to take place through shifts in the pattern of bilateral aid or in

Table 1.6 Grant Equivalent of Concessional Commitments to Countries Over $200 Per Capita by Income Group and Level of Commitment, 1973/74

1970 Income Group	1970 Population (million)	1970 Per Capita GNP (US$)	Grant Equivalent Per Capita (US$)	Grant Equivalent Total ($ million)	Grant Equivalent Percent of 1973 GNP
$200-300 Per Capita Income					
A. Over $14 Per Capita					
Papua and New Guinea	2.4	300	113.7	272.9	26.0
Jordan	2.3	250	81.2	186.8	21.5
Syria	6.1	290	50.6	309.0	11.0
Mauritius	.8	240	39.0	32.8	9.1
Congo	.9	300	35.7	32.1	7.8
Senegal	3.9	230	32.5	126.7	10.9
Tunisia	5.1	250	32.5	165.7	6.5
Paraguay	2.4	260	24.6	59.0	5.9
Egypt	33.3	210	20.3	677.4	7.7
Honduras	2.5	280	18.8	47.0	5.3
Liberia	1.5	240	16.2	24.3	5.4
Algeria	14.3	300	14.1	201.9	2.4
Subtotal A	75.5	230	28.3	2,135.6	7.4
B. All Other in $200-300 Range	93.8	240	8.4	788.0	2.4
C. Group Total	169.3	240	17.3	2,923.6	4.7
$301-500 Per Capita					
A. Over $10 Per Capita					
Nicaragua	2.0	430	28.5	56.8	5.4
Fiji	.5	430	27.6	13.8	3.8
Ivory Coast	4.9	310	27.1	132.9	5.9
Zambia	4.1	400	26.3	107.9	5.3
Guyana	.8	370	17.6	13.2	4.1
Dominican Republic	4.1	350	14.7	60.4	2.6
Subtotal A	16.4	360	23.5	385.0	4.6
B. All Other in $301-500 Range	216.6	380	3.8	818.2	0.5
C. Group Total	233.0	380	5.2	1,203.2	0.7
Over $500					
A. Over $7 Per Capita					
Gabon	.5	630	54.4	27.2	4.0
Barbados	.3	610	41.5	10.8	4.5
Israel	2.9	1,960	39.6	114.8	1.2
Costa Rica	1.7	560	27.0	45.9	3.5

Table 1.6 (continued)

			Grant Equivalent		
1970 Income Group	1970 Population (million)	1970 Per Capita GNP (US$)	Per Capita (US$)	Total ($ million)	Percent of 1973 GNP
Lebanon	2.7	590	26.8	72.3	2.6
Cyprus	.6	950	23.0	13.8	1.5
Panama	1.5	730	21.9	32.9	2.3
Jamaica	1.9	670	14.4	27.3	1.4
Singapore	2.1	920	11.9	25.0	0.6
Chile	9.8	720	10.4	102.3	1.4
Trinidad and Tobago	1.0	860	9.5	9.5	0.7
Yugoslavia	20.5	650	7.5	153.4	0.7
Subtotal A	45.6	760	13.9	635.2	1.2
B. All Other over $500	129.0	900	1.8	237.5	0.1
C. Group Total	175.2	870	5.0	872.7	0.4
Total of Groups A	136.5	430	23.1	3,155.8	3.5
Total All Other	440.0	770	4.2	1,843.7	0.5
All countries over $200 Per Capita	576.5	690	8.7	4,999.5	1.1

decisions by those donors to channel more concessional funds through multilateral institutions.

There may, however, be a case for some reallocation of conventional official capital to countries with relatively low receipts in the $200-500 income groups—especially to those where productivity of aid appears relatively high. Countries in this income group with per capita commitments of less than $7 on a grant equivalent basis in 1973/1974 include Brazil, Colombia, Peru, Philippines, and Turkey. For this group of countries, of course, another relevant consideration in any aid reallocation would be the extent of their access to private capital markets on reasonable terms.

It is of interest to see what the impact on growth and welfare might be from the potential shift in aid to the poorest countries discussed.

On the assumption that the illustrative $1 billion reallocation by 1980 were reached gradually, it would produce a cumulative shift of $4.4 billion during the six-year period, within an aggregate aid total of $38.4 billion for the fifteen oil importers identified in Table 1.5 plus the thirty high aid recipients listed in Table 1.6. The average incremental capital output ratios (ICORs) for the past decade produce a handy (if limited) proxy of the productivity of aid for purposes of this illustration. For the poorest group, the average was about 5.5 for 1965 to 1973, while for the thirty high aid recipients, the ICOR averaged about 4.0 (For the three largest countries in this group—Algeria,

Egypt, and Yugoslavia—the ICORS were 3.9, 4.6, and 4.2, respectively, while in most of the other countries, the ICOR was under 4.0.)

Using these two sets of assumptions, the total growth in GNP attributable to aid in this period for these forty-five countries works out at 4.2 percent with constant shares and 3.8 percent after the assumed reallocation in favor of the poorest. However, as shown in Table 1.7, using population weights to aggregate country growth, the annual increase in W would be 3.5 percent on constant shares and 3.9 percent after the assumed reallocation.

Even more substantial increases in total welfare than these could be achieved by an increase in the real level of aid, and/or increased productivity. For example, if total aid could be increased in real terms by 5 percent annually over the 1973/1974 level for the total of the forty-five countries considered in this illustration, their 1979/1980 level would rise to $9.1 billion, compared with $6.4 in 1973/1974, and the cumulative difference for the six years would be $7.3 billion. If this increment were allocated entirely to the poorest group, it would represent a 38 percent increase in the cumulative total for 1975 to 1980 projected on the assumption of a constant real level. The annual growth in welfare (based on population weights) would be 4.4 percent. The impact of a reduction in the ICOR for aid for the poorest

Table 1.7 Illustrative Impact of Aid Reallocation on Growth and Welfare for 45 Countries

	15 Poorest[a]	30 Upper and Middle Income[b]	Totals
Base Period GNP (billion $)	110	90	200.0
Base Period Population (million)	899	148	1047
Assumed ICOR (for aid)	5.5	4.0	
Assumed Aid 1975-80 (US$ million, 1973-74 prices)			
A (constant shares)	19.2	19.2	38.4
B (reallocated)	23.6	14.8	38.4
Percentage Growth in GNP, 1974-80			
A (constant shares)	3.17	5.33	4.15
B (reallocated)	3.90	3.73	3.82
Percentage Growth in W, 1974-80 (population weighted)[c]			
A (constant shares)	3.17	5.33	3.47
B (reallocated)	3.90	3.73	3.87

[a]From Table 1.5.

[b]From Table 1.6 (group A countries).

[c]As the identity between the GNP and population weighted growth rates for each group indicates, population weighting is applied here only to the totals for the two groups and not within each group.

group from 5.5 to 4.0 would be almost exactly the same.

Productivity of aid measured in terms of its contribution to GNP growth is only one element in determining the welfare impact of aid. Another important element is the allocation of aid in relation to per capita income levels. Substantial progress has been made during recent years in reallocating aid in favor of countries with (1970) income levels below $300 per capita. However, the major beneficiaries have been in the $200 to $300 range. There remains a significant potential for further reallocation to the group under $200 per capita. The main "target" countries consist of a limited number (ten to fifteen) now receiving a comparatively low per capita level of assistance. The role of concessional aid is particularly important for these countries, which typically have very limited creditworthiness for private borrowing.

The objective of increasing welfare in the developing countries as a whole will be best served by simultaneous efforts on the part of the donors to increase both the real level of total concessional assistance and the share of the total going to this limited group of poor countries. As a practical matter, however, achievement of the latter objective will also require that the poorest countries improve their ability to make productive use of this aid. In determining the outcome for the poorest group as a whole, the performance of India, which comprises about two thirds the population of all countries in this category, will be crucial.

Notes

The views in this article represent those of the authors, and not necessarily those of the World Bank. We are indebted to Julian Bharier, Ian Little, Marcelo Selowsky, and Joris Voorhoeve for helpful comments. Pisei Phlong and Sayeed Sadeq assisted with the statistical analysis.

1 Measured on a 1967-1969 price base, the terms of trade loss between 1970 to 1972 and 1975 amounted to 14 percent of 1975 imports for oil importing countries with incomes under $200 per capita. The loss for middle-income oil importers in the same period correspond to 10 percent of 1975 imports.

2 Analyses of the factors leading to this conclusion are given in Chenery (1975), Tims (1975), McNamara (1975), and Holsen and Waelbroeck (1976).

3 See, for example, Little and Mirrlees (1968) and Squire and van der Tak (1975).

4 This function has also been used by Kuznets (1972), who showed that for the 1960s the value of W was about 1 percent lower than the value of G because of the higher growth rates of the richer countries.

5 For example, assume that Mexico has a level of per capita income (in purchasing power terms) four times that of India and that a loan of $10 million will yield a net increase in Mexican GNP twice as large as that in India. On these assumptions, the allocation of a loan to India would produce twice as large an increase in W even though the allocation to Mexico would yield twice as great an increase in G. It should also be noted that application of the same criteria would lead to a reallocation away from low-income countries
e marginal productivity of aid is very low to countries with moderately higher in-
with substantially higher marginal productivity of capital.

6 OECD (1975) and OECD (1976).

7 Inclusion of concessional assistance from OPEC countries yields a commitment total that we have labeled official concessional assistance (OCA), as shown in Table 1.1.

8 The latter tabulation is shown in Table 1.1. Our smaller sample is limited to countries that are active borrowers from the World Bank. The bulk of the difference between the two is accounted for by the countries of Indochina and the dependent overseas territories of France, Netherlands, the United Kingdom and the United States.

9 Failure to use this quadratic form may account for the findings of Cline and Sargen (1975) that per capita income had no influence on the allocation of World Bank commitments in grant equivalent term for a sample of nineteen countries from 1969 to 1972. Separate regressions using the quadratic form prepared by the bank staff for a larger sample of World Bank commitments from 1970 to 1974 show per capita income was significantly correlated with per capita commitments measured on both a nominal and grant equivalent basis. However, it is possible that even with the use of the quadratic form, per capita income may not have been significant for the time period chosen by Cline and Sargen.

10 Preliminary tests were also made on a number of other variables: losses or gains from terms of trade, savings rates, GNP growth rates, and several subjective measures of performance in equity and economic management. Results of these tests have so far proved inconclusive and are not discussed here.

11 Little and Clifford (1965), Strout (1966), OECD (1969), Henderson (1971), Isenman (1975).

12 This decline is reflected in a fall in the negative elasticities given by the population coefficients for these two time periods in the regression results.

13 The population coefficients have high T ratios (ranging from 6 to 8) indicating that these results are quite stable and would not be much affected by the elimination of a few extreme country cases.

14 Dudley and Montmarquette (1976) argue that the entire small country bias in bilateral commitments can be explained by factors such as these.

15 Comprehensive commitment data on a comparable basis are not available prior to 1967. However, flow data for net official assistance compiled by OECD indicate that the share of countries with incomes under $200 per capita income in 1970 declined from 43 percent in 1960 to 1966, to 42 percent of the total in 1968 to 1970. However, there were major shifts within this group during the period, with the share of India and Pakistan dropping from 26 to 21 percent and that for Nigeria and Indonesia increasing from 2.5 to 7.5 percent.

16 As indicated in Figure 1.1, the coefficients for the income variables in the regressions on the full sample for 1970 to 1972 are not statistically significant at the 10 percent level. However, they are marginally significant for the other two time periods, and for the reduced sample they are highly significant in all three periods.

17 The supporting statistical evidence regarding the statements in the text is available from the authors.

18 The list of these countries is available from the authors.

References

Ahluwalia, M. S., and Hollis B. Chenery in *Redistribution with Growth*, by Chenery Ahluwalia, Bell, Duloy, Jolly. Oxford University Press, London, 1974.

Chenery, Hollis B., "Approaches to Development Finance" in Symposium on a New International Order, The Hague, Netherlands, May 1975.

Chenery, Hollis, B., and M. Syrquin, *Patterns of Development 1950-1970*, Oxford University Press, London, 1975.

Clifford, J. M., and Ian M. D. Little, *International Aid.* George Allen and Unwin, Ltd., London, 1965.

Cline, William R., and Nicholas P. sargen, "Performance Criteria and Multilateral Aid Allocation," *World Development*, Vol. 3, No. 6, June 1975.

Dudley, L., and C. Montmarquette, "A Model of the Supply of Bilateral Foreign Aid," *American Economic Review* March 1976, 66, 132-142.

Henderson, P. D. "The Distribution of Official Development Assistance Commitments by Recipient Countries and by Sources," *Bulletin*, Oxford University Institute of Economics and Statistics, Vol. 33, February 1971, pp. 1-20.

Holsen, John A., and Jean L. Waelbroeck, "LDC Balance of Payments Policies and the International Monetary System," World Bank Staff Working Paper No. 226, February 1976.

Isenman, P., "Biases in Aid Allocations Against Poorer and Larger Countries," *World Development*, Vol. 4, No. 8, 1976.

Kuznets, S., "The Gap: Concepts, Measurement and Trends" in *The Gap Between Rich and Poor Nations*, ed. G. Ranis, MacMillan, London, 1972.

McNamara, Robert S., Address to Board of Governors, World Bank Group, September 1975.

Organization for Economic Cooperation and Development (OECD), *Development Assistance, 1969 Review*, Paris, 1969.

OECD, *Development Cooperation, 1974 Review*, Paris, 1974.

OECD, *Development Cooperation, 1975 Review*, Paris, 1975.

OECD, Press Release of the Development Assistance Committee, June 29, 1976.

Squire, Lyn, and Herman G. van der Tak, "Economic Analysis of Projects," Johns Hopkins University Press, Baltimore and London, 1975.

Strout, A., and P. Clark, "Aid, Performance, Self-Help, and Need," AID Discussion Paper No. 20, Washington, D.C., 1969.

Little, Ian M. D., and James A. Mirrlees, *Manual of Industrial Project Analysis*, OECD, Paris, 1968.

2
Debt Relief as Development Assistance
Peter B. Kenen

It was agreed that I would survey here old and new sources of development assistance. It soon became clear to me, however, that the rescheduling of international indebtedness deserves the most urgent attention. There are two reasons. First, the debt-service problems of developing countries and proposals to relieve them are drifting to the top of the international agenda, and we must confront such problems analytically before seeking to resolve them politically. Second, debt relief may be the most promising way to increase the flow of resources to developing countries.

This work, then, concentrates on the debts of developing countries and ways to reduce debt-service burdens. It begins by describing the problem in general terms that will be familiar to many readers, but it offers new data that may alarm even those who have been watching the problem. It goes on to survey proposals for debt relief and to assess their short-run impact on debt-service flows. It concludes with some thoughts on financing debt relief.

The Sources of Development Assistance

Transfers of resources by gross lending have been taking place on a scale unforeseen a few years ago. In 1969, the Pearson Commission projected gross borrowing and debt-service payments for developing countries. Hypothesizing terms slightly more liberal than those prevailing in the late 1960s, the commission predicted that debt-service flows on official development assistance would reach $6 billion in 1981. (Pearson, et al., 1969, Chart 7, assumption 1.) They have already reached that rate. To make matters worse, borrowing from private lenders has grown very rapidly, raising total debt-service flows above $10 billion in 1974, and, I fear, above $17 billion in 1976. Let us look more closely at some of these trends, using the data on debts and debt-service flows in Tables 2.1 through 2.3.

By the end of 1973, the sixty-seven countries included in the World Bank's reporting network (and in the statistics summarized in Table 2.1) had accumulated long-term debts larger than $70 billion, and short-term debts to U.S. banks and other U.S. lenders larger than $8 billion.[1] Two years later, after the increase in oil prices and the commodity-price cycle, their long-term debts exceeded $105 billion, and their short-term debts to U.S. lenders totaled $18 billion.[2] Borrowing from private sources increased rapidly from

Table 2.1 The Debts of Developing Countries, 1973 and 1975 (All Developing Countries Except Oil Exporters) ($ billion)

Type	1973	1975
Disbursed Long-Term Debt		
To Private Creditors		
Suppliers' Credits	7.1	7.9
Bank Credits	10.9	22.4
Other Credits	6.8	7.5
To Public Creditors		
International Organizations	11.9	20.9
DAC Governments	29.3	35.6
East Bloc Governments	3.6	5.1
Other Governments	1.2	6.2
Total	70.8	105.6
Short-Term Debt to U.S. Creditors		
To U.S. Banks	6.0	14.5
To U.S. Nonbanking Concerns	2.1	3.4[a]
Total	8.1	17.9

Source: Long-term debt in 1973 from World Bank, *World Debt Tables*, October 1975 (EC-167/75), Table 7; long-term debt in 1975 estimated in accordance with methods detailed in the Appendix. Short-term debt from Treasury Department, *Treasury Bulletin*, February 1976, Tables CM-II-2 and CM-IV-2. Short-term debts to banks exclude U.S. claims on the Bahamas, Panama, and Other Latin America, as well as on oil-exporting countries (1973 claims on Middle Eastern and African oil exporters estimated at $300 million and $75 million, respectively); debts to nonbanking concerns exclude claims on the Bahamas and Other Latin America, Indonesia, and Venezuela. Short-term debts include those of countries and private entities not covered by the World Bank data on long-term debt.
[a]September 1975.

1967 to 1973 (World Bank, 1975a, Table A), and this faster rate of increase has compounded the borrowers' problems. Private credits are available only on market-related terms, and the growth of borrowing from banks, private capital markets, and suppliers has hardened average terms. Interest rates are higher and maturities shorter than those forecast a few years ago.[3]

The figures in Tables 2.2 and 2.3 dramatize the size and urgency of the debt-service problem. In 1976, interest and amortization payments on long-term debts will probably exceed $14 billion, an increase of almost $5 billion in two years. They will be larger than gross loan disbursements were just two or three years ago.[4] If, in addition, some of the short-term debt incurred in 1974/1975 has to be repaid, as assumed in Table 2.3, total debt-service payments will climb to $17 billion, a figure far higher than anything projected five years ago.

There is no need to belabor the obvious. To exchange current for future

Table 2.2 Projected Debt-Service Flows, 1976

Type of Debt	Implicit Service Rates		Projected Service Flow in 1976 ($ million)		
	Interest (percent)	Amortization (years)	Interest	Amortization	Total
Suppliers' Credits	5.42	4.67	428	1,692	2,120
Bank Credits	7.72	7.30	1,729	3,068	4,797
Other Private Credits	5.52	9.17	414	818	1,232
International Organizations	4.86	23.25	1,016	899	1,915
DAC Governments	2.90	17.24	1,032	2,065	3,097
East Bloc Governments	1.66	9.43	85	541	626
Other Governments[a]	2.90	17.24	181	360	541
Total, Long-term Debt	–	–	4,885	9,443	14,328
Estimate, 1974[b]	–	–	3,126	6,459	9,585
Increase, 1974 to 1976	–	–	1,759	2,984	4,743

Source: Implicit rates from same source as those in Table 2.10 of the appendix; debt-service flows calculated using implicit service rates and debt projections in Table 2.1.

[a] Actual implicit service rates were 2.89 percent and 10.42 years in 1973; it is assumed here, however, that the relevant rates for this category, dominated now by debts to oil-exporting countries, resemble rates on debts to DAC governments.

[b] Sum of projected flows from Table 2.10 of the appendix.

resources at recent rates and on current terms is not a prudent way to foster larger flows of resources to developing countries. To do so would only exacerbate a problem that may now be acute.

There is, then, only one way to transfer more resources. Developed countries must give them away by larger grants and grant-equivalent transfers. It is, of course, fashionable to be pessimistic about their willingness to do so, and nothing in the numbers can allay that pessimism. The growth of bilateral development assistance has barely kept pace with world inflation, and no large donor has achieved the target accepted by the majority of OECD countries—an annual transfer of official development assistance equal to 7/10 of 1 percent of GNP.[5]

The international political atmosphere is hardly conducive to enlarging grant and grant-equivalent transfers. Nations, like individuals, can be persuaded to part with resources only by appealing to their self-esteem or self-interest, and much has happened recently to weaken the donors' belief that development assistance serves their self-interest.

Denunciations, declarations, and diplomatic opposition to policies of the United States have led many Americans to reappraise the commitment to global values that has been a mainspring of public support for U.S. bilateral

Table 2.3 An Estimate of Debt-Service Flows on Short-Term Debt 1974 and 1976

		Amount ($ million)	
Item	Rate	1974	1976
Interest on Short-Term Debt			
To U.S. Banks	7.72 percent[a]	463	1,119
To U.S. Nonbanking Concerns	5.42 percent[b]	114	184
Total Interest		577	1,303
Amortization of Increase in Short-Term Debt			
To U.S. Banks	7.30 years[a]	–	1,164
To U.S. Nonbanking Concerns	4.67 years[b]	–	278
Total Amortization		–	1,442
Total Interest and Amortization		577	2,745
Debt-Service Flow, All Debt[c]		10,166	17,073

Source: Debt data from Table 2.1; implicit service rates from Table 2.2.

[a] Average rate for long-term bank credits.

[b] Average rate for long-term suppliers' credits.

[c] Sum of short-term debt, above, and long-term debt from Table 2.2.

aid and for U.S. contributions to multilateral aid agencies. It would be wrong to suppose that the blunt words of U.S. representatives at United Nations' meetings reflect only momentary anger with particular resolutions. They convey a deeper disenchantment that may be hard to dispel.

Current Third World rhetoric, moreover, can hardly revive support for development assistance. Demands for reform of the international economic system that are prefaced by catalogs of past wrongs convey the distressing suggestion that international economic relations are a zero-sum game. An increase in the power or wealth of Third World countries is to be accomplished by diminishing the power or wealth of First World countries. Whether this inference is right or wrong, it is influential, and its implications are discouraging to those who would advocate an enlargement of development assistance.

Finally, the new demands for equity seem sometimes to border on hypocrisy. Governments that have done little indeed to rectify internal inequality are not embarrassed to demand an international rectification. Governments that invoke the liberal values of the West to justify their aims and programs are themselves sinners against those values, and their sins also tarnish what is left of the belief that development promotes democracy. We have long known that poverty breeds tyranny. We are beginning to realize that this proposition has no neat obverse. And we have seen too many instances in which growth has been ultrabiased toward guns, not butter.

I do not say these things to excuse the faults of the rich, at home or abroad. I recite them only to warn that extravagant rhetoric and conduct inconsistent with what one asks of others are here, as in all things, counterproductive. Now I turn to debt relief as one of the few devices that may evoke perceptions of self-interest and solicitude and may thereby generate a larger flow of development assistance.

The Case for Debt Relief

During the last two decades, several developing countries have sought and received debt relief in varying amounts.[6] Others will do so in the next few years. Judging from the growth of total debt-service flows and other indexes, debt burdens are higher now than ever before for many developing countries. Bankers and financial journalists are predicting large-scale defaults, and some developing countries are themselves hinting that they will default if relief is not forthcoming.

Defaults by developing countries, even if widespread, would not seriously threaten the stability of the international financial system, loose talk to that effect notwithstanding. Some banks and other private lenders would be hurt. A few might be wounded mortally. But there is little justification for the fear that defaults would wreck the Eurocurrency market or would do grave damage to national financial systems.

There are good reasons, however, for seeking to head them off. First, unilateral defaults would injure relations between developed and developing countries at a time when those relations are already strained by the policies and attitudes of many developing countries toward foreign investors and creditors. Private lenders who believe that they have been mistreated turn to their own government for support. The governments are forced to interpose themselves—to represent the interests of their citizens abroad—in a manner that often invites and sometimes earns the accusation of interference. Second, the prospect of default can have inequitable effects on the level and distribution of resource transfers. Lenders who worry about their debtors' ability to pay sometimes throw good credits after bad to keep them afloat, and borrowers whose own policies have impaired their ability to pay are rewarded, not punished, for their imprudence. Third, piecemeal default, when it takes place, is also apt to reward improvidence. Those who have borrowed too heavily or pursued policies inconsistent with their debt-service obligations escape those obligations. More importantly their conduct tarnishes the creditworthiness of others. Defaults by a handful of developing countries with relatively small debts would make it difficult for many others with good records and prospects to borrow anew.

Some of these objections to defaults are also objections to case-by-case debt relief. It, too, can favor the improvident and damage the creditworthiness of others. There is, at the very least, the need for agreed upon international rules to govern debt relief. There may be need for new multilateral institutions.

Above all, in my judgment, there is need to regard debt relief as a form of development assistance, not as a device for protecting the integrity of the lenders' balance sheets.

This last point is emphasized frequently by those who direct our attention to the problem. Summarizing debt-relief operations in the last two decades, Islam (1975, p. 34) has written:

Debt relief in the past was mainly related to service payments due in the immediate future. In some cases, it related only to a part of the total debt burden. Most of the creditor countries preferred a "short leash" approach, and kept their options open to review debt service problems after a few years. In some cases, the debt rescheduling exercises were undertaken more than once. A very long-term rescheduling, it was feared, might not ensure sufficiently strict economic discipline and sound debt management policies. In many cases, the interest rate applied to the rescheduled debt was the commercial rate; only in a few cases was it a concessional rate.

If there is any principle which may be said to guide debt relief operations, it is that relief afforded should be the minimum needed to ensure the early resumption of debt service payments and that the cost to the creditors of any postponement of amortization and interest payments, whether by means of rescheduling or refinancing, should be matched by additional interest charged at commercial rates. . . .

The debt relief I have in mind would be more comprehensive in scope and larger in grant content than has been typical heretofore. It would be a way of easing ex post the terms of official and private lending over the last twenty years.

Proposals along these lines were made by the Pearson Commission (1969, pp. 156-160) and have received official sanction. At its Seventh Special Session, the United Nations General Assembly called for comprehensive debt relief (Res. 3362, II, para. 8):

The burden of debt on developing countries is increasing to a point where the import capacity as well as reserves have come under serious strain. At its fourth session the United Nations Conference on Trade and Development shall consider the need for, and the possibility of, convening as soon as possible a conference of major donor, creditor and debtor countries to devise ways and means to mitigate this burden, taking into account the development needs of developing countries, with special attention to the plight of the most seriously affected countries. . . .

Anticipating the discussion at UNCTAD IV, the Group of 77 made a formal proposal at their Manila meeting in February 1976. I quote the operative paragraphs in their entirety:

3. Debt relief should be provided by bilateral creditors and donors in the form of waivers or postponement of interest payments and/or amortization, cancellation of principal, etc., of official debt to developing countries seeking such relief. In that framework, the least developed, the developing landlocked and the developing island countries should have their official debts cancelled. . . .

4. Multilateral development finance institutions should provide programme

assistance to each developing country in an amount no less than its debt service payments to these institutions.

5. Agreement should be reached to consolidate commercial debts of interested developing countries and to reschedule payments over a period of *at least* 25 years. The consolidation of commercial debts and the rescheduling of payments would require the establishment of suitable financial arrangements or machinery which might include, *inter alia*, a multilateral financial institution, such as a fund or a bank, designed to fund the short-term debts of interested developing countries.

This resolution addresses itself to a number of economic and political questions: Who should receive debt relief? Who should grant it? What form should it take? It is silent on certain other questions, including the one most often raised by those who are asked to grant relief: Can conditions be attached to debt relief to discourage developing countries from borrowing themselves back into difficulty very soon again?

No single set of answers to these and other questions will satisfy debtors and creditors. It may be difficult to satisfy even the debtors. Notice how often the ministerial resolution qualifies its own proposal with references to "interested" countries and to special claimants like landlocked and island countries. There are large differences, too, in the interests of lenders and in the characteristics of their claims. Loans by East Bloc countries, for example, bear lower interest rates but shorter maturities than those of Western governments (see Table 2.2).[7]

All of these differences lead some observers to despair of reaching any comprehensive agreement. They propose instead ad hoc arrangements subject only to loose principles and guidelines. This is the position taken by Bitterman (1973, pp. 228-229):

> The practical problems of refinancing à la Pearson, or generally refunding for all willing debtors, are formidable. It has taken long and difficult negotiation to get international agreement in the acute refunding cases. More general agreements would be practically impossible without the establishment of an international debt refunding agency financed pro rata by the creditors. Otherwise the refunding countries or those giving equivalent grants or soft loans would pay off the harder creditors. . . .
>
> In sum, a general refunding for all the aid recipients is not feasible either by consolidation or the Pearson method. From the standpoint of both creditors and debtors refunding should not be carried beyond necessity. Economic development will have to muddle through with a combination of credits, soft loans and grants punctuated by refundings as needed. . . .

I am not much more optimistic. But the problem itself has grown graver, and support for a comprehensive approach seems also to be growing. In my view, moreover, debt relief is one of the few policy domains in which developed countries can be forthcoming rather than reluctant in responding to demands from developing countries. Debt relief is not a zero-sum game. It can confer economic and political benefits on grantors and grantees and on the international system. It will at least remove a major irritant from the international body politic.

I do not minimize the difficulties or depth of differences in view that continue to separate developed and developing countries. The answers one gives to the questions I raised—to whom, from whom, and how—depend importantly on one's views about the role of debt relief.

If relief were granted, as in the past, primarily to preserve the integrity of the lenders' balance sheets, the following might be the answers: Relief should be granted only to countries that are now or will soon be unable to honor their obligations at an acceptable internal political cost. It should be granted directly by the creditors whose claims are in jeopardy. It should defer current debt-service payments but should not reduce substantially the present value of creditors' claims—it should not have a large grant element. On this view, moreover, countries that qualify for debt relief should agree to abstain from new borrowing, or, at the very least, to subordinate new obligations to those of their existing creditors. These answers are less generous than those implied by some of the arrangements made in recent years, but are not gross caricatures of those arrangements.

If relief is viewed instead as a form of development assistance, whether as a substitute or complement to others, the answers are different indeed. All developing countries should be eligible, although they need not be equally eligible. Relief should be granted by the chief suppliers of concessional assistance, even those that are not large creditors, and it should reduce significantly the present value of future debt-service flows, not just postpone current flows. Finally, the conditions imposed on the recipients should not be especially onerous, nor should they subordinate new borrowing to the claims of creditors that grant debt relief.

The questions I have raised and answered are not truly independent. The form in which debt relief is granted, for example, will determine in large measure the incidence of benefits. Turning the same point on end, distributional desiderata must figure prominently in the design of a debt-relief proposal. This point is recognized explicitly by the ministerial resolution quoted earlier, when it proposes canceling the debts of the least developed countries. The same point can be made quite plainly by asking what countries would benefit most from various forms of debt relief.

Using statistics furnished in the appendix, working with three country classes (based on the countries' incomes per capita), and expressing the reductions in first-year debt-service flows as percentages of debt disbursements, consider the effects of two proposals:[8]

1. A one-year forgiveness of interest on all long-term debt covered by the World Bank's debt tabulations would have reduced the debt-service payments of the higher-income countries by $2,155 million in 1974, that is, by 37 percent of concurrent debt disbursements. It would have reduced the payments of the lower-income countries by $519 million, in other words, by only 24 percent of debt disbursements. The higher-income countries have the largest debts at the highest interest rates and would have been the largest beneficiaries.

2. A one-year forgiveness of all interest on long-term bilateral debts to governments would have reduced the debt-service payments of the higher-income countries by $877 million, or 15 percent of disbursements. It would have reduced the payments of the lower-income countries by $392 million, or 18 percent of disbursements. The lower-income countries would have captured a larger share of the reduction in debt-service payments because they are the larger debtors to governments. The size of the reduction, however, is much smaller for all countries, absolutely and in relation to disbursements.

Clearly, any comprehensive plan that seeks to decrease substantially the probability of default by large debtor countries, but also to afford meaningful assistance to the lower-income countries, must include several types of concessions, tailored to the needs of the various countries.

The ministerial resolution calls attention to another set of issues impinging on one's answer to my question about sources of debt relief. It is not difficult to say who should grant relief in respect of debts to governments. The creditors themselves are the ones to do so. The answer is not as obvious, however, when one comes to the claims of multilateral lenders, especially the World Bank and regional development banks. These are financial intermediaries, obtaining most of their loanable funds from private financial markets. They cannot grant relief to their debtors without impairing their ability to service their own debts. Recognizing this particular difficulty, the ministerial resolution distinguishes clearly between bilateral creditors (para. 3) and multilateral institutions (para. 4), although the solution it proposes in respect of the latter seems to me unsatisfactory, because it could freeze new lending into a pattern that would discriminate against the newest, poorest countries.

Turning to credits from private institutions, it is easily argued that suppliers' credits should be refinanced by the creditors' national governments. Suppliers' credits finance exports and are not different in purpose or form from official export credits. As a matter of fact, many of these credits (and some bank loans) are insured or guaranteed by governmental entities. The fiscal, legal, and administrative arrangements required for something resembling refinancing are already in place. Most bank loans, however, pose difficult problems. Even those that financed exports to developing countries may bear no geographic congruence to the corresponding flows of goods. Loans by U.S. banks, for example, finance exports from many developed countries (and from one developing country to another). Furthermore, the largest long-term bank loans have been made recently by non-national (Eurocurrency) banks.

In debates about the regulation of these institutions, it is argued that responsibility for their integrity should rest with the governments of the countries from which they come. On this principle, the burden of refinancing credits extended by the foreign branches of U.S. banks would rest with the United States. This line of argument makes some sense when the aim is to defend the solvency or liquidity of the banks concerned; the U.S. government or one of its instrumentalities should be the lender of last resort to U.S. banks, wherever located. (Even in this somewhat different context, however, there are problems at the fringes. Who should be lender of last resort to banks that are truly non-national, like the so-called consortium banks?) Applied to the problem of debt relief, moreover, the principle itself is less cogent. The burden of concessional debt relief, a form of development assistance, should be allocated in accordance with some agreed upon notion of equity, not borne by those countries whose banks and their branches happen to have been large lenders to the developing countries. The refinancing of bank credits, to the extent that it occurs, should be handled multilaterally, as suggested by the ministerial resolution (para. 5).

Finally, what should be done about other forms of debt, including the bonds issued by developing countries in national and international capital markets? Were these to be refinanced, they might be treated like bank credits. There are reasons, however, for excluding them entirely from any comprehensive plan. First, an attempt to refinance or otherwise to modify the terms of bond issues would undo the progress made so slowly and painfully to open international capital markets to developing countries. I would prefer to proceed in a different direction—to adopt some of the measures proposed recently for easing access to private capital markets, including interest subsidies and guarantees.[9] Second, the bond issues of developing countries are marvelously heterogeneous. It would be very difficult to grant significant debt relief on terms that would be comparable across securities, let alone countries or groups of countries.

There is no way to guarantee that countries relieved of their debts will not immediately borrow again so heavily and on such terms that they will soon confront debt-service obligations as large as those they bear today. Once relief is granted, after all, the creditors' leverage is greatly diminished. It should not be impossible, however, to devise rules for new borrowing that would keep debt-service flows from growing more rapidly than current-account receipts (to keep so-called debt-service ratios from rising much above the levels to which they would be pared in consequence of debt relief). A country might still experience an unanticipated increase in its debt burden on account of a shortfall of export earnings. Such a country, however, would qualify for compensatory financing from the International Monetary Fund. In fact, the same moving average of export receipts that is used to measure shortfalls in current-account receipts and qualify a country for such financing might also be used to define the permissible rate of growth in debt-service payments and, therefore, the permissible level of new borrowing.[10]

A solemn undertaking to obey this rule would probably be honored by most governments, but sanctions might help. These could include denial of access to compensatory financing and to new official development assistance when a country borrows excessively or fails to meet its debt-service obligations once these are scaled down. The international community has by now acknowledged explicitly and liberally that developing countries should receive preferential treatment and should be exempted from certain obligations. But they cannot be allowed to renege on obligations assumed freely or to claim that all commitments made in the past were undertaken out of weakness and dire need. There can be no international order, old or new, if the doctrine of "changed circumstances" is allowed to prevail over fundamental principles of law. Countries that repudiate obligations cannot be permitted to claim rights and privileges.

Finally, one cannot guarantee that debt relief will increase the net flow of resources to any or all developing countries. Some of the funds required may well be diverted from other aid programs—including those that may be judged to be superior developmentally or distributionally. Debt relief is "high quality" aid in that it is untied. If administered in the fashion suggested here, moreover, it would have a large grant content. Yet it would also be unencumbered by conditions on its use, apart perhaps from limitations on new borrowing of the type proposed above, and the manner in which some developing countries have spent their freely available funds—on guns, not butter—has led many advocates of aid to retreat from their earlier belief that aid should be entirely unconditional.

Critics of debt relief have emphasized these points, and I do not minimize their importance. Nor do I know of any way to obviate the possibility of substitution. It is naive to suppose that governments or legislatures can be deceived. It is morally wrong and stupidly arrogant to propose deception.[11] I do suggest an unconventional method of financing relief toward the end of this paper, but even this may not prevent substantial substitution. In my judgment, however, the threat of substitution is not a decisive objection. My own reasons for urging that debt relief receive consideration—reasons set out above—have to do with the political and economic consequences of wide-spread default. A general debt crisis would prolong and intensify North-South confrontation and most certainly would cause a sharp reduction in resource flows of all types, public and private, to all developing countries. On this view, debt relief is a defensive measure, not a device to enlarge the flow of resources.

The Size and Distribution of Benefits from Debt Relief

Several attempts have been made recently to gauge the effects of debt relief on debt-service burdens and on the net flow of resources to developing countries (UNCTAD, 1976). The one examined here is designed to show who would gain and by how much if there were a comprehensive international agreement reflecting the considerations I have already mentioned, if all developing countries took advantage of it, and if there were no substitution for other forms of aid. The proposal deals subsequently with four classes of long-term debt. The analysis asks what such an agreement would do to first-year debt-service flows, absolutely and in relation to gross flows of credit (measured as before by disbursements of long-term loans projected for 1974). I look at two base years, 1974 and 1976. Using 1974, the last year for which we have data broken down by groups of countries, I am able to ask *who* would benefit. Using 1976, I am able to ask how large the benefits would be, given current levels of debt and debt-service flows.[12]

The specific proposal analyzed here is not necessarily best. It is not a recommendation, merely an example on which to base an estimate of changes in debt-service burdens. It embodies the following features:

1. The governments of all developed countries would forgive absolutely fractions of their own long-term claims on developing countries. The fractions would be 25 percent for higher-income debtors, 50 percent for middle-income debtors, and 75 percent for lower-income debtors. In addition, the creditors would reduce the interest rates and lengthen the maturities on their remaining claims. The interest rates and maturities used here are based on averages attaching to bilateral DAC government loans at the end of 1973, listed on line 1 of Table 2.4. Interest rates would be reduced by one-half of one percent and maturities lengthened by about 50 percent for all debtors taken together, as shown on line 3 of Table 2.4.

2. Multilateral institutions would not forgive any of their claims but would agree to a similar reduction of interest rates and lengthening of maturities. In some instances, this would require new lending by a soft-loan agency such as the International Development Association (IDA) to pay off quasi-commer-

Table 2.4 Rates Used to Estimate Effects of Alternative Debt-Relief Proposals, 1974

Rate Structure	Interest (percent)			Amortization (years)		
	Higher Income	Middle Income	Lower Income	Higher Income	Middle Income	Lower Income
1. Actual Official Bilateral[a]	3.50	3.00	2.25	13	16	27
2. Actual Official Multilateral[b]	6.25	5.50	2.25	19	22	37
3. Reduced Official Bilateral	3.00	2.50	1.75	20	30	40
4. Reduced Official Multilateral	5.75	5.00	1.75	25	35	50
5. Hypothetical Supplier	5.00	4.50	3.75	10	15	20
6. Hypothetical Bank	6.25	5.50	2.25	10	15	20

[a]Based on rates for DAC governments in Table 2.10 of the appendix.
[b]Based on rates for international organizations in Table 2.10 of the appendix.

cial loans by, say, the World Bank; relief would be accomplished by substituting one form of indebtedness for another. Actual interest rates and years to maturity are shown on line 2 of Table 2.4; proposed rates and maturities are shown on line 4.

3. Governments would agree to take over or refinance long-term suppliers' credits granted by their nationals. They are not likely to do so, however, on terms as generous as those proposed to consolidate governmental loans. Here, then, I examine the consequences of two proposals. The first and more generous assumes governments that would offer terms resembling those actually attaching to governmental loans at the end of 1973 (line 1 of Table 2.4). The second and less generous proposal assumes that they would offer terms more liberal than those offered by suppliers but less generous than those offered on their own loans (line 5 of Table 2.4).

4. A new multilateral institution would be established to furnish debt relief in respect of long-term debts to banks. Here, as with suppliers' credits, two sets of terms are studied. The first and more generous are those actually offered by multilateral institutions at the end of 1973 (line 2 of Table 2.4). The second and less generous set of terms contains the same interest rates but requires more rapid repayment (line 6 of Table 2.4).

Table 2.5 shows what would have happened if the most generous option had been offered in each instance above, and all developing countries had taken advantage of it. It assumes the progressive forgiveness of official bilateral debt, and the consolidation of suppliers' and bank credits at the relatively low interest rates and long maturities shown on lines 1 and 2, respectively, of Table 2.4 The table also shows what would have happened had less generous terms been offered (consolidation of official bilateral debt without progressive forgiveness, and consolidation of suppliers' and bank credits on the terms shown by lines 5 and 6, respectively, of Table 2.4).[13]

Table 2.6 calibrates the calculations detailed in Table 2.5. It expresses the reductions in first-year debt-service flows as percentages of total debt-service flows and of loan disbursements in 1974. Three points emerge at once.

First, unless consolidation is accompanied by the progressive forgiveness of governmental loans, there will not be substantial relief for lower-income countries. Compare the first-year reductions with and without forgiveness. Second, relief in respect of suppliers' and bank credits on the terms described here would be most helpful absolutely to the higher-income countries, but the gains to the middle- and lower-income countries would not be inconsiderable as fractions of total debt-service flows or loan disbursements. Third, debt relief may be well worth the effort. A comprehensive consolidation of long-term indebtedness on the best terms described above, taken together with the progressive forgiveness of governmental loans, could have increased the flow of resources to developing countries by $4.5 billion in 1974 and by $6.7 billion in 1976. Each of these numbers was slightly larger than 45 percent of total debt-service flows in the corresponding year.

Table 2.5 Estimated First-Year Effects of Alternative Debt-Relief Proposals, Long-Term Debt, 1974 and 1976 ($ million)

Proposal	Estimated Debt-Service Flows, 1974					Projected All Countries, 1976
	Higher Income	Middle Income	Lower Income	All Countries	Im-plicit Rates[a]	
Consolidation of official bilateral debt with forgiveness:						
Interest	314	78	61	453	2.65[b]	621[c]
Amortization	524	104	87	715	23.87[b]	982[c]
Reduction in debt service	741	459	764	1,964	—	2,660
Consolidation of official bilateral debt without forgiveness:						
Interest	419	156	243	818	2.40	1,126
Amortization	699	208	346	1,253	27.20	1,725
Reduction in debt service	461	277	322	1,060	—	1,412
Consolidation of official multilateral debt:						
Interest	360	74	72	506	4.26	890
Amortization	251	42	83	376	31.57	662
Reduction in debt service	117	33	53	203	—	363
Consolidation of suppliers' credits at actual official bilateral rates:						
Interest	155	50	23	228	3.19	252
Amortization	340	104	39	483	14.78	534
Reduction in debt service	673	289	182	1,144	—	1,332
Consolidation of suppliers' credits at hypothetical suppliers' rates:						
Interest	221	75	39	335	4.69	370
Amortization	442	111	52	605	11.80	669
Reduction in debt service	505	257	153	915	—	1,081
Consolidation of bank credits at actual official multilateral rates:						
Interest	578	46	18	642	5.88	1,317

Table 2.5 (continued)

| Proposal | Estimated Debt-Service Flows, 1974 | | | | | Projected |
	Higher Income	Middle Income	Lower Income	All Countries	Im-plicit Rates[a]	All Countries, 1976
Consolidation of bank credits at actual official multilateral rates: *(continued)*						
Amortization	487	38	22	547	19.95	1,123
Reduction in debt service	908	131	109	1,148	–	2,357
Consolidation of bank credits at hypothetical bank rates:						
Interest	578	46	18	642	5.88	1,317
Amortization	925	56	41	1,022	10.68	2,097
Reduction in debt service	470	113	90	673	–	1,383
Summary for Selected Categories						
Bilateral and multilateral debt Reduction with forgiveness	858	492	817	2,167	–	3,023
Reduction without forgiveness	578	310	375	1,263	–	1,775
Suppliers' and bank credits Reduction on actual official terms	1,581	420	291	2,292	–	3,689
Reduction on hypothetical terms	975	370	243	1,588	–	2,464
Total reduction on best terms[d] With forgiveness	2,439	912	1,108	4,459	–	6,712
Without forgiveness	2,159	730	666	3,555	–	5,464

Source: Based on debt and debt-service data in Tables 2.1 through 2.3 and Table 2.10 of the appendix and terms proposed in Table 2.4.

[a]Calculated service payment as a percentage of multiple of all-country debt in 1973.

[b]After deducting forgiveness from all-country debt.

[c]After deducting debt forgiveness (at all-country average of 50 percent).

[d]Best terms are actual official terms applied to suppliers' and bank credits.

Table 2.6 Perspectives on Debt-Relief Proposals, 1974 and 1976

Proposal	Estimated Debt-Service Flows, 1974				Projected All Countries, 1976
	Higher Income	Middle Income	Lower Income	All Countries	
Reductions as Percentages of Total Debt-Service Flows					
Bilateral and multilateral debt					
With forgiveness	13.6	29.5	51.2	22.6	21.1
Without forgiveness	9.1	18.5	23.5	13.2	12.4
Suppliers' and bank credits					
Official terms	25.0	25.2	18.2	23.9	25.7
Hypothetical terms	15.4	22.2	15.2	16.6	17.2
Total reduction on best terms[a]					
With forgiveness	38.6	54.7	69.4	46.5	46.8
Without forgiveness	34.2	43.8	41.7	37.1	38.1
Reductions as Percentages of Loan Disbursements					
Total reduction on best terms[a]					
With forgiveness	41.5	50.5	50.4	45.1	—
Without forgiveness	36.7	40.4	30.3	35.5	—

Source: Debt-service reductions from Table 2.5; debt-service flows and loan disbursements from same source as Table 2.10 of the appendix.

[a]Best terms are actual official terms applied to suppliers' and bank credits.

The distribution of benefits from debt relief, even with progressive forgiveness, would not be strongly skewed in favor of the poorest countries. When first-year reductions are compared to total debt-service flows, the outcomes appear to be skewed in their favor. Using my 1974 figures, the lower-income countries would have garnered a 69 percent reduction in debt-service flows, compared with only 39 percent for the higher-income countries. But when the same reductions are compared to loan disbursements—the current gross flow of resources are a better measure for this purpose—the benefits appear to be distributed quite uniformly. The same figures for 1974 imply (in the absence of substitution) a 50 percent increase in gross flows to middle- and lower-income countries and a 41 percent increase in gross flows to higher-income countries. Without progressive forgiveness, moreover, debt relief would have been regressive. The absolute and relative benefits would have been largest for the higher-income countries.

Table 2.7 shows calculations for three countries, Argentina, Korea, and India, one from each country class in Table 2.6. The summary statistics

Table 2.7 First-Year Reductions in Debt-Service Flows, Selected Countries, 1973 ($ million)

Item	Argentina	Korea	India
Consolidation of official bilateral loans			
With forgiveness	30	41	375
Without forgiveness	22	6	141
Consolidation of official multilateral loans	23	6	22
Consolidation of suppliers' credits			
Official terms	166	134	45
Hypothetical terms	141	116	38
Consolidation of bank credits			
Official terms	68	32	22
Hypothetical terms	49	29	20
Total reduction on best terms[a]			
With forgiveness	287	213	464
Without forgiveness	279	178	230
Total as percentage of 1973 debt service			
With forgiveness	41	58	73
Without forgiveness	40	48	36
Total as percentage of 1973 loan disbursements			
With forgiveness	34	29	55
Without forgiveness	33	24	27

Source: Debt and debt-service data from World Bank, *World Debt Tables*, October 1975 (EC-167/75), Table 9; debt-relief proposals from Table 2.4.
[a]Best terms are actual official terms applied to suppliers' and bank credits.

shown there suggest that the conclusions drawn above for broad country classes are valid also for important members of those classes. Once again, progressive forgiveness is required if India, the lowest-income country, is to obtain substantial relief and if the distribution of benefits is not to be skewed in favor of the wealthier countries.

The Costs of Debt Relief

I conclude with some numbers and thoughts on the costs of the analyzed proposal. The costs, like the benefits, are expressed on a first-year basis, not as present values. They are, then, readily comparable to figures on annual aid flows, but not to figures on grant equivalents.

Table 2.8 shows how much it would cost developed countries to forgive

Table 2.8 First-Year Costs of Debt-Relief Proposals ($ million)

Item	Cost 1974	1976
Consolidation of official bilateral loans with forgiveness		
Interest forgiven	430	649
Amortization forgiven	972	1,483
Cost of forgiveness[a]	1,402	2,132
Interest foregone	61	27
Interest cost of deferred amortization[b]	37	38
Total costs	1,500	2,197
Consolidation of official bilateral loans without forgiveness		
Interest foregone	126	171
Interest cost of deferred amortization[b]	70	93
Total costs	196	264
Total costs of other proposals		
Consolidation of official multilateral loans	81	144
Consolidation of suppliers' credits		
Official terms	233	263
Hypothetical terms	117	135
Consolidation of bank credits		
Official terms	272	558
Hypothetical terms	236	485
Total costs of best terms[c]		
To governments		
With forgiveness	1,733	2,460
Without forgiveness	429	527
To multilateral institutions	353	702

Source: Based on debt-relief proposals outlined in Table 2.4.

[a]If computed as the interest cost of borrowing the principal of total debt forgiven, using a 7.5 percent interest rate, the figures would be $1,276 million for 1974 and $1,759 million for 1976.

[b]Cost of borrowing at a 7.5 percent interest rate to cover the reduction in first-year amortization payments.

[c]Best terms are actual official terms applied to suppliers' and bank credits.

progressive fractions of their claims on developing countries and to consolidate the remaining claims on more generous terms. The costs are (1) interest forgiven, (2) amortization forgiven, (3) interest foregone in consequence of lower interest rates, and (4) interest incurred by lengthening maturities (that is, the cost of borrowing at 7.5 percent to cover the first-year difference between old and new amortization payments). The total first-year cost of this package would have been $1.5 billion if implemented in 1974 and about $2.2 billion if implemented in 1976. The largest part of the cost is interest and amortization forgiven. Without progressive forgiveness, the package would have cost about $200 million in 1974 and some $256 million in 1976.

Table 2.8 also shows the total costs of the other components (each of which consists of interest foregone on account of reduced rates and interest incurred on account of longer maturities). The totals at the bottom of the table assume that governments take responsibility for consolidating official bilateral loans and suppliers' credits and that multilateral institutions (including a new one to deal with bank credits) take responsibility for the other two components.

Costs to governments have to be borne in the usual way—by budgetary appropriations or public borrowing. Costs to multilateral institutions, which have no power to levy taxes and cannot borrow on terms as favorable as those on which they would be lending, have to be financed some other way. In the short run, the financing might be made available from the Trust Fund established with profits from gold sales by the International Monetary Fund. In the long run, however, there is need to tap new sources of revenue.

I close with one suggestion along these lines. It borrows from one frequently made for the use of royalties generated by the exploitation of seabed resources.[14] Producers of all nonrenewable resources, wherever they may be, should be taxed on their output, and the proceeds should be used in aid of development. It is by now generally acknowledged that the world's nonrenewable resources are or should be subject to global regulation for purposes of conservation. It is a simple, logical extension of this principle to assert that rents arising from ownership and exploitation are or should be placed at the disposal of the international community. If the accident of ownership does not justify reckless exploitation, neither can it justify unilateral appropriation.

I do not propose that all of these rents be devoted to international use. I would not even know how to calculate them. Instead, I suggest that a tax be levied at one percent of the value of output and that some of the revenue raised be used to finance the multilateral institutions' share of the costs of debt relief.

Table 2.9 attempts to show how much revenue could be raised by a tax on twelve commodities and the countries that would pay it. It derives from calculations based on output in 1971 and prices in 1971 and 1974. A one percent tax would have raised $1.3 billion at 1971 prices and $3.5 billion at

Table 2.9 Revenues from a One Percent Tax on Outputs of Nonrenewable Resources ($ million)

Commodity or Producer	1971 Prices	1974 Prices
Total, Twelve Commodities[a]	1,276.2	3,551.4
Coal[b]	798.5	1,519.6
Petroleum[c]	333.3	1,778.7
Metals[d]	117.9	212.4
Chemicals[e]	26.9	40.7
United States	271.9	811.9
European Community	134.6	253.6
Other Developed Countries	95.0	225.2
Eastern Europe	97.5	184.6
Oil-Exporting Countries[f]	199.6	1,065.4
Other Developing Countries	89.5	169.8
Unallocated[g]	388.5	840.9

Source: Output and price data from published sources; details available on request.

[a]Excludes production in the U.S.S.R., the People's Republic of China, East Germany, North Korea, and North Vietnam.

[b]Valued at the German export price.

[c]Valued at the price for light Iranian crude.

[d]Aluminum, copper, iron, lead, tin, and zinc. Outputs of nonferrous metals were valued arbitrarily at 75 percent of the price for final (refined) output quoted on the London Metals Exchange; iron ore is valued at the Lake Superior price.

[e]Nitrates, phosphates, potash, and sulphur, valued at U.S. domestic prices.

[f]Includes revenue from products other than petroleum.

[g]Revenue from countries producing less than one percent of world output; country composition varies across commodities.

1974 prices (because most commodity prices were higher). The United States would have paid one-fifth of the tax. The oil-exporting countries would have paid about 15 percent at 1971 prices and about 30 percent at 1974 prices. This distribution reflects the fact that oil and coal, the two nonrenewable fuels included in the calculation, account for most of the revenue. The large contributions of the United States and OPEC are neither unreasonable nor punitive. These countries sit on precious resources whose worth is in no way due to the genius, industry, or abstinence of their citizens. Resources are the gift of God, no matter what language we use to address Him.

The one percent tax proposed here would have covered twice over the costs to the multilateral institutions of the debt-relief plan outlined above, even if the tax were based on 1971 prices. No one, however, would have trouble devising ways to use the rest of the revenue. A tax of this type, indeed, may be the most promising way to finance interest subsidies on future borrowing by the developing countries, including their borrowing through multilateral institutions. Subsidies may be required over the long term to prevent an early reemergence of debt-service problems, even with guidelines and sanctions to limit extravagant borrowing.

Notes

I am indebted to several colleagues for comments on the first version of this paper, especially to C. Fred Bergsten, Hollis Chenery, Richard Cooper, Charles Frank, Lawrence Krause, John Lewis, W. Arthur Lewis, and Paul Streeten. Some gave me their comments personally; others raked me over the coals at the MIT Workshop. They may notice some change in the tone of this revised version, but it will be too large to satisfy some of them and not large enough to satisfy others. I am grateful to Nancy Marion of Princeton University for gathering and processing the data used to illustrate the tax proposal made at the end of the paper.

1 There are no comprehensive data on the short-term debts of developing countries. The U.S. data used in this paper, however, account for a large slice of total short-term bank credit and may also serve to gauge the trend in total short-term suppliers' credit.

2 The 1975 projections in Table 2.1 use data and methods described in the appendix. The increase of long-term debt in 1974/1975, $35 billion, may understate net borrowing during those years, but does not fall far short of the figure produced independently by Holsen and Waelbroeck (1976) reproduced in the Appendix.

3 Several readers have urged me to recognize that worldwide inflation has reduced real interest rates, offsetting in whole or part the tendency described in the text. The point is well taken but needs qualification. It is the improvement in a debtor's terms of trade, not the rate of inflation *per se,* that reduces real *external* indebtedness, and the terms of trade of developing countries were not much better at the beginning of 1976, after the recent price cycle, than in 1971, before it started.

4 World Bank (1975a), Table 1D. Gross disbursements to developing countries (other than oil-exporting countries) totaled $11.8 billion in 1972 and rose to $15.6 billion in 1973, averaging $13.7 billion in the two years together.

5 Recent trends are summarized in World Bank (1975b), p. 8. There is one cause for guarded optimism—a gradual increase in the grant component of official development assistance—but it was not sustained in 1974.

6 The major cases are surveyed by Bitterman (1973).

7 Some of them, moreover, are repayable in the debtors' own currencies, which is to say that they are in effect repayable in the debtors' exports.

8 Here and hereafter, I use disbursements to calibrate debt relief, because they can be deemed to measure to a first approximation the level of gross flows of development assistance. The debt-service flows and debt disbursements used in this particular calculation are those projected by the World Bank, using debt data through 1973. Actual disbursements may have been quite different in 1974, since new borrowing was large (and some of it was utilized quickly to finance the current-account deficits resulting from the increase in oil prices and the decline of other raw-material prices). For present purposes, however, projected disbursements may be the better yardstick, as they were not so heavily influenced by the need for balance-of-payments financing, reflecting instead the distribution of undisbursed credits and, therefore, the distribution, ex ante of development assistance. The country classification used here and later is the one in World Bank (1975a); the countries labeled lower-income include most of those classified as Most Seriously Affected in UN usage.

9 See, for example, Michalopoulos (1975) and the proposals made in the resolution of the Ministerial Meeting of the Group of 77 (para. 12). One reader suggests that this option be pursued to its logical limit: the poorest developing countries should be granted debt relief (approaching debt cancellation); the more affluent should not be granted any debt relief but should be afforded easier access to credit and export markets in the developed world.

10 I admit to slighting one major difficulty. Some governments do not know how much their countries owe, and many do not have comprehensive controls to keep total borrowing, including private borrowing, in line with permissible levels.

11 I would still urge that development assistance be funded on a long-term basis, not annually through complex legislative processes. The aim, however, is not to bypass the legislature, but rather to reduce the costs and uncertainties involved in guiding an appropriation through the legislature each and every year (and exposing aid programs to volatile swings in public opinion concerning the policies of individual foreign governments).

12 The analysis for 1974 uses the statistics on debt and debt-service payments shown in Table 2.10 of the appendix; the totals for all countries are sums of the subtotals for the three country groups that are analyzed separately. The analysis for 1976 is based on global figures; I had neither the resources nor data to project separately the debts and debt-service payments of the three country groups. To obtain the results for 1976, I have had to assume that the reductions in interest rates and extensions of maturities that were applied to the three country groups individually in respect of 1974 would give the same global changes in interest rates and maturities in 1976 as they did in 1974. This assumption is inaccurate, as the pattern or borrowing has changed, but I had no other way to estimate effects of debt relief on current debt-service burdens. The calculations for 1974 and 1976 are independent, not consecutive. If the proposals analyzed here had been applied in 1974, debts and debt-service flows would have been different in 1976, invalidating my calculations for 1976. In other words, each set of calculations assumes that the year to which it refers is the first year of debt relief. Another methodological qualification: I have not tried to calculate the *total* relief afforded by each component of the proposal (to calculate the change in the present value of future debt-service flows, thereby to measure the concessional element in each component). But because each component involves a reduction of interest rates as well as an extension of maturities, each one probably contains a significant concessional element.

13 One cannot estimate the effects of consolidating short-term debt, since there are no comprehensive data with which to work. A partial calculation, however, shows that the effects are large. If short-term debts to U.S. banks and suppliers were refinanced at 6 percent and if all of the increase in 1974/1975 were amortized across ten years, not on the terms shown in Table 2.3, these would be the first-year effects in 1976:

Interest	1,074
Amortization	890
Reduction in debt service	781

14 See Oda, *et al.* (1976). Proposals similar to my own have been made before, as by Ul Haq (1975, p. 161).

References

Bitterman, H. J., 1973, *The Refunding of International Debt* (Duke University Press, Durham).

Holsen, J., and J. Waelbroeck, 1976, LDC Balance of Payments Policies and the International Monetary System (World Bank Staff Working Paper No. 226).

Islam, N., 1975, *New Mechanisms for the Transfer of Resources to Developing Countries* (United Nations Economic and Social Council, Doc. E/AC.54/L.83).

Kenen, P. B., and C. S. Voivodas, 1972, Export Instability and Economic Growth, *Kyklos*, 25, 791-804.

Michalopoulos, C., 1975, *Financing Needs of Developing Countries: Prospects for International Action* (International Finance Section, Princeton University, Princeton).

Oda, S., et al., 1976, *A New Regime for the Oceans* (Trilateral Commission, New York).

Pearson, L. B., et al., 1969, *Partners in Development: Report of the Commission on International Development* (Praeger, New York).

Ul Haq, M., 1975, Negotiating a New Bargain with the Rich Countries, in G. Erg and V. Kallab, eds., *Beyond Dependency* (Overseas Development Council, Washington).

UNCTAD, 1976, *International Financial Co-operation for Development: Debt and Debt Service* (United Nations Conference on Trade and Development, Doc. TD/188/Supp.1, Ch. III).

World Bank, 1975a, *World Debt Tables* (EC-167/75).

World Bank, 1975b, *Annual Report*.

Appendix
Projecting Long-Term Debts to 1975

Under normal circumstances, two years are not long to wait for a definitive statistical compilation like the one provided by the World Bank in *World Debt Tables*. But the events of 1974/1975 caused large changes in the volume, and, no doubt, the composition of international indebtedness. Thus, the effort to project long-term indebtedness summarized in Table 2.1 of the text and described in more detail by this appendix.

The appendix discusses line-by-line the entries in Table 2.1, and uses the following abbreviations to denote data sources:

BIC *Borrowing in International Capital Markets*, World Bank, November 1975 and January 1976 (EC-181/753 and 754).
IFS *International Financial Statistics*, International Monetary Fund, February 1976.
TB *Treasury Bulletin*, U.S. Treasury Department, February 1976.
USW *The U.S. and World Development*, Overseas Development Council, 1975.
WB *World Bank Annual Report*, World Bank, 1974, 1975.
WDT *World Debt Tables*, World Bank, October 1975 (EC-167/75, I & II).

The benchmark figures mentioned below are those that appear in Table 7 of WDT; unless otherwise indicated, they refer to total *disbursed* debt at the end of 1973 and exclude the debts of oil-exporting countries.

Suppliers' credits were projected directly from the 1973 bench mark figures by assuming an invariant relationship between the number in WDT and the corresponding country total for the long-term claims of U.S. *nonbanking concerns* in TB. (There has in fact been some slight decrease in the WDT-TB ratio since 1970, but no allowance was made for a further decline in 1974 or 1975.) In September 1975, the latest date for which TB data were available, the long-term claims of U.S. nonbanking concerns were $1,880 million. Multiplying by the WDT-TB ratio, we obtain as the 1975 projection the $7.9 billion in Table 2.1.

Private bank credits were projected separately for U.S. and other banks. Credits owed to U.S. banks are represented by the long-term claims of U.S. banks in TB. In December 1973, the total for developing countries was $3,358 million; in December 1975, it was $5,529 million. The difference between the 1973 bench mark in WDT and the TB figure was taken to represent total credits owed to other banks, including Eurocurrency banks, and was projected on the following assumptions: (1) that undisbursed credits at the end of 1973 were distributed between U.S. and other banks in the same proportion as total disbursed credits; (2) that published Eurocurrency credits in BIC were the only new credits extended by banks outside the United States in 1974 and 1975; (3) that new debt disbursements in each quarter of 1974 and 1975 were 25 percent of the sum of undisbursed credits at the start of the quarter and new Eurocurrency credits extended during the quarter; and (4) that annual repayments to banks outside the United States bore the same relationship to total disbursed debt that repayments projected for 1974 in WDT bore to total disbursed debt in December 1973 (that they were 15.3 percent of disbursed debt at the start of each year).

To illustrate the application of these assumptions, consider the annual estimates for 1974 (in millions of U.S. dollars):

Undisbursed credits, December 1973 (69.2 percent of
total undisbursed credits in WDT) $1,941
New Eurocurrency credits, 1974 (from BIC) 8,222
Disbursements in 1974 (sum of quarterly estimates) 5,589
Repayments in 1974 (15.3 percent of disbursed debts
in December 1973, WDT less TB) 1,156
Net increase in disbursed credits owed, 1974 4,433
Estimate of undisbursed credits, December 1974 4,574

The 25 percent disbursement rate is somewhat larger than the one implied by the annual projections of disbursements in WDT. It is nevertheless reasonable to assume some acceleration of disbursements in the special circumstances of 1974/1975. Performing the corresponding calculation for 1975 and adding the two-year increase in disbursed credits owed to the 1973 total in WDT, disbursed credits from all banks outside the United States were projected at $16,905 million in December 1975.

Other private credits were projected on the assumption that new international and foreign bond issues were the only source of other private credit in 1974 and 1975, that these were fully disbursed, and that there was no amortization of the new bonds in whole or in part during 1974 or 1975. Thus, the projection in Table 2.1 is the sum of the projection in WDT (which allows for the disbursement and repayment of credits extended before 1974) and of new bond issues listed in BIC.

Loans from international organizations were projected by amending the projection in WDT. That projection allows for the disbursement and repayment of loans approved before 1974. Four amendments allow for disbursements of loans approved in 1974 and 1975:

1. Disbursements of new loans by the World Bank and its affiliates were projected by assuming that half of the loan commitments made in fiscal 1974 came before December 31, 1973, and are included in the WDT projection (the rest being made in the first half of 1974), and that half of the commitments made in fiscal 1975 were made before December 31, 1974 (the rest being made in the first half of 1975). The World Bank and its affiliates committed approximately $3,650 million in fiscal 1974, apart from new commitments to oil producers, and another $5,300 million in 1975. Thus, an additional $1,830 million was deemed to be available for disbursement by June 30, 1974, and 10 percent was assumed to be disbursed in the second half of 1974. Similarly, $4,400 million of newly committed funds was deemed to be available by December 31, 1974 ($2,650 million of commitments in the first half of fiscal 1975 and 90 percent of the balance from 1974), and 10 percent was assumed to be disbursed in the first half of 1975. Carrying this procedure forward, disbursements of new credits were projected at $1,250 million for the two years ending in December 1975.

2. Disbursements of new loans by other development banks were projected crudely by assuming that they were one-fourth the size of new-loan disbursements by the World Bank and its affiliates. This ratio was derived from data on commitments in WDT, Table B. (Commitments by regional development banks and other multilateral institutions averaged 27.8 percent of commitments by the World Bank and IDA from 1970 to 1973 but the percentage was falling with the rapid growth of World Bank lending.)

3. Disbursements by the multilateral aid agencies established by the OPEC countries were projected arbitrarily at $250 million per year for two years.

4. Obligations to the IMF oil facility, excluding those of developed countries, are given in IFS at SDR 3,015 million for December 31, 1975, and this was equivalent to $3,530 million. (As this facility did not exist before 1974, all of its lending must be added to this debt category.)

The sum of these amendments is $5,590 million, bringing the total for the whole category to the $20.9 billion in Table 2.1.

Loans from DAC governments were projected on the basis of net lending reported or forecast in OECD data on the flow of Official Development Assistance (ODA) from DAC countries. This rubric does not include official export credit or lending for arms purchases. Some ODA, moreover, is destined for countries omitted from the totals in Table 2.1. In fact, the growth of ODA bears only a crude statistical relationship to the growth of total debt reported in WDT. From 1971 to 1973, for example, net bilateral lending reported as ODA amounted to $4.9 billion, while the increase of debt to DAC governments in WDT was $7.8 billion (including the increase of undisbursed debt but excluding oil-exporting countries). At the same time, lending reported as ODA was larger in 1974 than what is implied by the projection in Table 7 of WDT (a projection that makes no allowance for disbursements of new credits).

Development lending by DAC governments will be known with certainty by 1977, but the data for 1975 were not at hand when the projections were made. The figure in Table 2.1 is the sum of the actual number for 1974 (the $2,970 million in WB, 1975) and a forecast for 1975. The latter was obtained by assuming that actual ODA will exceed the forecast for 1975 in USW, Table D-4, by the same percentage that actual ODA exceeded the forecast for 1974, and that the bilateral loan component will be 26.3 percent of total ODA, its actual share in 1974. These assumptions give a loan forecast of $3,306 million for 1975 and, therefore, a two-year total of $6,276 million, the figure used in Table 2.1.

Loans from East Bloc governments were projected to grow slightly faster than in 1972/1973, when total debt, including undisbursed debt, rose by only $900 million. Table 2.1 shows an increase of $1.5 billion for 1974 and 1975 taken together. This is in the same neighborhood as the one implied by the extrapolation in WDT, Table 7. There, the projections from known commitments yield an increase of $660 million for 1974. Making only small allowance for disbursements of new loans—small because the data in WDT suggest that there are long lags between commitments and disbursements of East Bloc credits—one comes to the $750 million rate implied by the projection in Table 2.1.

Loans from other governments were projected by assuming that the only "other" governments making new loans in 1974/1975 were those of the OPEC countries and by amending the projection in WDT for disbursements of new credits by those governments. There is, however, much uncertainty concerning these disbursements. OECD figures in USW, Table D-9, put disbursements at $2.0 billion in 1974, and this number is not much different from the one implied by more recent data in WB, 1975. (Gross disbursements are given there at $5.0 billion, including $2,680 million to the World Bank and IMF. Subtracting this last sum and the $250 million mentioned above as the annual rate of disbursement through other multilateral aid agencies, one comes out with $2.1 billion for 1974.) But we know very little about disbursements in 1975. Bilateral commitments were very large in 1974 (they are put at $7.2 billion in USW, Table D-9), and there were additional commitments in 1975, some of which may have been disbursed. Here, then, it is assumed that disbursements in 1975 were half again as large as in 1974, so that total debts to "other" governments are listed as being $5.0 billion larger than the projection in WDT.

The two-year increase of debt shown in Table 2.1 is $34.8 billion, and, though it was estimated from fragmentary data, it is not vastly different from an estimate compiled by Holsen and Waelbroeck (1976) from more comprehensive and up-to-date sources:

Consolidated Balance of Payments for Non-Oil Developing Countries, 1974/75 ($ billion)
Goods and Services Deficit $69.7
Official Grants 8.2
Direct Investment 9.8
Long-Term Public Borrowing (including oil facility) 40.3
Other Borrowing (including errors and omissions) 9.9
Reserve Use (including other IMF drawings) 1.5

The figures shown here for long-term borrowing are similar to those shown in Table 2.1. Reclassifying the net changes shown there to match the components used by Holsen and Waelbroeck, we find:

	Holsen and Waelbroeck	Table 2.1
Loans from Banks	13.9	11.5
Loans from OPEC Sources	6.8	5.5
Other (including oil facility)	19.6	17.8

It would appear, then, that the estimates developed here are deficient chiefly in underestimating bank loans (because they rely entirely on U.S. and Eurocurrency data) and are too low also in respect of OPEC disbursements.

Note, finally, that the "other borrowing" estimated by Holsen and Waelbroeck comes close to the estimate of short-term borrowing from U.S. banks and nonbanking concerns that appears at the bottom of Table 2.1.

Table 2.10 Disbursed Long-Term Debt and Debt-Service Data by Country Class and Type of Debt, 1973

Type of Debt	Amount (in $ million)			Implicit Service Rates	
	Princi-pal in 1973	Projected Service Flow		Inter-est (percent)	Amorti-zation (years)
		Inter-est	Amorti-zation		
Higher-Income Countries					
Total disbursed debt[a]	39,624	2,155	4,165	5.44	9.5
Suppliers' credits	4,417	237	931	5.37	4.7
Bank credits	9,249	715	1,258	7.73	7.3
Other private credits	5,716	326	546	5.71	10.5
International organizations	6,265	400	328	6.39	19.1
DAC governments	12,875	445	961	3.46	13.4
East Bloc governments	771	19	94	2.47	8.2
Middle-Income Countries					
Total disbursed debt[a]	10,817	452	1,216	4.18	8.9
Suppliers' credits	1,673	104	399	6.21	4.2
Bank credits	844	66	149	7.77	5.7
Other private credits	589	30	130	5.12	4.5
International organizations	1,476	82	67	5.53	21.9
DAC governments	4,638	139	288	3.00	16.1
East Bloc governments	1,066	18	151	1.66	7.0
Lower-Income Countries					
Total disbursed debt[a]	20,352	519	1,078	2.55	18.9
Suppliers' credits	1,047	46	198	4.38	5.3
Bank credits	820	62	87	7.54	9.4
Other private credits	491	19	65	3.85	7.6
International organizations	4,128	95	113	2.30	36.7
DAC governments	11,800	266	445	2.25	26.5
East Bloc governments	1,783	23	138	1.31	12.9

Source: World Bank, *World Debt Tables*, October 1975 (EC-167/75), Table 7.

[a]Includes debts to other governments not shown separately.

Comment
Paul Streeten

"Let bygones be bygones." This is certainly misleading advice in economics. Bygones exercise a powerful influence on the future through their effects on expectations and incentives. All debt-relief problems have two sides, one facing the past and the other, the future. But the way in which we deal with the past affects powerfully expectations and incentives for the future. Frequently there is a conflict between the two. The writing off of past debts on the principle that we will let bygones be bygones may reduce the flow of capital in the future because we may expect the same thing to happen again.

Although loans at concessionary interest rates are a new, post-World War II, phenomenon, it is likely that the effective average interest rate on commercial loans before 1914 was low—if we take into account default on debts resulting from bankruptcies, wars, and other misadventures. A novel feature of the current debt situation is that defaults are no longer permitted to occur. Refinancing and rescheduling have taken their place.

In discussing how to tackle the debt problem, I would draw a sharper distinction than does Professor Kenen between commercial debts and development debts. The typical commercial debt used to be Ghana's. Examples of commercial debts now are those of Chile, Argentina, Peru, Bolivia, Uruguay, Zaire, Zambia, the Philippines, Brazil, Mexico, and South Korea. Examples of development debts are those of India, Pakistan, and Bangladesh. There is a danger that running up commercial debts on hard terms creates the expectation that relief will be given later. Such relief, if it comes out of the aid budget, may be aid to creditors in rich countries at the expense of worthier, poor aid recipients. It favors unworthy exporters and their bankers rather than development. I would also subdivide commercial debt into loans that are guaranteed and those that are not guaranteed by the creditor country's government. Guaranteed loans should, of course, be paid by the government if the debtor does not pay, but not out of the aid budget. In Britain, the Export Credits Guarantee Department (ECGD), and in the United States, the Export-Import Bank, are the guaranteeing institutions. Such an institution should be run like an insurance company and should be self-financing. There need be no aid element in guaranteed commercial debt. The introduction of the principle of insurance and of the clear liability of ECGD to accept the risks will introduce a note of caution into the lending processes and will obviate a situation in which aid bails out rash, rich lenders.

As far as nonguaranteed debt is concerned, we should allow, and occasionally encourage, default. There is the danger that manufacturers and their bankers push junk on developing countries and that these manufacturers and bankers then get compensated by the creditor countries' tax payers. The whole transaction then appears as a contribution to development aid. I can see no reason why we should not let debtors default and let this default be a warning to other lenders. Otherwise we set up wrong expectations and incentives, and aid flows to the wrong people. If anyone were to reply that we should respect the principle "caveat emptor," my reply would be that it is part of the syndrome of underdevelopment, that the countries lack experience and are understaffed in government offices.

It may be and often is asked in what sense aid is a burden. If the yield of the debt-financed project exceeds the interest rate, there is no problem about losing through debt service; if it falls short of it, it is foolish to borrow. I think it was Göran Ohlin who reminded us of an illustration of chutzpah: a boy murdered both his parents and then pleaded for mercy on the ground that he was an orphan. Some pleas for relief from the debt "burden" may sound rather like the plea of that boy.

But such an approach to the debt problem misses the point that developing countries, compared with domestic borrowers, must overcome three additional hurdles, and this is why the analogy between internal and international loans is misleading. (I shall not discuss the well-known fact that many loans are tied to procurement from the donor country, whereas debt service has to be in convertible currency.)

First, developing countries must pay the debt through increased exports or reduced imports, and what appears as a debt crisis is often in reality a balance of payments crisis. It is true that the secondary transfer burden (which consists in payment across the exchanges) can be negative. If the price of exports can be raised in the face of inelastic demand, the terms of trade will improve, and there will be a secondary benefit instead of a burden. On the other hand, and more normally, if the developed countries impose import restrictions, the secondary debt burden may become large and service of the debt may even become impossible. The ability to service it therefore depends partly upon the policies of creditor countries.

The second hurdle for intergovernmental debts is the budget. The developing country has to raise enough in taxes to service the debt, and for well-known reasons this may be difficult or impossible.

The third hurdle arises from the fact that internal loans at the same interest rate as those that apply to international loans have a lighter burden because the interest rate can be deducted from taxable income. In the absence of an international tax, the burden is therefore higher than for the same domestic debt. At a 50-percent profits tax, the burden of international debts is doubled. This argument does of course assume either that public services equivalent to its tax payments are received by the firm or that the tax can be passed on to consumers under a regime of administered prices.

As far as suppliers' credits are concerned, it is important that the restraint on excessive lending be exercised by creditor countries; and not, as Professor Kenen suggests, left entirely to the developing countries. This must be done jointly by the donor countries in order to resist the pressures of export lobbies and their bankers.

A final point: the mounting debt problem presents serious difficulties for aid recipients. Yet budgetary appropriations for aid present many donors with difficulties. The following proposal is an attempt to contribute simultaneously to the solution of both problems.

Repayments of principal and interest on previous loans should be credited to a separate aid budget, instead of returning to the exchequer. In this way, the budgetary requirements for new aid appropriations would be reduced. If donors were not willing to contribute aid, it would be possible for them to reduce new appropriations in proportion to the growth of the separate aid budget. But if they were serious in saying a budgetary, not a real resource, constraint prevented them from doing more, such an arrangement would make it possible to give a greater volume of aid without additional budgetary appropriations.

3

SDRs: The Link
John Williamson

The link may be defined as an arrangement whereby newly created reserve assets are injected into the international economy according to a distribution formula designed to promote the flow of development finance. Such a definition requires a criterion of a neutral distribution formula. The obvious definition, well established in the literature (Grubel, 1972), is that distribution is neutral if it is proportionate to countries' long-run demands for reserves. It has generally been accepted that IMF quotas provide a rough measure of countries' long-run reserve-demand levels, from which it follows that the existing basis for allocating newly created SDRs between countries, in proportion to IMF quotas, is roughly neutral. (Hawkins and Rangarajan, 1970, argued that IMF quotas were in fact biased against LDCs, but the conventional assumption that quotas provide an approximately neutral distribution formula will be accepted in what follows.) The link, then, implies that LDCs receive a larger proportion of newly created reserve assets than they obtain under the existing arrangement for allocating SDRs.

The purposes of this work are to review the development of the link proposal, to provide a critical survey of the arguments that have been developed concerning the desirability of a link, and to outline the progress of the link proposal in international negotiations, with a view to drawing conclusions regarding the potential role of the link as one element of a new international economic order.

Origins

The first proposal for a link was contained in the British proposals for an International Clearing Union (ICU) advanced during the pre-Bretton Woods negotiations. Keynes, the author of the British proposals, envisaged the ICU playing a role in financing "international bodies charged with post-war relief, rehabilitation and reconstruction" through the grant of overdraft facilities, which might be serviced out of the Reserve Fund of the ICU and a levy on surplus credit bancor balances (Cmd 6437, 1943, para. 39, 1). This proposal provoked Kalecki and Schumacher (1943) into suggesting the creation of a special Investment Account in the ICU from which industrializing countries might borrow directly for development purposes. They argued that this would not only facilitate development, but also would strengthen the defenses against the expected postwar deflation.

The modern debate on the link was initiated by Sir Maxwell Stamp (1958). In order to remedy the prospective shortage of international liquidity, he proposed that the IMF be empowered to create fund certificates that would rely for their acceptability on the agreement of all fund members to accept them as reserve assets in settlement of payments deficits. Noting the difficulty of persuading members to borrow from the fund, he suggested that an appropriate way of introducing fund certificates into circulation would be for the IMF to buy IBRD bonds with the newly issued certificates, thus permitting an expansion of IBRD lending for development. A revised version of his proposals in 1962 suggested the IDA as a suitable recipient for newly issued certificates and disburser of aid, and sought to provide safeguards against the inflationary impact of fund certificates on fully employed economies by allowing countries to contract out of the first-round spending of certificates and by placing a limit on the volume of certificates that a country was obliged to accept from any source.

A major debate on the possible prospective inadequacy of international liquidity was sparked by Triffin's *Gold and the Dollar Crisis* (1960). Triffin proposed converting the IMF into a deposit-issuing institution. This would have provided some scope for a link, since he envisaged IBRD bonds as one medium for IMF investments; although it should be noted that whether in fact it would have resulted in a link, in comparison with a neutral distribution formula, would have depended on the proportions in which the obligations of developed countries and of the IBRD were combined in the IMF's portfolio. Several of the numerous other plans advanced in the course of the debate also would have provided some scope for a link, but this was not true of those plans that initially had the most influential support; the multiple currency proposal initially favored by the United States, the composite reserve unit proposal of Bernstein (1963), and the French version of the composite reserve unit, would all have excluded the LDCs from participation in the distribution of newly created reserve assets, and therefore would have involved what has since been termed a "reverse link."

Variants

A number of variants of the link proposal have been advanced. These may be classified according to (1) the type of reserve asset to which they applied, (2) the source of link-created funds, (3) the "organic" versus the "inorganic" link, (4) the imposition of restrictions on the use of link-generated funds, and (5) the formula for distributing the proceeds of the link.

Question 1 is only of historical interest. The world now has its fiduciary reserve asset in the form of the SDR, and seems highly unlikely to get another one. Recent discussion has concentrated on the desirability of amending the SDR allocation formula so as to implement a link. This paper will be restricted to this version.

Question 2. It has normally been assumed that the link would be applied to newly created SDRs designed to increase the world supply of reserves. Maynard (1972) seems to have been the first to point out that, if a substitution operation were to lead to the replacement of reserve currencies by SDRs and if the former reserve centers were to amortize their debts to the substitution facility, the additional SDRs that would need to be created to prevent amortization leading to a depletion of the world reserve stock could also be distributed according to the link principle. There seems to be no reason for distributing any such SDRs on a basis other than SDR allocations designed to increase the world reserve stock; the case for linking such SDRs must stand or fall with the general case. It will be assumed therefore that any SDR allocations made to offset amortization would be treated in the same way as those made to expand world liquidity.[1]

Although a full link has not been accepted, several other proposals designed to increase the access of LDCs to IMF credit have in fact been implemented. The first step in this direction was the establishment in 1963 of the compensatory financing facility. This permitted a country experiencing a shortfall in export receipts (below the level indicated by a formula based on previous experience) to borrow from the fund without the usual conditions and beyond the normal limits. This facility was liberalized in 1966 and again in 1976, while a parallel facility to assist in the financing of buffer stocks was established in 1969. An Extended Fund Facility, under which LDCs could receive longer-term balance-of-payments finance in support of policies designed to correct "structural imbalances in production, trade, and prices," was created in 1974. Finally, the Trust Fund, to be financed by the profits on sales of redundant IMF gold, was established in 1976 with the object of providing assistance to needy LDCs. The remainder of this paper, however, will be confined to consideration of the SDR link.

Question 3. The "organic" link would involve a change in the IMF Articles so as to alter the formula governing the distribution of SDR allocations. The "inorganic" link, first suggested by Patel (1967), envisaged SDRs allocated by the IMF on the basis of existing quotas, but proposed that the developed countries should voluntarily contribute a proportion of their allocations to the IDA whenever new SDRs were created. This could be accomplished either by the IDA accepting the SDRs directly (provided, of course, that the IDA/IBRD were designated a holder of SDRs), or by the developed countries depositing equivalent quantities of their own currencies with the IDA. The main attraction of the inorganic link has always been the highly pragmatic one of not making introduction of the link dependent on the time-consuming process of amending the IMF Articles. Supporters of the link have taken it for granted that the inorganic link was a second best, principally because of the doubt as to whether all of the developed countries could be relied upon to contribute to IDA on the occasion of SDR allocations if this were voluntary. The version discussed here is the organic link.

Question 4. A number of economists, starting with Stamp (1962) and including Scitovsky (1966) and Karlik (1969), have proposed the imposition of restrictions on the countries where link generated funds may be spent. Their motive was the desire to keep the link from aggravating inflationary pressure in economies already operating at full capacity. Stamp proposed that individual surplus countries be allowed to contract out of the obligation to accept first-round expenditures of fund certificates, while Scitovsky and Karlik suggested that individual DCs desiring larger reserves should be allowed to buy newly issued reserve assets with their currency, which in turn would be placed with a development finance institution (DFI) for lending to LDCs who might then purchase goods in the specific country whose currency was lent to them. The main criticisms of the proposal are that tying is unlikely to be very effective (since IDA could divert its nontied funds to support purchases from those countries not eligible for tied expenditures); that, to the extent the first criticism is not applicable, tying would reduce the real value of aid; that in any event the tying is restricted to the first round of expenditure, so that reserve creation would still indirectly intensify the pressure of demand in fully employed economies; and, most fundamentally, that the availability of reserves on preferential terms to deficit countries would impair operation of the adjustment process (Haan, 1971, p. 145). Here, we will assume that there are no restrictions on first-round expenditure of link-generated funds.

Question 5 concerns the issue of how link-generated funds should be distributed to the developing countries. Most proposals prior to the 1970s envisaged the use of one or more of the DFIs as an intermediary for distributing link funds to the LDCs, presumably in the form of project aid. (Kalecki and Schumacher, 1943, provided an early exception: they envisaged individual developing countries borrowing directly from the Investment Account of the ICU.) However, when the LDCs came to formulate their common position on the link, in the course of the C-20 negotiations, they resolved instead to support a change in the country distribution of SDR allocations, under which developing countries would have a weighting factor (greater than unity) applied to their quotas for the purpose of determining entitlement to SDR allocations. (The "least developed countries"—twenty-five of the poorest countries, the largest of which is the Sudan—would, it was proposed, be entitled to an even greater weighting factor.) The LDC preference for this version of the link is easy enough to understand. First, it would place the responsibility as to how to use link-generated funds on the countries themselves, avoiding the need to negotiate with the DFIs. Second, borrowing from IDA has been heavily concentrated among a limited number of LDCs, notably Indonesia and the Indian subcontinent, which have a relatively minor voice among the LDCs in the IMF; the majority of the LDCs had a clear financial interest in a quota-based system of distribution. (The other LDCs that could be expected to lose from a quota-based distribution were compensated by the special provision for the least developed; the Indians were simply outvoted.) It is quite clear that the developed countries were at best unenthusiastic about this mutation of the link proposal, for reasons that were the direct converse of those that appealed to the LDCs. First, the elimination of DFI control over the spending of the proceeds of the link would have reduced the assurance that the funds would actually be spent to promote investment rather than to increase consumption (although the usual reasons for doubting the effectiveness of tying suggest that this factor is of limited consequence).[2] Second, since quotas are broadly proportionate to economic wealth while IDA aid goes to the poorest, the resulting income redistribution is liable to be less progressive under the LDC-favored version of the link (Cline, 1976, pp. 74-77). For the purpose of focusing discussion on a single version of the link proposal, it will be assumed hereafter that, if an aid link were to be instituted, it would take the form of weighting factors whereby the less developed and least developed would receive greater direct allocations of SDRs than under present arrangements. The reason for this assumption is that, where conflicting views are held by different groups of countries, usually the views of the countries with the greater interest in the question at stake can be expected to prevail.

The variant of the link to be considered here is therefore one in which the entitlement to receive newly created SDRs (including any that might result from a decision to offset the amortization of reserve centers' debts to a substitution facility) is modified by the application of weighting factors to the quotas of developing countries. These weighting factors would serve to raise the proportion of SDRs allocated to all developing countries, and to raise even more the proportion accruing to the least-developed countries. This would be an organic link, and there would be no restrictions on the expenditure of the linked SDRs.

Monetary Consequences of the Link

Much of the debate as to the desirability of a link has been addressed to the question as to whether a link could be expected either to enhance or to impede the operation of the international monetary system, and in particular as to how it might affect the ability of the SDR to provide the major reserve asset in the system. The present section will present and consider these arguments, taking up first the arguments that have been advanced by the supporters of the link, and then those developed by critics.

Stamp's original argument (1958) was that a link was necessary in order to inject new reserve assets into circulation because of the reluctance of developed countries to borrow. In fact the developed countries did not display reluctance to accept their SDR allocations.

A second argument, originally used by Kalecki and Schumacher (1943) and subsequently endorsed to a greater or lesser extent by Stamp (1958),

UNCTAD (1965), and Scitovsky (1966), rested upon an assumption of insufficient demand, either on a world basis or in particular countries faced with a reserve shortage and insufficiently competitive prices. If there were a protracted insufficiency of demand on a global basis, clearly there would be a general gain from the distribution of SDRs to countries that could be relied upon to spend them. This hardly describes the postwar experience, however, and it seems distinctly unlikely that the post-Keynesian world will experience prolonged global demand deficiency in the future. Neither can "dilemma situations" (ones in which the demand-management policy needed to restore internal balance is the opposite to that needed to restore external balance at the given exchange rate, for example, in a deficit country experiencing unemployment) in individual countries provide a rationale for the creation of linked SDRs in an era when countries have overcome their reluctance to use exchange rate changes to facilitate the adjustment process. This argument is not, therefore, applicable in current circumstances.

A third argument is that the developing countries suffer from particular difficulties related to their economic structure—export instability, import incompressibility, debt servicing, lack of confidence—which impose greater adjustment burdens on them than on developed countries, so that world efficiency would be maximized by distributing new reserves to the LDCs in order to reduce their need for adjustment (Cohen, 1966, Márquez, 1970). To the extent that this is true, it is rational for LDCs to hold larger reserves, and neutrality would require that these larger reserve holdings be reflected in larger SDR allocations and therefore larger IMF quotas. The question of a link is, however, whether it is desirable to go beyond neutrality, and this argument is irrelevant to that question.

A fourth argument in favor of the link asserts that, because the developed countries all have ambitions of running current-account surpluses, the injection of additional SDRs into the system through unearned allocations cannot succeed in reconciling payments objectives, whereas the injection of linked SDRs, which would require the developed countries to earn their reserve growth through current-account surpluses, could do so (Haan, 1971, Maynard, 1972). It cannot be denied that spokesmen for the developed countries sometimes talk as though exporting real resources were in itself a privilege rather than a burden, and it is possible to conceive of circumstances under which there might be a conflict of national interests caused by a general desire to achieve current account surpluses. This could occur if many countries were trying to stimulate their growth rates and concluded that the factor limiting investment was the incentive to invest rather than the availability of savings, and if they concluded that internal measures to stimulate investment were difficult, for example, because of downward stickiness of the interest rate. It is also plausible to suppose that the sudden rise in global ex ante savings caused by the oil price increase may have resulted in a period of inconsistent current account targets. There are therefore some reasons for giving a certain weight to the argument that the link would lubricate the adjustment process by permitting payments objectives of all countries to be satisfied simultaneously.

Nevertheless, if the case for the link rested on its contribution to the effective operation of the international monetary system, it would be a very weak one indeed. Most proponents of the link, at least in recent years, have based their case rather on the desirability of promoting the flow of aid, and hence have felt that in order to establish their case all they needed to do was demonstrate that a link could be constructed without adverse repercussions on the international monetary system. In contrast, most opponents of the link have based their case on the adverse monetary consequences of introducing a link. Therefore the arguments that have been developed in the opposite direction are the crucial ones.

One line of argument runs directly counter to the final argument considered above in favor of the link. Stek (1974) argued that a link would actually serve to increase the degree of inconsistency in payments objectives. He viewed these objectives as being determined entirely by reserve needs. This would seem to imply that the current-account objectives of the developed countries would rise pari passu with the SDR allocations they no longer received because they were being injected via the link instead, but then suggested that under the link these objectives would in fact rise more than pari passu because the lack of assurance that countries would succeed in earning linked SDRs would result in their adding a safety margin to their current-account objectives. The latter part of the argument is vulnerable, not only to a de minimis counter, but also to the charge of neglecting stock factors; once countries had achieved a higher reserve stock, the need for a safety margin would disappear, so that a permanent intensification of current-account inconsistency would ensue only if (contrary to the normal assumption) SDR supply were unresponsive to the higher demand for reserves to hold. The former part of the argument stands or falls with the assumption that current account objectives are determined by reserve needs alone; the arguments advanced above all depended on countries desiring current surpluses for some purpose other than to satisfy their liquidity requirements. If valid, Stek's first conjecture without the succeeding argument implies that the link is irrelevant either way to the question of reconciling payments objectives.

A more popular argument for holding that the link would impede the adjustment process asserts that, because linked SDRs would tend to be earned by countries that were already in surplus, payments imbalances among the developed countries would be aggravated by the link. Cline (1976) has undertaken calculations of the quantitative importance of such an effect, and concluded that it could be dismissed on de minimis grounds. However, de minimis provides a reason for attaching a low rather than a zero weight to a factor. The more fundamental point is whether it is proper to reward countries for failing to correct their deficits. This is what is implied by allowing the distribution of reserves to be influenced by a concern to assist the liquidity position of countries simply because they are in deficit. Such a criterion strikes me as entirely improper.

Another popular argument against the link concerns its inflationary potential. There are two points here. One, which will be considered below, concerns the possibility that the link would lead to an excessive volume of SDR creation. The other is that the first-round impact on world aggregate demand of a given volume of SDR creation would be greater if one distributed SDRs to those who would plan to spend, rather than to hold, them. This is true,[3] but, it might seem easily countered by an offsetting change in the quantity of SDRs created. However, Polak (1970, pp. 517-518) has observed that this counter would be incomplete if reserve creation were intended to persuade countries to ease payments restrictions rather than to stimulate demand. It has also been argued (Bauer, 1973, Stek, 1974) that the first-round impact of a given volume of aid distributed through the link would be greater than that of an equal volume of aid distributed through conventional channels, since in the former case countries would fail to make budgetary provision for the increased spending. Kahn (1973) replied that demand management policy is determined by the overall state of demand rather than by particular elements of additional expected expenditure; an increase in link-financed exports would be as visible as any other exports, and hence could be expected to lead to offsetting deflationary action as and when the need arose.

Perhaps the most serious criticisms of the link have been based on a conviction that the link would undermine the monetary integrity of the SDR. It has been envisaged that this might occur in four ways.

The way most emphasized is that the essentially limitless needs for development finance might lead to SDR allocations that are excessive from a monetary standpoint (Group of 10, 1965, para. 138). Supporters of the link have done their best to still this fear by accepting that decisions on SDR creation should be made solely with a view to satisfying global liquidity requirements and should in no measure be dependent on the needs for resource transfer of the beneficiaries of the link. (See, for example, UNCTAD, 1969, or the statements of the Group of 24 during the C-20 negotiations.) But, while the principle is never challenged, the criteria that govern SDR allocations are so imprecise that it is understandable if agreement on the principle is not particularly reassuring to skeptics. For example, the LDCs continued to press for a new allocation of SDRs even in 1972/1973, when the world was positively bloated with excess liquidity by just about any standard. If the LDCs were in a position to determine the volume of SDR allocations, this would undoubtedly be a powerful argument. But in fact the decisive voice in determining SDR creation is that of the developed countries, since a decision on SDR allocation requires an 85 percent vote, and, even after the latest quota revisions, the LDCs will have only 31 percent of total fund quotas. Furthermore, some critics have tended to undermine this case by arguing the opposite proposition that the link would lead to inadequate SDR creation because the advanced countries would be unwilling to sanction adequate SDR allocations if they had to earn their own reserve increases through resource transfer (Johnson, 1972, p. 119). This reasoning has been inverted by Haan (1971, pp. 122-127) to argue that the need to earn reserves on the part of the countries with the decisive voice in SDR creation is just what is needed to restrain inflationary issues of SDRs. This logic has even been used to suggest (though not, to my knowledge, in public) that beneficiaries of the link might volunteer to surrender their right to vote on proposals regarding SDR allocations.

Second, it has often been argued that the link would threaten the monetary prospects of the SDR by undermining confidence in it. This argument was expressed initially in terms of the inadequate backing for a reserve asset that would be provided by the obligations of LDCs (Altman, 1961). However, after Machlup (1965) had pointed out that the acceptability of a monetary asset depended on the willingness of third parties to receive it in payment of debts and not on what it is backed by, and after this philosophy had been incorporated in the decision to make the SDR an asset with no counterpart liability, this argument fell into disrepute. What is needed to engender confidence in the SDR is not an orthodox balance sheet for the Special Drawing Account, but (1) assurance that other countries will always be willing to receive SDRs when a country needs to use them, and (2) assurance that those with the responsibility of paying the interest service on SDRs will continue to do so. If the second factor is unaffected by the link, there is no reason for the first to be affected; therefore the second one is crucial. It seems to me that the best case one can make for believing that the link might harm confidence in the SDR rests on the possibility that the LDCs might be tempted to default on their interest obligations (Williamson, 1972). A financial temptation to default would, after all, arise if it appeared that the present value of future interest obligations on past SDR allocations exceeded the present value of expected future SDR allocations. Although neither the IMF nor the IBRD has yet suffered a debt default, any belief on the part of potential SDR creditors that SDR debtors had a significant financial interest in default could hardly help but undermine confidence in the SDR. The argument is nonetheless unconvincing. If there is an incentive to default with a link, there will also be an incentive to default without one.[4] Also, default would be an offense to the international community that would be bound to threaten a whole range of international economic relationships, and so be a most unattractive course of action. Further, since the present value of future SDR allocations depends positively on the difference between the SDR interest rate and the cost of alternative sources of long-term foreign borrowing, and the latter is greater when the country's creditworthiness is lesser, the LDCs in general (and those with the greatest pressure to consider default in particular) will be the countries with the greatest interest in ensuring access to future SDR allocations, and therefore the ones with the greatest incentive to avoid default.

The third way in which a link could undermine the monetary prospects of the SDR has received relatively little attention, either in the literature or in official discussion. It concerns the need to provide a sufficiently high yield on the SDR to make it an attractive reserve asset for central banks to hold. The higher the interest rate on the SDR, the lower the real transfer (seigniorage) that would accrue to LDCs as a result of the link. Hence one must expect that the LDCs would resist rises in the SDR interest rate even more vigorously than they did in 1973/1974. But, unless and until the SDR carries an interest rate broadly competitive with that on the dollar, it is highly improbable that central banks will be willing to replace dollar holdings by SDR holdings on a substantial scale, and hence that the SDR can become the major reserve asset of the system. This threat to the prospects of the SDR would, however, be relatively easy to avoid. It would be necessary only to accompany the agreement to introduce a link with a simultaneous agreement to base the SDR interest rate on an appropriate formula.[5]

The fourth possible threat to the SDR arises from the fact that nonbeneficiaries of the link would have their financial incentive to support the establishment of an SDR-based system eroded by introduction of the link. One of the major incentives to support an SDR-based system is found in its financial attractiveness to many countries—an attractiveness based on the insignificance of the real resource costs involved in creating reserve assets in the form of SDRs and the wide distribution of the seigniorage from reserve creation. If, however, seigniorage is concentrated in a limited number of countries, the likelihood is lessened that a winning coalition of countries with a financial stake in the adoption of an SDR-based system can be formed. How much weight should be attached to this factor depends critically upon what the alternative to an SDR-based system is perceived to be.

SDR creation was originally perceived as an alternative to an increase in the price of gold. Since gold mining absorbs real resources, the substitution of SDRs for a gold price increase would have led to a real resource saving, and hence to scope for distributing a substantial part of the saving to a particular group of countries (the LDCs) without destroying the incentive for the others to support the SDR. However, as Cline (1976) has observed, the position has changed in recent years. Cline perhaps goes too far in arguing that a rise in the official price of gold toward the free market level would increase international liquidity at a zero resource cost; not only does he understate the probability that such a move would induce a rise in the market price, and thereby attract additional resources into gold production (p. 81, n. 1), but he completely ignores the welfare cost of withholding monetary and hoarded gold from release for industrial and artistic purposes. Nevertheless, he is right to argue that the financial attractiveness of the SDR as compared to gold is marginal for many countries in present circumstances. It follows that, by reducing the financial attractiveness of an SDR-based system, the link might make its realization less likely.

However, Johnson (1972) has argued that the realistic alternative to an SDR-based system is not a reversion to gold, but perpetuation of the reserve-currency system. As between these two systems there is no saving of real resources. There is still, of course, a certain benefit in receiving the command over resources that is the counterpart to reserve creation; that is, seigniorage still exists. (Some comments on its magnitude appear below, under "Prospects for the Future.") However, the choice between different systems of reserve supply involves a zero-sum game (Cline, 1976, p. 79). If the LDCs get more seigniorage as a result of the link, others will get less, and hence will find the SDR system less attractive. This general proposition does not, however, pinpoint what is really the key element in the situation. One country, the United States, has a financial interest in the preservation of the dollar as the principal reserve asset; the other industrialized countries (as well as the LDCs) have a financial interest in replacement of the dollar by the SDR. The interest of the United States in preserving the role of the dollar would be marginally greater if there were a link, while that of Europe and Japan in establishing an SDR-based system would be somewhat less if there were a link, but within a quite wide margin the direction of their interests would be unaffected by the presence of a link. Hence, if the United States were willing to acquiesce in the establishment of an SDR-based system and introduction of the link, there would be little reason to fear that the link would jeopardize the acceptability of the SDR-based system to other countries (on financial grounds). These were, of course, precisely the reforms that the United States was unwilling to countenance in the Committee of 20, although a financial motive for this resistance was never admitted and may even have been unrecognized.

Aid and Income Distribution

The principal argument for the link rests on the desirability of recasting the international economic order so as to achieve a more egalitarian distribution of world income among countries. The seigniorage resulting from the creation of fiduciary reserve assets is one instrument that could be directed by collective international action in accordance with explicit distributional aims, and the link is based on the proposition that it should be so directed.

It has been argued at times that, because the SDR system permits a neutral distribution of seigniorage, it ought to be operated in this way. (The leading exponents of this view are, or have been, Machlup, 1965, Grubel, 1969, and Johnson, 1972.) This position seems to be treated by its adherents as a self-evident truth—a treatment usually reserved for indefensible propositions. According to the normal argument, neutrality would be desirable if either

(1) the initial income distribution were optimal, or (2) desirable non-neutrality were necessarily associated with sufficiently unfortunate allocational effects. The most charitable comment on someone prepared to defend the existing world income distribution as optimal would be that he betrayed a lack of ethical sensibility.[6] The argument that redistribution through the SDR system should be avoided because it could have unfortunate allocational effects, specifically by undermining the monetary integrity of the SDR, does contain an element of truth: the analysis in the preceding section implied, for example, that a decision to hold down the interest rate on the SDR so as to maximize the redistributive impact of the SDR system could have disastrous consequences for the SDR. There is a perfectly respectable case for arguing that the efficiency of the monetary system should not be jeopardized by redistributive objectives. This case rests on the reasonably firmly established result that monetary manipulation is an inefficient method of achieving distributional ends. (See, for example, the literature on the inflation tax surveyed in Laidler and Parkin, 1975, Part 6.) There is no case for arguing that redistribution should be avoided insofar as it can be achieved without prejudicing monetary efficiency.

The mere fact that reserve creation and resource transfer are different things (Group of 10, 1965, para. 138) does not, therefore, imply that it is improper to design a system that will promote both objectives, to the extent that they are not competitive with each other. Whether there would in fact be any seigniorage from reserve creation to redistribute, under a monetarily efficient system, is a question that will be examined under "Prospects for the Future." What remains to be examined here is whether redistribution of seigniorage would be an effective mechanism for promoting the flow of aid.

One reason, advanced by supporters of the link, for believing that it would provide an effective method of providing aid is that the increased level of aid would not carry with it the balance-of-payments burden associated with an increase in bilateral aid (Maynard, 1972). It is true of course that the same can be said of any increase in multilateral aid (Cline, 1976, p. 71), but the organization of multilateral aid programs has its own problems.

A key question raised by opponents of the link goes under the ugly title of "additionality." Unless, it is argued, the link succeeds in "tricking" national parliaments, it cannot lead to an increase in the total aid flow, since a parliament which understands what is happening will promptly reduce other aid flows by an equal sum (Haberler, 1971, Johnson, 1972). There are two distinct questions at issue here. The first is whether the link would in fact lead to an increase in the flow of aid; the second is whether any increase that did occur would conform to democratic proprieties. So far as the first point is concerned, ther are few economists whose views deserve great weight, but one such must surely be Congressman Henry Reuss, who once observed:

... if you pursue the so-called nonorganic link, I do not see ... how you have accomplished very much in political terms that could not be accomplished by a more heroic frontal attack, namely induce the U.S. Congress to pass a law which says we up our miserable present IDA contribution by three times. . . . If, however, we get organic . . . then you may be able to achieve some fiscal monkey business, which would be all to the good. (U.S. Congress, 1969, p. 70)

The question remains whether "fiscal monkey business" is an affront to democracy. To those who view the nation-state as the sole source of legitimate political authority, presumably the answer must be that it is entirely improper. To those, on the other hand, who view nation-states as one type of social institution among many, and, moreover, a type that has acquired far too much power for the good of mankind, there is no similar proscription on welcoming devices that would mark a move toward redistributing income among the citizens of different countries as a matter of right rather than of charity.

International Negotiations

When the creation of a fiduciary reserve asset was first discussed in official circles in the mid-1960s, discussion was concentrated in the Group of 10. Many of the initial proposals would actually have excluded the LDCs from their scope. The Ossola Report argued against the link (Group of 10, 1965, paras. 137-138) on the grounds that development finance and reserve creation were different things, that the link might impair confidence, and that variations in world liquidity needs might subject the flow of aid to irrelevant shocks if a link were in operation. However, the report also reflected an implicit sympathy for the view that reserve creation should be distributionally neutral (para. 136), and this no doubt helped pave the way for ultimate agreement to set up the SDR system in a manner that would allow the developing countries to be full participants. At least a "reverse link" was avoided.

The LDCs first began organizing themselves into a coherent pressure group in international economic affairs with the founding of UNCTAD in 1964. One of this organization's early acts was to issue a report (UNCTAD, 1965) endorsing a link as an integral part of the desirable mechanism of reserve creation. The Alliance for Progress (1966) then endorsed the link. Not surprisingly, the LDCs, as the prospective beneficiaries of the link, were quick to support the idea.

The first developed country in which significant political support for the link emerged was, paradoxically, the United States. By 1967 the Subcommittee on International Trade and Payments of the Joint Economic Committee of the United States Congress was endorsing the link as one element of a desirable international monetary reform. The following year, Finance Minister Colombo of Italy suggested an inorganic link in the course of his address to the IMF Annual Meetings. Other developed countries gradually modified their opposition to the link in the succeeding years. The Commonwealth

Finance Ministers' Annual Meeting, which traditionally precedes the IMF Annual Meetings, became an occasion primarily devoted to lobbying Britain and the other developed members of the Commonwealth for their support. By the time the C-20 started work, only the United States (government), Germany, and Australia still opposed the link—and Australian opposition was reversed on the election of a Labor government in 1973.

The major forum in which the link has been discussed is the Committee of 20, which met from 1972 to 1974. The principal LDC aim in the C-20 was the establishment of a link. This aim was pursued unremittingly, and considerable diplomatic skill and patience were exercised in lining up the hundred-odd LDC members of the IMF in a united front, articulated through the Group of 24. Not only did the LDCs achieve agreement on the principle of a link, which was perhaps unremarkable, but they also reached a decision on the form of the link they preferred: namely, the basis of SDR allocation should be changed so as to allocate a greater proportion of newly created SDRs to developing countries than they would have been entitled to on the basis of quotas. The only bargaining counter the LDCs used to promote the link was the implicit threat to refuse to ratify any reform that did not include the link, and that had no great bargaining value, until such time as the industrial countries agreed on a reform they were anxious to see translated into an amendment of the IMF Articles. That stage was, of course, never reached. Whether the LDCs might have fared better if they had been prepared to engage in real bargaining for the link, for example, by offering to accept controls on reserve placements in the Euro markets in return, is an interesting but entirely hypothetical question.

Most of the developed countries were prepared, if hardly anxious, to concede the link. The exceptions were Germany and the United States, both of which held out, at the cost of courting considerable unpopularity, to the bitter end. The German objections were based on the possible inflationary implications of the link, and were therefore consistent with the major German preoccupation in the C-20—the objective of eradicating the inflationary bias that the Bretton Woods system had manifested in its dying years. The Germans were concerned about both the greater first-round impact on aggregate demand of a given volume of SDRs, if these were allocated to countries expecting to spend them rather than to hold them, and the pressure for greater SDR allocations, if these were going to provide aid. It was much less easy to see what underlay the U.S. resistance to the link. The reason always given was that the link would tend to undermine confidence in the SDR. It may well be true that one or two important potential SDR creditors were suspicious of the SDR on account of its lack of "backing," and that their suspicions would have been aggravated by the link. But such solicitude for the SDR was unconvincing when accompanied, as it was, by opposition to asset settlement and to a change in the basis of valuation and improvement in the yield of the SDR. One possible motive for U.S. opposition to the link was the financial one: more SDRs for LDCs would have meant less seigniorage for the United States. The sum potentially involved was, however, so trivial, especially in comparison with the shortfall of the U.S. aid program below the internationally agreed target of one percent of GNP, that it is very difficult to believe that it justified the loss of goodwill among the LDCs. It is also possible that the United States objected to the loss of the power of patronage provided by the ability to disburse aid. Or the administration may have feared congressional opposition to the erosion of its authority over aid implicit in the link.

Prospects for the Future

It has been argued here that there is nothing improper about a link—provided that a concern for distributional objectives does not lead to distortions that would impede monetary efficiency. The question that arises is how much redistribution could occur without violating this criterion. This amounts to asking how much seigniorage there would be in an efficient system. The answer is that there would be about as much seigniorage as there is in the present system. Any attempt to extract more seigniorage than this would enable the dollar to out-compete the SDR; and any system which enabled the SDR to dominate the dollar would be vetoed by the United States.

It is sometimes argued that the United States reaps no seigniorage from the present system, because dollar assets are supplied competitively and interest rates therefore rise to the point where all seigniorage is competed away. This argument would be correct only in a world of perfect capital mobility. In a world of imperfect capital mobility, the fact that certain holders of short-term assets (namely, foreign monetary authorities) hold dollars rather than something else implies that interest rates on dollar assets are lower than they would be otherwise, and it is this interest saving—for a given distribution of world wealth—that measures the seigniorage reaped by the United States. Measurement of a seigniorage gain involves, in principle, a comparison between two general equilibrium positions. One is the present situation, in which the United States is able to get help in financing the excess of its long-term foreign investments over its accumulated foreign surpluses by the official holdings of short-term assets of other monetary authorities. The other is a situation where all reserves are held in SDRs rather than in dollars, and, in order to enable it to redeem its official dollar liabilities for SDRs, the United States is obliged to borrow on private capital markets a sum equal to its present official liabilities.[7] Only if the United States were an atomistic competitor on the world capital market would this change not impose a cost on the United States. Since not even the most extreme monetarist models have typecast the United States as a negligibly small part of the world economy, one must conclude that the United States does indeed reap some seigniorage from the system.

There is, therefore, a certain element of seigniorage that could be redistributed away from the United States by replacement of the dollar by the SDR, and further redistributed from the developed countries to the LDCs by adoption of the link. However, although there is every reason to argue that this seigniorage exists, there is also reason to be cautious about its size. The gain to a country through receiving SDR allocations stems from the difference between the SDR interest rate and the opportunity cost of alternative sources of long-term foreign borrowing. If the SDR interest rate were set at a rate close to the rate at which developed countries can borrow, which is where it would need to be set if the SDR were to become the principal reserve asset without detailed regulations prohibiting central banks from holding reserve currencies, then the benefit of receiving SDR allocations to an individual developed country would be very small.[8] The benefit to an LDC would be somewhat larger, insofar as the borrowing rates faced by LDCs are typically higher; but the grant element of the link would nonetheless be only a fraction, and perhaps quite a small fraction, of the volume of linked SDR allocations.

Recognition of the limited value of a link as a vehicle for redistribution in the presence of a competitive interest rate has led some economists (Isard and Truman, 1974) to suggest schemes whereby the interest charged on LDC use of linked allocations would be subsidized by the developed countries. For example, a link could be introduced by amending the formula for allocating SDRs in favor of the LDCs, while maintaining the obligation to service SDRs unchanged on the basis of IMF quotas. The attraction of this scheme is that it would be consistent with a competitive interest rate on the marginal use and accumulation of SDRs by all countries, while substantially increasing the redistributive impact of the link. Its disadvantage is that it probably would make the move from a dollar-based system to an SDR-based system financially disadvantageous to the developed countries (other than the United States, to whom such a move would be costly in any case). It might, perhaps, be argued that this is precisely the type of change the developed countries should be prepared to endorse, despite its cost, if they are in earnest about an egalitarian recasting of the international economic order.

However, the obstacles blocking this solution are formidable. It is not just the probable reluctance of the DCs to concede an interest subsidy, nor even the continued resistance of the United States and Germany to the principle of a link, that provide the principal reason for doubting that the link has a future. The major reason lies in doubt as to whether the SDR has a future. With the present elastic supply of reserves, it seems unlikely that sufficient reserve stringency could develop to convince the necessary 85 percent of the IMF membership that new SDR allocations are called for. Hence, without conscious major reforms to the system, involving in particular the introduction of asset settlement, the debate about the link is academic. The responsibility for preventing such reforms lies overwhelmingly, if not exclusively, with the country that happens to have an unadmitted and perhaps unrecognized financial stake in the preservation of the existing nonsystem, the United States. Since the sums at stake are not large, moreover, it must be judged unlikely that other countries will make the sorts of threats that might persuade the United States to modify its opposition to the establishment of an SDR-based system.

The developing countries would be well advised therefore to pay less attention to their potential gains in an ideal system, whose creation is most unlikely, and more attention to exploiting in their own interests the nonsystem that presently exists and that seems likely to persist indefinitely. Even under existing arrangements, there is in fact one way in which the LDCs can get some slight seigniorage benefit: a substantial number of LDCs have established their creditworthiness in recent years, and emerged as significant borrowers in the Euro markets. Thus, by placing reserves in the Euro market rather than in a reserve center, an LDC may get not only a somewhat higher rate of interest, but also may do something to expand the lending potential of a market in which LDCs as a group are major borrowers. The gains from this strategy are not comparable with those that would stem from the link, since (1) many DCs do not place reserves in the Euro markets on principle, in the interests of controlling international liquidity, and (2) the borrowing rates for LDCs in the Euro markets are higher than the SDR interest rate would be. Nevertheless, the comparatively small gains are immediately available. Furthermore, the strategy might increase marginally the probability of establishing the link inasmuch as, if the DCs ever decide they are not satisfied with an international monetary nonsystem, one element of the desired reforms will surely be control of reserve placements in the Euro markets, and the more such placements they have, the greater will be the bargaining strength of the LDCs. It is, admittedly, sad to end by recommending that, in lieu of a new international economic order, the LDCs should deliberately exploit the existing disorder.

Notes

1 The proposal that amortization payments be linked should be sharply distinguished from a proposal advanced by some countries in the C-20, which envisaged the Substitution Account lending out the currencies paid in to LDCs, who would then spend these currencies in the issuing country and assume responsibility for subsequent amortization. (See IMF, 1974, pp. 175-176.) This proposal, of course, exhibited a complete failure to understand the economic rationale for substitution, that is, to protect the liquidity position of a reserve center during the time span when it could not be expected to make restitution for its past borrowings in the form of real resources.

2 A version of this point was accorded major importance by some participants in the workshop, who argued that, unless link proceeds were distributed by a DFI, there could be no presumption that a link would improve the world personal distribution of income.

3 However, Cline (1976) has again undertaken calculations which confirm that any such impact is of minimal quantitative importance.

4 Let i be the SDR interest rate, r = opportunity cost of foreign borrowing, at which the LDC discounts future income, p the present moment of time, S_t the total volume of SDRs allocated at time t, and ρ_k the share of the kth country in SDR allocations. Then the kth country has to compare:

P. V. of future interest payments on past SDR allocations

$$= \int_p^\infty ie^{-rt} \sum_0^p S_t^k \, dt = \rho_k \int_p^\infty ie^{-rt} \sum_0^p S_t \, dt,$$

and P. V. of future SDR allocations $= \rho_k \sum_p \int_p^\infty (r - i)e^{-rt} S_t \, dt.$

The point at which the value of these two expressions is equal is independent of ρ_k, which proves that a link (an increase in ρ_k) will not create an incentive to default where otherwise none would exist.

5 My own version of an appropriate formula would be a weighted average of the short-term interest rates on the currencies composing the SDR basket (with the weights for the interest rate basket corresponding to those of the SDR basket), minus a "security discount" of perhaps one to one and a half percent to allow for the attraction of holding a more stable asset (in terms of a typical country's import composition) than any single currency can provide. See Polak (1974) for a discussion of this question.

6 A related argument presented during the workshop was referred to in note 2: it holds that there is no presumption that an international redistribution of income in favor of the governments of poor countries will achieve anything in terms of redistributing income to poor people. My own view is that although no doubt there will be instances where additional resources are largely or even entirely appropriated by privileged elites, there is not much reason to believe that this is generally true; and that it is proper to judge by the average, rather than the worst, behavior pattern.

7 This hypothetical comparison is not intended to deny that immediate implementation of such a change would be totally unacceptable to the United States, and therefore that any attempt to move in this direction would require the creation of a Substitution Account which, so long as it existed, would prevent the United States from bearing the full cost of being deprived of its seigniorage.

8 In the extreme case, if the SDR interest rate were equal to the DC borrowing rate, a small DC would gain no benefit through receiving SDR allocations. This does not, however, imply that the DCs collectively would accept no burden through sacrificing their SDR allocations in favor of the LDCs. Collectively they would have to curtail absorption to the extent needed to earn their reserve increases from the LDCs; they could redistribute this burden among themselves through borrowing and lending, but the group of DCs as a whole would not have this option. Of course, if the social marginal product of investment in the DCs were in fact equal to their borrowing rate and the latter were equal to the SDR interest rate, the DCs would not suffer a welfare loss through seeing a given volume of domestic investment replaced by a similar level of foreign investment in the LDCs. In this case there would be a welfare gain to the world as a whole as a result of the replacement of low-yield investment in DCs by high-yield investment in LDCs—a gain permitted by socialization of the risk of lending to the LDCs.

References

Altman, O. L., "Prof. Triffin on International Liquidity and the Role of the Fund," IMF *Staff Papers*, April 1961.

Bauer, P. T., "Inflation, SDRs and Aid," *Lloyd's Bank Review*, July 1973.

Bernstein, E.M., "A Practical Program for International Monetary Reserves," *Quarterly Review and Investment Survey of Model, Roland and Co.*, 1963 (4).

Cline, W. R., *International Monetary Reform and the Developing Countries*, Brookings, Washington, D.C., 1976.

Cmd 6437, *Proposals for an International Clearing Union* (Keynes Plan), HMSO, London, 1943.

Cohen, B. J., *Adjustment Costs and the Distribution of New Reserves*, Princeton Studies in International Finance, No. 18, Princeton, 1966.

Group of 10, *Report of the Study Group on the Creation of Reserve Assets* (Ossola Report), Rome, 1965.

Grubel, H. G., "The Distribution of Seigniorage from International Liquidity Creation," in R. A. Mundell and A. K. Swoboda, eds., *Monetary Problems of the International Economy*, University of Chicago Press, Chicago, 1969.

_____ , "Basic Methods for Distributing SDRs and the Problem of International Aid," *Journal of Finance*, December 1972.

Haan, R. L., *Special Drawing Rights and Development*, Stenfert Kroese NV, Leyden, 1971.

Haberler, G., "The Case Against the Link," Banca Nazionale del Lavoro *Quarterly Review*, March 1971.

Hawkins, R. G. and C. Rangarajan, "On the Distribution of New International Reserves," *Journal of Finance*, September 1970.

Inter-American Committee of the Alliance for Progress, *International Monetary Reform and Latin America*, Washington, D.C., 1966.

Isard, P. and E. M. Truman, "SDRs, Interest and the Aid Link: Further Analysis," Banca Nazionale del Lavoro *Quarterly Review*, March 1974.

IMF, *Documents of the Committee of Twenty*, Washington, D.C., 1974.

Johnson, H. G., "The Link that Chains," *Foreign Policy*, Fall 1972.

Kahn, R. F., "SDRs and Aid," *Lloyd's Bank Review*, October 1973.

Kalecki, M. and E. F. Schumacher, "International Clearing and Long-term Lending," *Oxford University Institute of Statistics Bulletin*, August 7, 1943.

Karlik, J. R., *On Linking Reserve Creation and Development Assistance*, a staff study prepared for the Subcommittee on International Exchange and Payments of the Joint Economic Committee, U.S. Congress, Washington, D.C., 1969.

Laidler, D. E. W., and J. M. Parkin, "Inflation–A Survey," *Economic Journal*, December 1975.

Machlup, F., "The Cloakroom Rule of International Reserves," *Quarterly Journal of Economics*, August 1965.

Márquez, J., "Reserves, Liquidity and the Developing Countries," in IMF, *International Reserves*, Washington, D.C., 1970.

Maynard, G. W., *Special Drawing Rights and Development Aid*, Overseas Development Council, Washington, D.C., 1972.

Maynard, G. W., and G. Bird, "International Monetary Issues and the Developing

Countries: A Survey," *World Development*, September 1975.

Park, Y. S., *The Link Between Special Drawing Rights and Development Finance*, Princeton Essays in International Finance, No. 100, Princeton, 1973.

Patel, I. G., "The Link Between the Creation of International Liquidity and the Provision of Development Finance," UNCTAD, Geneva, 1967.

Polak, J. J., "Money: National and International," in IMF, *International Reserves*, Washington, D.C., 1970.

_____ , *Valuation and Rate of Interest of the SDR*, IMF, Washington, D.C., 1974.

Scitovsky, T., "A New Approach to International Liquidity," *American Economic Review*, December 1966.

Stamp, M., "The Fund and the Future," *Lloyd's Bank Review*, October 1958.

_____ , "The Stamp Plan—1962 Version," *Moorgate and Wall St.*, October 1962.

Stek, P., "SDR Creation, Development Aid and the Adjustment Process," *De Economist*, 1974 (5).

Triffin, R., *Gold and the Dollar Crisis*, Yale University Press, New Haven, 1960.

UNCTAD, *International Monetary Issues and the Developing Countries*, UN (Sales No. 66, 11.D.2), 1965.

_____ , "International Monetary Reform and Cooperation for Development," UN, TD/B/285, October 13, 1969.

U.S. Congress, *Linking Reserve Creation and Development Assistance: Hearings*, May 28, 1969, Subcommittee on International Exchange and Payments of the Joint Economic Committee of the U.S. Congress, Washington, D.C., 1969.

Williamson, J., "SDRs, Interest and the Aid Link," Banca Nazionale del Lavoro *Quarterly Review*, June 1972.

Comment
Alexandre Kafka

1. Professor Williamson has written an excellent paper. I agree with his views on the monetary consequences of the link and with his conclusions that for the immediate future there appears to be little, if any, "percentage" in the link and that the LDCs may have wasted their ammunition in the reform negotiations in concentrating preponderantly on the link.

2. I do not, however, agree entirely with the nature of his doubts regarding the prospects for the link and its value to LDCs, if it were established. First, if a link providing additional funds could be established, it would be a good deal more helpful to the LDCs than Professor Williamson seems to believe. Second, the SDR may have even less of a short-term chance than it seems to have at present. However, third, even if there were new SDR allocations, there would still be little chance in present conditions for the link to provide additional development assistance. Let us take these points in order.

3. If additional link finance were to become available, that would be a good deal more useful than Professor Williamson believes. Even if the SDR and therefore link finance carried a fully competitive interest rate, link aid would be highly useful because of its availability. Only in a perfect capital market can one say that there is no problem of availability provided the interest rate is right. Moreover, link aid has a maturity, which, in the absence of reconstitution, is limited only by balance of payments surpluses, and this type of maturity would perhaps be the most useful quality of link aid.

4. Professor Williamson rightly attributes the improbability of additional SDR allocations at this moment to the fact that reserve supply is elastic. But there is an additional reason in the confused state in which the partial reform of the international monetary system has left gold.

It seems unlikely that gold will become a fully usable reserve asset in the next few years. One cannot expect the United States soon or perhaps ever to abandon its opposition to pegging the price of gold again, now that the partial reform has abolished the official price for it. For the foreseeable future therefore the function of gold will be limited to serving as collateral for loans obtained by central banks. But the mere fact that large quantities of gold will continue to lie around in central bank vaults and could at any time be activated by an agreement to peg the price of gold at a sufficiently higher level than the present official price will increase the reluctance of monetary authorities to solve any reserve supply problem through SDR allocations.

On the other hand, the present system, in which floating is managed rather than free, but in which there are practically no usable primary reserve assets, may prove unstable. Today, intervention does take place on a scale which is not always small but intervention is entirely voluntary. Consequently, an intervening monetary authority has no right to expect balances of foreign currencies which it acquires to have their value in terms of other currencies in any way guaranteed (as they were in the former par value system, ultimately through the obligation not to change a par value except with the permission of the Fund). However, if in the future intervention is intensified, outside the return to a par value system, but perhaps in the form of what the President of France has called a "more viscous system" of exchange rates, the problem of a value guarantee for currency balances will arise (the viscosity of exchange rates may not be adequate to induce the degree of intervention required to maintain it). In a world with perfect foresight the interest to be earned on currency balances would always compensate for changes in exchange rates and therefore avoid the problem of value guarantees, but this is not our world. This implies that a future, more intensified intervention system would have to be run with a system of exchange rate guarantees for currency balances acquired or that, alternatively, intervention would have to be limited to countries whose currency is depreciating and who would intervene with funds borrowed from other central banks, which implies an automatic if partial exchange rate guarantee for the lenders.

But the extent to which central banks will be prepared to intervene with borrowed funds may be too limited for intensified intervention. Depreciating currencies may be protected by restrictions instead, hardly a desirable outcome. On the other hand, a system of exchange rate guarantees is inherently clumsy. Thus, in the end, if the world will not countenance unmanaged floating (or a return to gold), it may have to go forward (or backward) after all to the SDR, not as a medium of intervention but as something into which currency balances acquired in intervention may be converted.

5. Even if it should do so, however, one could not be sure in present circumstances that the link would provide additional development finance. It would be a mistake to believe that only parliaments are reluctant to increase development assistance in general, which is what the link would do. There is perhaps more awareness today than earlier of, and more disposition to deal with, the problems of the poorest LDCs. But what is lacking is the recognition that even the more fortunate LDCs cannot meet all of their financial needs by borrowing in the markets. There is also more recognition than ever before that financial assistance for resource development in the LDCs is in the interest of the DCs. Occasionally, it may seem that there is some disposition to help the LDCs help themselves through offering them wider trading opportunities. But, as far as development aid in general is concerned, we may have come to the end of an era of goodwill on the part

of the industrial countries toward the developing countries in general. Not only parliaments but also governments must take this attitude into account. Hence, under present circumstances, we cannot be sure that link finance will not be offset by the reduction of other finance, except for resource development and for the benefit of the poorest LDCs.

6. Regarding the reasons for the failure to get the link accepted in the reform negotiations, I have a slight disagreement with Professor Williamson. I mention it only because of its possible historical interest. He states that the LDCs frightened developed countries with the specter of inflationary allocations by pressing for SDR allocations for 1972 and 1973 when liquidity was growing rapidly. But despite the huge increase in dollar reserves, the Group of 10 would have been prepared to accept a modest allocation at that time in order to keep the SDR alive. The LDCs, however, did not want to agree to that.

7. There remain two questions:

The first is what should the LDCs have aimed at in the last stage of the reform negotiations, when the link was dead?

It seems to me that the Outline of Reform of the Committee of 20 contained two modest provisions, the retention of which in the partial reform would have been useful. One was the provision that, in the establishment of current account or capital account restrictions, LDCs should be exempt insofar as possible. At the same time there was a provision that the Fund should give consideration to the special problems faced by LDCs in judging the justification for restrictions these countries may need to impose.

A second question concerns the action the LDCs should take now to promote greater financial assistance in the context of the partial reform.

Professor Williamson mentions the desirability of the LDCs depositing their reserves in the offshore currency markets so that a future regulation of that market would not hit them too hard. This is being done. Also important would be insistence on a large increase in quotas for all countries in the forthcoming Seventh General Review of Quotas that is to take place within three rather than five years after the Sixth General Review. This has a much better chance of acceptance than SDR allocations, because it represents conditional, not unconditional, liquidity. At present, quotas are so small that the Fund has lost influence even over countries in deficit, unless they are small, or, if large, in a really desperate financial situation. This means that the Fund is of interest to only a limited group of countries. The lack of interest major and even medium-sized countries have in the rules under which the Fund grants financial assistance carries the danger that the Fund will be increasingly severe with countries that still find it useful to appeal to it.

It would be unrealistic to believe that the problem of the small size of quotas can be solved, as it has to some extent been solved in recent years, by a proliferation of special facilities, including those addressed to LDCs. The liquidity of the Fund is not unlimited and lenders to the Fund will impose, in the present context, increasingly severe conditions. It would be better for the LDCs to insist on a large increase of the Fund for the benefit of *all* of its members, to be made available to all in similar conditions, even if this would be not development but rather balance of payments finance. The availability of the latter is helpful to development and to developing countries, both directly and indirectly, just as the availability of development finance reduces the need for balance of payments finance.

4

The Oceans as a Source of Revenue
Richard N. Cooper

Along with Antarctica, radio frequencies, and space orbits, the high seas have traditionally been the property of no state. They have in principle been accessible to all. In 1970 the United Nations General Assembly passed a resolution (with no dissents but with the United States and thirteen others abstaining) declaring that the ocean floor should be regarded as "the common heritage of mankind." By extension, we should regard all the unappropriated resources and potential resources of the earth and its surroundings as the common heritage of mankind.

A potential resource takes on economic value only when it is in practice accessible and when it is not in infinite supply. With the growth of population and income, and with continuing advances of technology, many parts of the global environment that formerly were either inaccessible or seemingly inexhaustible have become both accessible and exhaustible, and as such they now command economic rent. The clearest example in the oceans is fish, many stocks of which have now become "overfished," a term to which we give more precise meaning below. We can also observe incipient congestion in ocean shipping and in ocean dumping, that is, the use of the ocean as a medium for waste disposal. "Exhaustion" of these two uses remains largely localized at the present time, and can be remedied by traffic control of shipping and by local regulations for land-based pollution plus liability rules to cover such matters as major oil spills. The economic rents implicit in these uses of the oceans remain small.

Petroleum can be extracted from the ocean floor, and in the future manganese nodules and perhaps other minerals will also be harvested from the seabed and perhaps from the ocean itself. Extraction of minerals may or may not generate economic rents—that depends on costs and on alternative sources of supply—but any such rents are generated in a different way from the rents on fisheries or shipping congestion or waste disposal, all of which involve externalities, that is, instances in which the economic activity of one party affects (in these cases, raises) the costs to others undertaking the same activity or using the oceans in other ways.

The oceans have still other uses: for scientific research and as a concealing medium for strategic forces. But none of these uses yet commands an economic rent. The ocean is still "inexhaustible." This paper will therefore focus on fishing and on mineral extraction as the major sources of oceanic rents for the rest of this century.[1]

Aspects of Resource Use

Management of the oceans involves a complicated array of issues. For concreteness, initial observations will focus on fishing, but with appropriate changes they will apply to mineral extraction and other resource uses of the oceans as well.

It is useful to distinguish four conceptually different aspects of resource use: (1) the product (fish), (2) the economic activity (fishing), (3) the net revenue derived from the product, and (4) decision making regarding the regime to govern the activity, the disposition of the product, and (where different from disposition of the product) the net revenue. Part of the difficulty in international discussions of ocean management is that these quite different aspects are not adequately differentiated; or, in more sophisticated discussion, that the protagonists want all four, ignoring the likelihood that there may be important trade-offs among them—greater access to the activity, for instance, probably resulting in lower net revenue or in less product.

This paper will focus on the net revenues to be derived from the oceans, on the assumption that a "transfer of resources" is mainly what is needed by less developed countries from the international community, at least insofar as management of the oceans is concerned. This emphasis takes for granted a relatively free world market, so that developing countries both have access to needed goods on the international market and can readily sell their surplus production to the world market. The emphasis on revenues, on this assumption regarding markets, can be justified by arguing, in brief, that with maximum revenues less developed countries will if necessary be able to buy the product (say, fish) on the world market, and will be able to get it more efficiently, that is at lower cost, that way than if they engage in the fishing activity directly. If it should happen, as increasingly may be the case, that some developing countries are low-cost fishermen, then they will be the ones to engage in the activity and they can sell their product on the world market. In other words, not engaging in the activity does not preclude access to this important source of protein so long as there is a relatively efficient world market in fish. Put in this way, a problem evidently does arise if the leading fishing nations—one of which is the Soviet Union—do not sell their output on a world market. Conceivably such countries could preempt an important world resource. But under the scheme developed below, they would have to pay a high price for that privilege in terms of other goods and services as valued in the world market—high enough to induce other nations to give up the privilege of fishing.

Moreover, while the activity of fishing is certainly a prospectively important source of employment for the burgeoning labor force of developing countries, the revenues derived from fishing could provide even greater and more productive employment when channeled through properly managed national development plans, or even through domestic government expenditure that is not especially well managed. So here, too, to focus on the activity is to miss alternative, potentially more effective ways of achieving economically useful activity through the use of revenues.

Finally, participation in decision making for all nations will be assured by procedures developed below for the efficient management of ocean resources.

Harvesting Living Marine Resources

Let us turn now to the question of raising revenue from ocean fishing.[2] Economists for years have bemoaned the necessary evil of "deadweight losses" associated with most systems of taxation. It is difficult to find a tax that in some fashion or other does not blunt economic incentive or distort patterns of consumption, in either case resulting in allocative losses in welfare. Thus there is generally a trade-off between revenue raising and efficient resource allocation. A distinctive feature of proper management of fisheries is that such management can generate revenue while *improving* rather than worsening the allocation of resources. This possibility arises because unrestricted access to a commercially valuable fishery will lead to "overfishing," that is, fishing activity greater than is desirable either from a conservationist or an economic point of view. This overfishing arises because of the "externality" involved in fishing: the cost of harvesting a given amount of fish varies inversely with the total stock of fish, since fishing is essentially a search and gather activity. The smaller the stock, the higher the cost of a given harvest. Yet when fishermen harvest, they make no allowance for the social cost they impose on others by reducing the stock. They will fish as long as the price exceeds their own marginal costs. As a result, there is excessive entry into fishing until the scarcity rents that should accrue to each fishery are dissipated by excessive depletion of the stock of fish, raising costs for all.[3]

To avoid the dissipation of rents through cost-increasing overfishing, access to the fishery must be limited. Conservation regulations aim to do this in a variety of ways, usually by putting a ceiling on the allowable annual catch from a given fishery or by limiting the fishing season to a certain period of time. But a generally more efficient method for limiting entry is to impose a tax or royalty per unit of harvest. An optimal tax captures the scarcity rents that should accrue to a commercially valuable fishery, thus generating revenue, and simultaneously limits entry. After allowance for costs of collection and enforcement of such a tax, and for improving our knowledge about ocean ecology (since our information on the dynamics of fisheries in response to intense harvesting is in most cases only rudimentary), net revenues could be used for transfers to developing countries to foster economic development through the International Development Association or some comparable agency.

My proposal is this: every fishery (defined on the basis of ecological considerations focused on commercially valuable marine products, sometimes including a single species but sometimes including the entire "biomass" of valuable material), should be managed by a regional commission established for that fishery, with global representation but with disproportionate weight in decision making to go to the coastal states nearest the fishery. Each commission would establish the economically optimal harvest from its fishery and would license access to the fishery, levy taxes on the harvest, and supervise the gathering of scientific information on the fishery. The appropriate tax would of course vary from fishery to fishery, and might vary from species to species within a fishery where harvesting techniques varied according to species. Moreover, each commission would vary its tax rates as economic conditions or new knowledge about the fishery altered the optimal harvest.[4] Any revenues in excess of operating costs would be turned over to the international community for economic development, to be dispersed through such agencies as the UNDP, IDA, or the various regional development banks.

In principle the regulations should apply to all harvesting within a given fishery, including harvesting in what are now territorial waters. In practice it would probably be both desirable and practicable to exclude from regulation traditional coastal fishing activity in less developed countries, on the grounds that the pressure on fish stocks of major fisheries from such traditional fishing is likely to be de minimus. Thus traditional ways of life in poor countries would not be jeopardized by the new tax scheme, and indeed would be preserved and improved insofar as the scheme protected stocks that would otherwise be depleted by more modern fishing fleets.

How much revenue could such a scheme, applied to the world's fisheries, be expected to generate? This is impossible to estimate with any exactitude, since the requisite knowledge for establishing an optimal tax does not exist for most fisheries. But the studies that have been done on particular fisheries show an impressive amount of waste in resources at the present (see Table 4.1). The method typically used to derive an estimate of excess costs is to compare the yields (harvest per some unit of input, such as man-days or boat-days or fathoms of net) in the recent period with yields at some earlier time when the fishery was mature but not evidently overfished. Such yields have sometimes dropped by extraordinary amounts. For instance, Crutchfield and Pontecorvo report that the Alaskan salmon catch in Bristol Bay dropped from around forty tons per fisherman per season in the 1930s to ten tons in the mid-1960s, and the harvest per fathom of net fell even more, to about one sixth what it was in the 1930s.[5] If allowance is made for productivity increases in fishing gear during this thirty-year period, the drop in output per unit of effort is even more startling. A rough indication of the nature of productivity increases can be drawn from the whaling industry: between 1930 and 1963 the average size of the catcher boat, the boat that actually catches the whales, grew from 219 gross tons to 703 gross tons, and the average horsepower per catcher increased from 729 to 2,957.[6] In addition,

Table 4.1 Excess Resource Costs on Various Fisheries

Fishery	Percent Excess Cost
North Atlantic cod, 1965[a]	10-20
All United States fisheries, circa 1970[b]	20-30
Groundfish on George's Bank, 1971[c]	31
Norwegian winter herring, 1967[d]	45
Yellowtail flounder in New England, circa 1970[e]	62
Alaskan salmon, 1965[f]	83

[a] Since 1965 effort has increased and yield has declined, so the excess cost would be much greater today. Source is a bioeconomics working group of the International Commission for North Atlantic Fisheries (ICNAF). See FAO (1947); also Christy (1973), p. 17.

[b] Based on a comparison of high and low levels of catch per day of effort from the 1940s to the 1960s, assuming all rent to be dissipated in the latter period. See Robert Nathan Associates (1974), pp. 64-65.

[c] Excess cost over maximum sustainable yield, which in turn would involve excess cost over the economically optimum yield. Cited in Christy (1973), p. 17.

[d] Assumes a 50 percent increase in productivity of herring fishing gear from the early 1950s, due especially to the introduction of nylon nets and power blocks, and no decline in catch per unit of (productivity adjusted) capacity. See Pontecorvo and Vartdal (1967), p. 81.

[e] Based on a production function for the fishery constructed from biological data and certain assumptions about the natural growth of the stock. See Gates and Norton (1974), Table 7. It is noteworthy that the same model shows that harvesting at the "maximum sustainable yield," a favorite objective of biologists, would involve excess costs of 54 percent.

[f] Assumes a 50 percent increase in productivity in the salmon industry between the early 1930s and the late 1950s, applied to the decline in catch per fathom of net in Bristol Bay. See Crutchfield and Pontecorvo (1969), p. 115.

catchers now carry radar, asdic, and variable pitch propellors, all of which make it easier to detect whales and to maneuver to catch them. Despite these substantial improvements in technique, the total whale tonnage harvested per catcher-day dropped by 27 percent between 1935 and 1965.

Many overfished fisheries have now come under some form of regulation to prevent further depletion of the stocks, but the regulations typically take the form of prescribing technology or limiting the fishing season, with the result that the rents continue to be dissipated through inefficiency. For instance, the allowable season in the areas under jurisdiction of the Inter-American Tropical Tuna Commission is now down to about nine weeks, compared with a season of some nine months in the mid-1960s, despite a doubling of the allowable catch.[7] Such a shortening of the season means that the fishing fleet is idle for much of the year.

Over half of the world's marine fishing is now under some form of regulation, and part of the remainder is overfished. If we assume, conservatively on the above figures, that there is today an excess cost of 25 percent on about 60 percent of the world's marine fishing, the total excess cost would be something in excess of $2 billion a year. This is a substantial sum. It compares, for example, with 1975 disbursements by the International Development Association, the leading source of development assistance on very easy terms, of $1 billion, and it exceeds the recent annual disbursements by the World Bank. It would of course take some years to realize these rents, since taxes would have to be introduced gradually to avoid sharp short-term disruption both to fishermen and to consumers of fish; or they would have to be introduced at full force only after the stocks had been rebuilt through restrictions on harvesting achieved in some other way. But the potential rent from marine harvests is even greater than this, for it has been estimated that the sustainable yield of the oceans of species that currently have commercial value could under proper harvesting conditions double or even triple existing harvests,[8] and by bringing in additional species or by engaging in primitive "aquaculture," that is, man-made improvements to the marine environment, yields could be increased even further.

At this writing, the Third Session of the United Nations Conference on Law of the Sea is in progress. The outcome of this conference is not yet clear, but substantial consensus has developed around the creation of an "exclusive economic zone" extending 200 nautical miles (about 230 statute miles) from the coasts into what is now the high seas. Whatever such a zone ends up entailing for other uses of the oceans, it gives coastal states exclusive rights to the fish within the economic zone. When allowance is made for the enclosure of high seas by archipelagic states (for instance, Indonesia), this extension would appropriate about one third of the ocean area, and about 90 percent of the current marine harvests, to national control. (Whales and tuna are the only major species at present harvested from regions beyond 200 miles.)

One rationale for extending coastal state jurisdiction over a wide economic zone is that it will permit rational conservation measures to be applied to depleted fisheries. The history of purely national regulation of limited wildlife stocks is not very encouraging in this regard, however.[9] If anything, the international record is slightly better. Moreover, many fisheries will cover two or more national economic zones, so the problems (and possibilities) of international regulation are not in any case avoided.

A major irony in the baffling politics of North-South relations is that originally less developed countries insisted on a wide extension of national jurisdiction into the oceans, a notion at first resisted by the major "powers," including the Soviet Union. But the latter gradually reversed their position as they realized the intensity of pressure by less developed countries on the issue and as they did their quantitative homework: nearly half of the ocean territory to be appropriated under the 200-mile economic zone will go to developed countries (including the Soviet Union), which together have less than a quarter of the world's population. Certain developing countries, such as Peru and Somalia, will fare very well under the proposal, but it is difficult in terms of economic development to understand why less developed countries as a group supported it so strongly in the early stages of the conference.

Roughly fifty landlocked and shelflocked[10] nations finally launched a major effort in the spring of 1976 to reduce the exclusivity of the economic zone concept, but their efforts probably came too late, after the exclusive economic zone concept had become widely accepted and indeed entrenched in the thinking of most coastal states.

In the absence of global agreement on a proposal to internationalize the world's open water fisheries, it still might be possible for the developed countries among themselves to agree on a modified version of such a scheme, either for all of their fisheries or at least for those fisheries which overlap national economic zones. An appropriate tax on harvest is the most efficient method for limiting access to each fishery, for unlike other forms of regulation it does not inhibit the development of new technology[11] or result in excessive application of capital, as is the case with variable harvesting seasons. The "common heritage" of the open ocean fisheries could then be acknowledged (1) by encouraging participation by the Food and Agriculture Organization or other relevant international bodies in the decision making of the regulatory bodies of each fishery and (2) by earmarking some substantial portion of the revenues from the fisheries for internationally agreed upon purposes such as peace keeping or economic development. Such an arrangement would dilute the exclusivity of the economic zone to each coastal state and would thereby put other countries on notice that their jurisdiction over the economic zone was a privilege conferred by the international community of nations rather than an absolute right of the coastal states. In addition, those fisheries that extend beyond 200 miles, such as tuna and (if it remains commercially viable) whaling, could be established in a similar way.

Oil and Minerals

In addition to fish, the ocean offers petroleum and other minerals, mainly at present the so-called manganese nodules. Oil and minerals pose different analytical issues than do fish, since in general there are no "externalities" associated with them.[12] The "rents" associated with mineral extraction will therefore be nonexistent if the market price just covers the costs of extraction, which are generally high for underwater operations. In any case, unlike in the case of fishing, the rents cannot readily be tapped without some uneconomic discouragement to the activity.

Petroleum

Petroleum is found in sedimentary material and is therefore limited to continental land masses and their underwater extensions, called the continental margin.[13] In 1974 just under one fifth of world petroleum production was offshore, most of it close to shore and all of it in relatively shallow waters, under 200 meters in depth. But substantial petroleum deposits do exist outside of presently defined territorial waters, generally three to twelve miles in width. This is true of North Sea oil, for example. In principle, all such oil could be regarded as part of the common heritage, owned by all peoples. Under the Continental Shelf Convention of 1958, however, exclusive jurisdiction over the seabed was conferred on the coastal state in areas "adjacent to the coast . . . to a depth of 200 meters or, beyond that limit, to where the depth of the waters admits of the exploitation of the natural resources." On one interpretation, this would seem to extend national jurisdiction to the middle of the oceans as technology permitted ever deeper exploitation. The key to restriction therefore hinges on a legal interpretation of the phrase "adjacent to the coast."

In 1970 the United States proposed that all oil beyond the depth of 200 meters be managed by the nearest coastal state, but held in trust for the international community, and that a third to a half of the net revenues from its exploitation be set aside for international uses. Coming from a country with a long coastline, this was an extraordinarily generous proposal, and it is only one of the many baffling aspects of the politics of relations between developed and less developed nations that this proposal was received very coolly by the less developed countries[14] and that it was never seriously considered.

The National Petroleum Council has estimated that 30 to 45 percent of offshore oil reserves, which are perhaps one quarter of total world oil reserves, lies below 200 meters.[15] Assuming that offshore production by 1985 were to double from an estimated 1976 offshore production of 3 billion barrels, and that one third of this output were to be drawn in seas over 200 meters deep (compared with virtually none at the present time), gross revenues at eleven dollars a barrel would amount to $22 billion on this deep-water oil. Costs rise rapidly with the depth of the water and with the turbulence of the seas, but if costs amounted to 80 percent of this, it would still leave net revenues of $4.4 billion, half of which would be $2.2 billion, to be set aside for international uses under the U.S. proposal of 1970.

Discussion at the UN Conference on Law of the Sea has concentrated on creation of a 200-mile economic zone, including the bottom below the sea. The negotiating text of the conference contained a provision for international royalties on oil taken beyond 200 miles. The National Petroleum Council estimates that only 5 to 20 percent of offshore reserves lie beyond 200 miles, so this provision would generate very much less revenue, and none until far into the future. Some participants at the conference want seabed rights all the way to the edge of the continental margin, which in a few places around the world is 500 to 600 miles from shore; this extension would effectively "nationalize" all the offshore oil.

A task force of the Trilateral Commission has suggested that the developed countries establish a trust fund into which they pay 50 percent of the net revenues on all oil produced in their waters beyond a twelve-mile territorial sea.[16] That would be more generous than the United States' proposal in its proximity to the coasts, but would exclude the oil-rich, less developed countries. A rigorous application of the notion of common heritage would include those countries as well. To do so would generate revenues of roughly $6 to $7 billion by 1985.

Manganese Nodules

Manganese nodules are potato-sized metallic nodules, about 30 percent manganese by weight, that can be found over large areas of the deep ocean floor. From an economic point of view the interest in them arises from their 1 to 2 percent content of nickel, as sulfide ores are depleted, and copper, and to a less extent from cobalt and various trace metals. At present, nickel alone accounts for about 70 percent of the value, and as a practical matter nodules can be considered potential nickel mines, on current estimates being somewhat more expensive than existing sulfide ores but apparently less expensive to mine than the laterite ores to which the world must otherwise increasingly turn for its supplies of nickel in the years to come. Nodules can be found in all the oceans, but the nickel and copper content is economically high only in the Pacific, as far as is now known.

How far and how fast nodule extraction will develop depends very much on the legal regime that is established over mining operations on the deep ocean floor; a number of American, Japanese, and European firms apparently stand ready to start serious exploration and pilot operations as soon as they can get adequate financing, which in turn hinges on reduction of legal uncertainties.

There seems to be little question that the nodules represent a promising source of nickel, copper, and cobalt; but production will rise only slowly, even when the legal issues are settled. By the year 2000 perhaps 50 million tons of ore will be extracted from the sea, up from perhaps 10 million tons in 1985. At today's prices and estimated costs, the net revenue per ton would be about twenty dollars, yielding $200 million by 1985 and $1 billion by 2000.[17]

Projections regarding an untried technology always entail much uncertainty, but on present estimates deep-sea mining seems economically feasible, if not exceptionally profitable. The capital requirements both for extraction of the nodules and for processing them are high. High taxes on the activity will therefore not tap exceptionally high rents, but rather will simply discourage development effort. Two approaches, not mutually exclusive, would be suitable for generating revenues for the international community from nodule mining.

1. Treat the corporations that engage in mining as *international* corpora-

tions for tax purposes and apply the conventional profits tax of about 50 percent. On the above estimates this would generate about $100 million in revenues by 1985 and perhaps $500 million by 2000. National treasuries would agree to credit this tax against national tax liabilities, just as they do now for profits taxes paid to foreign jurisdictions by home corporations or their subsidiaries. With this arrangement, the tax would not discourage deep-sea mining compared with other normal investments.

2. Ration the mining sites through auction, with the bidding to involve both an initial entry fee and a royalty (or profits tax rate) on all output. In bidding, the companies would bet on what they think each site is worth, but they would share the risk (through the profits tax rate) with the auctioning authority. A fair auction presupposes a number of competing prospectors and also that the principal uncertainty lies in the quality of the site and not in the nature of the extraction technology, so reliance on this second technique should wait until nodule mining has been economically tested.

In the UN Law of the Sea Conference the majority of less developed countries have been urging a quite different approach: to establish a new international organization which would have exclusive rights to undertake the actual mining of the nodules, if necessary by contracting for services, and with authority to restrict the output. The latter consideration seems to be governed by a desire to protect present exporters of the relevant minerals from experiencing reductions in prices as a result of seabed mining. The contribution of manganese nodules to world output of nickel and copper would still be less than 1 percent on the above calculations, with a negligible effect on prices, but they would contribute nearly half of the world supply of cobalt.[18] Only Zaire is dependent on the export of cobalt, however, and that product accounts for only 5 percent of Zaire's export earnings at present, and presumably less as Zaire diversifies its economy in the next quarter of a century. Given the timing involved, Zaire's economic progress cannot be seriously affected by the influence of deep-sea mining on cobalt prices. In any case, if necessary, adequate compensation could be paid from the international profits taxes, with much to spare for general development financing.

Summary

An approach to the oceans that regards what is now the high seas and the seabed below as the common heritage of mankind, owned by the world community rather than by individual coastal states, could with proper implementation generate considerable revenue for the international community, to be used for internationally agreed upon purposes, for which transfer of resources to developing countries would surely be the principal contender. The time profile of the revenues available depends of course on the rate of development of the resources of the oceans as well as upon the stocks of resources available. In the cases of offshore oil and nodule mining, the amounts of revenue available would presumably grow year by year until maximum exploitation was achieved some time in the next century. In the case of fish an interval of time is required to establish the proper regulatory regimes and in some cases to rebuild depleted stocks of fish; but, once established, the regime could generate a steady amount of revenue (at a constant relative price for marine products) for an indefinite period. A rough estimate of the magnitudes involved within the relatively near future, say, by 1985, suggests that a full capture of rents on fish at 1974 levels of output would yield $2.2 billion, a fifty percent profits tax on offshore oil coming from waters more than 200 meters deep would yield $2.2 billion, and a 50 percent profits tax on manganese nodules would yield $0.1 billion, for a total of $4.5 billion in revenues from the oceans. It is a magnitude that deserves serious consideration. If a new Law of the Sea Convention merely metes out these resources to coastal states in the form of exclusive economic zones, it will represent one of the major missed opportunities for mankind to build toward a world community.

Notes

1 Charles Pearson has suggested that disposal charges might be an important source of revenue. He identifies two very different principles on which to base such charges: the first arises from negative external effects on fisheries and other users, such as those discussed; the second involves charging a "monopoly rent" to those who want to use the ocean and have no other low-cost method of disposal. As Pearson recognizes, the second principle would involve a misallocation of the world's resources, since the oceans frequently do represent the channel of waste disposal that is socially least expensive. So long as that is so, and in many localities it is likely to be so for a long time, it would not be desirable to levy these monopoly rents. See Pearson (1973), pp. 221-237.

2 "Fishing" here means the harvesting of any living resources from the oceans. In practice not only fish but also mammals, crustaceans, mollusks, and even seaweed are taken from the oceans. But fish proper account for about 80 percent of the value and 90 percent of the weight of the total harvest of living resources.

3 This basic characteristic of a fishery was first pointed out in the economic literature by H. Scott Gordon (1954), pp. 124-142. Gordon's analysis was in terms of a single time period. For a simple model of a fishery including all future time periods, and hence the future implications of present changes in stocks, see the appendix.

4 Setting the optimal tax requires knowledge of the ecological characteristics of the fishery, of the cost characteristics of the potential fishing fleets, and of a social rate of discount. See the appendix. If a regulatory commission's knowledge of fishing costs is limited, and if collusion among prospective bidders is unlikely, instead of setting a tax, the commission might establish an allowable harvest and auction it on a royalty basis for a period of, say, five years; or it could auction transferable licenses subject to an annual tax proportional to the prevailing market value of the licenses.

5 See Crutchfield and Pontecorvo (1969), pp. 202-205.

6 See Small (1971), p. 67.

7 See Rose (1974), p. 813.

8 See Holt (1975), p. 79.

9 Sidney Holt reports that the catch of shrimp per boat in the Gulf of California had declined by 1973 to less than 20 percent of its level in 1950, for instance, despite the fact that the fishery is under exclusive Mexican jurisdiction. U.S. regulation of oysters and lobsters in territorial waters also gives little encouragement to the notion that national jurisdiction will assure rational management.

10 Nations with some coast, but whose "economic zone" is truncated to less than one third of what it would otherwise be by the zones of other nations.

11 The development of cost-reducing technology would of course call for a higher tax, but under competitive conditions incentives would still be present to develop such technology.

12 With the manageable exceptions of drilling into a common pool of oil and exploration of a nodule-rich zone on the deep ocean floor.

13 The continental margin is composed of three roughly distinguishable parts: (1) the relatively flat *shelf*, a direct underwater extension of the continent; (2) the steeper *slope*, the face that drops from the shelf toward the deep ocean floor; and (3) the more gentle *rise*, a sometimes extensive layer of debris that has rolled down the slope and covers the deep ocean floor, or the abysmal deep, as it is sometimes called. Petroleum deposits possibly exist on all parts of the continental margin.

14 Understandably, the Soviet representative to the UN Seabed Committee dismissed the proposal as reflecting "unjustified optimism" by the United States. Less understandably, the Indian representative also dismissed the proposal, emphasizing the monopoly of technology by a relatively few companies: "in effect, therefore, some foreign companies rather than the coastal state concerned would become trustees." This statement misses the enormous possibilities of the proposal for generating revenue. Quoted from Lawrence Juda (1975), pp. 119-120. On the bureaucratic politics of the U.S. proposal, see Hollick (1974), pp. 26-40.

15 See Gardner (1976), p. 2.

16 See Hardy, Hollick, Holst, Johnston, and Oda (1975), p. 46.

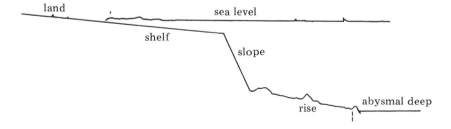

Figure 4.1

17 Calculations based on Robert R. Nathan Associates (1974), pp. 18-27, and on conversations with C. G. Welling, Manager of Ocean Mining, R&D Division, Lockheed Missiles & Space Co. For an earlier and more optimistic calculation of net revenue per ton, see Mero (1972), pp. 191-203. Mero estimates that 10 to 500 billion tons of nodules would be ultimately recoverable, at costs in 1970 prices of forty-six to eighty-five dollars a ton. At the lower value and at 1975 metals prices the net revenue would be about thirty-five dollars a ton.

18 See Nathan Associates, Tables 4 and 5.

References

Cooper, R. N., "An Economist's View of the Oceans," *Journal of World Trade Law*, Vol. 9, July/August 1975.

Christy, F. J., Jr., *Alternative Arrangements for Marine Fisheries: An Overview*, Washington: Resources for the Future, May 1973.

Crutchfield, J. A., and G. Pontecorvo, *The Pacific Salmon Fisheries: A Study in Irrational Conservation*, Baltimore: Johns Hopkins University Press, 1969.

FAO Fisheries Reports No. 142, Suppl. 1, Rome, March 1974, pp. 8-9, *The Scientific Advisory Function in International Management and Development Bodies.*

Gardner, R. N., "Offshore Oil and the Law of the Seas," *New York Times*, March 14, 1976.

Gates, J. M., and V. J. Norton, "The Benefits of Fisheries Regulation: A Case Study of the New England Yellowtail Flounder Fishery," University of Rhode Island, Marine Technical Report No. 21, Kingston, R.I., 1974.

Gordon, H. S., "The Economic Theory of Common Property Resource: the Fishery," *Journal of Political Economy*, Vol. 62, 1954.

Hardy, M., A. Hollick, J. Holst, D. Johnston, and S. Oda, *A New Regime for the Oceans*, New York: The Trilateral Commission, December 1975.

Hollick, A. L., *New Era of Ocean Politics*, Baltimore: Johns Hopkins University Press, 1974.

Holt, S., "Marine Fisheries and World Food Supplies," in A. Bourne (ed.), *Man/Food Equation*, Academic Press, 1975.

Juda, L., *Ocean Space Rights*, New York: Praeger, 1975.

Mero, J. L., "Potential Economic Value of Ocean-Floor Manganese Nodule Deposits," in David R. Horn (ed.), *Ferromanganese Deposits on the Ocean Floor*, Lamont-Doherty Geological Laboratory, Columbia University, Palisades, New York, for the National Science Foundation, January 1972.

Robert R. Nathan Associates, *The Economic Value of Ocean Resources to the United States*, prepared for Senate Commerce Committee, 93rd Congress, 2nd Session, Government Printing Office, December 1974.

Pearson, C., "Extracting Rent from Ocean Resources: Discussion of a Neglected Source," *Ocean Development and International Law Journal*, Vol. 1, 1973.

Pontecorvo, G., and K. Vartdal, Jr., "Optimizing Resource Use: The Norwegian Winter Herring Fishery," *Statsøkonomisk Tidsskrift*, September 1967.

Rose, A. D., "The Tuna Example: Is There Hope for International Cooperation?" *San Diego Law Review*, Vol. 11, May 1974.

Small, G. L., *The Blue Whale*, New York: Columbia University Press, 1971.

Appendix
Simple Model of a Fishery, and a Guide to Optimum Management

Suppose the population dynamics of a single-species fishery can be characterized by

$$f(s) = \dot{s} + h, \, f''(s) < 0 \tag{1}$$

where s is the stock of fish, $\dot{s}$ is the change in s per unit time, and h is the harvest per unit time.

Suppose the costs of fishing on this fishery can be characterized by a cost function

$$C = C(h, s), \, C_h > 0, \, C_s < 0, \, C(o, s) = 0, \tag{2}$$

where C_h represents the incremental cost per unit of harvest, stock being held constant, and C_s represents the change in costs of a given harvest resulting from an increase in the stock. In general, C_h and C_s will depend in value both on the size of the stock and on the size of the harvest. This cost function consolidates the cost functions of individual fishing units into a relationship for the industry as a whole. In competitive equilibrium, marginal harvesting cost C_h will apply to each fishing unit, and will also equal average harvesting cost (inclusive of normal return to capital), which also depends on the stock of fish.

Suppose finally that the market price of fish is a constant, p. Under these circumstances, competitive access to the fishery will lead to a level of activity such that $p = C_h$ and profits are at the competitive level, that is, until marginal (and average) cost equals price.

The economically optimal harvest is the one that maximizes the present value of the fishery, assumed here to depend only on its present and future yield of fish. Thus we want to choose the stock s^* and the harvest h^* that maximizes:

$$\int_o^\infty [ph - C(h, s)] \, e^{-it} \, dt \tag{3}$$

where i is the social rate of discount (assumed to be constant).

Maximizing (3) is a problem in the calculus of variations and gives rise to the Euler condition for maximization:

$$p = C_h + [C_s + \frac{dC_h}{dt}] \, \frac{1}{f'(s) - i} \tag{4}$$

The term $\dfrac{dC_h}{dt}$ is transitory, so for a sustained yield from the fishery we have

$$p = C_h + \frac{C_s}{f'(s) - i} \, . \tag{4'}$$

The second term on the right-hand side, which for $i > f'(s)$ will be positive, indicates the extra social cost associated with the "stock externality" of the fishery. At the maximum sustainable yield, $f'(s) = 0$, it is simply the present discounted value of the extra costs imposed for present and all future fishing by reducing the stock by one unit.

Equation (4') shows that in setting $p = C_h$ competitive access to the fishery leads to a marginal cost C_h that is above that called for by optimal management: the stock is depleted below the optimal level, raising C_h. To prevent this overfishing, a royalty tax must be levied equal to the second term on the right-hand side of equation (4'). This tax will vary inversely with the stock.

The optimal sustainable harvest of the fishery can be shown graphically as in Figure 4.2.

Here eq.(1) shows the biological yield of the stock, and eq.(4') shows the economically optimum relationship between harvest and stock, neglecting the transitory term in eq.(4). The optimum sustainable harvest is h^*, which in general will be lower than the maximum sustainable yield, shown by the

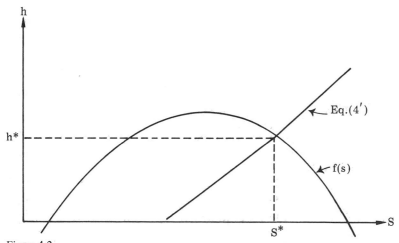

Figure 4.2

maximum height of the curve of eq.(1). The optimum stock may be either larger or smaller than the stock that supports a maximum yield.

For further discussion, including relaxation of the constant price assumption, see R. N. Cooper (1975), pp. 372-377.

Comment
Nurul Islam

Professor Richard Cooper analyzes very clearly the financial resources or revenues that might be available for the development of the poor countries from the exploitation of three types of ocean resources—sea fisheries, offshore oil and gas production, and deep seabed mining. He recommends in the case of fishing the appropriation of the entire economic rent by means of taxes, whereas in the case of offshore oil and gas and seabed mining he suggests 50 percent tax on profits. In the case of fishing there is a complication. It will be necessary to abandon the existing method of regulating sea fishing for purposes of conservation and prevention of overfishing by means of fixing the seasons and duration of fishing. The coastal states should accept price mechanism that is, taxation as against direct control over fishing activity as the optimum method of regulation. Professor Cooper makes undoubtedly the most effective case for such a changeover.

Rough orders of magnitude of resources available from these three sources by 1985 are estimated to be about $4.5 billion. An annual total of $4.5 billion does compare favorably with the $11 to $12 billion of official development assistance that has been made available to the poor countries in recent years. Considerably more than official development assistance has been provided by multilateral agencies, about $3 billion in 1974. In view of the stagnation in the flow of conventional sources of development assistance, any proposal for tapping new sources or mechanism for increasing the flow of resources to the developing countries deserves highest consideration. From the point of view of the recipient countries, it would be development assistance of a higher quality since it would not be tied to sources of procurement.

The basis of these estimates is the imposition of the same percentage rate of taxes on the net revenues of all the coastal states, irrespective of the amount of revenues involved; there is no progressiveness in burden sharing among the coastal states. The question of equity in burden sharing in development assistance is neglected. Furthermore, it is not clear whether these estimates should include revenues earned by the developing coastal states as well, which are expected to be the recipients, not providers, of development assistance. It is not explained by Professor Cooper why, in the case of offshore oil and gas revenue, he restricts his proposals to waters beyond 200 meters in depth. The logic of his argument for using the "common heritage of mankind" for the development of the poor nations could easily be extended to include revenue from all the offshore oil and gas beyond territorial waters. Since this is the most important source of revenue among the three different resources mentioned by him, it is of critical importance as to whether one includes revenue from all oil and gas production beyond territorial waters or only from production in waters more than 200 meters in depth. Professor Cooper's logic of argument should also be extended to include rents from all natural resources whether they are land based or are exploited from ocean. The rents from scarce natural resources, that is, the excess over the supply price for the exploitation of natural resources, which includes a reasonable rate of profit for the exploiters, is an income which is not due to the ability, genius, or hard work of the countries in which these natural resources happen to be located. The location of natural resources across the nation-states is an accident of geography and the appropriation of rents from them by a nation-state is no different in the ultimate analysis from the appropriation of profits from ocean resources. There is one difference, neither in economics nor in logic but in law, that is, ocean resources have not yet been legally appropriated whereas land resources were appropriated long ago. This has been recognized by international law.

As the author rightly points out, whether the resources estimated by him would in fact be available for development assistance depends upon a large number of factors, including institutional arrangements and the principles of demarcation of various zones in the ocean such as territorial waters, economic zones, and deep-sea waters. These issues are under negotiation in the Law of the Sea Conference which has just ended one of its sessions in Geneva without any agreement. It must, however, be noted that revenue sharing from ocean resources is only one of the many considerations involved in the negotiations for the demarcation of zones for national, international, and joint controls. These considerations include rights of navigation and of overflight, scientific research or protection of environmental pollution, and so forth. International negotiations on all these matters are interrelated. There are obvious trade-offs between the various objectives, which are both economic as well as political and strategic in nature. No clear analysis of trade-offs seems to be available to date to determine the criteria of choice between economic and noneconomic objectives.

While the author's analysis, as he himself points out, deals exclusively with the possible transfer of financial resources to the developing countries, the latter are interested not merely in financial transfers but also in other economic objectives. Again, the trade-off between different economic objectives is not clear. How much financial transfer would offset the surrender of their objective, for example, of gaining access to or physical control over ocean resources, has not been worked out. No such "deal" has been offered by the developed countries in terms of alternative combinations of the various objectives, so that the developing countries could reveal their preference. They are interested not only in obtaining or sharing in revenues from ocean resources but also in their prices, and in direct participation in their exploitation. They would like to acquire technology and know-how for the exploitation of ocean resources and to participate in the decision-making process that sets the international rules for the exploitation of ocean resources.

The author advocates an international regime that would ensure access to ocean resources, irrespective of whoever exploits or engages in productive activity, being available without discrimination and restriction to all countries and being priced competitively. Apart from the fact that optimum pricing policy for nonrenewable natural resources remains a matter of controversy even among theoretical economists, the developing countries are interested in outputs and prices of the ocean resources, partly because the very same resources are produced on land in many developing countries, and consequently the output and price policy relating to the ocean resources would affect their income from the land-based resources. While it is true, as the author reminds us, that on the basis of existing knowledge, the proportion of the available ocean resources to land-based resources is quite small for the former to have any significant impact on the prices of and incomes from the latter, this might not be true in the future when more knowledge about ocean resources is likely to be available.

It has been pointed out that the support on the part of the developing countries for a 200-mile economic zone under exclusive national control is not in their best interests. The 200-mile economic zone is supposed to contain 90 percent of the known ocean resources and would result in handing over the bulk of the world's ocean territory to the developed countries, since the latter happen to be the large coastal states. Even among the developing countries, distribution of economic zones is highly unequal. If the developing countries are interested only in financial resources to be derived from ocean, they should support the case for the narrowest economic zone under exclusive national control leaving a major part of ocean resources to be exploited under international auspices, especially since they do not have the necessary capital and technology to exploit ocean resources. At the same time they should negotiate for a significant share in the income derived from the exploitation of ocean resources under international control. One can advance several reasons why they do not do so. First, they are not certain they would benefit from the international control over a larger area more than they would from the national control over a small part of the ocean, that is, economic zone of 200 miles under national jurisdiction. Experience with negotiations on the International Seabed Authority, which is concerned with the exploitation of manganese nodules beyond 200 miles, seems to have created misapprehensions in developing countries about the ability of international agencies to protect or promote their interests. The developed countries have opposed the suggestion that the international Seabed Authority should be governed by the principle of "one man—one vote," rather than by the weighted voting of the industrialized countries. Neither do they agree to allow the authority direct responsibility for the production of seabed minerals, nor do they want it to undertake the regulation of output and of prices fixed by the multinational corporations that are to be licensed to produce the manganese nodules. This has tended to strengthen the impression that the developed countries are not willing to vest an international authority under majority control with adequate powers, even though the seabed resources involved constitute so small a part of the total world supply of the specific minerals. Second, the developing countries may be under the impression that in view of the much discussed prospects of scarcity of natural resources in the future and in view of increasing dependence of the developed countries on imports from the developing countries, they would be able to bargain on the basis of ocean resources under their national control, if not in terms of prices of their exports or a share in the revenues from resources under the control of the developed countries, but at least to obtain a better deal on other economic and noneconomic issues relating to the ocean regime.

The present trends indicate that economic zones of 200 miles under exclusive national control are going to be internationally accepted. A few coastal states have already unilaterally appropriated 200 miles without any promise or obligation to the effect that they would share resources with the developing countries. Professor Cooper suggests that in the case of fisheries the developed countries should offer unilaterally to share revenues with the developing world. This is probably the only way under the present circumstances that a share in revenue from resources within a 200-mile limit could be made available to the developing countries. The concessions obtained by the landlocked states from the coastal states for participating in the resources of the latter's economic zone, may provide a precedent in persuading the rich coastal states to give a share to the poorer states in their ocean resources. But then if it is left to the developed countries to agree to share their resources with the poor countries, that is no different from sharing revenue from other national resources, excepting that the ocean resource is a newly acquired national resource.

5

Taxing the Brain Drain: A Global Point of View
Koichi Hamada

Introduction

In recent years, the migration of skilled, professional people from less developed countries to developed countries has become a matter of importance. It is estimated that the total stock of the immigrants of professionals and technicians from less developed countries to the United States, accumulated during the ten years from 1962 to 1971, amounts to more than 200,000. It is evident that the Immigration Act of 1975, which eliminated the earlier racial-origin quotas, has reinforced the increase in the immigration from the LDCs (less developed countries). In Canada, the estimate of accumulated skilled immigrants during the ten years from 1963 to 1972 amounts to 40,000; and in the United Kingdom, a similar estimate during the nine years from 1964 to 1972 amounts to more than 60,000 (Bhagwati, 1976).

This substantial increase in the migration of professionals and technicians has led to concern in LDCs and to attention from economists. For, the migration of skilled labor, better known as the "brain drain," is alleged to result in gain to the DCs (developed countries), as well as to the emigrants, but only at the cost of those who remain behind in the LDCs. Thus the migration of skilled labor is discussed fashionably in UN debates as the "reverse transfer of technology" from LDCs to DCs.

Of course, the freedom of movement of people across national borders can be regarded as a dimension of progress in a humanistic society. With freedom of choice in residence, one can have more freedom to choose living conditions and a cultural environment, and to engage in preferred religious or political activities. In the present situation, however, it is mostly the people with skills who can migrate easily whereas those without professional skills face quite strict restrictions of entry into DCs. This asymmetry in the opportunity for migration aggravates the unfavorable welfare effects for those who are left behind in the LDCs.[1]

Humanistic consideration of the welfare of those in the LDCs has recently led Bhagwati to propose a surtax on the earnings of skilled emigrants in DCs. This proposal (for a supplementary income tax on such earnings to be routed to LDCs via the UN for developmental spending) has been supported by theoretical and empirical arguments on the nature of gains and losses of the

parties, such as original residents in the recipient country, migrants themselves, and those who remain behind in the home country. Rationales for the
proposal are based on separate considerations of these gains and losses, and
on an equity principle between those who gain and those who lose by
migration (Bhagwati and Partington, 1976).

On the other hand, the counterargument, which has not been systematically
developed but has nonetheless appeared sporadically, stresses the freedom of
labor mobility and its welfare effect on international efficiency. However,
most arguments seem to rely on the general principle that factor mobility
improves efficient allocation of resources, and they do not pay explicit
attention to the interdependent nature of the gains and losses of the parties
involved.

The main purpose of this paper is to broaden our perspectives on the
interdependent nature of gains and losses, and to analyze simultaneously the
aspects of efficiency and equity in a unified, global picture. Instead of
concentrating on the *distributional* question of losses to any specific party as
a rationale for the tax proposal or appealing merely to the principle of global
efficiency, I shall consider how the principle of equity can be implemented in
a design of international taxation that has the least distorting effect on the
amount of migration.

Special attention will be paid to the device suggested by Oldman and Pomp
(1975), that is, the device of extending to emigrants the regular tax schedule
of the country of origin, with relief from double taxation. It will be shown
that this device not only promotes the transfer of income from those who
gain to those who lose, but also helps to realize the amount of migration
judged efficient from the international point of view, as long as there is no
exogenous restriction on the entry of skilled workers. If some restriction on
entry is binding effectively, then the scheme of global extension of tax
schedule does not achieve efficiency, and a rationale for a variant of the
Bhagwati tax proposal arises. It will be shown, however, that our analytical
framework can indicate an algorithm to determine the proper rate of tax,
which was left as arbitrary in the original surtax proposal.

In Section 2, I present the original Bhagwati tax proposal with its possible
variants and also the estimates for the proceeds from such a surtax obtained
by various authors. In Sections 3 and 4, I examine rationales for and
counterarguments against the tax proposal. In Section 5, I present a simple
framework to examine gains and losses of the parties simultaneously, to
analyze the relationship between efficiency and equity. Section 6 discusses
the practical problems in implementing the global extension of domestic tax
schedule. In the appendix, a game-theoretic analysis will be carried out
concerning the mutual interplay of tax policies of a DC and an LDC.

In short, this paper is an attempt to show that a global theoretical
framework clarifies several issues concerning losses and gains due to migra-

tion, and helps to design a tax scheme that appeals to the criterion for international efficiency as well as to our moral principle regarding equity.

The Original Proposal

The proposal for taxation on the income of the "brain drained" was originally sketched by Bhagwati (1972), and was developed with its economic rationales and with estimates for the revenues in the U.S. case in Bhagwati and Dellalfar (1973).

The original proposal essentially stated that a supplementary income tax should be levied on the income earned by the professionals, technicians, and kindred persons (PTKs) who emigrate from LDCs to DCs, and that the tax should be collected by the tax authority of the host DC and eventually be routed to LDCs of origin or LDCs en bloc, preferably via the UN, for developmental spending.

Several features of this proposal need to be noted:

1. The tax is to be paid primarily by the *emigrants* themselves, though some additional tax *on the DC of immigration* to share its benefit from emigrants with the LDC of origin was also suggested.

2. The tax is levied on the actual earned income of the emigrant after emigration, and *not* at the time of departure (as in the unpopular exit tax of the Soviet type). The brain drain tax may work as a deterrent to emigration, but it does not work as a prohibitive tax, while the Soviet exit tax is quite likely to function as prohibitive in the environment of an imperfect capital market. Accordingly, freedom in the choice of location is much less violated in the brain drain tax proposal than in the Soviet exit tax. The two taxes differ also in their justifications. The Soviet Union considers its exit tax as a compensation for its domestic investment in education. The brain drain tax, on the other hand, is considered as a means of compensation for the (more general) loss imposed by the emigrant on those left behind, and, more important, as a means of transferring a part of the improved incomes of the emigrants to those in LDCs who could not so improve their incomes in a world of imperfect mobility—thanks to DC (immigration) restrictions on free movement of migrants.

3. The tax is calculated as a surtax on the net income (after-income tax of the DC) of the emigrants. The rate for such a surtax is assumed tentatively as 10 percent in the numerical estimates of revenues, but how to determine the rate of the surtax remains an open question.

4. If the brain drain tax is to be effective, it should be at least *collected* by the authority of the DCs. However, the question of who *levies* it gives rise to serious constitutional issues to be considered below.

5. The revenue resulting from the tax is to be distributed to the LDC of origin, or, alternatively, to an international agency, such as the UNDP,

to be transferred in a generalized fashion to LDCs for developmental purposes.

This proposal was under extensive and critical discussion by economists and lawyers in Bellagio in February 1975. It turned out, especially from the examinations by lawyers, that if the tax was levied by the tax authorities of DCs, this would raise serious constitutional and political problems. Therefore the original proposal was modified to take the following form: "LDCs would legally levy it, DCs would collect it and the tax would be ratified by a special treaty at the UN with the provision that the proceeds from the tax would go to the UN to be disbursed *via* UNDP or the proposed new UN Special Fund on LDCs en-bloc for development purposes" (Bhagwati, 1976).

Estimates for the tax revenues from such a surtax have been made by Bhagwati and Pelcovits (1976) for the United States, by De Voretz and Maki (1975) for Canada, and by Balacs and Gordon (1975) for the United Kingdom. The total revenues come to an annual sum of approximately U.S. $300 million in 1972 (see Table 5.1). The revenues from Australia and the EEC and from extension of the tax to LDC-national professionals employed permanently or on long-run assignments in international agencies, such as the UN, OECD, IMF, and IBRD, would bring the total revenues to $400 million in 1972 values. If we adjust for post-1972 inflation, Bhagwati concludes that the estimate for 1976 would reach U.S. $500 million.[2] This is a sizable sum of resource transfer to LDCs, especially when it is noted that it is all a "grant equivalent" flow and hence equivalent to about three to four times' that magnitude of average "aid dollars."

In this paper, I shall be concerned however not so much with the actual estimates of revenues raised by the proposal as with the critical examination of the pros and cons of this proposal from economic, legal, political, and ethical viewpoints. In particular, a variation of the proposal will receive special attention. In their paper presented at Bellagio, Oldman and Pomp (1975) considered the extension of relief against double taxation to the brain drain taxation problem. In general, the possibility of double taxation occurs when an individual or a firm has tax obligations to more than one country. Most countries allow some type of credit relief to such a person. In the simplest form of relief, a taxpayer computes his tax liability and then takes as a credit against that liability the amount of foreign taxes he has paid to foreign authorities. Suppose that an LDC levies its regular income tax on the income of PTKs emigrated from the LDC to a DC, and the effective DC tax rate on the income of the PTK is lower than the effective LDC rate. Then, under the double-taxation relief provision, PTKs should pay tax to the LDC at a rate equal to the excess of the effective LDC rate over the effective DC rate.[3]

This consideration led to the following variation of the brain drain tax proposal. The LDC would extend its tax jurisdiction over income from foreign sources as long as individuals remained citizens of the LDC, and possibly, by an international treaty, for some years after they lost the citizenship of the LDC of origin. The regular schedule of the domestic income tax (with some adjustment for the living standards) would then be extended to the emigrated PTKs. However, with the double-taxation relief, the tax paid to the DC would be credited against the tax obligation to the LDC.[4] The reason why this version attracts our serious attention will be discussed in more detail later.

Rationale for the Tax Proposal

The Bhagwati proposal for taxing the brain drain is partly (though not wholly) a reaction to the adverse effects of the brain drain and accordingly it is typically justified on moral grounds or on principles of equity. A justification on grounds of efficiency, in particular those of international efficiency rather than domestic efficiency of the LDC of origin, is hardly to be found in the literature and would appear at first to be improbable. However, I shall present in later sections a rationale for extending the regular tax schedule of the LDC with relief for double taxation precisely on the ground of international or cosmopolitan efficiency.

It is best to quote Bhagwati on the moral rationale of the proposed brain drain tax (Bhagwati and Partington, 1976, p. 22):

The rationale behind the tax implementation would consist of two arguments; in order of their importance: (1) Firstly, one would assert the moral principle that, in a world of imperfect mobility, those few who manage to get from LDCs into DCs to practice their professions at substantially-improved incomes ought to be asked to contribute a fraction of their gains for the improved welfare of those left behind in the LDCs; this would effectively be extending the usual principle of progressive taxation across national borders. (2) Moreover, since there is a widely-held presumption, based on several sound arguments and embodied in numerous international resolutions, that the brain drain creates difficulties for the LDCs, it would also constitute a simple and rough-and-ready way for the emigrating professionals to compensate the LDCs for these losses. In fact, the moral obligation to share one's gains with those who are unable to share in these gains would be reinforced if these others were also hurt by one's emigration.

Any moral principle depends on a value judgment. Thus one cannot objectively say whether the above moral principles are right or wrong. However, one can safely say that they are likely to appeal to quite a few policy makers in DCs as well as to many of those in LDCs. Now let us turn to the examination of the components of gains and losses relevant to these moral arguments: What are the gains of DCs?, What are the losses to LDCs of origin?, What are the gains to emigrants?

Gains to DCs

One well-known source of gains to DCs is the effect of immigration in nonmarginal finite magnitudes. Even though immigrants are paid their marginal product, gain for the indigenous nationals of the recipient country still accrues as long as the returns to skilled labor fall with PTK immigrants.

The second source of gains is the external economies due to the inflow of PTKs. If the social marginal product of the human capital embodied in the immigrating PTKs is well reflected in the wages of immigrating PTKs, then this problem does not arise. However, if the marginal product of human capital is not duly reflected in the market price, then a gain from externalities will accrue to the nationals of recipient DCs.

Losses to LDCs

In contrast to the sparse literature on the welfare gains to DCs, there is much written on the possible welfare losses to LDCs losing PTKs. Since the comprehensive survey by Bhagwati and Rodriguez (1975) covers this subject in a systematic and detailed fashion, we shall be content with the summary of the possible sources of losses to LDCs. The welfare criterion is usually based on the per capita national income of those who remain behind, or their well-being, taking into account income-distributional considerations.

1. The loss due to finite rather than marginal outflow of skilled labor. For an infinitesimal outflow of PTKs from LDCs, it can be argued that an emigrant neither harms nor helps the nonimmigrants because the emigrant has been contributing his marginal product to national income, and, at the same time, earning his marginal product (Grubel and Scott, 1966). For finite changes, however, the process is the reverse of what we have argued already for the recipient country (Berry and Soligo, 1969, and Tobin, 1974). This loss, of course, disappears when diminishing returns disappear, for example, because of incomplete specialization in international trade for a small country (Johnson, 1967).

2. The loss (or gain) due to the outflow of factors of production other than labor. If an emigrant carries with him factors of production other than labor, then the income of those left behind will deteriorate or improve depending on the relative proportion of the factor endowment of those who emigrate compared with those who remain behind (Johnson, 1967, Bhagwati and Rodriguez, 1975).

3. The loss due to the emulation effect. If unemployment exists in LDCs of origin, then several new aspects of losses will emerge. In the presence of sticky wages, if the wage level of the skilled labor is adjusted upward in some way to international standards, then this emulation effect will reduce the welfare of those remaining behind. This emulation effect can be serious if only those who possess special skills can migrate and those who possess ordinary skills are denied the opportunity (Bhagwati and Hamada, 1974).

4. The loss due to externalities attached to the service of PTKs. One of the characteristics of LDCs is that various kinds of market distortions, such as rigidity of wages and immobility of labor between sectors, exist in the domestic economy. In general, the social marginal benefit due to skilled labor

is not fully reflected in the private marginal benefit accruing to it. The relevant externalities differ from profession to profession, and from country to country. It has been pointed out (Hamada and Bhagwati, 1975) that while the phenomenon of overqualification of workers for jobs may mitigate the welfare loss of LDCs, the existence of an "internal diffusion" process between rural and urban areas, as well as the lack of screening power of skilled labor in LDCs, will aggravate the welfare loss to LDCs of origin.

5. The welfare loss in the presence of income taxation in LDCs. The LDCs of origin also engage in income redistribution policies through taxation and transfer payments. If an LDC desires to increase its marginal rate of taxation to achieve more equality in income, then this gives an incentive for PTKs to emigrate. Since only those who are earning more than average income will emigrate in usual cases, the implementation of progressive taxation will be obstructed by the possibility of brain drain. This conflict between equity and efficiency (in the light of domestic objectives) was noticed by Cooper (1973) and was analyzed by Hamada (1975). Recently it has been shown that the implementation of brain drain taxation greatly helps the simultaneous achievement of the objectives of income equality and efficiency (Bhagwati and Hamada, 1976).

Gains to Emigrants

It is almost obvious that an emigrant reveals the existence of his welfare gain, economic, political, or other, by the very act of emigration.[5] Since it is quite likely that those who are left behind will be hurt by emigration, the moral principle sketched above indicates that some compensation to them should be made from the gain of emigrants if the gain is economic in nature.

In the typical case where DCs restrict the inflow of PTKs from LDCs, the PTKs who fortunately can immigrate are often able to enjoy some quasi-rent from the restriction. In this case, the taxation of their income further takes on the nature of taxation on rent.

Frequently, however, the curbing of the number of migrating PTKs is counted as one of the objectives. However, it is an open question whether the actual number of emigrants is in itself excessive. This question can be answered only after one specifies the welfare function to evaluate the consequences of the brain drain, and only after one knows whether some compensation for the possible loss to LDCs can be made without changing the magnitude of migration of PTKs.

Argument against the Brain Drain Taxation

As compared to abundant writings, particularly by Bhagwati, which support and rationalize the brain drain tax proposal, few works so far criticize it. In fact, I know of no systematic attempt to rebut it. However, in several places some common issues are raised against the tax proposal or at least against particular forms of it. I shall therefore examine here possible economic or legal criticisms of the Bhagwati proposal.

Economic Argument

One basic criticism is that there is a brain drain phenomenon but no brain drain problem. The emigrants and the DCs of immigration almost certainly benefit. And the loss to the LDCs of origin can be neglected if outflow of skilled labor is marginal. This is the "cosmopolitan" view, expressed in various ways by Grubel and Scott (1966) and also by Johnson (1972).

A criticism of the proposal itself would be that such a tax deters the amount of migration, so that it distorts the efficient amount of the movement of skilled labor. According to this view, such a tax not only interferes with the freedom of movement and choice of occupation, but also distorts the efficient allocation of labor among countries. It is interesting to notice that lawyers also raise this objection. "At the least, the rate should be low enough so that it does not affect the individual's decision to migrate" (Oldman and Pomp, 1975, p. 752).

One can readily construct a rejoinder to these criticisms by referring to several factors that could lead to adverse impact on LDCs of origin, including the fact that not all labor but only that in a highly skilled category has reasonable scope for mobility in the actual world. It is not my intention however to contrast here the pros and cons on the proposal and to render a verdict. Rather, I will discuss later in a global and international framework to what extent these two opposing views can be reconciled.

Legal Argument

In the useful communication between lawyers and economists in Bellagio, several points emerged concerning the feasibility of some particular form of the brain drain tax proposal.

1. A most serious question is whether it would be constitutional for DCs to levy a tax on professional immigrants from LDCs. The paper by Oldman and Pomp (1975) makes it clear that the Fourteenth Amendment to the U.S. Constitution is a strong obstacle to such a tax being levied by the United States. According to the amendment, the law should be structured and actually operated so as to ensure that all citizens and residents of the United States are treated in a similar way. Therefore the imposition of a different rate of tax on a particular group of taxpayers on the basis of their national origins would in all probability be rejected as discriminatory by the U.S. Supreme Court (see also Partington, 1976).

2. Even if such a tax levied by a DC were constitutional, as in the United Kingdom, political and practical difficulties might make implementation of the proposal difficult. In particular, given the racial origins of most LDC professional immigrants, the tax might be objected to as racially discriminatory (Partington, 1976).

3. Finally, such a tax may be regarded as a violation of basic international human rights. For example, it may be regarded as a violation of the UN Declaration on Human Rights that there should be "equal pay for equal work." But, as Newman (1976) emphasizes, international law is not yet framed into a doctrine so rigid that it would constitute a barrier to the implementation of a brain drain tax, as proposed.

The Political Economy of the Tax Proposal

The rationale for the tax proposal, as we have seen, is based mainly on the moral principle of equity. In particular, it is derived from a consideration of equity between skilled emigrants and the nonmigrants in the LDCs. The counterarguments against such a tax proposal would seem to be grounded in alleged interference with human rights and in the economic desirability of preventing any distortion of the market-determined amount of migration.

Moreover, the rationale for the tax is argued mainly from the viewpoint of the LDCs of emigration. In order to assess the desirability and political feasibility of the Bhagwati-type tax proposal, however, we need a *global framework* to analyze the gain to DCs and the loss to LDCs, and the effect of the tax on the amount of migration at the same time. We shall carry out this task with the aid of the simple diagram in Figure 5.1.

Let us assume a neoclassical environment where the marginal product of skilled labor is downward sloping in both the LDC and the DC.[6] Also let us assume that the partial-equilibrium analysis of skilled labor approximates the full gains and losses in national welfare. Then the distribution of gains and losses between the DC and the LDC due to the emigration of skilled labor from the latter to the former can be illustrated as follows.

Let O_1A and AO_2 be the endowment of skilled labor in the DC and in the LDC before migration, respectively. When the possibility of migration opens up, skilled labor equal to AB will migrate from the LDC to the DC. Therefore, the national income of the LDC will decrease by the area $QRAB$, and the income received by those who remain behind will decrease by the area of triangle WRT, reflecting the finite effect pointed out by Berry and Soligo (1969) and Tobin (1974). The national income of the DC will increase by $PABQ$, and the income received by those originally living in the DC will increase by PSQ. The gain obtained by emigrants themselves is clearly equal to $SRTQ$.

Figure 5.1 is a familiar diagram, used to illustrate the welfare-effect international capital movements (Kemp, 1969). If we were measuring capital on the horizontal axis, then the welfare gain due to free movement of capital amounting to triangle PQR would be distributed to the two countries in amounts PSQ and SRQ. Thus both countries would gain by the free movement of capital. On the other hand, in the case of migration, not only is the total gain distributed to the former residents of the DC and the new

Table 5.1 The Brain Drain Tax:
Estimates for U.S., Canada and U.K., and for all DCs

Item	U.S.
1. Period over which the stock of professional LDC immigrants is considered (tax estimate relates to the terminal year of the period)	1962-1971 10 years
2. Total stock of PTK immigrants in the terminal year of the relevant period[a]	208,309
3. Average after-(DC)-tax annual incomes of different categories of immigrants	Physicians, dentists, and surgeons $23,807 Scientists (natural) $11,415 Nurses $ 5,987 Engineers $12,550 Technicians $ 7,807 (calculated from Tables 1 and 2; income figures are based on *1972 salary levels*)
4. Estimated total revenue from a 10% tax on disposable incomes of professional LDC immigrants	*Year: 1971* $231.7 million (Table 2)
5. Total revenue (1972):[b] Sum of U.S., Canada, and U.K.	(⩾) $300 million
6. Total revenue (estimating additional 25% revenue from EEC, Australia, and other DCs)	(⩾) $375 million
7. Total UN receipts[c] (total revenue plus equal matching contributions by DCs from general revenues)	(⩾) $750 million
8. Total UN receipts: 1976[d] (additionally allowing for taxation of international civil servants and inflation during the 1970s)	(⩾) $1 billion

Canada	U.K.
1963-1972	1964-1972
10 years	9 years

Canada	U.K.
37,653	60,759
+18,315, if certain other pro-	New Commonwealth and alien
fessional and technical occupa-	LDCs
tions are not excluded	(Table 6)
(Table 2 and note 3)	

Physicians and dentists	$20,734	Doctors and dentists	£2,280
Nurses, medical, and		Nurses	£1,025
dental technicians	$ 5,692	Scientists (natural and	
Scientists (natural)	$13,438	social)	£2,050
Teachers	$ 7,582	Teachers	£1,823
Engineers	$13,794	Engineers	£2,054

(aggregation of categories and
calculation of weighted averages
are based on Tables 1 and 5; income
figures relate to *1972 salary levels*)

(calculated from Table 8; income
figures relate to *1973 salary levels*)

Year: 1972
$52.0 million
(of which $13.6 million is from
certain excluded professions)
(Table 7 and note 6)

Year: 1972
£10.8 million
(8.6 million, New Commonwealth)
+2.2 million, alien
(Table 10)

Sources: Bhagwati and Pelcovits, Appendix to Bhagwati and Dellalfar, for U.S.; Balacs and Gordon, for U.K.; DeVoretz and Maki, for Canada. Reprinted from J. N. Bhagwati and M. Partington, eds., *Taxing the Brain Drain: A Proposal*, North-Holland Publishing Company, Amsterdam, 1976.

The definition of LDCs in the three studies is broadly comparable. However, the definition of PTK or professional manpower are probably not that close. For Canada, the *detailed* estimates refer only to a subset. However, the *revenue* estimate has been calculated also for the full PTK set, and this is the $52.0 million figure (of which $13.6 million represents the professions omitted by the authors from their detailed calculations, these professions being listed in their Table 1). For definitions of professional immigrants used in the Balacs and Gordon paper for the U.K., given the data availability there, see their paper.

[a]The table references in each cell refer to the table numbers in the original by Bhagwati and Pelcovits on the U.S., by DeVortez and Maki on Canada, and by Balacs and Gordon on the U.K.

[b]An exchange rate of $2.5 to £1.00 has been used. The Canadian dollar has simply been treated as identical with the U.S. dollar.

[c]Row (7) contains estimates of the total receipts that the UN would get if the tax proceeds were matched by an equal contribution by DCs from their general revenues.

[d]This estimate is from Bhagwati's paper, "The Brain Drain," ILO World Employment Conference, Geneva, June 1976.

residents (the emigrants) but there is also a loss of an amount equal to the area of QRT, suffered by the nonmigrants in the LDC.[7]

Thus we have the following remarkable asymmetry between the case of foreign capital outflow and the case of emigration, arising obviously from the fact that we do not regard the income accruing to capital invested abroad as anything except income accruing therefore to those resident in the investing country (and hence owning the invested capital).[8] In brief, with the case of capital flows, we can decompose the total gains accruing from the flow of the factor from a low-MP (marginal product) country to a higher-MP country in Figure 5.1 as follows:

Total Gain $= PRQ = SRQ + PSQ$
LDC Gain $= SRQ$
DC Gain $= PSQ$

Whereas, in the case of migration, with the emigrants separated out as a welfare entity, we have in Figure 5.1:

Total Gain $= PRQ = SRQ(= SRTQ - RTQ) + PSQ$
Emigrants' Gain $= SRTQ$
LDC (excluding emigrants) Loss $= RTQ$
DC (excluding immigrants) Gain $= PSQ$

This asymmetry of distribution might well be regarded as the basic reason why moral concerns are raised in the case of brain drain: in contrast to the case of foreign investment where the gain from the international factor movement is divided by the two countries, the DC gains now at the cost of those left behind in the LDC. The emigrants similarly are seen to gain at the sacrifice of those left behind in the LDC. This surely legitimates a strong appeal to the moral principles enunciated by Bhagwati in defense of his brain drain tax proposal. In fact, the Bhagwati tax proposal can be regarded as a means of transferring part of the gains of emigrants $(SRTQ)$ to compensate the loss of those left behind (QRT). Under the simplified case of linear marginal-productivity schedules and abstracting from other taxes in the DC, the amount of tax should be equal to half of the gain of immigrants in order for the tax to compensate fully the loss incurred by those left behind in the LDC.[9]

Thus once one accepts the moral principle that those who gain at the cost of others should compensate those who lose, the taxation of the gain of migrants is the natural consequence—provided that one takes the state before migration as the original position from which the moral principle should apply. However, the question still remains whether this moral principle would be sufficient to persuade efficiency-oriented economists and particularly hard-nosed government officials of DCs to accept the proposed brain drain tax. In short, the rationale for the tax so far is grounded in morality, with the welfare loss to those left behind in the LDC being emphasized. The appeal is thus to one's moral sentiments and not to the efficiency principles of economics. I myself regard the moral principle as crucially important in this kind of international policy proposal. However, to officials of DCs, the moral reasoning may not be sufficient to spur them into implementing or administering a new tax on their residents. For the tax proposal to be internationally feasible, it would surely help to provide an additional *efficiency* rationale for the tax, as indeed I proceed to do.

If we use the terminology of game theory, when the structure of conflict is in the form of a zero-sum game, then any international policy proposal is a matter of negotiation, generosity, sympathy, and sometimes threat. But when the structure of conflict is in the nature of a nonzero-sum cooperative game, then incentives emerge for the parties to participate in implementing a new rule. The political economy of international negotiation suggests that, whatever the agreement is, we need a structure of payoffs to induce all the relevant parties to participate in the agreement (Hamada, 1976).

In this discussion therefore we shall show that a brain drain tax in the form of an extension of LDC tax schedules to skilled emigrants, with relief for double taxation, will simultaneously help to promote the efficient amount of migration between two countries. Thus, in addition to the moral principle, we will have the principle of efficiency legitimating this specific form of tax on

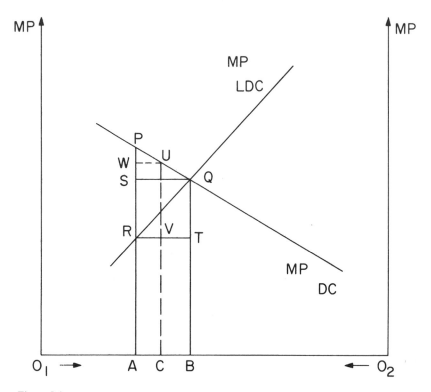

Figure 5.1

the PTKs migrated from LDCs to DCs. At the same time, this procedure will give us a criterion for determining the specific rate of taxation (which was left arbitrary in the original Bhagwati proposal).

Now let us introduce (domestic) income taxation by the DC and by the LDC into the picture. In Figure 5.2, D_D indicates the after-tax wage (or marginal product of labor) in the DC, and D_L indicates the after-tax wage in the LDC. In the absence of the brain drain, potential emigrants compare the after-tax income at home with the after-tax income abroad, so that migration takes place up to the intersection of D_D and D_L, that is, up to point M. Thus in Figure 5.2, which is drawn on the assumption that the tax rate in the LDC is higher than that in the DC, migration amounts to AD and is evidently larger than the efficient amount AB. If the tax rate in the DC is higher than that in the LDC, then AD will be smaller than AB.

When AD is smaller than AB, there is no convenient way of curing this inefficiency. However, when AD is larger than AB, as in Figure 5.2, the extension of the domestic tax schedule with tax credit to avoid double taxation will achieve the efficient amount of migration AB. This can be easily shown as follows.

With the migration of amount AB, emigrants will earn gross wage BQ in the DC of immigration. However, under the new regime of extension of LDC tax schedule to them, with double-taxation relief, they will be liable for overall taxation of amount QF, of which EQ will be collected by the DC under DC tax liability whereas the LDC will collect the remainder at EF, since the overall LDC tax liability of QF will be reduced by the amount accruing to the DC under the double-taxation relief. Clearly, therefore, AB represents an equilibrium amount of migration under the new regime; and it also is the optimal amount of migration that would equalize marginal products to skilled labor in both countries (at Q).[10] The beauty of the scheme is that, aside from leading to the efficient amount of migration, it also generates revenue for the LDC, as desired by the Bhagwati proposal: the LDC earns from the emigrants, in this instance, tax proceeds of amount $HJFE$. Clearly, therefore, this variant of the Bhagwati proposal to tax the brain drain is both efficient *and* raises revenue for the LDC of emigration in keeping with the moral principles enunciated by Bhagwati.

Consider now the more realistic case of migration already restricted by DC restrictions on entry. Suppose that the quota for immigrants is equal to AC as in Figure 5.3. When the extension of the tax LDC tax schedule with double-taxation relief is applicable, the disposable income of emigrants can be drawn as the curve D_E. Therefore at the level of migration amounting to AC, the disposable income of the emigrants equals CN that is larger than CI, the disposable income at home. Therefore, so long as the level of restriction of immigration is set below the efficiency level AB, the extension of the regular LDC tax schedule with double-taxation relief will generate revenue for the LDC but will *not* affect the level of immigration.[11]

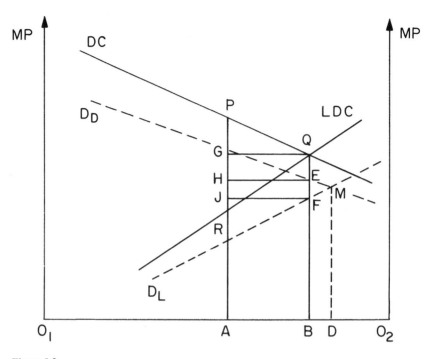

Figure 5.2

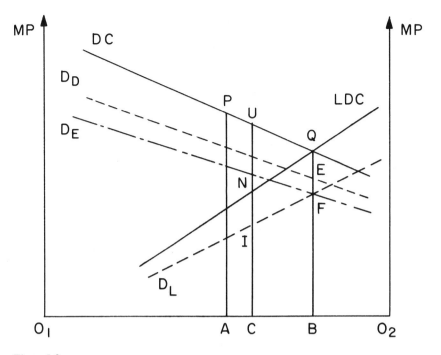

Figure 5.3

Thus we can conclude, *Proposition: Suppose that the income tax rate is higher in the LDC than in the DC in the relevant range of income received by emigrants. Then the extension of the LDC tax schedule to its emigrants with credit for the tax levied by the DC achieves the Pareto-optimal amount of migration. When there is a quota on immigration by the DC, this regime of extension of the LDC tax schedule with double-taxation relief will not affect the amount of migration, unless the quota is above the Pareto-efficient magnitude.*

This result gives us then a constructive way, or a kind of algorithm, for finding a proper rate of brain drain taxation. The first step is to extend the LDC tax schedule to emigrants along with the relief from double taxation in the form of foreign tax credit. If the magnitude of migration is reduced, then it shows that the extension of the LDC tax schedule with double-taxation relief will have helped to achieve the efficient amount of emigration. If, however, the amount of migration does not change, this shows that the effective restriction on entry lies at the doorstep of DC immigration policies and that the quota is restricting the immigration short of the Pareto-efficient amount of immigration. In the latter case, the extension of the LDC tax schedule with double-taxation relief to emigrants from LDCs will generate revenue from this variant of the Bhagwati brain drain tax without helping or hurting as far as the efficient level of migration is concerned: and the tax will have the effect of a tax on pure rents, providing us with an added perspective and rationale for the tax.[12]

Finally, we should notice the interdependent nature of income tax policies by the two countries. The mutual interplay of the tax policies presents us with an interesting strategic problem. Just as in the case of taxation of income from foreign investments (Hamada, 1966), one can formulate this bargaining situation as a nonzero-sum game, as is done in the appendix.

Practical Issues Concerning the Extension of the LDCs Tax Schedule

There are, of course, several practical problems to be cleared up before we can actually implement the extension of domestic income tax schedules to emigrants with relief to avoid double taxation.

First, it will not create serious legal problems to extend the domestic income tax schedule to nonresident citizens, although the enforcement may be difficult. In fact, several countries, such as the United States, Mexico, and the Philippines, are extending their tax jurisdiction over nonresident citizens, even though the tax rate is not identical between resident and nonresident citizens in the case of the Philippines.[13] An international treaty would be vital however to implement the general rule of extending LDC income tax schedules to their emigrants with multilateral relief against double taxation.

Second, for this proposal to be meaningful, the effective tax rate of LDCs over the relevant range of income should naturally be higher than that of

DCs. Tables 5.2 and 5.3 indicate a tentative calculation of effective tax rates of DCs and LDCs chosen on the ground that they have been either recipients or sources of the brain drain. Of course, many questions should be answered before we reach any definite conclusions on the relative magnitudes of tax rates: Should we credit the state or city tax in the United States, or the provincial tax in Canada? and What combination of deductions should be used in the comparison? But, roughly speaking, we can find the following tendencies: although the income tax rates in Mexico and Hong Kong are mainly lower than those in the DCs, and although the tax rate in Taiwan is not much different from that in the United States, the tax rates in other LDCs in the tables are generally higher than those in DCs.

This observation suggests the applicability of the scheme to many combinations of DCs and LDCs. At the same time, it shows the inapplicability of this modified form of the brain drain tax proposal to some LDCs with lower tax rates. Even for many LDCs with higher marginal rates, the actual enforcement is quite lax and the de facto tax rates may therefore be lower. However, where the resulting tax rates are then lower than those in DCs (after allowing for DC evasions!), the logical answer would be to seek better enforcement of legislated tax rates in LDCs. Clearly, it does not seem equitable to resort to a surtax on the brain drain when the tax rate in the LDC on the relevant range of income of emigrants is smaller than that in the DCs: a surtax in such a case would mean a discriminatory treatment of emigrants from residents by the LDC government.

Third, it is probably worth reiterating that our analysis indicates the critical importance of the LDC tax rate being higher than the DC tax rate. In this connection, we should note that, according to the game-theoretic "strategy" analysis of the appendix, the DC stands to gain by moving its tax rate on immigrants closer to that of the LDC when the latter exceeds the former. On the other hand, any fear of such a move materializing can be readily removed by noting that it is highly unlikely that the DC would levy a higher tax which would be discriminatory on immigrants from LDCs.[14]

Fourth, in the actual implementation of this scheme of extending the LDC tax schedules to emigrants, some attention will have to be paid to the fact of differences in living standards. As a conversion factor of foreign income to domestic income, there are several alternative measures: official exchange rate, de facto or sometimes black market exchange rate, cost of living index using some consumption basket, and so on. What is clear is that a straightforward extension of LDC tax schedules will be exorbitantly taxing (Oldman and Pomp, 1975).

Apart from these economic difficulties, there are social, political, and humanistic issues. In particular, some immigrants are political, religious refugees; yet some others are forced to leave LDCs because of the expulsion policies of their governments. They would not feel like paying a penny to their home countries. In such a case, the global extension of individual LDC

Table 5.2 Income Tax (1)

	U.S. Federal Tax	(a)	Canada Federal Tax	(b)	U.K.[c]
US$5000					(£2,000)
S[d]	$491 (9.8%)		$444.84 (8.90%)	$611.02 (12.22%)	$1,053.75 (21.08%)
M	322 (6.4)		152.24 (3.04)	229.17 (4.58)	918.75 (18.38)
M+2C	98 (2.0)		32.18 (0.64)	72.49 (1.45)	618.75 (12.38)
US$10,000					(£4,000)
S	1,530 (15.30%)	$1,984 (19.84%)	1,559.22 (15.59%)	2,065.28 (20.65%)	1,553.75 (25.54%)
M	1,190 (11.90)	1,519 (15.19)	1,204.42 (12.04)	1,602.27 (16.02)	2,418.75 (24.19)
M+2C	905 (9.05)	1,148 (11.48)	1,057.22 (10.57)	1,410.17 (14.10)	2,118.75 (21.19)
US$20,000					(£8,000)
S	4,255 (23.8%)	5,456 (27.28%)	4,470.45 (22.35%)	5,905.70 (29.53%)	6,381.25 (31.91%)
M	3,400 (17.0)	4,455 (22.28)	3,974.36 (19.87)	5,250.34 (26.25)	6,156.25 (30.78)
M+2C	3,010 (15.11)	3,918 (19.59)	3,761.56 (18.81)	4,969.22 (24.85)	5,677.88 (28.39)
Rate of exchange			US$1 = $1CDN		1 = US$2.5

aThis table includes the federal income tax, the New York State tax and the New York City tax. Deductions for the federal income tax are assumed at 15% of the total remuneration. For the New York State and City taxes standard deductions have been used.

bThis table includes the federal income tax and the provincial income tax at the minimum rate of 30.5% of the federal income taxes before the special federal 5% tax reduction.

cAssuming that both children are under 11 years old.

dS: single; M: married; M+2C: married with two children.

All data pertain to 1974.

tax schedules may turn out to be unfair, leaving aside the many administrative complexities that would attend it. Hence, on these grounds, the *practical* translation of the variant of the brain drain tax proposed here as both morally sound *and* economically efficient would seem to yield to the variant proposed in Bhagwati and Partington (1976): that is, where uniform tax rates would apply under an international treaty to all LDC emigrants in DCs, and the proceeds, collected by DCs, would be routed en bloc to LDCs via the United Nations for development spending.

Concluding Remarks

I believe in the freedom to choose one's location as a basic human right. Therefore, other things being equal, it is better to allow migration as freely as possible. However, if the migration of skilled labor takes place at the cost of those who are left behind in LDCs, it is natural to appeal to the moral principle of equity and to devise a plan to transfer incomes partially from those who gain to those who suffer from the migration.

Thus the Bhagwati tax proposal can be justified on moral principles alone. In this paper, however, I have tried to give a rationale for the taxation of emigrants' earnings by the authority of LDCs also from the *efficiency* point of view. I have succeeded in showing that in order to implement the efficiency criterion as well, the scheme of extending the LDC income tax schedule to emigrants with relief against double taxation is an ideal variant of the original brain drain tax proposal. Where barriers exist in DCs on immigration, as they often do, the efficiency question turns out to be irrelevant—as the entry restrictions violate efficiency unavoidably—and the brain drain tax would essentially be a revenue-raising device for LDCs and thus be justified on moral principles alone.

The variant of the brain drain tax, in the specific form of the extension of the LDC tax schedule to emigrants with double-taxation relief, has thus been demonstrated here to be of special interest to economists (on grounds of efficiency), even though it was suggested originally by lawyers. By appealing to efficiency norms, in addition to equity, this variant is likely to increase the acceptability of a brain drain tax in policy circles.

However, in contrast to this efficiency advantage, it would appear that this variant may not be appealing to public opinion because it ties in the revenues to specific LDCs, many of which individually may be offensive to the emigrants being taxed (Ali Mazrui from Uganda would not wish to have to pay a surtax to the government of Idi Amin); it would also be administratively complex to administer by DCs because of very diverse LDC tax rates. Hence, on balance, the present paper may be regarded rather as providing an efficiency rationale, *in broad terms*, for other variants of the brain drain tax proposal which are more readily acceptable on administrative and other grounds: that is, the "optimal" variant

Table 5.3 Income Tax (2)

	Argentina	Colombia	Mexico
US$5,000	($a25,000)	(112,500 pesos)	(62,450 pesos)
S[a]	$325.8 (6.52%)	$1,238.44 (24.77%)	$357.82 (7.16%)
M	257.4 (5.15)	1,197.33 (23.95)	357.82 (")
M+2C	135 (2.7)	1,164.44 (23.29)	357.82 (")
US$10,000	($a50,000)	(225,000 pesos)	(124,900 pesos)
S	1,629.8 (16.30%)	3,130.67 (31.31%)	1,094.26 (10.94%)
M	1,514.6 (15.15)	3,087.33 (30.87)	1,094.26 (")
M+2C	1,291.4 (12.91)	3,052.67 (30.53)	1,094.26 (")
US$20,000	($a100,000)	(450,000 pesos)	(249,800 pesos)
S	5,478.6 (27.39%)	7,205.11 (36.03%)	4,074.04 (20.37%)
M	5,325 (26.63)	7,158.44 (35.79)	3,923.44 (19.62)
M+2C	5,037 (25.19)	7,121.11 (35.61)	3,772.84 (18.86)
Rate of exchange	US$1 = $15.00 (official rate)	US$1 = 22.50 pesos	US$1 - 12.49 pesos

[a]S: single; M: married; M+2C: married with two children.
[b]Surcharge included.
All data pertain to 1974, except for Argentina and Colombia, where data
pertain to 1972.

Taiwan	Hong Kong	India[b]	Korea	Philippines
(NT$190,000)	(HK$282,500)	(Rs.39,550)	(2,400,000 won)	(P34,500)
$ 397.37	$ 248.89	$ 1,1566.53	$ 752.5	$ 807.6
(7.95%)	(4.98%)	(31.33%)	(15.05%)	(16.15%)
345.26	122.79	1,566.53	677.5	750.2
(6.91)	(2.46)	(")	(13.55)	(15.0)
275.79	69.69	1,566.53	602.5	663.0
(5.52)	(1.39)	(")	(12.05)	(13.26)
(NT$380,000)	(HK$56,500)	(Rs.79,100)	(4,800,000 won)	(P69,000)
1,398.42	1,194.69	5,287.67	2,615	2,813.9
(13.98%)	(11.95%)	(52.88%)	(26.15%)	(28.14%)
1,295.79	896.02	5,287.67	2,515	2,730.4
(12.96)	(8.96)	(")	(25.15)	(27.30)
1,145.26	743.36	5,287.67	2,415	2,591.3
(11.45)	(7.43)	(")	(24.15)	(25.91)
(NT$760,000)	(HK$113,000)	(Rs.158,200)	(9,600,000 won)	(P138,000)
4,672.63	3,000	14,329.20	7,290	8,416.2
(23.36%)	(15.0%)	(71.65%)	(36.45%)	(42.08%)
4,518.68	3,000	14,329.20	7,165	8,310.1
(22.59)	(")	(")	(35.83	(41.55)
4,292.89	3,000	14,329.20	7,040	8,136.2
(21.46)	(")	(")	(35.2)	(40.68)
US$1 =	US$1 =	US$1 =	US$1 =	US$1 =
NT$38	HK$5.65	Rs.7.91	480 won	P6.90

proposed, after the Bellagio deliberations, in Ch. 1 in Bhagwati and Partington (1976).

Notes

I am indebted to Jagdish Bhagwati for valuable comments. I also thank Mariko Ogawa for her assistance in preparing Table 5.2.

1 This asymmetry is less marked for Western Europe, which has admitted numerous "guest workers" of low skills in the postwar period, unlike the United States and Great Britain.

2 Moreover, Bhagwati considers a matching contribution of the DCs equaling this total amount, bringing the figure to $1 billion. But considering the political difficulty of realizing the surtax itself, I shall set aside this additional issue.

3 For an extensive legal account of the relief against double taxation, see Owens (1961).

4 As long as the tax liability to the LDC exceeds that to the DC, the emigrant would be paying a net, supplementary income tax, as is the essence of the Bhagwati proposal. However, the LDC of origin would get this revenue, ruling out the version whereby the revenues go to LDCs en bloc.

5 This is obviously not true of those who are "expelled," say, the Asians of Uganda. See Bhagwati (1976).

6 This implies that skilled labor is fully employed in the LDC as well as in the DC. For an analysis of situations with unemployment, see Bhagwati and Hamada (1974).

7 This contrast is less sharp when emigrants send some of their income back home.

8 Clearly, if we were to regard the emigrants as still members of the LDC of origin, for welfare analysis, this asymmetry would disappear. For arguments suggesting that this might well be appropriate, see Bhagwati and Rodriguez (1975), as also the discussion in Bhagwati and Hamada (1976).

9 In the same diagram, we could analyze the effect of immigration restrictions. If the DC imposes a quota on immigration by the amount of AC where C lies between A and B, the lucky emigrants will gain an amount of income equal to the area $WRVU$, this gain having the nature of quasi-rent arising from the restriction. The LDC (excluding the emigrants) will still suffer a loss of income, so that one can deduce from the previously mentioned moral principles that some of the emigrants' gain should be transferred to those left behind in the LDC.

10 This is what is called, in the public finance literature, the "neutrality" effect of double-taxation relief agreements. Cf. Richman (1963).

11 The diagram is drawn on the assumption of linear tax schedules in both countries. However, the reader can easily verify that the same conclusion also holds true under nonlinear tax schedules, provided that the marginal propensities to tax in both countries are less than unity.

12 I might also add that the brain drain tax has been approached from an altogether different perspective, in the context of a Mirrlees-Atkinson type of framework, by Bhagwati and Hamada (1976). It is shown there that the extension of the domestic tax schedule to emigrants will help achieve efficiency and equity from the viewpoint of the *LDC itself* when the optimal linear income tax is being considered in a context where the tax is necessary for redistribution and hence equity but affects incentives and hence effi-

ciency. The foreign tax rate is not considered explicitly there, but by a simple reasoning, the foreign tax does not change our result provided that foreign tax rate is lower than the tax rate of the country of origin, and provided that relief from double taxation is granted. As noted, the purpose of taxation in that model is to achieve domestic equity and it is different from the role of taxation considered in this paper; however, it is important to notice that the brain drain tax measure for the sake of vertical as well as horizontal equity can be consistently shown to take the form of an extension of the LDC tax schedule with double-taxation relief to its emigrants.

13 Oldman and Pomp (1975) examine possible complications, such as emigrants renouncing their LDC citizenships, and suggest legal remedies.

14 In fact, the reader will recall our earlier argument that, in the United States at least, such discriminatory tax *levied* by the DC itself would almost certainly be found unconstitutional by the Supreme Court. Cf. Oldman and Pomp (1975).

References

Atkinson, A. B., 1973, "How Progressive Should Income Tax Be?," in M. Parkin, ed. *Essays in Modern Economics* (Longmans, London).

Balacs, P., and A. Gordon, 1975, "The Brain Drain and Income Taxation: A UK Case Study," *World Development*, 3 (10), 677-703.

Berry, R., and R. Soligo, 1969, "Some Welfare Aspects of International Migration," *Journal of Political Economy*, 77.

Bhagwati, J. N., 1972, "The United States in the Nixon Era: The End of Innocence," *Daedalus*.

Bhagwati, J. N., and W. Dellalfar, 1973. "The Brain Drain and Income Taxation," *World Development*, 1, No. 182, 94-101.

Bhagwati, J. N., and K. Hamada, 1974, "The Brain Drain, International Integration of Markets for Professionals and Unemployment: A Theoretical Analysis," *Journal of Development Economics*, 1, No. 1; reprinted in revised version in Bhagwati (1976).

Bhagwati, J. N., and D. Rodriguez, 1975, "Welfare-Theoretical Analyses of the Brain Drain," *Journal of Development Economics*, Vol. 2 (3); reprinted in Bhagwati (1976).

Bhagwati, J. N., and K. Hamada, 1976, "Optimal Policy Intervention in the presence of Brain Drain: Educational Subsidy and Tax on Emigrants' Income," MIT Working Paper, No. 172.

Bhagwati, J. N. (ed.), 1976, *The Brain Drain and Taxation: Theory and Empirical Analysis* (North Holland, Amsterdam).

Bhagwati, J. N., and M. Partington (eds.), 1976, *Taxing the Brain Drain: A Proposal* (North Holland, Amsterdam).

Cooper, R. N., 1973, *Economic Mobility and National Economic Policy* (Almquist and Wiksell International, Stockholm).

DeVoretz, D., and D. Maki, 1975, "The Brain Drain and Income Taxation: Canadian Estimates," *World Development*, 3 (10), 705-716.

Hamada, K., 1966, "Strategic Aspects of Taxation on Foreign Investment Income," *Quarterly Journal of Economics*, 80, No. 3, 361-375.

Hamada, K., 1975, "Efficiency, Equity, Income Taxation and the Brain Drain: A

Second Best Argument," *Journal of Development Economics*, 2, 281-287.

Hamada, K., and J. N. Bhagwati, 1975, "Domestic Distortions, Imperfect Information and the Brain Drain," *Journal of Development Economics*, 2; reprinted in Bhagwati (1976).

Hamada, K., 1976, "On the Political Economy of Monetary Integration," in R. Z. Aliber, ed., *The Political Economy of Monetary Reform* (Macmillan, London).

Grubel, H., and A. Scott, 1966, "The International Flow of Human Capital," *American Economic Review*, May.

Johnson, H. G., 1967, "Some Economic Aspects of Brain Drain," *Pakistan Development Review*, 3.

Johnson, H. G., 1972, "Labor Mobility and the Brain Drain," in G. Ranis, ed., *The Gap between Rich and Poor Nations* (Macmillan, London).

Kemp, M. C., 1969, *The Pure Theory of International Trade and Investment* (Prentice-Hall, New York).

McCulloch, R., and J. Yellen, 1975, "Consequences of a Tax on the Brain Drain for Unemployment and Income Inequality in LDCs," *Journal of Development Economics*, 2; reprinted in Bhagwati (1976).

Mirrlees, J. A., 1971, "An Exploration in the Theory of Optimal Income Taxation," *Review of Economic Studies*, 38, 175-208.

Newman, F., 1976, "The Brain Drain Tax and International Human Rights Law," in Bhagwati and Partington (1976).

Oldman, O., and R. Pomp, 1975, "The Brain Drain: A Tax Analysis of the Bhagwati Proposal," *World Development*, 3 (10), 751-763.

Owens, E., 1961, *The Foreign Tax Credit* (Harvard Law School, International Tax Program, Cambridge, Mass.).

Partington, M., 1976, "Taxing the Brain Drain: A Report on the Bellagio Conference," in Bhagwati and Partington (1976).

Richman (Musgrave), P. B., 1963, *Taxation of Foreign Investment Income* (Johns Hopkins Press, Baltimore).

Tobin, J., 1974, "Notes on the Economic Theory of Expulsion and Expropriation," *Journal of Development Economics*, 1, No. 1; reprinted in Bhagwati (1976).

Appendix

Let the strategies be the (proportional) tax rates of the two countries, the payoffs being the income of the nationals originally resident in the DC and the income of those who remain behind in the LDC.

Let $F_1(L_1 + X)$ be the production function utilizing skilled labor in the DC, where L_1 and X are respectively the original stock of skilled labor and the amount of migration. Let $F_2(L_2 - X)$ be the production function of the LDC, where L_2 is the initial stock of skilled labor in the LDC. Let t_1 and t_2, which are taken as the strategies, indicate the tax rate in the DC and that in the LDC.

We shall take as the payoff of the DC the income of indigenous residents in the DC, that is,

$$Y_1 = F_1(L_1 + X) - (1 - t_1) \cdot F_1'(L_1 + X)X. \tag{1}$$

Let $\overline{X}$ be the upperbound of the amount of emigration, and $(L_2 - \overline{X})$ be the people who remain in the LDC under any circumstances. We shall define the payoff of the LDC as the income received by these people,[1] that is

$$Y_2 = F_2(L_2 - X) - (1 - t_2) \cdot F_2'(L_2 - X)(\overline{X} - X), \tag{2}$$

under the case where no extension of the LDC tax schedule is made.

1. In the absence of the extension of the tax schedule of the LDC to emigrants, the amount of migration is determined by the relationship:

$$(1 - t_1) \cdot F_1'(L_1 + X) = (1 - t_2) \cdot F_2'(L_2 - X). \tag{3}$$

One can derive the reaction curve of the tax authority of the DC, by maximizing Y_1 subject to (3) and with respect to t_1, given the value t_2. After substituting (3) into (1), one obtains as the first-order condition:[2]

$$F_1' = (1 - t_2)(F_2' - XF_2'').$$

which can be written, by virtue of (3), as:

$$F_2' = (1 - t_1)(F_2' - XF_2''),$$

or as:

$$1 - t_1 = F_2'/(F_2' - XF_2'') = 1/(1 + a_2\eta_2),$$

where $\eta_2(\equiv -(L_2 - X)F_2''/F_2')$ is the elasticity of the marginal productivity of skilled labor in the LDC, and $a_2(\equiv X/(L_2 - X))$ is the ratio of emigrants to the nonemigrants in the LDC. Therefore the reaction curve is written as:

$$t_2 = a_2\eta_2/(1 + a_2\eta_2). \tag{4}$$

Here a_2 is an increasing function of t_2, and accordingly t_1 tends to be an increasing function of t_2 within the range of constant η_2. From (4), one can see that t_2 lies between zero and unity. Thus the reaction strategy of the DC, given the tax policy of the LDC, is similar to monopsonistic behavior.

Also one can derive the reaction curve of the LDC by maximizing Y_2 subject to (3) and with respect to t_2, given the value to t_1. By a similar procedure to that used to derive equation (4), one obtains:

$$t_2 = a_1\eta_1/(1 + a_1\eta_1), \tag{5}$$

where $\eta_1(\equiv -(L_1 + X)F_1''/F_1')$ is the elasticity of marginal product of skilled labor in the DC, and $a_1(\equiv (\overline{X} - X)/(L_1 + X))$ is the ratio of potential emigrants in the LDC to all the skilled workers in the LDC. Since a_1 is an increasing function of t_1, t_2 in (5) tends to be an increasing function of t_1 within the range of constant η_1. And t_2 also lies between zero and unity. The reaction strategy of the LDC, given the value of the income tax rate in the DC, is thus similar to monopolistic behavior.

In Figure 5.4a, the reaction curve of the DC, $R1$, is drawn as an upward sloping curve, and that of the LDC, R also as an upward sloping curve. The intersection N of these two curves gives the Nash (or Cournot) solution of this game.[3] This noncooperative solution does not generally lie on the Pareto-efficient combination, which is indicated by the 45-degree line from the origin, $t_1 = t_2$, that is,

$$F_1'(L_1 + X) = F_2'(L_2 - X).$$

Therefore, in this hypothetical world where the tax policies of the two countries are determined only by the consideration relating to migration, the noncooperative behaviors would produce a situation similar to the interplay of tariff retaliations and would let the amount of migration diverge from the Pareto-efficient amount. Thus the structure of conflict has the nature of the prisoner's dilemma, well known in game theory.

2. Now suppose the LDC tax schedule is extended to emigrants, and that the agreement to avoid double taxation in the form of foreign tax credit is reached between the two countries. Then, instead of (3), we have the following relationship that determines the amount of migration:

$$\text{If } t_2 \geqslant t_1, \quad F_1'(L_1 + X) = F_2'(L_2 - X), \tag{6}$$

$$\text{if } t_2 < t_1 \quad (1 - t_1)F_1'(L_1 + X) = (1 - t_2)F_2'(L_2 - X). \tag{3}$$

The payoff of the indigenous people in the DC is expressed as before as:

$$Y_1 = F_1(L_1 + X) - (1 - t_1)F_1'(L_1 + X)X, \tag{1}$$

but the payoff of those remaining behind in the LDC is expressed as:

$$Y_2 = F_2(L_2 - X) - (1 - t_2)F_2'(L_2 - X)(\bar{X} - X)$$

$$+ (t_2 - t_1)F_1'(L_1 + X)X \qquad\qquad \text{if } t_2 \geqslant t_1. \tag{7}$$

$$Y_2 = F_2(L_2 - X) - (1 - t_2)F_2'(L_2 - X)(\bar{X} - X) \qquad \text{if } t_2 < t_1. \tag{2}$$

Consequently, as long as t_2 is no less than t_1, the Pareto-efficient amount of migration given by the solution of equation (6) is achieved. Let us denote this Pareto-efficient amount of migration by $\hat{X}$. Then, when $t_2 \geqslant t_1$,

$$Y_1 = F_1(L_1 + \hat{X}) - (1 - t_1)F_1'(L_1 + \hat{X})\hat{X}, \tag{6'}$$

Without the Extension of the LDC Tax to Emigrants

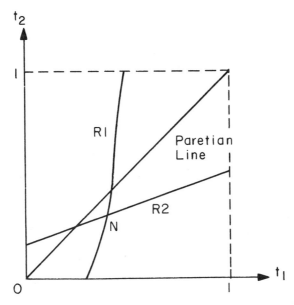

Figure 5.4a

With the Extension of the LDC Tax and the Double-Taxation Relief

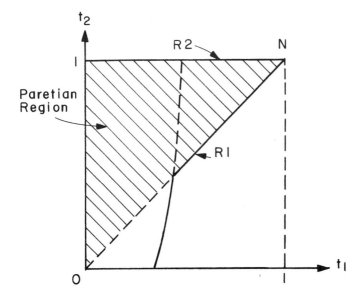

Figure 5.4b

$$Y_2 = F_2(L_2 - \hat{X}) + \left\{ (1 - t_1)\hat{X} - (1 - t_2)\bar{X} \right\} F_2'(L_1 + \hat{X}). \tag{7'}$$

Therefore, it can be easily seen that the reaction curve of the DC is $t_1 = t_2$ whenever $t_2 \geqslant t_1$, and that the reaction curve of the LDC is $t_2 = 1$.

When t_2 is less than t_1, the reaction curves are equations (4) and (5), just as in the absence of the extension of the LDC tax schedule. Noting that the strategy $t_2 = 1$ for the LDC dominates the strategy expressed by equation (5) in any case,[4] we can draw the reaction curves as in Figure 5.4b. In this hypothetical world where income taxation is solely used to adjust the revenues from migrants and to adjust the number of migrants, the Nash noncooperative solution is an unrealistic solution $t_1 = t_2 = 1$.[5]

It should be emphasized, however, that the structure of conflict is much more improved in this case than in the previous case where the LDC tax schedule is not extended. In Figure 5.4a, only the 45-degree line through the origin is the set of the Pareto-efficient magnitude of migration. On the other hand, in this case depicted in Figure 5.4b, all the points included in the shaded area above the 45-degree line result in the Pareto-efficient amount of migration. The degree of freedom in choosing the Pareto-efficient combination is much larger in this case. It seems therefore, that there is ample possibility in this case for both parties to choose *some* point in the shaded area, that is, in the set of cooperative solution.

Two remarks are to be made concerning this comparison of strategic structure. First, we have so far neglected the welfare of the emigrants themselves. As the combination of the tax rates, (t_1, t_2) approaches the northeast corner of the diagrams, the emigrants are exploited more intensively. If they have political power of negotiation or lobbying, they may have some influence in keeping the rates from rising. Of course, whether or not they can actually organize and express themselves is yet an open question. At any rate, this indicates the importance of perhaps preventing the socially discriminatory treatment of emigrants by the LDC as well as by the DC, in order to protect the human rights of migrants. Needless to say, however, the variant of the proposal we are considering here is the extension of the *regular* tax schedule of the LDC and the tax credit for the *regular* tax paid to the DC.

Second, the above analysis reveals the close relationship between international agreements on rules and resource allocation. Just as the change in liability rules affects resource allocation and income distribution, the change in rules in the form of an agreement to avoid double taxation facilitates the realization of the efficient allocation of skilled labor and, at the same time, affects the relative strength of the bargaining powers of the parties in this situation of potential international conflict.

Notes

1 This definition may seem a little awkward, but we cannot use a simple concept such as average income because we want to grasp the effect of finite rather than infinitesimal

changes in skilled labor. This is the reason why we shall assume a fixed value of $\overline{X}$.

2 The second-order condition is satisfied when $F' > 0$ and $F'' < 0$ for $i = 1, 2$.

3 The Nash solution is stable if the absolute slope of $R1$ is larger than that of $R2$.

4 This can be seen by comparing the value of Y_2 obtained by substituting $t_2 = 1$ into (7), with the value of Y_2 in (2).

5 This Nash solution will not actually be realized because the tax rates are determined by many factors other than the mere consideration of migration and of the revenues relating to migration.

Editor's Note

During 1978, international attention was directed to the proposal to tax the brain drain. The UNCTAD convened an Intergovernmental Group of Experts in Geneva to discuss this and other related proposals concerning the international migration of highly skilled manpower. The Group of 77, representing the developing countries, in its agreed document of recommendations appended to the report of the group, endorsed the Bhagwati proposal in the format where the developing countries might extend their tax jurisdiction, as under the global tax system practiced by the United States, Philippines, Switzerland, and Mexico in particular, to their citizens working abroad rather than at home. They asked that the developed countries take steps to provide the necessary information and cooperation to enable developing countries that wished to exercise their tax jurisdiction abroad to do so.

For details, refer to (1) *Report of the Group of Governmental Experts on Reverse Transfer of Technology*, Meeting held at Palais des Nations, Geneva, 27 February to 7 March 1978, TD/B/C.6/28, UNCTAD, Geneva, 20 March 1978; (2) J. Bhagwati, "The Reverse Transfer of Technology (Brain Drain): International Resource Flow Accounting, Compensation, Taxation and Related Policy Proposals," TD/B/C.6/AC.4/2, UNCTAD, 1978; (3) Richard Pomp and Oliver Oldman, "Legal and Administrative Aspects of Compensation, Taxation and Related Policy Measures: Suggestions for an Optimal Policy Mix," TD/B/C.6/AC.4/7, UNCTAD, 1978; and (4) J. Bhagwati, "The Brain Drain, Compensation and Taxation," paper presented to the Conference on "Economic and Demographic Change: Issues for the 1980's," International Union for the Scientific Study of Population, Helsinki, August 28-September 1, 1978.

II
International Trade

6

Market Disruption, Export Market Disruption, Compensation, and GATT Reform
Jagdish N. Bhagwati

Introduction

This work addresses the issue of market disruption and suggests schemes for compensating the less developed countries (LDCs) who face what may aptly be described as export market disruption when the importing, developed countries (DCs) invoke protective devices, such as "voluntary" export restraints, to assist domestic industries seeking relief from foreign competition.

Section 1 deals with the problem of defining market disruption. Section 2 considers the GATT Article XIX on the subject and its relationship to national legislations. Section 3 goes on to outline the principal forms in which market-disruption-related restrictions have been invoked, focusing on "voluntary" export restraints (VERs) and the more sustained and formal multilateral arrangements (the LTA which restricts the exports of textiles). Section 4 discusses the welfare impact of the possibility of market-disruption-induced restrictions that LDCs face on their exports of manufactures. Section 5 assesses the need for compensation that the welfare losses to LDCs imply from this analysis, and develops specific proposals for such compensation. Section 6 suggests ways in which the GATT Article XIX could be modified to implement these suggestions. Appendix 1 contains a brief review of one precedent, where the "importing" country provided compensation to the "exporting" country for "export market disruption," so to speak. This is the case of the United States compensating Turkey for adjustment assistance to Turkish poppy farmers (the objective being to enable the farmers to shift to nonpoppy farming at no loss). Appendix 2, on the other hand, is a theoretical exercise, in a general-equilibrium framework, of the phenomenon of export market disruption and provides the necessary analytical support to the compensation schemes discussed in the text.

1. The Concept of Market Disruption

In a basic sense, market disruption is an old, protectionist concept: imports are considered disruptive of the domestic industry in the domestic market and hence must be curtailed and regulated. In this sense, virtually all imports are market disrupting, and indeed if one examines, in a "revealed preference" fashion, the demands for protection by many industries in almost all countries, this loose and all-embracing version is, in fact, what would most nearly reflect the intent of the spokesmen for these industries.

However, in an international economy, which, in the postwar, post-GATT world has been geared to increasing trade liberalization, the institutions governing the use of protective devices for manufactures have taken a narrower view of market disruption.

This is particularly true of the GATT, where Article XIX is designed to handle cases of "serious injury" to domestic industries and is set within the context of other rules designed to constrain the use of protection by member countries.[1]

It is correspondingly true also of national legislations enacted to correspond to Article XIX and related GATT provisions. Thus the United States had established corresponding "escape-clause" procedures by Executive Order 9832 from 1947 to 1951, by Section 7 of the 1951 Trade Agreements Extension Act between 1951 to 1962, and by Section 301 of the Trade Expansion Act from 1962.[2]

Under these legislations, for example, the successful invoking of protection required the public demonstration of injury, caused by tariff-concession-led imports, to the U.S. Tariff Commission which would, in turn, convey its finding to the president who, in turn, could act on it, consistently with the national legislation and the GATT rules.

On the other hand, the national executive has often been willing to sidetrack GATT restrictions and associated national processes for seeking relief under market disruption, and to invoke measures, outside of the GATT framework, to regulate the flow of such imports. The most potent such measure has been the VERs, which have tended to proliferate since the 1950s.

In consequence, it would be appropriate to say that, if we were to rank the different groups and institutions seeking to define market disruption and to seek relief from imports therewith, according to the degree of restrictiveness that they would apply to the concept, the ranking would be as follows:

$$
\left.\begin{array}{c}\text{Domestic}\\\text{Industry}\\\text{in}\\\text{Importing}\\\text{Country}\end{array}\right\} < \left\{\begin{array}{c}\text{National}\\\text{Executive}\\\text{in}\\\text{Importing}\\\text{Country}\end{array}\right. \gtrless \left.\begin{array}{c}\text{National}\\\text{Legislative}\\\text{in}\\\text{Importing}\\\text{Country}\end{array}\right\} < \left\{\begin{array}{c}\text{GATT}\\\text{(in}\\\text{particular,}\\\text{Article}\\\text{XIX)}\end{array}\right.
$$

That is to say, the domestic industry, seeking relief from imports, would apply the least restrictive criteria to define market disruption; and the highest, in restrictiveness, would be the GATT, which seeks generally to minimize interferences with expanding trade. In between are the national executives and legislatures whose relative actions and attitudes on the issue of market disruption are likely to vary. Thus, in the United States the executive has been, via VERs, de facto less restrictive in the interpretation of market disruption, whereas the legislative statutes have been closer to GATT. On the other hand, this is quite consistent with the legislative representatives, interested in specific industries in their constituencies, being the effective moving force in getting a free-trade-oriented executive to enact the VERs. Hence one must distinguish between executive actions and legislation, on the one hand, and the executive and legislative bodies' attitudes toward the issue of market disruption, on the other hand.[3]

It is clear that the loosest, industry-based view of market disruption would extend to all competition with imports in the domestic market and indeed no evidence of any serious injury would need to be established. Thus, as Metzger has noted, the provisions of H.R. 18970, the so-called U.S. Trade Act of 1970, if it had become law, would have effectively elevated this view of market disruption to the status of the operating criterion for invoking protection (thus going beyond what GATT Article XIX envisaged).[4] The escape clause would have retained a Tariff Commission investigation but reduced the definition of injury to one where the domestic industry's relative share in the domestic market had fallen, while also removing presidential discretion in vetoing Tariff Commission recommendations for escape-clause action.[5]

By contrast, Article XIX of GATT restricts the "emergency action on imports of particular products" to situations which satisfy three conditions: (1) that the alleged disruption should have been the result of "the obligations incurred by a contracting party under this Agreement, including tariff concessions"; (2) that the product must be imported in "increased quantities"; and (3) that conditions must exist which "cause or threaten serious injury to domestic producers." While these conditions, and shifts in their interpretation over time, are discussed in the next section, it is pertinent to note immediately that the GATT envisions a much narrower interpretation of market disruption and hence a correspondingly smaller scope for invoking legitimate interferences with imports.

In keeping with this view of the matter, the associated national legislation has been relatively strict in interpreting market disruption as well. Thus, in the United States, the invoking of the escape clause has had to involve a public inquiry by the U.S. Tariff Commission which had to apply legislated criteria, similar to those of Article XIX, to the case at hand: the U.S. industries going the escape-clause route have had to argue that concession-induced imports were causing serious injury, and have often failed to win their case.

The invoking of protective devices by industries seeking curtailment of imports despite the GATT Article XIX and corresponding national legislations has therefore taken the route of executive action, typically in the form of VERs, outside of this framework; hence, the de facto definition of market disruption has turned out to be substantially closer to the importing industry's viewpoint than the GATT rules might suggest.

A review of the existing VERs, including the LTA governing the trade in textiles, reveals that the concept of market disruption that can successfully be invoked to get political, executive action in DCs tends to include the following "weakly restrictive" features:

1. There need not be a sharp rise in imports; it is enough for the relative *share* of foreign imports to increase sharply in the domestic market.

2. It is usually helpful to appeal to the notion that foreign competition is from "low-priced" imports. The Europeans have the term "abnormal competition" to refer to this phenomenon and claim market disruption when, according to J. De Bandt, the import price is below the domestic price by "the portion of value added which they are unwilling to forego."[6] This is a strange notion indeed for economists to contemplate: after all, trade will reflect comparative advantage and imports will be effected when they are cheaper than domestic output. But it is a notion that is widely held and presumably is occasionally successful in getting protection.

The reliance on criteria such as decline in domestic industry's share in the domestic market and the need to compete with "low-priced" imports have thus replaced the need to show that there is "serious injury" in any other sense (that unemployment is rapidly resulting in the industry) and that it is attributable to increasing imports.

Hence the matter has become of serious concern to LDCs whose ("low-priced," "low-cost") exports have now come fairly significantly to face the prospect of market-disruption-induced restrictions, and, indeed, are in some important cases (such as the LTA) already under such restraints.[7] Therefore prior to discussing the manner in which such prospects can be regulated and compensated for, it is necessary to examine in greater depth the history and present status of GATT rules on the subject, proceeding then to a fuller exploration of the growth of VERs and other restrictions outside of the GATT-and-related framework.

2. GATT Rules and National Legislations

It is useful to put the current GATT rules on the phenomenon of "serious injury," as applicable to market disruption, in historical perspective as well as in relation to the rest of GATT articles.

It is fair to say that GATT has had built into its basic structure an asymmetry under which agriculture has managed to be relatively easy to protect but interferences with trade in manufactures have been made more difficult. Thus, for example, the GATT Article XI is explicit in ruling out quotas as follows:

1. No prohibitions or restrictions other than duties, taxes or other charges, whether made effective through quotas, import or export licenses or other measures, shall be instituted or maintained by any contracting party on the importation of any product of the territory of any other contracting party or on the exportation or sale for export of any product destined for the territory of any other contracting party.

2. The provisions of paragraph 1 of this Article shall not extend to the following:

(a) Export prohibitions or restrictions temporarily applied to prevent or relive critical shortages of foodstuffs or other products essential to the exporting contracting party;

(b) Import and export prohibitions or restrictions necessary to the application of standards or regulations for the classification, grading or marketing of commodities in international trade;

(c) Import restrictions on any agricultural or fisheries product, imported in any form . . . necessary to the enforcement of governmental measures which operate:

(i) to restrict the quantities of the like domestic product permitted to be marketed or produced, or, if there is no substantial domestic production of the like product, of a domestic product for which the imported product can be directly substituted; or

(ii) to remove a temporary surplus of the like domestic product, or, if there is no substantial domestic production of the like product, of a domestic product for which the imported product can be directly substituted, by making the surplus available to certain groups of domestic consumers free of charge or at prices below the current market level; or

(iii) to restrict the quantities permitted to be produced of any animal product the production of which is directly dependent, wholly or mainly, on the imported commodity, if the domestic production of that commodity is relatively negligible.

It is clear from the above that the essential exemptions contemplated under Article XI.2 relate to agricultural commodities (with domestic price support programs, and so forth) and do not help manufacturing industries desiring protection.

The basic *protective* outlet for manufactures (as distinct from articles such as XII relating to balance of payments and XXI concerning security exceptions) which seek protection from imports on alleged grounds of "market disruption" is provided under Article XIX whose full text states:

1. (a) If, as a result of unforeseen developments and of the effect of the obligations incurred by a contracting party under this Agreement, including tariff concessions, any product is being imported into the territory of that contracting party in such increased quantities and under such conditions as to cause or threaten serious injury to domestic producers in that territory of like or directly competitive products, the contracting party shall be free, in respect of such product, and to the extent and for such time as may be necessary to prevent or remedy such injury, to suspend the obligation in whole or in part or to withdraw or modify the concession.

(b) If any product, which is the subject of a concession with respect to a preference, is being imported into the territory of a contracting party in the circumstances set forth in subparagraph (a) of this paragraph, so as to cause or threaten serious injury to domestic producers of like or directly competitive products in the territory of a contracting party which receives or received such preference, the importing contracting party shall be free, if that other contracting party so requests, to suspend the relevant obligation in whole or in part or to withdraw or modify the concession in respect of the product, to the extent and for such time as may be necessary to prevent or remedy such injury.

2. Before any contracting party shall take action pursuant to the provisions of paragraph 1 of this Article, it shall give notice in writing to the CONTRACTING PARTIES as far in advance as may be practicable and shall afford the CONTRACTING PARTIES and those contracting parties having a substantial interest as exporters of the product concerned an opportunity to consult with it in respect of the proposed action. When such notice is given in relation to a concession with respect to a preference, the notice shall name the contracting party which has requested the action. In critical circumstances, where delay would cause damage which it would be difficult to repair, action under paragraph 1 of this Article may be taken provisionally without prior consultation, on the condition that consultation shall be effected immediately after taking such action.

3. (a) If agreement among the interested contracting parties with respect to the action is not reached, the contracting party which proposes to take or continue the action shall, nevertheless, be free to do so, and if such action is taken or continued, the affected contracting parties shall then be free, not later than ninety days after such action is taken, to suspend, upon the expiration of thirty days from the day on which written notice of such suspension is received by the CONTRACTING PARTIES, the application to the trade of the contracting party taking such action, or, in the case envisaged in paragraph 1 (b) of this Article, to the trade of the contracting party requesting such action, of such substantially equivalent concessions or other obligations under this Agreement the suspension of which the CONTRACTING PARTIES do not disapprove.

(b) Notwithstanding the provisions of subparagraph (a) of this paragraph, where action is taken under paragraph 2 of this Article without prior consultation and causes or threatens serious injury in the territory of a contracting party to the domestic producers of products affected by the action, that contracting party shall, where delay would cause damage difficult to repair, be free to suspend, upon the taking of such action and throughout the period of consultation, such concessions or other obligations as may be necessary to prevent or remedy the injury.

The GATT view of the invoking of "escape-clause" protection in the matter of market disruption, as implicit in Article XIX, was therefore traditionally a rather strict one. However, its interpretation has been somewhat less strict than the language would suggest.

Thus, the "unforeseen developments" in para. 1(a) have been interpreted as inclusive of situations deriving from the fulfillment by a member of its obligations (under Articles III or IX).[8] More important, the interpretation of the phrase "increased quantities" in para. 1 has been formally agreed to as including the case where imports may have increased only *relatively* to domestic production (as, in fact, was explicit in the corresponding Havana

Charter, Article 40 text).[9] Finally, the article clearly states that the relaxation of commitments under it will be "for such time as may be necessary": this, in turn, has been clarified to imply that while the expectation is one of short-term, temporary invoking of protection, the phrasing does allow for longer and continuous invoking of Article XIX.[10]

But, subject to these liberal interpretations, the scope of Article XIX is essentially narrow. Basically, it does require that concession-led increasing imports be a cause of serious injury. It also builds into the mechanism the *possibility* of compensation to the exporting member countries that thereby lose the tariff concessions to be suspended: reflecting, of course, the fact that Article XIX explicitly pertains to imports of articles on which a concession had earlier been granted and which is being suspended by the invoking of Article XIX.[11]

Of these two restrictive aspects of Article XIX, the former has caused the critical difficulty for industries seeking relief from imports, by claiming market disruption, under national legislations. Thus, in the United States (until the 1974 legislation), for example, the escape-clause actions (under the U.S. legislations, noted in Section 1) have been remarkably unsuccessful. Thus, of 134 investigations instituted by the commission until 1962, the process terminated in presidential invocation of the escape clause in only fifteen cases, with yet more dramatic failure rates for the post-1962 period!

The result has been a rather limited resort to GATT Article XIX for relief by industries alleging market disruption: national legislations and processes, reflecting the tougher criteria of Article XIX, have eliminated the bulk of the protectionist demands under the broad umbrella of "market disruption." The corresponding paucity of actions under Article XIX is therefore only natural.

It may also be noted that the invoking of Article XIX has generally taken the form of an increase in bound tariffs and, to a lesser degree (in about a third of the cases), of the imposition of QRs.[12] Furthermore, it has been estimated that the developing countries' exports were involved in more than half of the developed countries' invoking of Article XIX. The restrictions imposed in these cases were removed within a year in a third of the cases involving developing countries whereas in half the total number of cases the measures had been in force for over five years.

3. Growth and Existence of Principal Forms of Market-Disruption-Related Instruments of Protection

Basically, therefore, national governments in DCs responding to the protectionist pressures from their industries have responded in two principal ways: (1) by trying to weaken the restrictive nature of GATT rules on market disruption; and (2) by bypassing the GATT framework altogether.

Of these, the former has been the less important and has, in fact, not resulted in any major changes at the GATT to date. Apparently, the first public reference to "market disruption" specifically appears to have been made by the United States, via Mr. Douglas Dillon in Tokyo at the Fifteenth GATT Session in 1959.[13] This was to lead to the appointment of a GATT working party in June 1960 to examine the issue of market disruption. Their initial efforts amounted to defining market disruption to include four elements "in combination":[14]

(i) a sharp and substantial increase or potential increase of imports of particular products from particular sources;
(ii) these products are offered at prices which are substantially below those prevailing for similar goods of comparable quality in the market of the importing country;
(iii) there is serious damage to domestic producers or threat thereof;
(iv) the price differentials referred to in paragraph (ii) above do not arise from governmental intervention in the fixing or formation of prices or from dumping practices.

The working party advocated a multilateral and "constructive" approach toward this problem, one that would permit trade expansion. Its recommendation that there be a permanent Committee on Market Disruption was accepted and this committee, in collaboration with the International Labor Organization, was to consider the economic, social, and commercial aspects of market disruption and report on the matter.[15] As it happened, this report never materialized, and, in fact, the most important market-disruption-type restriction that soon materialized, the LTA (Long-Term Arrangement Regarding International Trade in Cotton Textiles), was to be negotiated in 1962 quite without regard to this committee! In the years that have lapsed since then, the GATT has not managed to regulate market disruption any more than the DCs have managed to alter the basic GATT framework to accommodate less restrictive criteria for invoking market-disruption-related protection.

The fact is that the alternative route, of bypassing the GATT altogether to seek successfully restraints on trade in cases of market disruption defined far more weakly than in GATT, is the one that has been chosen by DCs. And the most fashionable policy instrument chosen has been the VERs, ironically described as "voluntary" but, in fact, imposed on reluctant exporting countries threatened with more drastic treatment in the absence of the VERs. And the most serious of the VERs, those on cotton textiles, have been formally signed multilaterally into continuing quantitative restrictions under the LTA.

Before discussing the scope of these VERs, it is interesting to note that an analysis of the U.S. VERs, as in Table 6.1, shows how industries that failed to win protection by the escape-clause route then proceeded, through executive action, to secure VERs on imports (from Japan): the correlation is revealing. At the same time, note that several industries with VERs have not even bothered to go the escape-clause route first; this is true, for example, of cotton textiles in the United States, now under the LTA! In fact, the great

Table 6.1 The Relationship Between Japanese Voluntary Export
Restraints and United States Escape-Clause Investigations

Items Subject to Japanese Voluntary Export Restraints	Items in Previous Escape-Clause Action	Finding in Previous Escape-Clause Action
1. Bicycle parts	Bicycle parts	Negative
2. Malleable cast-iron joints	Cast-iron soil-pipe fittings	Negative
3. Bicycles, assembled	Bicycles	First investigation: Negative Second investigation: Positive (president invoked escape clause) Third investigation: Negative
4. Thermometers	Clinical thermometers	Positive (president invoked escape clause)
5. Wood screws	Wood screws	First investigation: Negative Second investigation: Negative Third investigation: Evenly divided (president declined to invoke escape clause)
6. Gloves, woolen, knitted	Knit gloves and mittens, wool	Dismissed (at applicant's request)
7. Scarves, silk and rayon	Screen-printed silk scarves	Positive (president declined to invoke escape clause)
8. Silk fabrics	Silk woven fabrics	Dismissed (after preliminary inquiry)
9. Flatware, stainless steel	Stainless steel table flatware	Positive (president invoked escape clause)
10. Gloves and mittens, baseball use	Baseball and softball gloves	Positive (president declined to invoke escape clause)
11. Raincoats, vinyl	Plastic raincoats	Negative
12. Smoking accessories	Tobacco pipes and bowls	Positive (president declined to invoke escape clause)
13. Tableware, hard porcelain	Household china tableware	Negative
14. Umbrellas	Umbrellas	Dismissed (at applicant's request)
15. Umbrella frames	Umbrella frames	First investigation: Positive (president declined to invoke escape clause)

Table 6.1 (continued)

Items Subject to Japanese Voluntary Exports Restraints	Items in Previous Escape-Clause Action	Finding in Previous Escape-Clause Action
		Second investigation: Dismissed at applicant's request)
16. Glass- and crystal-ware	Handmade glassware	First investigation: Evenly divided (president declined to invoke escape clause) Second investigation: Negative
17. Rosaries	Rosaries	Negative
18. Tiles, mosaic, unglazed	Ceramic mosaic tiles	Positive (president declined to invoke escape clause)

Source: Constructued from Lynch (1968, p. 200) and Kelly (1963, pp. 169-173) by John Cheh (1974, Table VI-2).

advantage of VERs is that the industry does *not* have to satisfy the relatively stringent requirements such as the demonstration to an officially designated agency (say, the U.S. Tariff Commission) of serious injury from concession-led increase in imports: all that is truly necessary is sufficient political clout with one's government, and, in turn, the latter's clout with the government and/or traders of the exporting countries. As Metzger has put it pointedly in relation to the historical Potato Agreement of 1948 between the U.S. and Canada, an early example of a VER:

On the U.S. side, strong domestic interests desired to protect themselves against competitive imports. They either believed that they could not qualify for escape clause relief (i.e., Cotton Textiles, Man-made Textile Fibers, Shoes), or, if they might qualify for National Security Amendment relief (i.e., Steel), they were aware of the foreign relations problems involved in imposing unilateral quotas, which are often considered to be "unfriendly" acts by America's trading partners. Cognizant Congressional Committees, made aware of these problems by their own experience no less than by that communicated by the Chief Executive, have not desired to force the Administration's hand by passing mandatory legislative quotas; indeed, they have had grave doubts that in the last analysis they could muster the strength to repass such a bill over a determined Chief Executive. Yet, they, like the Administration, have been loathe to treat all domestic industries—those with and those without major political strength—alike. Those without sufficient domestic political strength have simply had to live with the foreign competition which cannot be stemmed under generally applicable domestic legal criteria. Those with such strengths have secured the extraordinary remedy of the United

States raising to the highest international negotiating levels the matter of securing curtailment of imports from friendly foreign countries, developing and developed alike, in the interest of those who can not show, or at any rate have not attempted to show, serious injury in consequence of increased importation.

Indeed, similar exertion of political muscle by industry and, in turn, by government against the exporting country were to mark the four early VERs between Japan and the United States in the 1930s.[16]

Information regarding VERs is, by the standards of international trade data, occasionally difficult to come by: this is in the nature of the case, given the extra-GATT-framework, political arm twisting that precedes their incidence. For the United States, we have Magee's estimates that are seen, in Table 6.2, to yield an estimated value of trade (affected by VERs) as exceeding $5 billion in 1971: a figure that, as one would expect, exceeds greatly the Canadian 1968 estimate of $57 million (Canadian). On the other hand, Canada and the United States are only two of many DCs practicing VERs.

By far the most important existing, as distinct from potential, VERs relate to textiles and currently are embodied in the Arrangement Regarding International Trade in Textiles, negotiated by some fifty governments in 1973 and entering into force on January 1, 1974. This arrangement goes back proximately, in essence, to the initial Short-Term Arrangement (STA) negotiated in 1961 at U.S. initiative and remaining in force between October 1961 and September 1962, and then succeeded by the LTA which was to be repeatedly renegotiated. The original agreements were restricted to cotton textiles whereas the latest agreement extends to "wool, man-made fibres, or blend thereof."[17]

The VERs, including the Arrangement on Textiles, suggest certain broad characteristics and conclusions.

Table 6.2 Major U.S. Imports Subject to Voluntary Export Restraints and Import Quotas, 1971 (in millions of dollars)

	VERs	QRs
Petroleum		3,278
Sugar		813
Dairy products		70
Total		4,161
Cotton textiles	590	
Synthetic and woolen textiles	1,840	
Steel	2,009[a]	
Meat	598	
Total	5,037	

Source: Stephen P. Magee (1972, p. 662); cited also in Fred Bergsten (1975).
[a] 1969 figure, excluding several categories of steel products covered by the VERs. Thus the figure for total VER coverage should be somewhat higher. In 1973, the total coverage approximated $2.3 billion.

1. They can be invoked successfully at extremely low levels of imports, both absolutely and as a share of domestic absorption. Thus, the early VERs on textiles from Japan, imposed by the United States in the 1930s, were at a time when total imports of textiles into the United States were no more than 3 percent of domestic production and total imports from Japan were only about 1 percent.[18] From 1951 to 1962, straddling the renewal of such VERs in the mid-1950s, the shares were, if anything, even lower. Similarly, the steel VERs invoked by the United States have also been in the face of imports as low as 17 million tons against domestic production of 141 million tons in 1969.[19]

2. The industries profiting from VERs almost always allege fears of "low-price" imports offering undue competition and *threatening* injury, rather than actually causing it.[20]

3. The length of duration of the VERs, at a time, would seem to be around one year but can extend to five years. In several cases, they have been renewed beyond the period of first imposition.[21] Some have been allowed to lapse as well.

4. The VERs are an inefficient instrument, compared to domestic tariffs or quotas, in restricting imports. The principal cause is that VERs apply to specific exporters and they cannot effectively rule out new suppliers from entering the market. In consequence, the progress of most VERs on specific countries (with notable exceptions as in the case of U.S. VERs on steel) has been toward increasing coverage of other exporters and, in the case of textiles, to a fully multilateral arrangement of exporters and importers.[22] In other cases, for instance, Canada, there is "back-up" legislation in case VERs fail to hold back imports effectively.[23]

5. While the VERs build in permissible rates of growth of exports from specific countries, these are invariably controlled at low levels. Thus the latest Arrangement on Textiles builds in a ceiling of 6 percent (as against the earlier 5 percent), but, at the same time, allows for an escape route (seized under the earlier arrangement by Canada, for example, at 3 percent) under which a "lower positive growth rate may be applied."[24]

6. Furthermore, there is literally no sanction against the expansion of capacity in the domestic industry of the importing country while the VERs operate. This is the case even for the 1974 Arrangement on Textiles; and, in fact, while the earlier LTA operated, the exporting LDCs noted and complained about the growth of such capacity in member DCs to no avail. Therefore VERs are, in this respect, one-sided.

7. Finally, unlike the compensation *possibility* in the GATT Article XIX, there is practically no evidence that any of the existing and past VERs have incorporated explicit compensation to the countries whose export markets are being disrupted.[25]

4. Impact of "Export Market Disruption" on Welfare of Exporting LDCs

The *threat* of protectionist restrictions being invoked by the importing countries, on grounds of market disruption, can be shown to impose a welfare loss on the exporting countries, as is in fact done in the theoretical Appendix 2.

It is shown there that, taking expected utilities, economic welfare of the exporting country will be less in the absence of such a threat. It is also shown that if the exporting country, in turn, reacts with an optimal policy intervention in the nature of restricted exports so as to reduce the probability of VERs or other such market-disruption-related restrictions being invoked, then the reduction in welfare from the *threat* of such invocations will be less than if the exporting country took no such action: but the loss will still be there. And, furthermore, if investment allocations cannot be costlessly readjusted, once in place, then the presence of such "adjustment costs" will further increase the loss of welfare from the threat of such trade restraints. Finally, the *actual* invoking of the trade restraints would inflict a welfare loss on the exporting country that would exceed the expected loss from the *threat* of such an invocation at a future date.

From these general theoretical propositions, certain compensatory proposals would seem to follow.

First, there is a case for asking importing DCs to compensate the exporting LDCs faced with mere *threats* of market-disruption-related trade restraints. The DCs can reasonably be asked to "buy," with compensation payments, the right to invoke a market-disruption-related trade restraint on a product, and to forego the right to resort to such trade restraints on all products *not* so bought for. Thus a list of "restrainable" items can be prepared under multilateral auspices, such as GATT, and the compensation required for affected exporting countries, whose welfare is correspondingly reduced, would have to be paid to put a product on such a list.

Second, the actual invoking of such restraints, by imposing a greater loss, would equally call for further compensation to the affected exporters.

Compensation, for potential and actual export market disruption, to the exporting countries affected by trade restraints related to market disruption would thus be the natural consequence of our analysis. In Section 5, therefore, we consider the possible rules in this regard in greater depth, proceeding in Section 6 to consider the implications these rules would have for modifications in GATT Article XIX and related provisions.

5. Compensation for Export Market Disruption, Potential and Actual: Suggested Rules

The rules for compensation for market-disruption-related trade restraints can then be defined on a number of dimensions as follows.

1. *Penalty/compensation for potential restriction.* In accordance with the arguments of the preceding section, a list of "items potentially subject to

market-disruption-related trade restrictions" ought to be maintained. This list might be described as the *list of potentially restrainable items.*[26] For putting an item on such a list, the DCs would be required to pay a "penalty" which could be utilized to compensate the exporting countries subject to welfare loss from the threat of trade restraints on the item.

2. *Penalty compensation for actual invoking of trade restraints on potentially restrainable items.* Moreover, as and when the trade restraints are actually invoked, a further penalty should be used for compensating the exporting country whose export market is thus restrained.[27] The penalty so imposed, if it is to reflect the compensation to be paid to the exporting countries, must then be less than the actual cost of the trade restraint by the adjusted sum already paid for putting the item, in the first place, on the list of potentially restrainable items.

3. *Escape clause from list of potentially restrainable items.* While the preceding two rules should, in principle, divide all items into those that are restrainable and those that are not, this is politically inadequate. There will almost certainly be cases where unforeseen *and* politically unmanageable difficulties will arise on items not already put on the list of potentially restrainable items and the DC of importation will be unable to avoid responding to political pressures for trade restraint.

An escape-clause action for items not on this list would therefore be appropriate. At the same time, given the fact that this should not provide an incentive to escape from the option of putting such items on the restrainable list, it would be equally appropriate to make the invoking of this escape clause both more difficult and more costly. Thus, the escape clause should require that the importing DC be allowed nonetheless to invoke a trade restraint on items not on the list of potentially restrainable items, provided that (a) it makes a demonstrable case, under multilateral (GATT) auspices, of the existence of serious injury (as under the current GATT Article XIX) *and* (b) it then makes a considerably larger penalty payment for the compensation of the exporting countries. It may also be noted that one would, in practice, need a substantial time limit for an item to be on the restrainable list before permitting the invoking of trade restraints under it. Otherwise, when this period could be a few weeks or months, it would pay countries to go this route rather than the proposed escape-clause route where the proposed penalties are higher.

4. *Automaticity of compensation.* The penalty/compensation would be automatic under the preceding rules, rather than constituting a mere possibility as in the current GATT Article XIX. This would rule out the use of political muscle to get out of this obligation when invoking trade restraints.

5. *Financial form of compensation.* Moreover, the above rules require financial compensation. This is in contrast, for example, to the Article XIX variety of "compensation," which takes the form of either grant of a new tariff concession (on something else) or of withdrawal of a tariff concession

by the exporting country. This latter method reflects the tariff-bargaining framework in which GATT rules are enmeshed; it makes little sense since compensation to the exporter in the form of enabling the latter to raise a tariff in retaliation, for example, presupposes that the latter is advantageous while in fact, it is likely to cause yet more damage by further restraining trade; at the same time, it disrupts yet another market in seeking redress for the original market disruption. The financial form of penalty/compensation provided for in the rules suggested above is free from these obvious defects.

6. *Compensation to exporting country.* Furthermore, the financial compensation is designed here for payment to the exporting *country*, rather than to the exporting industry: as called for by the theoretical analysis of Appendix 2. In turn, the payment is to be made by the importing country. It may be noted that the latter, financial penalty to be paid from the budget would, in turn, serve to generate executive counterpressures against the industrial pressure groups for trade restraints, potential and actual.

7. *Compensation only for LDCs.* The preceding rules in regard to compensation may be applied only to exporting LDCs. They are, after all, the countries which have been seriously affected by the textiles restrictions and by VERs, as we have already seen.[28] Further, there is greater willingness, as part of the new international economic order, to grant LDCs reasonable accommodation via framing new rules regarding their trade. Moreover, the flows of funds to be so generated are far more likely to be significant, relative to their needs, for LDCs than for DCs. Finally, discriminatory adjustment of trade rules, in favor of LDCs, is well-embedded in GATT reform, as in the enactment of Article XXIII for them at GATT.

The foregoing set of rules, involving essentially compensation for exporting LDCs by importing DCs, are not entirely novel in their reference to the *potential* use of trade restraints since the well-established practice of the "binding" of tariffs does imply that the potential use of restrictions is given up. In regard to the notion of the compensation itself, however, there are no obvious precedents. At the same time, a precedent of sorts, which certainly suggests that what is being proposed here is fully feasible, relates to the payment by the United States of compensation to the Turkish government of a sizable sum in order to enforce the ban on poppy production: by using this money to compensate Turkish farmers, in turn, this would theoretically have made it possible for them to shift to other cultivation at no financial loss.[29] This "precedent" is spelled out in some detail in Appendix 1. There would therefore appear to be nothing insuperable, politically, in putting the suggested compensatory rules here onto the agenda for GATT reform.

At the same time, it would be useful to note that; in complementarity to the rules suggested above, two DC policies would be extremely valuable, only one of which is being gradually extended in scope.

Insofar as the response to foreign imports, or to domestic decline due to other reasons, is to provide domestic adjustment assistance to assist factors of production to retrain and relocate, this will correspondingly reduce the need to resort to trade restraints by making the pressures for such restraints from the industry both less intense and politically less difficult to resist. In this regard, the easing of the criteria for such adjustment assistance in the recent U.S. Trade Act of 1974 is welcome news for the exporting LDCs.[30]

Next, it is clear from elementary principles that trade restraint, to protect the production level of the domestic industry, is inferior to the use of a production subsidy: from the viewpoint of the importing DC itself.[31] Equally, it is obvious that the use of the production subsidy will increase the overall market in the DC for the imported item while a tariff, by increasing the price for consumers, will reduce it. Hence, given the fact that domestic production must be maintained at a desired level, the use of a production subsidy by the importing DC will be preferable, from the viewpoint of the exporting LDC, than the use of a trade policy.[32] Thus it would be useful if the overall reform in regard to the phenomenon of market-disruption-related trade restraints, as suggested in this section, were to include a multilateral agreement by DCs to use production subsidies rather than tariffs or trade quotas, whenever trade restraints are invoked under the rules specified above.[33] The only exceptions to this code could include emergency situations where an immediate trade quota may be necessary: in this case, the quota could be phased out and replaced gradually by a production subsidy on a multilaterally agreed schedule.

6. Proposed Modification in GATT Article XIX

If the rules suggested in Section 5 are to be implemented, the logical place for them is the GATT; and there, the logical candidate for replacement by these rules is Article XIX.

The GATT is already being reexamined—as, in fact, it has been continuously since its inception in regard to new phenomena such as the growth of customs unions—in regard to the manifestation and growth of new problems such as the use of export quotas,[34] for example, to hold back commodities for an objective such as anti-inflationary policy. The recent thrust toward a new international economic order also provides an ideal climate in which to reexamine long-standing issues, for instance, market disruption, which have been addressed but for which suitable solutions have not been provided.

The rules suggested in Section 5 therefore provide an agenda for replacing the basic content of Article XIX, in an international economic climate where such a concrete proposal is likely to be examined without immediate hostility on the part of DCs. At the same time, in being concrete and specific, the suggested changes provide the necessary content and shape to the long-standing demands by LDCs that something be done about the phenomenon of market-disruption-related trade restraints from DCs. They constitute therefore an essential and useful input into the basic agenda for reforming GATT as part of a new international economic order.

The formal adoption of such rules, replacing Article XIX, would also have to bring the *existing* VERs, including the 1974 Textiles Agreement, into line with them. This would be done most naturally by formally sanctioning them, but insisting on the payment of the penalty by the importing DCs to compensate the LDCs whose exports are being constrained by these restraints. Otherwise, there would be an advantage to invoking VERs prior to the reaching of agreement on the new rules.[35] Also, there would be an advantage in bringing *all* such trade restraints under one institutional umbrella, where they can be watched, monitored, and regulated according to the suggested, new rules.

The dynamics of reaching an agreement on these rules, finally, presumably would have to involve an initiative by the LDCs themselves, as they are the parties injured by the current and potential market-disruption-related trade restraints. The logical place for their initiative is therefore the UNCTAD, to be followed by action by the LDC members of the GATT at the GATT. The proposals advanced here certainly provide an alternative and consistent set of reform rules that needs to be considered seriously alongside the suggestions in regard to market disruption recently aired by the LDCs.[36]

Notes

This paper was originally commissioned by the UNCTAD, Geneva, Switzerland, but does not represent or reflect the UNCTAD Secretariat's views. Thanks are due to Michael Pelcovits and Paul Krugman for excellent research assistance and to T. N. Srinivasan for co-authoring Appendix 2, which is an abbreviated version of a full-length theoretical analysis, published in the *Journal of International Economics*, November 1976. Helpful comments on an earlier draft were received from Robert Baldwin, Fred Bergsten, Charles Blitzer, Peter Diamond, Murray Kemp, Hendrik Houthakker, R. Krishnamurti, C. P. Kindleberger, Gerry Helleiner, Jan Tumlir, Stanley Metzger, John Williamson, Bela Balassa, Wolfgang Mayer, and Koichi Hamada.

1 Article XIX is one of several, so-called "safeguard" provisions in GATT which enable the contracting parties to reenact trade barriers for a number of specific reasons. Article VI, for example, allows the enacting of countervailing and antidumping duties.

2 Cf. Stanley Metzger (1971, p. 168).

3 It is thus well known that the U.S. executive has been generally more liberal on trade barriers reduction than the U.S. Congress, and that the VERs were imposed often so as to prevent more serious protectionist legislation from becoming enacted in the Congress.

4 Metzger (1971, p. 173).

5 This notion of market disruption as occurring whenever the domestic industry loses its relative share in the domestic market is implicit or explicit in trade legislation introduced earlier in the U.S. House of Representatives. Thus H.R. 2511, introduced on January 8, 1969, begins typically as follows: "A Bill to provide for the orderly marketing of flat glass imported into the United States by affording foreign supplying nations a *fair share* of the growth or change in the United States flat glass market . . ." (91st Congress, 2nd

Session, Committee Print, Committee on Ways and Means, U.S. House of Representatives, June 1970, U.S. Government Printing Office, Washington, 1970, p. 172, italics inserted). Or take H.R. 993 which begins with: "A Bill to provide for *an equitable sharing* of the United States market by electronic articles of domestic and of foreign origin . . ." (ibid., p. 150, italics inserted).

6 See Caroline Pestieau and Jacque Henry (1972, pp. 139-140). The work referred to here is by Henry.

7 Thus, according to Pestieau and Henry (1972), Canada had official VERs in 1971 with twenty countries, of which only six were DCs.

8 Thus a Working Party at GATT had concluded that "developments occurring after the negotiation of the relevant tariff concession which it would not be reasonable to expect that the negotiations of the country making the concession could and should have foreseen at the time when the concession was negotiated." Cf. GATT (1970-1971, p. 107).

9 GATT (1970-1971, p. 107).

10 GATT (1970-1971, p. 107). In fact, in the case of Germany, in regard to hard coal, the 1958 invoking of Clause XIX was in force as late as 1975.

11 The article builds in provision for consultations with interested contracting parties, which is the usual forum for granting the compensation if indeed granted. (Where the action is taken prior to consultation, the interested contracting parties may retaliate. However, such retaliation has been quite rare, having occurred only in three cases to present date.) Furthermore, as corroborated by unpublished tabulations at GATT, compensation is only a possibility, as noted in the text, and is often *not* provided when Article XIX is invoked. In fact, dissatisfaction with the compensation aspect of Article XIX has prompted occasional suggestions to do away with it and instead modify Article XIX so as to insist on the following of certain stricter criteria by the country invoking the article.

12 In some cases, the action taken took the form of establishing minimum valuations for imports, thus effectively raising the tariff rate for items with actual values below these minimums.

13 GATT (1961b, p. 25). In fact, it was at the United States' initiative that Article XIX had been included in GATT originally.

14 Cf. GATT (1961a); also cited in Pestieau and Henry (1972, pp. 137-138), in Metzger (1971, pp. 175-176), and discussed in GATT (1961b, pp. 25-26).

15 Cf. Pestieau and Henry (1972, pp. 137-138).

16 Metzger (1971, pp. 170-171). "As Henry states, the 'entire story shows clearly that the U.S.-Japan voluntary export restraint agreements of the 1930's resulted mainly from American pressures and threats of unilateral, permanent, and possibly more restrictive action. Nothing indicates,' he asserts, 'that this pattern has changed since.' The Japanese, for their part, accepted the agreements as the most practicable means of preserving a portion of their textile exports to the United States, and in the interest of political harmony in this sphere of their relationships with the United States."

17 Cf. GATT (1974), Article 12, pp. 17-18.

18 Cf. Metzger (1971, p. 170).

19 Cf. Metzger (1971, p. 182).

quotas under uncertainty shows that if the uncertainty comes from foreign supply, the welfare superiority of tariffs over quotas as methods of restricting imports to a given level if the tariff rate is high: precisely 100 percent in the case of linear supply and demand schedules. Cf. the interesting work of Michael Pelcovits (1975).

21 Pestieau and Henry (1972) note that the duration of a formal agreement is not identical with its incidence: occasionally, as with GATT Article XIX as well, the restriction will go into force before formal papers are exchanged. They also note that most Canadian VERs have duration of one year.

22 Besides, export quotas have always been known to earn the monopoly rents (from restriction) for the exporters whereas domestic quotas will earn them for the importer under competition.

23 Pestieau and Henry (1972, p. 168): "Several Canadian laws include clauses that can be used to supplement or reinforce VERs, and the various amendments enacted in the context of the present government's textile policy lessen the previous dependence on exporters' voluntary collaboration. Prior to January, 1969, subsection (7c) of section 40A of the Customs Act was used to apply special values for duty in instances where imports were found to have injured the interest of Canadian producers. However, this subsection was repealed and replaced on January 1, 1969, by the new section 8 of the Customs Tariff Act. As stated in section 37 of the Anti-dumping Act (1969), the new section authorizes the imposition of a surtax on imports that cause or threaten to cause injury to Canadian producers of similar or directly competitive goods. The Export and Import Permits Act has also been amended to permit unilateral imposition of import-licensing quotas to deal with problems of disruptive imports whenever VER arrangements would not be feasible. Furthermore, section 5(c) of this Act enables the federal government to control imports and 'to implement an intergovernmental arrangement or commitment'— clearly opening up a method for making VER arrangements more effective.

"These are the powers on which the efficiency of the Canadian VER system rests."

Examples can be found in U.S. Legislation as well, as in the Public Law 87-488 (H.R. 10788) which amended Section 204 of the Agricultural Act of 1956 by the insertion of the following sentence:

In addition, if a multilateral agreement has been or shall be concluded under the authority of this section among countries accounting for a significant part of world trade in the articles with respect to which the agreement was concluded, the President may also issue, in order to carry out such an agreement, regulations governing the entry or withdrawal from warehouse of the same articles which are the products of countries not parties to the agreement.

This legislation was approved on June 19, 1962.

Note that both the United States and Canada have back-up legislation for VERs in cases of textiles and meat.

24 Cf. GATT (1974, Annex B, p. 22).

25 However, from a theoretical standpoint, it may be noted that VERs, as contrasted with import QRs, will transfer the monopoly rents from the trade restriction to the exporters, so that one may well consider this to constitute an implicit compensation under a VER arrangement. In fact, as Bergsten has pointed out, textile export quota tickets are actively sold throughout the Far East at a premium that reflects this rent. See Fred Bergsten (1975, pp. 239-271).

26 An analogue to this recommendation may be found in the practice of "binding" tariffs in advance.

27 The loss inflicted by actual invoking of restraints is, of course well understood in trade-theoretic literature. For measurement of the cost of sugar protectionism to exporting LDCs, for example, see the work of Snape and Johnson, reviewed in H. G. Johnson (1967).

28 VERs have also affected Japan seriously; and, in some cases, such as the steel VERs in the United States, the impact was felt by the developed country exporters and imports were initially diverted to developing countries which thereby benefited.

29 The compensation rules suggested for trade restraints in this paper, however, relate only to financial compensation to the exporting *country*, and *not* to the exporting industry. For other contrasts, refer to Appendix 1.

30 For an excellent account of the U.S. policies in regard to adjustment assistance, and evidence on the efforts to ease the criteria for it until 1973, see Robert Baldwin and John Mutti, "Policy Issues in Adjustment Assistance: The United States," in Helen Hughes, ed. (1973), especially Section IV. Adjustment assistance in the EEC is also discussed in Ch. 7 of this volume.

31 This is one of the important policy prescriptions from the theory of optimal policy intervention in the presence of "noneconomic" objectives and follows from the fact that the tariff imposes a consumption cost (by raising prices for consumers) which is avoided, while equally protecting domestic output, by a production subsidy. Cf. J. Bhagwati and T. N. Srinivasan (1969).

32 This conclusion would have to be modified, but is not altogether nullified, if the domestic industry wishes to maintain a certain *share* of sales in the domestic market. The optimal policy intervention in this case, from the DC viewpoint, would be the combination of an import tariff and a production subsidy.

33 A code of conduct, along these lines, is mentioned also by Henry (1972, p. 175), who states that this "has been suggested in various places" and cites one example from Bela Balassa.

34 See, in this regard, the excellent pamphlet by C. Fred Bergsten (1974). Bergsten does not consider VERs or market-disruption problems in this study.

35 For a long-standing restraint such as the Textiles Arrangement, it may be politically easier and also quite sensible to have the penalty enacted at the time of the next renewal, since there has been a short time limit on each such arrangement.

36 The latter have been neatly summarized in UNCTAD document TC/B/C.2/R.4.

References

Baldwin, R., and J. Mutti, 1973, "Policy Issues in Adjustment Assistance: The United States," in Helen Hughes (ed.), *Prospects for Partnership*, IBRD, Johns Hopkins University Press, Baltimore.

Bergsten, C. F., 1974, *Completing the GATT: Toward New International Rules to Govern Export Controls*, British-North American Committee, United States, October.

_____ , 1975, *On the Non-Equivalence of Import Quotas and "Voluntary" Export Restraints*, Technical Series Reprint T-009, Brookings Institution, Washington, D.C.

Bhagwati, J., and T. N. Srinivasan, 1969, "Optimal Intervention to Achieve Non-

Economic Objectives," *Review of Economic Studies*, January.

Cheh, J., 1974, *U.S. Trade Policy and Short-run Domestic Adjustment Costs*, Ph.D. dissertation, M.I.T.

Dominion Bureau of Statistics, several years, *Trade of Canada, Imports by Commodities*, Queen's Printer, Ottawa.

GATT, 1961a, *Basic Instruments and Selected Documents*, 9th Supplement, Sixteenth and Seventeenth Sessions, February, Geneva.

———, 1961b, *The Activities of GATT, 1960/61*, April, Geneva.

———, 1970-1971, *Analytical Index, Third Revision, March 1970, Notes on the Drafting, Interpretation and Affirmation of the Articles of the General Agreement*, Geneva.

———, 1974, *Arrangement Regarding International Trade in Textiles*, Geneva.

Johnson, H. G., 1967, *Economic Policies Towards the Developing Countries*, Brookings Institution, Washington, D.C.

Kelly, W., 1963, *Studies in United States Commercial Policy*, University of North Carolina Press, Chapel Hill.

Lynch, J., 1968, *Toward an Orderly Market*, Sophia University; Voyager's Press, Tokyo.

Magee, S. P., 1972, "The Welfare Effects of Restrictions on U.S. Trade," *Brookings Papers on Economic Activity*, 3 (edited by A. Okun and G. Perry).

Metzger, S., 1971, "Injury and Market Disruption from Imports" in *United States International Economic Policy in an Interdependent World*, U.S. Commission on International Trade and Investment Policy, Vol. 1, Washington, D.C., July.

Pelcovits, M., 1975, "Tariffs *versus* Quotas," M.I.T. *mimeo.*, September; forthcoming in the *Journal of International Economics*, November 1976.

Pestieau, C., and J. Henry, 1972, *Non-Tariff Trade Barriers as a Problem in International Development*, Canadian Economic Policy Committee and the Private Planning Association of Canada, Canada, April.

UNCTAD, Document No. TD/B/C.2/R.4.

Appendix 1
On Compensating for Market Loss of a Bad:
The Turkish Poppy and the United States

Outside of the GATT Article XIX framework (where compensation is nonautomatic and furthermore applies only if the market disruption being nullified is a result of "obligations incurred by a contracting party under this Agreement, including tariff concessions," and whose applicability in any event has been emasculated by actions such as the LTA and VERs undertaken outside of its domain), the only major example of an importing country paying compensation to the exporting country when trade is sought to be eliminated or reduced is that of the United States paying Turkey a significant compensation to enforce the ban on Turkish poppy cultivation.

This precedent is not perfect, although it illustrates what is feasible. Its major difference from the compensation proposed for export market disruption is that its objective is to *induce* adjustment by compensating the exporting activity so that the exports will *in consequence* effectively cease, whereas the proposed compensation here is when exports have *already* ceased (or been reduced) and the compensation is for the adjustment that *has to occur* with the decline in exports. This difference, of course, stems from the fact that the case deals with trade in a bad, rather than a good, and hence with illegal trade that was sought to be eliminated at source through banning the production activity itself. Its similarity, however, with the proposed compensation for export market disruption (for goods) consists in the fact that the importing country provided the compensation to the farmers in the exporting country for the adjustment necessary if the heroin trade was to be curtailed. Hence, a brief account and review of the salient features of the case of Turkish poppy and the U.S. adjustment assistance is relevant.

The United States had for a long time been putting pressure on Turkey to reduce poppy cultivation. In response to this pressure, the number of provinces in which cultivation was legal was reduced from forty-two (out of seventy) in 1960 to seven in 1970, and four in 1971.[1] On June 30, 1971, the United States and Turkey announced a total ban on poppy cultivation. On February 14, 1974, Turkey unilaterally lifted the ban.

The logistics of the poppy trade before the ban were as follows. By a simple process poppies can be turned to opium gum, which can in turn be manufactured into morphine base. Turkey produced around 120,000 kilograms of opium gum per year. Legally, all of this was supposed to be sold to a state marketing agency, at thirteen dollars a kilo. But about half of the crop went on the black market, selling at around thirty-five dollars a kilo. (Refined into morphine base—a cheap process—this became $550 to $600 a kilo in Marseilles.)[2]

The agreement to ban cultivation called for U.S. payments of $15 million a year, plus $20 million for agricultural development investments in the affected regions. This was to compensate the farmers, and also the Turkish government, for the $3.5 million a year it earned from morphine export. The Turkish marketing organization was to pay farmers a compensation of forty dollars per kilo for poppies not grown.[3]

For more than a year after the ban, there was little impact on the flow of heroin, as dealers drew down their stockpiles.[4] But eventually the ban had a major effect, doubling heroin prices in the United States.[5]

The ban was unpopular with farmers, and politicians in a seven-province area agitated for an end.[6] In the October 1973 elections all political parties promised to review the ban.[7] When cultivation was resumed, the Turkish government said that it was because of hardships to the peasants, that it was unfair to ask Turkey to bear this burden.

It would appear that the Turkish farmers were compensated only at the legal prices presumably available on their poppy, so that the premium from illegal sales for heroin was lost by them under the ban, despite the compensation; hence the discontent. Furthermore, it is apparent that the ban was somewhat sudden and so little of the developmental aid was actually spent in the poppy-growing region by the time the discontent surfaced.[8] Finally, the ban having been forced initially on a reluctant Turkey by the United States, which was naturally frantic to stem the heroin traffic, questions of Turkish sovereignty appear eventually to have played some role also in termination of the ban.[9]

Notes

1 *New York Times* (February 21, 1974).

2 *New York Times* (August 9, 1973).

3 *New York Times* (August 9, 1973).

4 *New York Times* (October 10, 1972).

5 *New York Times* (February 21, 1974).

6 *New York Times* (August 9, 1973).

7 *New York Times* (February 21, 1974).

8 *New York Times* (February 21, 1974).

9 *Wall Street Journal* (June 23, 1974).

Appendix 2 (jointly with T. N. Srinivasan)
Optimal Trade Policy and Compensation under Endogenous Uncertainty: The Phenomenon of Market Disruption

Introduction
The fact that "market disruption" permits or prompts importing countries to invoke quantitative import restrictions (or, what is now more fashionable, voluntary export restrictions by the exporting countries, at the urging of the importing countries) immediately implies that the exporting country faces a situation of endogenous uncertainty: where its own export level can affect the probability of such quantitative restrictions (QRs) being imposed. It simultaneously raises the following analytical questions which have obvious policy implications:

1. What is the optimal trade policy for an exporting country which is faced by such potential QR-intervention?

2. Since the possibility of such QR-intervention must restrict the trade opportunity set relative to that which would obtain in the absence of the QR-possibility, can one meaningfully define the loss that such a QR-possibility imposes on the exporting country and therefore the compensation that could be required to be paid to the exporting country under, say, a modified set of GATT rules?

1. Optimal Trade Policy: 2-Period Model with Zero Adjustment Costs

To analyze the problem of optimal trade policy for the exporting country in the presence of market-disruption-induced possibility of QR-intervention, we will deploy the usual trade-theoretic model of general equilibrium, but will extend it to a 2-period framework in Sections 1 to 4. In Section 3, we will also introduce adjustment costs, beginning with a simple formulation which has putty in period 1 and clay in period 2.[1]

Thus, consider a 2-commodity model of international trade. We then assume a 2-period time horizon such that the level of exports E in the first period affects the probability $P(E)$ of a quota $\bar{E}$ being imposed at the beginning of the next period.[2]

Let $U[C_1, C_2]$ be the standard social utility function defined in terms of the consumption C_i of commodity i $(i = 1,2)$. By assumption, it is known at the beginning of the next period whether the quota $\bar{E}$ has been imposed or not. Thus, the policy in the next period will be to maximize U subject to the transformation function $F[X_1, X_2] = 0$ and the terms of trade function π if no quota is imposed and with an additional constraint $E \leqslant \bar{E}$ if the quota is imposed.

Let now the maximal welfare with and without the quota be $\underline{U}$ and $\bar{U}$ respectively. Clearly then, we have $\bar{U} > \underline{U}$ when the quota is binding. The expected welfare in the second period is then clearly:

$$\underline{U} P(E) + \bar{U} [1 - P(E)].$$

The objective function for the first period therefore is:

$$\phi = U[X_1 - E, X_2 + \pi E] + \rho[\underline{U} P(E) + \bar{U} [1 - P(E)]]$$

where ρ is the discount factor. This is then to be maximized subject to the domestic transformation constraint, $F[X_1, X_2] = 0$. In doing this, assume that $P(E)$ is a convex function of E, that is, the probability of a quota being imposed increases at an increasing rate as E is increased, and that, in the case where π depends on E, πE is concave in E. Then, the first-order conditions for an interior maximum are:

$$\frac{\partial \phi}{\partial X_1} = U_1 - \lambda F_1 = 0 \tag{1}$$

$$\frac{\partial \phi}{\partial X_2} = U_2 - \lambda F_2 = 0 \tag{2}$$

$$\frac{\partial \phi}{\partial E} = -U_1 + U_2 \{\pi + E\pi'\} - \rho(\bar{U} - \underline{U})P'(E) = 0. \tag{3}$$

Now, eqs. (1) and (2) yield the familiar result that the marginal rate of substitution in consumption equals the marginal rate of transformation.

Eq. (3) moreover can be written as:

$$\frac{U_1}{U_2} = (\pi + \pi'E) - \frac{\rho\{\bar{U} - \underline{U}\}}{U_2} \; P'(E). \tag{3'}$$

If (A) monopoly power is absent ($\pi' = 0$) and if (B) the first period's exports do not affect the probability of a quota being imposed in the second period, then (3') clearly reduces to the standard condition that the marginal rate of substitution in consumption equals the (average = marginal) terms of trade. If (A) does not hold but (B) holds, then $\dfrac{U_1}{U_2}$ equals the marginal terms of trade ($\pi + \pi'E$), leading to the familiar optimum tariff. If both A and B are present, there is an *additional* tariff element: $\dfrac{\rho[\bar{U} - \underline{U}]}{U_2}P'(E)$. This term can be explained as follows: if an additional unit of exports takes place in period 1, the probability of a quota being imposed and hence a discounted loss in welfare of $\rho(\bar{U} - \underline{U})$ occurring, increases by $P'(E)$. Thus, at the margin, the expected loss in welfare is $\rho(\bar{U} - \underline{U})P'(E)$ since there is no loss in welfare if the quota is not imposed. Converted to numeraire terms, this equals $\dfrac{\rho(\bar{U} - \underline{U})P'(E)}{U_2}$, and must be subtracted from the marginal terms of trade ($\pi + \pi'E$), the effect of an additional unit of exports on the quantum of imports.[3]

It is then clear that the market-disruption-induced QR-possibility requires optimal intervention in the form of a tariff (in period 1). It is also clear that, compared to the optimal situation *without* such a QR-possibility, the resource allocation in the QR-possibility case will shift against exportable production: that is, comparative advantage, in the welfare sense, shifts away, at the margin, from exportable production. Moreover, denoting the utility level under the optimal policy intervention with quota possibility as ϕ_Q^{OPT}, that under laissez-faire with the quota possibility as ϕ_Q^L, and that under laissez-faire without this quota possibility as ϕ_{NQ}^L, we can argue that:

$$\phi_Q^{OPT} > \phi_Q^L; \; \phi_{NQ}^L > \phi_Q^L.$$

This result is set out, with the attendant period-wise utility levels achieved under each option, in Table 6.3 which is self-explanatory.[4]

For the case of a small country, with no monopoly power in trade (except for the quota possibility), the equilibria under alternative policies are illustrated in Figure 6.1.[5] Thus, U represents the utility level in the absence of a quota, $\underline{U}$ the utility level when the quota is imposed, and U^* the first-period utility level reached under the optimal policy intervention option. Note that

Table 6.3 Alternative Outcomes under Different Policies

	Alternative Outcomes		
	Optimal Policy Intervention with Possible Quota	Laissez-Faire with Possible Quota	Laissez-Faire with No Quota Possibility
Period 1 .	U^*	$\bar{U}$	$\bar{U}$
Period 2	$\rho[\underline{U}P^* + \bar{U}(1-P^*)]$	$\rho[\underline{U}P + \bar{U}(1-\bar{P})]$	$\rho\bar{U}$
ϕ: social utility level	ϕ_Q^{OPT}	ϕ_Q^L	ϕ_{NQ}^L

$$\phi_Q^{OPT} > \phi_Q^L \; ; \; \phi_{NQ}^L > \phi_Q^L$$

Notation:

(1) $\underline{U}$ is utility level if quota is imposed;

(2) $\bar{U}$ is utility level if quota is not imposed;

(3) U^* is utility level with optimal policy intervention when quota can be imposed in second period;

(4) $P(E)$ is the probability of second-period quota of $\bar{E}$ being imposed, as a function of the first-period exports, E. With optimal policy intervention in the situation with possible quota, the exports of the first period result in a value of P^* for $P(E)$. With laissez-faire, the exports in the first period will be different and the corresponding value for $P(E)$ is $\bar{P}$.

(5) ρ is the discount factor.

(6) $\phi_{NQ}^L > \phi_Q^{QPT}$ necessarily only for small countries with no influence on terms of trade.

(7) ϕ_{NQ}^{OPT}, when the country is optimally exercising its monopoly power in trade and there is no QR possibility, is not listed above.

equilibrium with U^* naturally requires that the export level is being restricted below the level that would be reached with nonintervention (at $\bar{U}$), while exceeding the level reached in equilibrium when the quota is invoked (at $\underline{U}$). Also, note that the optimal policy for restricting the first-period level of exports is a tariff: a conclusion that is, of course, familiar from the theory of optimal intervention under noneconomic objectives as considered in Johnson (1965) and Bhagwati and Srinivasan (1969).

2. Defining the Loss from Market-Disruption-Induced QR-Possibility

Consider now the measure of the loss to the exporting country from this possibility of a market-disruption-induced QR. One can think of alternative ways in which this loss could be defined:

Measure 1. Taking expected utilities, one can define the loss of welfare to the exporting country as the difference between ϕ_{NQ}^L and ϕ_Q^L: that is, the loss

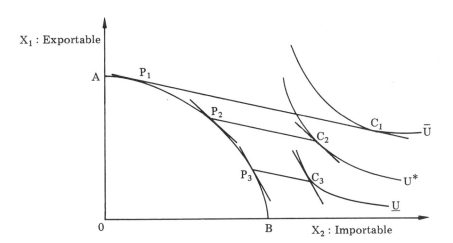

Figure 6.1

in expected welfare that follows, in the absence of optimal intervention by the exporting country, from the QR-possibility.

This measure clearly is: $\rho \overline{P} \left\{ \overline{U} - \underline{U} \right\}$ and is, of course, nothing but the expected loss in period 2 from the possible imposition of the quota, duly discounted.

Now, it is also clear that this measure will lie between the ex-post period-2 loss if the quota *is* invoked (which loss, duly discounted, is $\rho(\overline{U} - \underline{U})$) and the ex-post period-2 loss if the quota is not invoked (which loss is, of course, zero). Thus, one must regard the actual period-2 loss when the quota *is* invoked as an upper bound on the loss in this model.

It also follows that there is a welfare loss, measured as $\rho \overline{P} \left\{ \overline{U} - \underline{U} \right\}$ *even if the quota is not actually invoked in period 2*, and (in our 2-period model) the actual equilibrium allocations in each period are identical between the QR-possibility and the no-QR-possibility situations. This follows clearly from the fact that in period 1 consumers face the prospect of uncertain prices in period 2, as the QR may or may not be invoked.

Measure 2. Alternatively one may measure the loss to the exporting country as the difference between ϕ_{NQ}^{OPT} and ϕ_{Q}^{OPT}: the difference between expected welfare when there is no QR possibility but the optimal tariff to exploit monopoly power *is* being exercised and that when the government of the exporting country intervenes with optimal policy to maximize expected welfare when there *is* a QR-possibility. This alternative measure would be more meaningful for exporting countries with governmental trade agencies or exporters' associations with ability to regulate their overall export levels, whereas Measure 1 would be more meaningful for exporting countries with (only) atomistic exporters.

3. Adjusting for Adjustment Costs: A Putty-Clay Model

So far, our analysis was based on the assumption that the choice of optimal production in period 2 was not constrained by the choice of production in period 1. Thus, in Figure 6.1, the economy could move from P_1 or P_2 in period 1 to P_3 in period 2, along the (long-run) transformation curve AB. However, this procedure fails to take into consideration possible adjustment costs: that is, we were essentially dealing with a putty model.

However, this procedure eliminates an important aspect of the problem raised by market disruption. So, in this section, we modify our model and analysis to allow for adjustment costs. However, to simplify the analysis, we take initially the extreme polar case of a putty-clay model, where the production choice made in period 1 cannot be modified *in any way* in period 2.

With this modification, the choice variables now are: X_i, the production of commodity i in periods 1 and 2 ($i = 1,2$); E_1, the net exports of commodity 1 in period 1; and E_2, the net exports of commodity 1 in period 2 when *no* quota is imposed. As before, $\overline{E}$ is the net export of commodity 1 when the quota *is* imposed. Superscripts refer to periods 1 and 2.

Clearly then, the expected welfare ϕ is now as follows:

$$\phi = U^1 [X_1 - E_1, X_2 + \pi E_1] + \rho P(E_1) \underline{U}^2 [X_1 - \overline{E}, X_2 + \pi \overline{E}]$$
$$+ \rho \left\{1 - P(E_1)\right\} \overline{U}^2 [X_1 - E_2, X_2 + \pi E_2]$$

This is then maximized subject to the implicit transformation function, $F(X_1, X_2) = 0$, as before. The first-order conditions for an interior maximum then are:

$$\frac{\partial \phi}{\partial X_1} = U^1_1 + \rho P(E_1)\underline{U}^2_1 + \rho \left\{1 - P(E_1)\right\} \overline{U}^2_1 - \lambda F_1 = 0 \tag{4}$$

$$\frac{\partial \phi}{\partial X_2} = U^1_2 + \rho P(E_2)\underline{U}^2_2 + \rho \left\{1 - P(E_1)\right\} \overline{U}^2_2 - \lambda F_2 = 0 \tag{5}$$

$$\frac{\partial \phi}{\partial E_1} = -U^1_1 + \left\{\pi(E_1) + E_1 \pi'(E_1)\right\} U^1_2$$
$$- \rho P'(E_1) \left\{\overline{U}^2 - \underline{U}^2\right\} = 0 \tag{6}$$

$$\frac{\partial \phi}{\partial E_2} = \rho \left[-\overline{U}_1^2 + \left[\pi(E_2) + E_2 \pi'(E_2) \right] \overline{U}_2^2 \right] \left\{ 1 - P(E_1) \right\} = 0 \quad (7)$$

where $\quad U_j^1 \quad = \dfrac{\partial U[X_1 - E_1, X_2 + \pi E_1]}{\partial X_j}$,

$$\overline{U}_j^2 \quad = \frac{\partial U[X_1 - E_2, X_2 + \pi E_2]}{\partial X_j}, $$

$$\underline{U}_j^2 \quad = \frac{\partial U[X_1 - \overline{E}, X_2 + \pi \overline{E}]}{\partial X_j}, \text{ and}$$

λ = the Lagrangean multiplier associated with the constraint
$F(X_1, X_2) = 0.$

The interpretation of these first-order conditions is straightforward. Condition (7) states that, *given the optimal production levels*, the level of exports in period 2 *when no quota is imposed* must be such as to equate the maringal rate of substitution in consumption to the marginal terms of trade. Condition (6) is identical in form to the one obtained earlier: the optimal exports in period 1 must *not* equate the marginal rate of substitution in consumption in *that* period to the marginal terms of trade, but must instead also allow for the marginal change in expected welfare arising out of the change in probability of a quota being imposed: the latter equals $P'(E_1)(\overline{U}^2 - \underline{U}^2)$ where $\overline{U}^2 = U[X_1 - E_2, X_2 + \pi E_2]$ and $\underline{U}^2 = U[X_1 - \overline{E}, X_2 + \pi \overline{E}]$. Thus, condition (6) ensures the optimal choice of exports in period 1, *given the production levels*. Conditions (4) and (5) then relate to the optimal choice of production levels and, as we would expect, the introduction of adjustment costs does make a difference. Writing (4) and (5) in the familiar ratio form, we get:

$$\frac{F_1}{F_2} = \frac{U_1^1 + \rho P(E_1) \underline{U}_1^2 + \rho \left\{ 1 - P(E_1) \right\} \overline{U}_1^2}{U_2^1 + \rho P(E_1) \underline{U}_2^2 + \rho \left\{ 1 - P(E_1) \right\} \overline{U}_2^2}. \quad (8)$$

Clearly therefore the marginal rate of transformation in production (in periods 1 and 2, identically, as production in period 1 will carry over into period 2 by assumption), that is, F_1/F_2, must *not* equal the marginal rate of substitution in consumption in period 1, that is, U_1^1/U_2^1 (unlike our earlier analysis without adjustment costs in Sections 1 and 2). Rather, F_1/F_2 should equal a term which properly takes into account the fact that production choices once made in period 1 cannot be changed in period 2 to suit the state (the imposition or absence of a quota) obtaining in period 2. Eq. (8) can be readily interpreted as follows.

The *LHS* is, of course, the marginal rate of transformation in production. The *RHS* represents the marginal rate of substitution in consumption, if *reinterpreted* in the following sense. Suppose that the output of commodity 1, the exportable, is increased by one unit in period 1 (and hence in period 2 as well, by assumption). Given an optimal trade policy, then, the impact of this on welfare can be examined by adding it to consumption in each period. Thus social utility is increased in period 1 by U_1^1 while in period 2 it will increase by $\overline{U}_1^2$ if no quota is imposed and by $\underline{U}_1^2$ if the quota is imposed. Thus, the discounted increase in period-2 welfare is given as: $\rho \left[\underline{U}_1^2 P(E_1) + \overline{U}_1^2 (1 - P(E_1)) \right]$. Thus, the total expected welfare impact of a unit increase in the production of commodity 1 is:

$$U_1^1 + \rho \left[\underline{U}_1^2 P(E_1) + \overline{U}_1^2 (1 - P(E_1)) \right] .$$

Similarly, a decrease in the production of commodity 2 by a unit in period 1 (and hence in period 2 as well) reduces expected welfare by

$$U_2^1 + \rho \left[\underline{U}_2^2 P(E_1) + \overline{U}_2^2 \ 1 - P(E_1)) \right] .$$

Hence, the ratio of these two expressions, just derived, represents the "true" marginal rate of substitution, and this indeed is the *RHS* in eq. (8) to which the marginal rate of transformation in production$-F_1/F_2$, the *LHS* in eq. (8)$-$is to be equated for optimality.

The optimal policy interventions in this modified model with adjustment costs are immediately evident from eqs. (6) to (8) and the preceding analysis. Thus, in period 1, the ratio U_1^1/U_2^1 is clearly the relative price of commodity 1 (in terms of commodity 2) facing consumers, while $\pi(E_1)$ is the average terms of trade. Thus U_1^1/U_2^1 differs from $\pi(E_1)$ by $[\pi' E_1 - \dfrac{\rho P'(E_1) \left\{ \overline{U}^2 - \underline{U}^2 \right\}}{U_2^1}]$ and this difference constitutes a consumption tax on the importable, commodity 2. An identical difference between F_1/F_2, the relative price facing producers, and $\pi(E_1)$ would define a production tax on commodity 2 at the same rate, so that a tariff at this rate would constitute the appropriate intervention in the model with no adjustment costs. However, *with adjustment costs*, eq. (8) defines, for period 1, the appropriate production tax-cum-subsidy which, in general, will diverge from the appropriate consumption tax: so that the optimal mix of policies in the model with adjustment costs will involve a tariff (reflecting both the monopoly power in trade and the QR possibility) *plus* a production tax-cum-subsidy in period 1.[6] In period 2, in both the models (with and without adjustment costs), an appropriate intervention in the form of a tariff (to exploit monopoly power) would be called for; however, with production fixed at period-1 levels in the adjustment-cost model, a consumption tax-cum-subsidy would equally suffice. Specifically, note that in period 2, with adjustment costs, the price-ratio facing consumers would be $\overline{U}_1^2/\overline{U}_2^2$ if no quota is imposed, with the average terms of trade at $\pi(E_2)$, and the producer's price-ratio (as defined along the putty-transformation frontier) would be F_1/F_2; on the other hand, if the quota is imposed, these values change to $\underline{U}_1^2/\underline{U}_2^2$, $\pi(\overline{E})$ and F_1/F_2, respectively. The consumption tax-cum-subsidy and the equivalent tariff (with no impact on production decision, already frozen at period-1 levels) are then defined by these divergences, depending on whether the quota obtains or not.

A tabular comparison of the characteristics of the optimal solution, with and without adjustment costs, is presented in Table 6.4 and should assist the reader.

Note that the above results are quite consistent with the basic propositions of the theory of distortions, as developed in Bhagwati and Ramaswami (1963), Johnson (1965), and Bhagwati (1971): the first-best, optimal policy intervention for the case with adjustment costs requires a trade policy to adjust for the foreign distortion (represented by the effect of current exports on the period-2 probability of a quota being invoked) and a production tax-cum-subsidy to adjust for the existence of adjustment costs in production. It also follows, from the equivalence propositions, that the combination of the optimal tariff and the optimal production tax-cum-subsidy can be reproduced identically by a tariff set at the "net" production tax-cum-subsidy required by the optimal solution plus a consumption tax-cum-subsidy. Similarly, while our analysis has been focused on first-best policy intervention, the fundamental results of the theory of distortions and welfare on second-best policies also can be immediately applied to our problem. Thus, if there are zero adjustment costs so that there is only the foreign distortion in period 1, then clearly a production tax-cum-subsidy will *improve* (but not maximize) welfare. Similarly, if there are adjustment costs as well,

Table 6.4 Characteristics of Optimal Solutions in Models With and Without Adjustment Costs[a]

	No Adjustment Costs	Adjustment Costs
Period 1	$DRS_1 \neq FRT_1$	$DRS_1 \neq FRT_1$
	$DRS_1 = DRT_1$	$DRS_1 \neq DRT_1$
Period 2	$DRS_2 = DRT_2$	$DRS_2 = FRT_2$
	$= FRT_2$	(DRT_2 not relevant as production is frozen at period-1 levels)

[a]DRS, DRT, and FRT represent the marginal rates of substitution in consumption, domestic transformation, and foreign transformation, respectively. For an earlier use of these abbreviation see Bhagwati, Ramaswami, and Srinivasan (1969). Since we are considering an interior maximum, the inequalities do *not* include corner equilibria, of course. The subscripts refer to the periods, 1 and 2.

then there will be *two* distortions and then we would have applicable here the Bhagwati-Ramaswami-Srinivasan (1969) proposition that no feasible, welfare-improving form of intervention may exist if both of the policy measures that will secure optimal intervention cannot be used simultaneously.

Notes

1 The full-length *JIE* paper also extends the analysis to lesser rigidity and to steady state analysis.

2 This method of introducing market disruption presupposes that the QR-level is pre-specified but that the probability of its being imposed will be a function of how deeply the market is penetrated in the importing country and therefore how effective the import-competing industry's pressure for protection will be vis-à-vis the importing country's government. The effect of modifying this simplifying assumption so as to allow for varying levels of quota is noted later in this section.

3 Instead of assuming that the fixed quota of $\overline{E}$ will be imposed with probability $P(E)$, one could assume that a quota of $\overline{E}$ will be imposed with probability density $P(\overline{E}, E)$. In other words, the quota level $\overline{E}$ is variable and the probability of imposition depends both on the level $\overline{E}$ and on the quantum of exports E in the first period. Let $f(\overline{E})$ denote the maximum of $U(C_1, C_2)$ subject to $F(X_1, X_2) = 0$ and $E \leqslant \overline{E}$ where $C_1 = (X_1 - E_1)$ and $C_2 = (X_2 + \pi E_1)$. Then the expected welfare in period 2, given the export level E in the first period, is $\int f(\overline{E}) P(\overline{E}, E) d\overline{E}$. Let us denote this by $h(E)$. Thus the maximand ϕ now becomes $U[X_1 - E, X_2 + \pi E] + \rho h(E)$ and condition (3′) becomes $\dfrac{U_1}{U_2} = \pi + \pi' E + \dfrac{\rho h'(E)}{U_2}$. Now $h'(E)$ is the change in expected welfare in period 2 due to an additional unit of export in period 1 and this has to be added to the marginal terms of trade $\pi + \pi' E$. Nothing substantive therefore changes. Note however that if we allow for *many* exporting countries and if the *share* in the overall quota level granted in period 2 to *one* exporting country will increase with the export level achieved by that country in period 1, this would produce an incentive to *increase*, rather than decrease, the export level in period 1, ceteris paribus. Hence, our analysis based on one exporting country would need to be modified correspondingly.

4 However, we cannot assert that $\phi_{NQ}^L > \phi_Q^{OPT}$ except in the case of a small country with no influence on the terms of trade; this follows from the fact that ϕ_{NQ}^L is no longer the first-best policy in the presence of monopoly power in trade, so that $\overline{U}^*$ may well exceed $\overline{U}$ in Table 6.3.

5 Needless to say, for a country with no monopoly power, it is not meaningful to think of market disruption leading to QR's: if the country is indeed atomistic in foreign markets, its exports surely will not cause market disruption. Our analysis, of course, allows for monopoly power; only Figure 6.1 illustrates the simple case of a small country.

6 It should be pointed out that atomistic firms in period 1 are assumed to respond to that period's prices only. This assumption can be justified on the ground that they are likely to assume that these prices will carry over into the next period, since there is no other, obvious mechanism by which they can anticipate the "true" period-2 prices.

References

Bhagwati, J., and V. K. Ramaswami, 1963, "Domestic Distortions, Tariffs and the Theory of Optimum Subsidy," *Journal of Political Economy*.

Bhagwati, J., and T. N. Srinivasan, 1969, "Optimal Intervention to Achieve Non-Economic Objectives," *Review of Economic Studies*, January.

Bhagwati, J., V. K. Ramaswami, and T. N. Srinivasan, 1969, "Domestic Distortions, Tariffs, and the Theory of Optimum Subsidy: Some Further Results," *Journal of Political Economy*.

Bhagwati, J., 1971, "The Generalized Theory of Distortions and Welfare," in Bhagwati et al. (ed.), *Trade, Balance of Payments and Growth*, North Holland Co., Amsterdam.

Brecher, R., 1974, "Optimal Commercial Policy for a Minimum-Wage Economy," *Journal of International Economics*, May.

Haberler, G., 1950, "Some Problems in the Pure Theory of International Trade," *Economic Journal*, June.

Johnson, H. G., 1965, "Optimal Trade Intervention in the Presence of Domestic Distortions," in R. E. Caves, P. B. Kenen, and H. G. Johnson (ed.), *Trade, Growth and the Balance of Payments*, North Holland Co., Amsterdam.

Mayer, W., 1974, "Short-run and Long-run Equilibrium for a Small, Open Economy," *Journal of Political Economy*, September/October.

Comment
Isaiah Frank

One of the many things I have always liked about Jagdish Bhagwati is that he is an economic theorist who never loses sight of the ultimate purpose of the analytic work in terms of its application to issues of public policy. This paper is no exception.

Bhagwati demonstrates that even the *threat* of protectionist measures by importing countries on grounds of market disruption imposes a welfare loss on exporting countries, though less of a loss than the *actual* imposition of restrictions. From this proposition, plus a critical analysis of U.S. legislation on import relief and the GATT escape clause, Bhagwati comes up with a novel and highly imaginative proposal for the reform of the present approach to the problem of safeguards against market disruption.

One basic fact stands out with respect to both U.S. domestic escape-clause legislation and GATT Article XIX. Over the past thirty years the number of cases in which restrictions have been imposed on the basis of those provisions has been remarkably small. I need not cite the numbers—it is all documented in detail in Bhagwati's paper.

In the case of the United States, there have been a fair number of escape-clause applications, but very few have successfully satisfied the stringent criteria of U.S. law. Until recently the law required not only that the injury to the domestic industry had to be primarily due to increased imports, but that the increased imports in turn had to be primarily caused by a trade agreement concession. Few cases could satisfy the latter criterion. The Trade Act of 1974 eliminated the requirement of a causal link between increased imports and concessions, and loosened considerably the required link between serious injury and increased imports. It is doubtful, however, whether the present more accommodating provisions will lead to a substantial increase in the number of U.S. escape-clause restrictions.

Article XIX of GATT has also rarely been invoked by any country. As explained by Jan Tumlier in an incisive article published recently, the reasons are primarily the GATT requirement that escape-clause action be applied on a nondiscriminatory basis to all exporters, and the GATT sanctioning of retaliatory action in the form of the withdrawal of equivalent concessions by any adversely affected exporter.

Unfortunately, the infrequency of resort to these escape-clause provisions does not reflect a happy state of affairs. On the contrary, import restrictions in cases of market disruption have in fact been widely applied by many countries, but without benefit of formal invocation of escape clauses, including their criteria for determining injury and other substantive and procedural constraints. One particularly insidious form of such restrictions has been so-called "voluntary export restraints" (VERs), including those embodied in the Arrangement Regarding International Trade in Textiles.

Bhagwati's remedy calls for a radical overhaul of Article XIX of GATT insofar as it applies to developing countries. Without going into the details of his proposals, they would in essence require that importing developed countries provide financial compensation to exporting LDCs for maintaining the right to invoke a market-disruption-related trade restraint on particular products. Additional compensation would be paid as and when trade restraints were actually invoked. With respect to products not on the "list of potentially restrainable items," import restrictions could nonetheless be imposed but only subject to a demonstration of serious injury under GATT auspices and a payment of still larger financial compensation to the exporting countries.

Despite the innovative nature of Bhagwati's proposals, I believe they overreach the goal of market disruption policy. Bhagwati is absolutely right that the mere threat of protective measures distorts resource allocation in the LDCs, discouraging investment in industries with export potential. One of our prime goals should, therefore, be to reduce the uncertainty of market access. But will developed countries agree to a system of financial compensation for maintaining what they regard as their legitimate right to invoke safeguards? And if so, would the requirement for compensation in itself serve as a major deterrent? And to what extent would the compensation be additional to rather than a substitute for conventional forms of resource transfers to LDCs? I confess to serious doubts on all these scores.

In designing public policies, I believe there is a great advantage in avoiding sharp breaks with the past; in trying to achieve our goals by building on what already exists. In an era when comparative advantage can shift very abruptly, safeguards are essential for reducing the economic and social costs of the transition to the new resource allocation and for containing and controlling domestic political pressures for severe import restrictions. The prime policy objective should be to gain international acceptance of firm limits on the duration as well as the severity of such restrictions. Precedent for such limitations already exists in the U.S. Trade Act of 1974. That legislation provides that import relief must be temporary in nature. It may be granted for a five-year period, with one possible extension for three years, but is to be phased down after the first three years. If the safeguard action takes the form of a quantitative restriction, the quota may not be less than the value of imports during a recent representative period.

I hold no particular brief for these precise provisions, but they do in my view suggest the general lines along which to consider a new GATT approach.

I would eliminate the most-favored-nation requirement for safeguard action as well as the sanction for retaliation. In their place I would substitute four elements: strict time limits on safeguard measures; degressivity of the restriction; a minimum level below which imports may not be reduced; and a system of multilateral surveillance of actions taken under the new rules. Such provisions, particularly if combined with liberal adjustment assistance, would go a long way toward reconciling the developed countries' legitimate need for a safety valve in cases of market disruption with the developing countries' need to minimize the uncertainty of market access. And for the United States at least, this type of multilateral approach would be basically in line with existing policy and practice.

One quick word on "voluntary export restraints" which, Bhagwati points out, are the main form that restrictive measures have taken in the past. Except for textiles (where a system of voluntary restraints has been built into a formal intergovernmental arrangement), such measures usually bypass existing national and international constraints on safeguard actions. They are adopted by exporting countries primarily because of the implicit or explicit threat by importing countries of more drastic formal restrictions in the absence of the so-called voluntary restraints. In the case of many Japanese voluntary restraints, however, resistance by exporters was tempered by the opportunities provided by the restraints for the cartelization of the industry, including sanction for the fixing of prices and the allocation of export markets.

My own view is that LDC exporters to the United States should not allow themselves to be bamboozled into adopting export restraints by the threat of formal import restrictions. Few cases of voluntary restraints would have stood up to the exacting provisions of U.S. law on import relief, and LDC exporters would be well advised to resist extralegal pressures. In order to reduce the temptation of importing countries to resort to this soft option, however, I would make the proposed new approach to a multilateral safeguard provision applicable to requests for voluntary export restraints as well as to mandatory import restrictions.

More generally, I believe public resistance to import restrictions, particularly on the type of labor-intensive consumer goods typically exported by the developing countries, is stiffer than ever in the industrial countries. Developing countries can count on strong counterpressures in importing countries— deriving from the concern about inflation and the growing strength of the organized consumer movement. Only last April the President rejected import restrictions on shoes (exported by Brazil, Taiwan, and South Korea, among others), despite a unanimous finding of injury by the International Trade Commission. Consumers' Union was active in opposing restrictions, and the President's decision was influenced heavily by the likelihood of higher prices for consumers if import restraints were imposed. Including shoes, there have been fourteen applications for import relief under the easier escape-clause provisions of the Trade Act of 1974, but only specialty steel has received relief. And this record reflects experience during a recession when one would have expected maximum pressure for import relief.

In short, I believe that LDC export pessimism as related to manufactured products is largely misguided insofar as it rests on the imminent U.S. imposition of trade restrictions if their export drive proves successful. This response has not been typical in the past, and is even less likely to be so in the future if the type of multilateral safeguard provision I have suggested is adopted. Except for textiles and clothing, the U.S. market for LDC manufactures is wide open in the sense that quantitative restrictions are nonexistent. And with flexible exchange rates and rapidly shifting comparative advantage, remaining tariffs are becoming progressively less important. (Japan and some European countries have been substantially more restrictive on the basis of administrative and informal controls. In such cases the objective should be to bring their actions within the purview of the proposed new set of multilateral safeguard provisions.)

Recent annual growth rates for LDC manufactured exports (15 percent by volume from 1965 to 1971; 20 percent from 1965 to 1973) attest to the tremendous opportunities for augmenting foreign exchange earnings by this route. Highest priority should be assigned, therefore, not only to the objective of maintaining open markets in the developed countries, but also to ensuring that, within the LDCs, full advantage is taken of these rapidly growing opportunities through internal policies designed to eliminate disincentives to appropriate supply responses.

Comment
John Williamson

When Jagdish Bhagwati sent me the first draft of this paper I responded by making two comments. The first was that I liked the idea in the paper very much. It uses economic theory in order to address an important problem which has received inadequate attention in the past, and devises a solution which appears to respect the realities of political pressures in the developed countries while playing on the guilt feelings which most of them suffer when they feel obliged to impede a successful program of LDC export promotion. I have since tried the idea out on one or two European officials, and I have encountered two criticisms. One is that it would be too easy for DCs to surrender to protectionist pressures, since payment of compensation would enable this to be done with a clear conscience. The force of this criticism obviously depends on the level at which compensation payments would be set. The other criticism stems from the fact that VERs have (at least in certain European countries) been directed principally against Japan, and it was made perfectly clear that any proposal to make compensation payments to Japan would be a nonstarter. Since the Bhagwati proposal is confined to compensation of LDCs, however, this criticism is not pertinent. Hence my limited soundings have not led me to modify my initial reaction that this proposal might be negotiable if the LDCs decided to push it.

My second comment was that the paper lacked an important section. The revised draft still omits that section, so I interpret my appearance as a discussant as a minimum-cost strategy for remedying this omission.

The missing section concerns the calculation of compensation payments. Given the problems of international negotiation and the lack of any executive international authority, I think we can take it as axiomatic that one must seek a set of general rules which can be agreed ex ante and then be applied quasi-automatically, rather than allowing compensation payments to be determined ad hoc in each individual case. The rules governing compensation payments should clearly be designed to build in pressures to liberalize trade, and they should also avoid the creation of incentives to distort trade by either developed or developing countries. The latter principle implies the desirability of at least roughly reimbursing the harm actually done by the imposition of export restraints.

The Bhagwati proposal envisages the classification of all trade flows from developing to developed countries into one of four categories: (1) unrestrained items; (2) potentially restrainable items; (3) protected items; (4) items protected under the escape-clause procedure. Items in category (1) do not require a compensation payment.

A natural way to calculate compensation for items in category (2) would be to charge a fixed percentage, α, of the value of imports of listed items. Since the harm actually done by placing items on the list of potentially restrainable items is the increase in risk to LDC exporters that access to DC markets will be curtailed, the charge would appropriately be fairly modest: I suppose that a rate of 5 percent of the value of listed imports would indicate the order of magnitude that might be involved.

Compensation for the actual imposition of protection, that is, the transfer of items into category (3), should be at a substantially higher rate β, both so as to introduce a pressure for trade liberalization and to reimburse the harm actually done. An appropriate value for β might, perhaps, be of in the order of 25 percent. The conceptually appropriate base against which to levy this charge is clearly the value of trade which is *prevented* by the constraint, again so as to provide an appropriate incentive for liberalization and to reimburse actual harm. Trade prevented is not, of course, an observable magnitude, so that it would be necessary to develop general principles which would permit reasonable estimates of trade prevention to be constructed. Since trade prevented is the difference between the hypothetical level that imports would have attained in the absence of restraints and the actual level of permitted imports, the problem lies in constructing a reasonable estimate of the nonrestrained import level. The latter might be estimated as the actual level on some base date t_o compounded by a growth rate g over the intervening period, rather than the actual level in a period immediately prior to the imposition of restraints, so as to avoid both any incentive for LDCs to artificially accelerate exports when it became apparent that restraint was probable, and to provide progressively larger compensation payments over time if import restraints were not relaxed. The growth factor g, which should in principle represent the expected growth rate of imports had restraints not been imposed, might be estimated on the basis of the growth of domestic consumption, and/or the growth of consumption of the item in all DCs, and/or the growth rate of all DCs' imports from LDCs. The base date t_o might be the time when the item was placed on the list of potentially restrainable items, or, if that date was so far in the past as to yield figures out of line with subsequent developments, a time some set period (say, two years) prior to the imposition of restraints.

The combination of the suggested rules for items in categories (2) and (3) might make it financially advantageous for a DC to impose a very mild import restraint, so as to pay compensation even at the high rate β on a very small base of trade prevented, rather than at the lower rate α on the much larger base of all trade. The simplest way of avoiding this undesirable incentive to distort and restrict trade would be to provide that the minimum payment on category (3) items be some fixed percentage larger than the sum that would be payable if the item were in category (2). This would provide an incentive to restrict the imposition of restraints to occasions when the domestic pressures for protection were very strong.

A penal rate would apply to items in category (4), which were protected under the escape-clause procedure. The penal rate should obviously be substantially higher than, say double, the value of β but in other respects the calculations could follow the principles for category (3) items. It would be necessary to specify a minimum length of time τ (two years?) for which an item would have to be in category (2) before it could be transferred to category (3), if DCs were to be prevented from evading the escape-clause penalty. And it would then be natural for the penalty rate to be applied for a period which would make the total time spent in categories (2) and (4) sum to the minimum period τ. One might even strengthen the penalty by continuing to levy the category (2) compensation *as well* for the remainder of the period τ.

The preceding discussion leads me to conclude that the Bhagwati proposal cannot be dismissed on the basis of any supposed impossibility of constructing ex ante general rules which would have the desired set of incentives and result in some sort of rough justice. On the other hand, the approach outlined by Isaiah Frank in his discussion, and the proposals being pursued by the LDCs in GATT (as reported by Gardner Patterson in the general discussion), would also seem capable of providing reasonably satisfactory solutions to this important problem.

7

Access to Supplies and the New International Economic Order
C. Fred Bergsten

Introduction

A major component of the proposed new international economic order (NIEO) is a revised set of institutional arrangements to improve the returns to developing countries from their exports of primary products. Indeed, the success of the OPEC countries in achieving such increased earnings was the proximate trigger of the entire debate over a NIEO.[1] New commodity arrangements could take a variety of forms: agreements among producing and consuming countries on individual products, the "common fund" proposed by UNCTAD to finance a series (originally eighteen, subsequently ten) of such producer-consumer agreements, or joint action by producing countries alone through "producers' associations." All such approaches have one common denominator: they envisage cutbacks in commodity exports whenever necessary to maintain, or increase, the earnings of the producing countries.

Four different techniques—export quotas, export taxes, quantitative limits on domestic production, and taxes on domestic production—have already been used to achieve such export cutbacks, with a number of notable successes.[2] Some OPEC members applied a total embargo on oil sales to some importing countries, and some have deliberately limited production to achieve and subsequently preserve the drastic increase in oil prices. Most members of the International Bauxite Association have levied sizable production taxes on bauxite output, which amount in practice to export taxes because virtually all of the output is exported, and thus have raised their bauxite earnings by factors ranging from four to seven.[3] Within the International Tin Agreement, producing countries maintained export quotas well into 1976 and pushed the price of tin to the ceiling then contained in the agreement. The members of the Union of Banana Exporting Countries (UPEB) levied new export taxes in an effort to raise their total revenues. Members of the Intergovernmental Council of Copper Exporting Countries (CIPEC) adopted explict export quotas in late 1974, and then production quotas in 1975—which contributed significantly to a rebound of about 20 percent from the previous sharp decline in the copper price.[4]

This particular component of the proposed NIEO thus runs directly counter to the traditional concerns of consuming countries to retain assured access to foreign supplies at reasonable prices. These concerns are most acute regarding necessary foodstuffs and industrial raw materials, particularly energy sources, and less so regarding more marginal commodities (such as tea and cocoa). They are most pronounced in countries which are heavily dependent on imports, such as Japan, and less so in countries which are at least partially self-sufficient (notably in United States[5]). Nevertheless, the concern is sufficiently widespread across commodities and countries to make it appear as a source of major bargaining strength for the developing countries.[6]

The issue of access to supplies thus enters the debate over a NIEO in several ways. It provides an important incentive for the industrialized countries to accede to some of the demands of the developing countries. Conversely, it offers a possibility for concessions by the developing countries—the acceptance of limitations on their use of export controls—which could move forward the whole NIEO negotiation. Third, it raises acutely the issue of the distribution of NIEO effects *among* developing countries because most of them would actually suffer from higher world commodity prices,[7] and thus calls for solution if the Group of 77 wishes to minimize its internal tensions.

This paper will examine in detail one component of a possible solution to the problem of assuring access to supplies: a reform of the GATT rules to limit the use of export controls. It will then suggest alternative ways in which such reform could be linked to other aspects of the commodity issue, a link that will probably be necessary if a lasting agreement is to be negotiated.

The Issue of Export Controls

The GATT rules, which have governed international trade throughout the postwar period, have from their inception suffered a major gap in coverage. GATT has focused almost wholly on the problem of access to markets. Its specific efforts have been devoted to deterring countries from increasing their barriers to imports (and, to a lesser extent, their subsidies to exports), and to sponsoring a series of negotiations to reduce existing barriers to imports. Through these efforts, the GATT has played a major role in preventing a repetition of the trade conflict of the interwar period, and has contributed to increased world welfare through the reduction of traditional trade barriers.[8] The dramatic success of the developing countries in expanding their exports of manufactured products, in particular, would almost certainly have been impossible in the absence of this liberal international regime.[9]

The GATT, however, has in practice virtually ignored the issue of access to supplies. Its stated prohibition of export quotas has been meaningless because of the numerous exceptions thereto, and there are no GATT references whatsoever to export taxes. Thus GATT has focused almost wholly on the problems of sellers, and paid little attention to the problems of buyers.

The historical evolution of the asymmetry between international treatment of import and export controls is curious. Rules were developed against import barriers because the erection of such barriers was perceived as playing a major role in broadening and deepening the Great Depression, and thereby contributing to the onset of World War II. The erection of export barriers also played a major role in world economics and politics, however, in the years just preceding both world wars.[10] issue of access to supplies was indeed one of the factors underlying the expansionist policies of Japan and Germany which caused the World War II, and Roosevelt and Churchill called, in the Atlantic Charter, for "access, on equal terms, to the trade and raw materials of the world." There had been numerous efforts to develop international rules to deal with the problem in the interwar years dating from Woodrow Wilson's Fourteen Points, one of which "contemplated fair and equitable understanding as to the distribution of raw materials," and twenty-nine countries signed a draft convention on Import *and Export* Prohibitions and Restrictions in 1929 (italics added).[11]

Nevertheless, the postwar economic institutions did nothing to deal with the issue. Conventional economic wisdom feared renewed recession or worse. The concerns of most countries centered on their ability to export sufficiently, especially to the United States, to purchase needed imports. There were few worries about excess demand. The political weakness of most of the countries (many of which were still colonies) that relied on primary products for their export earnings supported this sense of complacency.

The one powerful primary producer, the United States, supported a complete GATT ban on export restrictions but did not carry the issue. The charter of the proposed International Trade Organization did include a chapter on "Inter-Governmental Commodity Agreements," which while primarily aimed at avoiding price declines did call for equal voting rights for importing countries and "assure[d] availability of supplies adequate at all times for world demand," but of course this charter was never implemented. Hence the postwar economic order began with a major gap concerning the issue of access to supplies.

Access to supplies became a serious matter of international concern again during the commodity boom spurred by the Korean War. Concomitantly, GATT made its only serious effort to implement the existing rules on export controls (GATT, 1950). However, nothing came of the effort as commodity prices declined after 1951[12] and the use of export controls—except for strategic purposes by the United States and other COCOM countries against the Communist countries—faded into the past.

Why No Action?

Countries employ export controls for three basic purposes:

1. *Exportation of their inflation* to other countries, by keeping goods at home

and avoiding disruption of domestic price controls.[13] This was the purpose of the U.S. export controls on soybeans in 1973, and the less formal restraint on agricultural sales in both 1974 and 1975.

2. *Improvement of their terms of trade*, by restricting output or levying export taxes on products with low price elasticities of demand and by promoting domestic processing industries through giving them preferential access to local raw materials. This aspect of export controls is of course the focus of the NIEO debate.

3. *Politically inspired denial of their products to others*, as in the case of COCOM countries vis-à-vis Communist countries and Arab oil producers against the United States and Netherlands.[14]

The international community found little need to devise international rules to deal with export controls during the first postwar generation, because underlying economic and political conditions precluded the use of such measures for the first two purposes and controls of the third type were not in any event susceptible to trading rules. Except for the brief period surrounding the Korean War, world inflation was moderate until the early 1970s. Commodity prices were relatively stable, and some even declined relative to overall price indexes. Hence buyers had little concern over the possible use of export controls. Indeed, the United States periodically dumped sizable portions of its agricultural output on the world market through PL 480 and other concessional sales programs.

This prevalence of buyers' markets also sharply limited the opportunity of commodity sellers to use export controls to strengthen their terms of trade. Indeed, producing countries sought the help of consumers in several commodities (such as tin and coffee) to protect them against price declines. There was little effective collaboration among exporting countries until the early 1970s, although OPEC (1960) and CIPEC (1967) had been formed earlier.

Export controls inspired by political objectives could not be covered by the usual type of international trading rules. Most were based on contemporary perceptions of "national security," for which exemptions are provided in virtually all international economic covenants. Most of those adopted were aimed at countries basically outside the institutional arrangements maintained by the market economies, and hence not covered by their rules anyway.[15]

The New Situation

All three of these conditions have changed significantly in the 1970s, and much of the change seems likely to persist.

Inflation has moved up alongside unemployment as the cardinal domestic economic problem in most countries. Simultaneously, most countries are becoming increasingly enmeshed in the world economy and hence more exposed to external developments. Hence countries are increasingly seeking ways to use their foreign economic policies to avoid importing inflation, and even to export some of their home-grown inflation to others. As a result, export controls have reemerged as a major issue in international economic relations.

All of the large industrialized countries have employed such controls in recent years.[16] The United States has probably done so most frequently, with its repeated limitations on a wide range of agricultural products (soybeans and wheat) and industrial raw materials (logs and fertilizers). The EEC has used export taxes on a number of products to keep its food prices from rising to world levels. Japan, largely informally, checked sales of petroleum-based synthetics to processors in other countries during the height of the energy crisis. The use of export controls to export inflation has of course ebbed as the rate of price increase has declined with the recession and into the early phase of recovery, though the United States again imposed informal controls on wheat exports in 1975.

Export controls to improve national terms of trade have continued throughout the recession and decline in world inflation. To be sure, the sellers' markets for commodities which arise from rapid economic growth—especially when accompanied by rapid inflation—make such actions more feasible. But OPEC has limited the erosion of the world oil price by limiting production. The members of the International Bauxite Association maintained their higher production taxes throughout the recession.[17] The members of CIPEC cut production sharply and triggered some recovery in the price of copper, and the tin exporters maintained such tight export quotas that the agreement's ceiling had to be raised in mid-1976. Other efforts include the export quotas employed by a number of coffee producers (notably Brazil, which became a net importer from 1972 to 1973 and may shortly do so again), and the export taxes levied by the members of the Union of Banana Producing Countries since 1974.

Export controls are of course a standard policy tool of "producers' associations." In addition to the six groups already mentioned, associations have been formed for at least seven additional commodities: iron ore, natural rubber, mercury, tungsten, tropical timber (in both Africa and Southeast Asia), manganese, and pepper. The price elasticities of both supply and demand are quite low for many of these products, and appear to have declined further in recent years for both economic and political reasons.[18] OPEC and IBA have demonstrated that producer groups can succeed. The absence of an effective response by importing countries to either has further encouraged producer efforts.

Many analysts have expressed doubts over the lasting success of any such use of export controls.[19] In 1975 and early 1976, several of the efforts were indeed blunted by the weakening of the commodity markets. In addition, some of the North-South political tension which has triggered the cartel efforts has been eased by the shift of the United States from total unwillingness to even discuss commodity issues (as late as April 1975) to its high-level initiatives to discuss all important international commodities.[20] Virtually all agree, however, that frequent efforts to exercise such market power are highly probable. Hence the issue will undoubtedly remain important for international economic relationships, whatever the longer-term outcome of the various steps—especially as commodity markets strengthen with the recovery of the world economy and particularly if the United States fails to sustain its newly cooperative approach toward the producing countries.

The use of export controls to promote national terms of trade goes well beyond producers' associations, of course. It extends to individual countries in a position to exercise price leadership for a particular product. Recent examples include Malaysia in natural rubber, Morocco in phosphates, and Brazil in coffee. Such price leadership may coexist with either tight or informal cartel arrangements, or be conducted purely on its own. And many countries have used export controls in an effort to promote more domestic processing of their foodstuffs (soluble coffee in Brazil) and raw materials (leather goods in Pakistan and Brazil). Canada amended its Export and Import Permits Act in May 1974 to authorize export controls "to ensure that any action taken to promote the further processing in Canada of a natural resource that is produced in Canada is not rendered ineffective by reason of the unrestricted exportation of the natural resource."

Finally, the use of export controls for international political purposes also seems likely to proliferate. Increasing international economic interdependence has increased the vulnerability of practically every country to external economic forces, and hence increased the potential political leverage of export controls.[21] The onset of détente has nudged aside the security blanket that smothered many international economic disputes into the 1960s, as alliance politics dominated overall international relations.

Most importantly, historically novel asymmetries have developed between the military and economic power of individual nations. Traditionally, countries have been either great powers or weaklings in *both* realms. Now, however, we are witnessing the unprecedented emergence of relatively defenseless economic powers and economically destitute military powers. On the one extreme lies Abu Dhabi, with its oil wealth and total military vulnerability. On the other lies India, with its nuclear capacity and powerful conventional forces but also its poverty level of per capita income and constant susceptibility to mass starvation. Such asymmetries had already developed in the 1960s, on a lesser scale, between the United States and the other industrialized countries. Western Europe and Japan remained dependent on the United States for their military security, but became its equal (or, in some regards, superior) on international economic issues.

These developments provide an almost irresistible impulse to countries to link economic and political issues, thus destroying the "two-track system"— which underlay much of the stability of the early postwar economic order—in

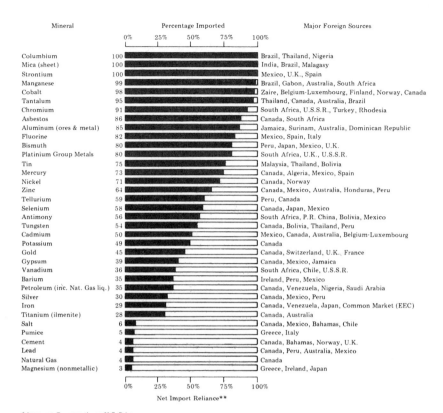

Mineral	Percentage Imported	Major Foreign Sources
Columbium	100	Brazil, Thailand, Nigeria
Mica (sheet)	100	India, Brazil, Malagasy
Strontium	100	Mexico, U.K., Spain
Manganese	99	Brazil, Gabon, Australia, South Africa
Cobalt	98	Zaire, Belgium-Luxembourg, Finland, Norway, Canada
Tantalum	95	Thailand, Canada, Australia, Brazil
Chromium	91	South Africa, U.S.S.R., Turkey, Rhodesia
Asbestos	86	Canada, South Africa
Aluminum (ores & metal)	85	Jamaica, Surinam, Australia, Dominican Republic
Fluorine	82	Mexico, Spain, Italy
Bismuth	80	Peru, Japan, Mexico, U.K.
Platinium Group Metals	80	South Africa, U.K., U.S.S.R.
Tin	75	Malaysia, Thailand, Bolivia
Mercury	73	Canada, Algeria, Mexico, Spain
Nickel	71	Canada, Norway
Zinc	64	Canada, Mexico, Australia, Honduras, Peru
Tellurium	59	Peru, Canada
Selenium	58	Canada, Japan, Mexico
Antimony	56	South Africa, P.R. China, Bolivia, Mexico
Tungsten	54	Canada, Bolivia, Thailand, Peru
Cadmium	50	Mexico, Canada, Australia, Belgium-Luxembourg
Potassium	49	Canada
Gold	45	Canada, Switzerland, U.K., France
Gypsum	39	Canada, Mexico, Jamaica
Vanadium	36	South Africa, Chile, U.S.S.R.
Barium	35	Ireland, Peru, Mexico
Petroleum (inc. Nat. Gas liq.)	35	Canada, Venezuela, Nigeria, Saudi Arabia
Silver	30	Canada, Mexico, Peru
Iron	29	Canada, Venezuela, Japan, Common Market (EEC)
Titanium (ilmenite)	28	Canada, Australia
Salt	6	Canada, Mexico, Bahamas, Chile
Pumice	5	Greece, Italy
Cement	4	Canada, Bahamas, Norway, U.K.
Lead	4	Canada, Peru, Australia, Mexico
Natural Gas	4	Canada
Magnesium (nonmetallic)	3	Greece, Ireland, Japan

Net Import Reliance**

*Apparent Consumption = U.S. Primary
+ Secondary Production + Net Import
Reliance

**Net Import Reliance = Imports − Exports
± Gov't Stockpile and Industry
Stock Changes

Figure 7.1 Imports supplied significant percentage of minerals and metals consumption in 1975.* Source: Bureau of Mines, U.S. Department of the Interior (import-export data from Bureau of the Census, July 1976)

which the two were kept largely separate.[22] Economic powers will use their comparative bargaining advantage to promote their security objectives, as the Arabs did with oil from 1973 to 1974. Military powers will be tempted to do likewise to extract economic concessions, as the United States did to some extent with Germany on the military offset issue throughout the 1960s. To the extent that countries possess economic power by virtue of their possession of key individual products, particularly raw materials, export controls will be used increasingly for broad political purposes. Unlike the long-standing use of such controls against Communist countries, any further proliferation will occur primarily among countries participating in the market-oriented world economy and hence could be covered by new rules that would govern the use of export controls.

There is thus a strong probability that export controls will be a frequently recurring problem in the world economy in the years ahead and limit the access of importing countries to foreign supplies. Some of their increased usage will be structural, as primary producing countries seek to improve their terms of trade and increase their domestic value added. Some will move with the economic cycle, correlating positively with world inflation. Some will also move with international politics, as countries seek to use their maximum bargaining leverage to influence world events. From the standpoint of the international economic system something needs to be done to better assure access to supplies and check the unbridled use of export controls.

National Interests

New international regimes seldom derive from systemic concerns alone, however. What are the national interests of different groups of countries on this issue? How does the question of export controls fit into the calls for a new international economic order?

Three sets of countries can be readily distinguished. The clearest situation obtains for countries that import the vast bulk of their food and industrial raw materials. Japan fits this category most precisely. Most of the Western European countries, except France, are in such a position. So are the large number of developing countries that export few primary products. These countries, including the majority of developing countries, would appear to have a strong interest in the institution of tough international limitations on the use of export controls.

At the other end of the spectrum lie those countries that are large net exporters of both food and industrial materials. Canada and Australia are the clearest examples, but a number of developing countries (for instance, Malaysia) fall into this category. If Brazil succeeds in its ambitious efforts to develop both food and oil, it could join this group within the next decade. These countries appear resistant to any international limitations on their freedom to employ export controls.[23]

A middle position is occupied by countries which are net exporters of farm products and net importers of raw materials, or vice versa. The United States fits the former description, and most OPEC countries the latter. They are likely to adopt more ambivalent, and even contradictory, positions—as indeed the United States has done in its vigorous opposition to the export controls of others (particularly OPEC) but frequent resort to their use itself.

The policy implications of the neat functional distinction between net exporting countries and net importing countries is upset, however, by North-South politics as well as the shadings of national economic positions and the differing potential of "commodity power" for different commodities. Although developed and developing countries fit into both categories—for example, Canada is clearly a net exporter and Korea is clearly a net importer—virtually all developing countries have maintained strong support for OPEC and the push for more producers' associations, even when the direct effects of those efforts redound to their own economic detriment. The reasons seem to be both political and economic: glee that the poor, nonwhite "south" has finally struck a solid blow against domination by the rich, white "north,"[24] and belief or at least hope that the nouveaux riches will be more generous than the titans of the ancien regime (notably the United States). [25]

In addition, it is generally believed that there is no real possibility that the food exporters would systematically limit their output, as the oil exporters and exporters of some other raw materials (for limited periods) have done, despite occasional calls within the United States for creation of a "counter-cartel." This is due partly to the humanitarian aspects of food, partly to generalized guilt feelings in the richer countries, which deter them from taking actions similar to those taken by poorer countries, partly to the domestic politics of agriculture in the producing countries, and partly to the unlikelihood of joint political action by the United States, Canada, and Australia. Whether rightly or wrongly, this asymmetrical assessment of the probabilities of the emergence of export controls in different sectors reduces the interest of countries which export industrial materials and import food in seeking new international rules to limit the use thereof.

The Case For Export Controls

Why not let the developing countries "get away with" the use of export controls, cartels, and the like to promote a transfer of wealth and income —the ultimate objective of those who propose a NIEO? It is highly improbable that such transfers will be provided through the budgets of the richer countries by traditional, or even novel, forms of foreign aid. Why not achieve the same result surreptitiously: from consumers in the richer countries through export controls and other price-propping devices for primary products sold by the poorer countries.[26]

Such a question should be answered in terms of two criteria. What would be the impact of such a world on international economic efficiency? What would be its impact on the equity of world income and wealth distribution? If a regime open to unfettered use of export controls met either criterion, it would be supportable in the political arena.

There are four conditions under which controls on the export (including production for export) of particular products might increase economic *efficiency*. The first two are straightforward applications of the theory of the second best, in which a new distortion is introduced to counter the impact of an initial distortion, and have analogous counterparts that traditionally have justified deviations from the standard prohibitions against the use of import controls.

One occurs when import controls in consuming countries generate scarcity rents which are captured in those countries (or anywhere outside the exporting country). In such instances, it is economically justifiable for producing countries to levy export controls to recapture the rents for themselves, because the likely result is to shift production back to where it is most efficient. For example, an increase in the OPEC price for oil would certainly have been justified (in purely economic terms) up to the level generated by the oil import quotas maintained by the United States into the early 1970s. The Netherlands and France instituted a wide range of controls on their agricultural exports for precisely this reason in the 1930s.[27]

In international commodity trade, higher import duties frequently exist for processed items than for the primary product itself. This "tariff escalation," which produces much higher effective than nominal protection for processing in the importing country, applies to both industrial raw materials (such as copper) and agricultural products (such as coffee). Producing countries are economically justified in countering such import protection by instituting export taxes (or other controls), to encourage domestic processing to the same extent that it is discouraged by the importers' duties. This is the analogy on the export side to the widely recognized right of importing countries to apply countervailing duties to offset the advantage provided to foreign producers by export subsidies.

The second efficiency-creating justification for export controls is the "infant industry" case. Export controls could promote efficient allocation of resources over time by protecting the supply, and perhaps the price, of imports to nascent processing industries which would be expected to become competitive without such preferences in the future. "Infant industry" protection via import controls has been one of the few cases where deviations from free trade can be justified on economic grounds, and an analogous justification applies on the export side.

The third and fourth cases are more conjectural, but under certain conditions may provide opportunities to enhance economic efficiency through the use of export controls. If price fluctuations are great enough to generate such uncertainty about future prices that investment (or consumption, or both) is deterred, then export controls adopted as part of an overall commodity agreement can promote economic efficiency. Price stabilization in such cases can enhance welfare, and export controls (instead of, or in addition to, the accumulation of buffer stocks) can contribute to that objective.

Finally, for exhaustible resources, export controls can under some conditions slow exploitation to a pace that more accurately takes account of the needs of future generations. Such excessive exploitation can occur because current prices are rising too slowly, so that the anticipated rise in the asset value of resources in the ground is less than the going rate of interest on alternative investment outlets. When such a situation exists, it may be cumulatively unstable because the "excessive" exploitation will further lower the expected future yield and encourage still more current production. (There are other reasons why exploitation may be too fast to produce optimality over time, including the existence of a market interest rate that is higher than the true social rate of time preference.) On the other hand, production would be inadequate if prices for such resources rose too rapidly and made the maintenance of reserves more attractive than alternative investments.[28]

Export and production controls may thus be economically justified in protecting future generations against excessive consumption in the present. However, excessive use of such controls can reverse the outcome and generate excessive costs to the present population. And the conditions under which such limits can be justified are quite limiting: there must be no reasonable likelihood of technical progress, including in the use of the resource, and there must be no reasonable likelihood of substituting alternative resources (shale oil or breeder reactors for fossil fuels) or alternative factors of production.

Nevertheless, there are thus four cases in which export controls can promote economic efficiency. Economic analysis could support their use in such instances, if ways could be found to institute adequate decision-making machinery for identifying the existence of one of the conditions.

There may also be an *equity* case for export controls in some cases, primarily those in which income was thereby transferred from richer to poorer countries. Even when the case is clearly desirable in terms of *international* redistribution, however, serious problems of *internal* distribution may remain. In some case, export (or other price-raising) controls could transfer income from poor consumers in richer countries to the wealthiest individuals in poor countries. In the extreme, this could redistribute income regressively even in absolute terms—for example, from unemployed users of home heating oil in New England to Arab sheiks.

In addition, the majority of world exports of primary products comes from the richer countries. Even for individual products sold largely by poorer countries, richer countries are usually important as well (Australia in bauxite, Canada in copper). Many more poor countries import primary products, on balance, than export them—and the net importers include most of the poorest countries. So a world of widespread export controls and producers' associations might well have a regressive impact on global income distribution, in purely intercountry terms, though particular instances of such policies could have progressive effects.

The Need for a Regime to Govern Export Controls

Thus the justification for export controls, on either efficiency or equity grounds, is highly selective. Such efforts can sometimes be justified, but many cannot. Given the limiting nature of each of the justifications, it seems likely that more potential uses of the instrument would violate the necessary criteria than would fulfill one of them. There is thus a strong case for general prohibition of export controls, on both efficiency and equity grounds, with exceptions to take care of cases where they can be justified. This has been the traditional approach for the regimes which have governed import controls, export subsidies, and international monetary actions such as exchange-rate changes.

In addition, any generalized effort to transfer income or wealth across national borders through impeding access to supplies could hardly remain surreptitious. Consumers in rich countries are quick to perceive price gouging by oligopolists at home or abroad, and seek to retaliate in whatever ways they can. In reaction to OPEC, for example, the U.S. Congress banned its members and those of any future cartels from eligibility for generalized tariff preferences—which can be of great importance to developing countries in their efforts to industrialize—and initially rejected the entire U.S. contribution to the fourth replenishment of the International Development Association. Aside from purely economic responses, which may undermine cartel efforts over the longer run in any event, direct retaliation would be highly probable if limitations on supply access were recognized to be a conscious, wide-ranging effort to transfer world resources with no quid pro quo for consumers.

So there are strong arguments against the feasibility of any effort to use export controls as a generalized component of any NIEO, though exceptions can be permitted for those instances where such controls would promote economic efficiency or income equity. More positively, virtually all countries—including most developing countries—would benefit from the creation of new international rules and institutional arrangements to limit the use of export controls because they are net importers of primary commodities.

Even net commodity exporters would generally benefit from international limitations on the use of export controls. In the first place, the longer-run economic interests of such countries are likely to be hurt by their own imposition of export controls. Use of such controls triggers reductions in demand for the product controlled, and production of substitutes in both the importing countries (as in energy) and in other exporting countries (as in soybeans). Nevertheless, short-run temptations will frequently induce countries in this position to apply such controls. As countries have learned painfully in the case of import controls, international barriers can often help them avoid self-defeating national actions.

Second, even countries that are net exporters rely on imports for a large number of key products. No country even remotely approaches complete self-sufficiency, except possibly China at its very low level of economic development, now that the United States has become dependent on imports for so many raw materials (including oil) and the Soviet Union on imports of food and technological help. Even those countries most prone to apply export controls can thus be badly hurt by the similar actions of others. This is particularly true because export controls can be applied to manufactured (including military) goods as well as primary products, as indeed occurred widely from 1973 to 1974 due to shortages in particular (especially energy-intensive) industries and the widespread use of price controls.

Finally, as with import controls and other instruments of international economic conflict, the application of export controls by one country spawns their application by another. Some of this reaction is defensive, as suppliers of a product whose sales were limited by other suppliers seek to protect themselves from unwanted deflections of demand in their direction. Some is defensive in a broader sense, as countries employ their own export controls to offset the adverse effects on them of the export controls used by others—as in the case of Jamaica, whose increased bauxite levy brought in just enough additional revenue to offset the impact on it of OPEC's increase in the price of oil (about $150 million). But overt retaliation is also a distinct possibility, and indeed was authorized in the United States when the Congress explicitly added the Mondale Amendments to the Trade Act of 1974 to counter OPEC-like actions with U.S. action in kind, and banned OPEC countries (and members of future cartels) from eligibility for U.S. tariff preferences.

In short, widespread use of export controls could trigger the same cycle of emulation and retaliation which resulted from the widespread use of import controls in the 1930s—when there existed no international rules or institutional arrangements to govern that type of economic aggression among countries. World inflation could be given a further upward push, just as world depression earlier was given a further downward push. International political hostilities would rise. Amendment of the existing rules, to provide effective multilateral surveillance over the use of export controls and other limitations on access to supplies, is thus needed to fill an important gap in current international economic arrangements.

Specific Proposals

A detailed set of rules to govern export controls would have three basic objectives: to deter unjustifiable uses of such tools of trade policy, to limit the scope and duration of those export controls that were adopted, and to provide institutional means of dispute settlement into which individual cases could be channeled when necessary. The rules themselves could range from modest requirements for international notification of, and consultation on, the imposition of such controls through binding limitations on their use except where certain specified criteria are met.[29] The following paragraphs sketch out the components of the more ambitious regime, in full recognition that it might be possible to adopt only less elaborate arrangements at first.[30]

Several procedural requirements should be a necessary component of any new "GATT for export controls." At present, countries are not even required to report internationally on their use of export controls. In addition to formal notification, they should be required to consult internationally prior to the imposition of such controls—just as they are required to consult on exchange-rate changes under the Articles of Agreement of the International Monetary Fund. And once any such controls were actually implemented, they should be subject to ongoing multilateral surveillance, either by the regular GATT machinery or by a special body created for this purpose, to monitor both their mode of operation and, periodically, whether their continuation is justified. In addition to reporting, consulting, and undergoing multilateral surveillance on any new controls that are contemplated, countries could be required to do so on existing controls—as was required of all countries participating in the Arrangement Regarding International Trade in Textiles within one year of its inception.

Such consultations and subsequent surveillance would be most effective if taken against the backdrop of agreement on the conditions which justified the use of export controls. Seven conditions can be envisaged. Four come from our earlier analysis of the cases in which export controls can increase economic efficiency (or, at least, reduce inefficiency): counters to import controls levied by consuming countries, especially cases of tariff escalation which deter processing in the producing countries; "infant industry" situations; reductions of excessive price fluctuation; and avoidance of exploitation of exhaustible resources that is too rapid from the standpoint of intertemporal considerations. One exception should cover cases where a political decision was made in both producing and consuming countries to use this device to improve international income distribution, particularly in the context of an international commodity agreement in which both sets of countries participated. Two should consciously rest on neither efficiency nor equity considerations, and simply emulate the existing rules which govern import controls: a national security exception, and an exception in cases of injury to a national economy if export controls are not imposed.[31]

Export controls should be banned in all cases where there is no international agreement that at least one of these criteria was met, and compensation required or retaliation authorized for any use thereof which was not approved. "Export controls," for this purpose, should be defined to include domestic measures with effects identical to explicit export controls, such as production controls and taxes, just as the "national treatment" provision of Article III of the GATT—from which exports are now explicitly exempted— rules out domestic taxes and government regulations that discriminate against imports. Any export controls that could be justified, and were adopted, should be subjected to strict time limits and tied to domestic adjustment measures that would make credible their temporary nature. Export (or production) taxes should be preferred to export (or production) quotas, and nondiscrimination among foreign purchasers should be required.

Negotiating Possibilities

There are several routes by which such new rules to govern export controls might become part of any NIEO. The simplest approach would be to include them as part of the Multilateral Trade Negotiations (MTN), confined solely to trade-offs within the GATT. A self-contained arrangement on the subject might even be achievable, if all countries were to recognize their interest in limiting the possible scope for using export controls, perhaps as one of the several codes to be negotiated to govern the use of nontariff distortions of trade. For example, it would seem that food importing countries would gain from accepting limitations on their own scope for using export controls in return for a similar commitment on the part of the United States and the other major food exporters. Nevertheless, enough countries envisage themselves as potential beneficiaries of the use of "commodity power" so that some wider trade-offs may prove necessary.

Two realistic possibilities emerge. As a quid pro quo for accepting limitations on their right to use export controls, primary producing countries could be granted tariff deescalation and reductions of nontariff barriers on products processed from their raw materials. Or, in recognition of the broader industrialization objectives of most primary producers, any (or all) of several steps could be taken on their behalf: additional liberalization of existing import barriers that now impede their industrial diversification, advance implementation of the trade liberalization to be negotiated more broadly in the MTN, liberalization of the existing systems of generalized tariff preferences, or tightening of the rules that permit the use of import restraints.[32] Any combination of these possibilities would represent a broad trade-off between increasing the access of the industrialized countries to foreign supplies and increasing the access of the developing countries to foreign markets.

Another option is to confine the issue to commodity trade, where export controls are most prevalent. In such a context, suppliers could accept limits on their use of export controls in return for alternative means to improve their terms of trade. One such quid, reduced barriers to products processed from the raw materials, has already been mentioned. Another would be a series of individual commodity agreements, in which floor prices and adequate financing for the accumulation of buffer stocks would give producers enough security so that they would accept commitments to keep selling—and permit the buffer stocks to do so as well—when prices bumped against agreed ceilings. A still greater commitment on the part of importers would be long-term purchase contracts, as agreed upon by the EC for sugar under the Lomé Convention. Still another, largely complementary, approach would be further liberalization of the IMF compensatory finance facility to provide income, rather than price, support for commodity producers. This approach could be pursued at two levels: global arrangements that applied to all countries, such as compensating financially at the IMF and new GATT rules, and through specific agreements on particular commodities.

There are thus a number of avenues through which the need for new international rules to govern the use of export controls could be achieved. The probability of achievement is higher than ever before because of the emergence of a balance of uncertainties. Producers and consumers are both uncertain about future price levels and price fluctuations. Producers are uncertain about their access to markets, and consumers are uncertain about their access to supplies. Both are increasingly aware of the need for new international arrangements to promote the economic security of each. Importing countries might well accept a modest transfer of resources through new international agreements if, in return, they received more secure access to foreign supplies. On this basis, rather than through unilateral confrontation, it might yet prove possible to include such a regime in any reform of the international economic order.

Notes

1 This was true for three reasons. First, the success of OPEC stimulated other developing countries to try to boost their own commodity earnings either through similar groupings of producing countries acting alone or through joint arrangements with consuming nations. Second, the non-oil developing countries were themselves hit hard by the higher price of energy and were thus forced to seek new ways to boost their export earnings. Third, the OPEC countries chose to use their new power to promote the NIEO; Gosovic and Ruggie (1976, p. 311) conclude that "the negotiations for a new international economic order gained prominence for the industrial countries as consumer-producer oil diplomacy became progressively linked to new economic order concerns."

2 For a schematic presentation, see Bergsten (1974a, p. 6).

3 For details, see Bergsten (1976).

4 See Mingst (1976) for an analysis of CIPEC.

5 Even the United States, however, has repeatedly voiced its concern—as Secretary of State Kissinger indicated in his "Address Before the Fourth Ministerial Meeting of the United Nations Conference on Trade and Development," Nairobi, May 6, p. 10, "we

need additional international arrangements to assure reliability of supply for the steady flow of raw materials is vital to every country."

6 And other producers of primary products, notably Canada and Australia, which frequently ally themselves quietly with the developing countries on these issues.

7 Regarding energy, for example, Tims (1976, p. 194) concludes that "higher oil prices have had a substantial adverse impact on the economic prospects of the developing countries." A paper presented by the German government to the Puerto Rico summit meeting in June 1976 reportedly concluded that only seventeen developing countries would benefit from implementation of the UNCTAD "integrated commodity program."

8 For a recent history of the GATT process, see Curzon (1976).

9 Manufacturing exports of developing countries (exluding oil exporters) grew by an average annual rate of 24.8 percent from 1965 through 1973. See Keesing and Plesch (1976, pp. 1-3).

10 See Rothschild (1974) and Gordon (1941, especially pp. 349-363). U.S. export controls against Japan were the most noted example prior to 1941, but most European countries also employed a large number of such measures in the late 1930s.

11 For a brief history, see League of Nations (1946), begun by Eugene Staley and completed by Klaus Knorr.

12 For a fascinating review of the accuracy of the commodity projections for the United States made at that time by the Paley Commission, see Cooper (1975).

13 In its postmortem analysis of the U.S. price controls from 1971 to 1973, the Cost of Living Council concluded that its greatest intellectual mistake was the failure to anticipate the huge shift into exports, whose prices were not controlled, of many U.S. producers of items whose domestic prices were controlled. Canada has faced the same problem even more acutely since its adoption of price controls in 1975. During World War II, however, the price controls of the U.S. Office of Price Administration applied to exports as well as domestic sales—and were designed, written and administered by Seymour E. Harris, as explained in Harris (1943).

14 For a more disaggregated analysis, with numerous examples of each type of action, see Bergsten (1974a, especially pp. 5-10). Another possibly distinct category is the use of production controls to conserve truly scarce resources; see below.

15 The controls that sought to limit exports to the Communist countries were in fact coordinated through a new international arrangement set up specifically for that purpose, the so-called Coordinating Committee (COCOM) associated with NATO.

16 One indication of the need for an international regime in this area is the absence of any comprehensive inventory of what countries are doing. There are no notification or other reporting requirements. Only the OECD has even compiled an unofficial list of the export controls employed by its members.

17 Jamaica in fact raised its levy further in 1975 and again in 1976, though it did have to relax the "minimum production levels" on which the tax was calculated.

18 The argument is elaborated in Bergsten (1974c).

19 For example, see Fried (1976), Mikesell (1974), and Varon and Takeuchi (1974).

20 As announced by Secretary of State Kissinger at the Seventh Special Session of the United Nations General Assembly, September 1, 1975. In response to his specific call for

consultations on copper, CIPEC reversed its traditional position and initiated a producer-consumer discussion in March 1976. Kissinger made specific proposals in December 1975 (at the Conference on International Economic Cooperation in Paris) and in May 1976 (at the UNCTAD meeting in Nairobi) to convene similar "forums" for bauxite and iron ore, respectively, but no such groupings had been launched at this writing.

21 For example, the United States now depends on imports for more than 25 percent of virutally all of the key industrial raw materials, and the percentages are growing rapidly. See Figure 7.1. Less than a generation ago, by contrast, the United States was a net exporter of raw materials.

22 As described by Cooper (1972).

23 Canada and Australia strongly resisted the inclusion of export controls in the OECD "standstill agreement" on trade barriers negotiated in 1974 and renewed in 1975, but eventually accepted the ban reluctantly.

24 As analyzed by Farer (1975).

25 There is not much parallel in the "North" for this dominance of politics over economics in the "South": Canada and Australia side largely with the producers on most commodity issues, even when this puts them at odds with the rest of the OECD.

26 Another surreptitious method is through increased host-country harnessing of multinational enterprises. An argument that such harnessing is in fact occurring, and raises similar problems as cited here regarding export controls, is in Bergsten (1974b).

27 Heuser (1939, especially Ch.9). For an analysis of the distribution between exporters and importers of the scarcity rents generated by import controls, see Bergsten (1975). Such recapturing of scarcity rents can of course be achieved through the use of export controls only for products where the price elasticity of demand is low. For price-elastic products, export *subsidies* may be a legitimate response to import controls in order to retain markets (rather than rents).

28 For a complete analysis see Solow (1974, especially pp. 3 and 6).

29 In late 1974, the Commission of the EC formally suggested three alternative possibilities: "A new notification and consultation procedure," a "Code of Conduct . . . at the level of general principles," or detailed "sectoral agreements aimed at a 'better management of supplies,' " perhaps generalized into international commodity agreements. Canada has also made proposals toward a sector approach. A less ambitious approach, which would not require formal amendment of the GATT, is advocated in Roessler (1975).

30 See Bergsten, (1974a), for full details of the proposed rules.

31 This could include the case of "countervailing export controls," where a producing country restricted its exports to offset import subsidies through which a consuming country sought to combat its internal inflation. See Bergsten (1974a, p. 39).

32 Such as the approach proposed by Bhagwati in Ch. 6.

References

Bergsten, C. F., 1974(a), *Completing the GATT: Toward New International Rules to Govern Export Controls* (British-North American Committee, Washington, D.C.).

_____ , 1974(b), "Coming Investment Wars?," *Foreign Affairs*, October 1974, 135-152.

_____, 1974(c), "The New Era in World Commodity Markets," *Challenge*, September/October 1974, 34-42.

_____, 1975, "On the Non-Equivalence of Import Quotas and 'Voluntary' Export Restraints" in Bergsten, ed., *Toward A New World Trade Policy: The Maidenhead Papers* (D.C. Heath and Co., Lexington, Mass.), 239-271.

_____, 1976, "A New OPEC in Bauxite," *Challenge*, July-August 1976, 12-20.

Bhagwati, J., 1977, "Market Disruption, Export Market Disruption, Compensation, and GATT Reform" in J. Bhagwati, ed., *The New International Economic Order* (MIT Press, Cambridge, Mass.).

Cooper, R. N., 1972, "Trade Policy is Foreign Policy," *Foreign Policy* 9, 18-36.

_____, 1975, "Resource Needs Revisited," *Brookings Papers on Economic Activity*, 1975, 1, 238-245.

Curzon, G., and V., 1976, "The Management of Trade Relations in the GATT" in A. Shonfield, ed., *International Economic Relations of the Western World 1959-1971*, Part II (Oxford University Press, London).

Farer, T. J., 1975, "The United States and the Third World: A Basis for Accommodation," *Foreign Affairs*, October 1975, 79-97.

Fried, E. R., 1976, "International Trade in Raw Materials: Myths and Realities," *Science*, February 20, 1976, 641-646.

GATT, 1950, *The Use of Quantitative Restrictions for Protective and Other Commercial Purposes.*

Gordon, M.S., 1941, *Barriers to World Trade: A Study of Recent Commercial Policy* (MacMillan, New York).

Gosovic, B., and J. G. Ruggie, 1976, "On the Creation of a New International Economic Order: Issue Linkage and the Seventh Special Session of the UN General Assembly," *International Organization*, 30, 2, Spring 1976, 309-345.

Harris, S. E., 1943, "Export Price Control," in *OPA, A Manual of Price Control* (Government Printing Office, Washington, D.C.).

Heuser, H., 1939, *Control of International Trade* (George Rutledge and Sons, London).

Keesing, D. B., and P. A. Plesch, 1976, "Recent Trends in Manufactured Exports from Developing Countries," mimeo, IBRD, March 19, 1976.

League of Nations, 1946, *Raw Materials and Policies.*

Mikesell, R. F., 1974, "More Third World Cartels Ahead?," *Challenge*, November/December 1974, 24-31.

Mingst, K., 1976, "Cooperation or Illusion: An Examination of the Intergovernmental Council of Copper Exporting Countries," *International Organization*, 30, 2, Spring 1976, 264-287.

Roessler, F., 1975, "Access to Supplies: The Role GATT Could Play," *Journal of World Trade Law*, January/February 1975, 25-40.

Rothschild, E., 1974, "1914 and Today's Trade Crisis," *New York Times*, June 23, 1974.

Solow, R. M., 1974, "The Economics of Resources or the Resources of Economics," *American Economic Review*, May 1974, 1-14.

Tims, W., 1975, "The Developing Countries," in E. R. Fried and C. L. Schultze, eds., *Higher Oil Prices and the World Economy* (Brookings Institution, Washington, D.C.).

Varon, B., and K. Takeuchi, 1974, "Developing Countries and Non-Fuel Minerals," *Foreign Affairs*, April 1974, 497-510.

8
Trade Policies of the Developed Countries for the Next Decade
Harald B. Malmgren

The trade policies of the developed nations affect the trading position of the developing nations in a number of ways. The import policies of the developed nations have received most of the attention, but their export policies are also important. For example, official assistance for export financing, widely used in exports from the OECD nations, constitutes an important element of trade competitiveness. Another example would be the periodic use by the economically advanced countries of export aids for agricultural products over the years, adding to the world market distortions which are so pervasive in agriculture.

The Problem of Nontariff Intervention

Trade policies have traditionally been thought of as policies that are designed to influence the volume or price, or both, of products that cross national boundaries. Much negotiating attention has therefore been given to tariffs, taxes, and other charges on imports, export subsidies, and quantitative limitations, particularly on imports. More recently, the focus of public policy debate has shifted toward the so-called nontariff distortions to trade or nontariff barriers. (A more recent term in wide use by trade negotiators is nontariff measures.)

Some of these distorting instruments of policy are deliberately applied at the border to regulate trade, but some are not aimed at trade objectives at all, and in a number of cases the trade distortion effects arise from the differences in domestic policy between trading nations. In this latter category, for example, are differences in health, safety, and consumer standards, and the methods used for testing and verification of such standards.

Domestic mircoeconomic policies aimed at sectoral, regional, or institutional problems also give rise to significant trade-distorting effects. These structural policies are becoming increasingly important. Governments are more and more being called upon to intervene, through the use of various economic devices, to shore up troubled segments of their economies and promote sectors which are politically judged to have high potential. As government responsibility has broadened, structural objectives have multiplied—to the point, in recent years, that structural policies often conflict with, or undercut, international rules as well as the arrangements which have emerged from multilateral bargaining.

This politicizing of structural changes in various markets creates a situation of instability and unpredictability. This in turn raises risks, and therefore investment costs, for both domestic producers and foreign exporters.

Thus there appear to be growing opportunities for distortion and even disruption of the interests among nations as a consequence of structural economic policies. An interesting case was the establishment in the early 1970s of a Michelin tire factory in Nova Scotia on the basis of a number of special tax incentives offered by national and regional authorities to entice Michelin to that location. The sales from this plant were approximately 80 percent to the United States and 20 percent to Canada. The U.S. market justified the establishment of the plant, and without the exports the project would not have been viable. Conversely, as the U.S. Treasury saw it, the regional location subsidies in effect constituted an export subsidy, since most of the output was for export, and the product price was very much affected by the array of tax incentives. Treasury therefore ordered the application of countervailing duties, treating the regional aids as export subsidies within the meaning of U.S. law.

Thus, international trade negotiations and policy discussions among governments are now going beyond border measures and are beginning to deal with ways in which policies can be limited by international agreement so that the external effects of domestic actions are subject to reasonable limitations. This approach, however, is not universally accepted. A debate has arisen between those who seek to minimize the distorting effects of policy differences through a degree of harmonization of domestic policy instruments, and those who favor elimination of all border measures affecting trade without any effort to discuss or change domestic policies. In the United States, for example, in the 1970s the Department of Agriculture took the latter position, refusing to have domestic agricultural policies discussed in international trade deliberations; while the European Community officials argued that discussion of border measures without reference to underlying domestic price supports, subsidies, and production limitations was meaningless. From a practical point of view, many of the policies and policy instruments that affect trade are embodied in national laws, administrative regulations and practices, and custom, and in regional or local variants of such laws, regulations, and practice. The internal politics and administrative procedures of each nation are therefore at issue. Addressing these questions enormously complicates intergovernmental discussions and negotiations.[2]

This complexity of forces at work in commercial transactions is itself a deterrent to the trade of developing nations. Institutionally, the larger international trading companies and transnational corporations are much better situated to deal with complexity and a variety of requirements than relatively small-scale exporting entities in developing countries. The trading companies and transnationals operate on a scale that allows specialization in diversity, in information collecting, in management of legal and institutional procedures in relation to national and local governments, and where necessary in location of production facilities to minimize what are perceived to be economically impeding forces. The developing nations do not have large-scale enterprises or trading companies that can operate in this way. To export, they must export through the complex systems of the industrialized countries, and that is difficult without an organized system.

Furthermore, the conflicting policies and procedures that vary from country to country, and that give rise to barriers and distortions to trade, do not remain fixed. As policies and instruments of policies change, the problems change. The complexity is thus more than a static problem; it is an everchanging, kaleidoscopic kind of complexity that the exporters in developing nations face.

From the developing nations' perspective, therefore, it would seem even more important, as compared with the position of the developed nations, that complexity be reduced and that the problems of nontariff distortions to trade be resolved. Through the mid-1970s, however, the developing nations in their various policy statements have not addressed the problem of complexity or the particular difficulties in the nontariff distortions area. Instead, in negotiations on nontariff issues, they have called for "differential treatment," focusing more on the exceptions to any new rules that might be negotiated than on the rules themselves.

Reform of the World Economic System and Economic Liberalism

It is customary in discussing the trade policies of the developed nations to concentrate on the need for liberalization of their markets. Among many economists this is simply a matter of pursuing the virtue of free trade. However, many of the spokesmen of developing nations do not perceive the problem as one of expanding the scope and depth of free trade forces and laissez-faire policies. On the contrary, much of the thrust of their declarations of the early and mid-1970s has been that governments must intervene in world markets to alter the terms, conditions, and patterns of world production and trade. The principle of preferential tariff treatment was an early element of this new approach. Now it can be seen in the calls for differential treatment in the application of all trade measures, price-fixing at high levels with subsequent indexation to bring about resource transfers, and other mechanisms for altering the pattern of world economic activity. In other words, while the industrialized nations are pursuing free trade, with less government intervention in markets, the developing countries favor an approach with more government intervention and less free play of market forces.

The governments of the developed nations have reacted with some alarm to the suggestions of developing countries for structural change, and some, particularly those of the United States and the Federal Republic of Germany, have argued that governmental intervention in world markets is per se a bad thing, bound to lead to greater distortions and economic inefficiencies. This argument seems to lose some of its force when account is taken of the various governmental actions taken by the developed country governments in protecting their domestic agricultural programs, or in their state trading activities, or in their periodic invocation of "safeguards" to protect particular sectors from international competition, in the invocation of export controls in connection with domestic objectives, in the subsidization of certain sectors, and so on. A doctrinal argument is also made in connection with exchange rate adjustment, but since there continues to be international controversy, especially among the developed nations themselves, over what kind of adjustments should take place, how fast and how often, and whether particular fluctuations are "stabilizing" or "destabilizing" adjustments, the doctrinal argument over exchange rates also seems to flag.

The important theoretical concepts put forward by Professors J. Bhagwati, H. G. Johnson, and others, concerning optimal levels and modalities of official intervention to correct distortions, have not figured prominently in the intergovernmental debate. There have been policy debates about the appropriate trade policies of the developing countries themselves, as between the so-called inward-looking and outward-looking strategies, with focus on tariff and subsidy strategies, but the assumption in this debate has tended to be that the developed nations would open their markets and act essentially as free markets.

While the outward-looking strategy appears to have worked well for a number of developing economies, it has been rejected or viewed with extreme caution by other nations. There are a number of points of controversy, but a prominent question raised by policy makers is whether the international market could be counted on as benign if all exporting developing nations followed the prescription of economic liberalism. Mahbub ul Haq has commented on this point that:

It is difficult to decide between the liberal academics and the complaining policy-makers in this case. Basically, outward-looking strategy, while attractive in principle, is still a very high-risk strategy. It assumes that developed countries are also likely to become outward-looking. . . . On the other hand, import-substitution strategy carries fewer risks for the harassed policy-makers because high-cost goods produced under protective walls can still be shoved down the throats of the local populations by closing down any decent alternative.[3]

Whether the trade policies of the developed nations will stay as they are, be further liberalized through international negotiation, or become selectively more protective, or whether some combination of liberalization and increased protection takes place is an open question. The uncertainty must itself be considered a hindrance to investment and trade expansion for developing countries.

Complexity, Uncertainty, and Market Management

The industrialized nations have liberalized their trading regimes very substantially since the establishment of the World Bank, IMF, and GATT systems. They have also maintained their sovereign rights to alter the conditions of trade as national circumstances require, and have sometimes acted unilaterally, in connection with sectoral as well as macroeconomic difficulties. An action taken to alter the level of protection, to shore up a sector, or perhaps the whole of trade account, is called a safeguard action.

So-called safeguards can take a number of forms, some consistent with international rules and some not. Safeguards explicitly provided for in the GATT include escape-clause or material injury safeguards, balance of payments safeguards, antidumping and countervailing duty safeguards, and national security safeguards. The GATT has also flexibly worked out other safeguard problems in a pragmatic manner. For example, the United States asked for and received a general waiver to cover its agricultural import restrictions. The textile import or export problems of many countries led to negotiation of a multilateral agreement governing the nature and extent of import restrictions of importing countries. Outside the GATT framework are the Common Agricultural Policy of the European Community, which has a continuously adjustable safeguard system, and the so-called voluntary restraint agreements on the part of exporting nations to limit their exports.

On the commodity front, some of the developed nations have acted to influence the supply of raw materials or provide for emergencies. In the U.S. case, enormous official stockpiles exist, and actions have from time to time been taken to limit the outflow of specific raw materials through the use of export controls. Freedom of action in this area seems to be highly prized by governments. International discussions aimed at limiting the freedom of action of developed country governments have made little or no progress (even when the discussions have been carried out within the restricted negotiating environment of the OECD).

In commodities, the operations of the market are not as competitive and open as economic theorists often postulate. In some cases, vertical integration from source to processed products, and high concentration internationally, have resulted in opportunity to manage or stabilize prices. When a large, integrated transnational enterprise sets and holds a "producer's price," by cumulating or drawing down inventories or stocks, or by buying back as well as selling on international commodity exchanges, the "market price" becomes an ambiguous concept. The market price in some cases becomes the producer's internal price, and in other cases it becomes a residual market price reflecting supply and demand only among the smaller, nonintegrated, entities in the market. Internal holdings of stocks, when called inventories, are considered legitimate by the economic liberals. On the other hand, official stockpiling is often considered dangerous by the same liberals in their doctrinal opposition to international buffer stocks—essentially because official stock management is unlikely to be motivated by long-term profit considerations but will be tempted or forced to follow political objectives as well.

Governments are highly active in the commodity area, and it is reasonable to suppose that they will be even more interventionist in the future, for a variety of reasons. This is not simply a matter of a widespread desire to stabilize prices. It is also a consequence of the desire to own and manage resources nationally, which gives rise to expropriation, threats of expropriation, and establishment of nationally owned enterprises. In the future, because of the growing governmental role, and the unlikelihood that the vertically integrated transnational enterprises will be able to remain intact or operate in the same manner as in the past to stabilize flows and prices internally, the trade policies of the developed country governments are likely to change. The freedom of action in private sector activities and methods of operation in the industrialized countries will become circumscribed, and governments will either seek new kinds of freedom of action, or will be forced to negotiate intergovernmental agreements that protect each nation's economy from disruptive (essentially, collusive) actions on the part of other nations.

Thus, when looking ahead at the potential or likely trade policies of the developed nations, one has to reckon with a number of evolving forces: the ups and downs of protectionism; the political need for interventionist economic policies, both macroeconomic and microeconomic; the evolution of administrative procedures, public information laws, and other influences on public decision-making systems; the international political climate and its influence on the desire of national governments to maintain freedom of action; the evolution of institutional mechanisms for dealing with international complexities and uncertainties in commercial policy and administrative practice, beyond the present framework of transnational enterprises, trading companies, state-trading entities, and highly complex distribution systems. For the potential exporter in a developing nation, this is a formidable array of uncertainties, posing risks that must be a major deterrent. Compared with the relative safety of well-protected home markets in the developing nations, the business of exporting must look rather unattractive.

Professor Bhagwati, in his paper in this volume, correctly points out that we must give greater attention to the *threat* of protectionist actions based on grounds of market disruption, because the threat of action itself imposes a welfare loss on exporting countries.[4] This economic loss is separate from and additional to the loss sustained from implementation of restrictions in specific cases. He also notes the tendency, in the U.S. case, to weigh injury in terms of the potential injury, or "threat of injury." In other words, potential exporters must weigh the rate of growth they would like to experience against the possible protectionist reaction to high rates of growth in the importing market.

The Trade Act of 1974 in the United States was intended to formalize the procedures for seeking safeguard protection, and to reduce the number of ad hoc efforts to bring about protectionism through lobbying and special legislation. Industries, farmers, and workers are encouraged, under this law, to follow specified procedures, and to work through an array of formal advisory bodies which would channel information and advice from the private sector. The Trade Act of 1974 did, however, also make the process of obtaining official safeguard action a little easier. On the one hand, the passage of the act forestalled the intense pressures for more severe and automatic regulation of commercial activity which were embodied in proposals such as the Burke-Hartke bill. On the other hand, the act opens new and complex avenues for safeguards and for administrative harassment.[5]

The case of agriculture is a microcosm of many of the conflicting concepts and political forces at work. In international negotiation of agricultural trade, it is conventional for many governments to argue that "agriculture is different." The social problems implied in the gradual decline in the number of rural families relying on farming for their incomes, together with the transition difficulties associated with rural migration to cities, have led many governments to argue that the transition, or structural adjustment, takes time and the pace cannot be accelerated. Therefore, it is argued, special protection against importation of products from other economic systems is required. It is also argued that conservation policies must inherently differ among nations, and that this gives rise to legitimate governmental intervention. It is argued further that government must assure a high degree of self-sufficiency so that a nation is not overly dependent on imports in time of crisis, such as war or international food shortages. In association with all these arguments there is usually some type of proposition that the balance between rural and urban incomes is adverse to farmers because their bargaining power is less, and that farmers' incomes must be supported, often through price supports and "indexation" of farm prices in relation to prices of the industrial sector (that is, purchasing power parity). Heavy fixed costs, rising capital costs, and high risk are noted in defense of subsidies, price supports, and trade protection. So we see governments heavily involved in most countries. Even in the United States, where the policy revolution of the 1970s has reduced the government's involvement in agriculture drastically, the apparatus of target price guarantees and administrative support stands ready to intervene as and when the levels established by the market forces become politically unacceptable.

When looking at this listing of specific issues and arguments, agriculture does not look all that unique. Similar arguments prevail in the provision of regional and sectoral aids to industries, and in the intervention of governments in the employment and production policies of private enterprise.

The structural adjustment question is, of course, at the center of most microeconomic intervention policies. Governments intervene because the pace of adjustment is too fast or too slow, relative to national and regional economic and social objectives. Some sectors change faster than others. The reasons vary from location to the flexibility and scale of the capital commitments (moving sewing machines is easier than rearranging steel mills or chemical processing facilities), from labor skill requirements to rate of technological change. Microeconomic adjustments occur in modules, and the modules for different economic activities do not always match up in time. Inventories and order books and capital expansion activities take up some of the slack, as does unemployment, but in the final analysis there are always pockets of disequilibrium. It is the economic "frictions" that are the focus of governmental incentives and disincentives, and we find ourselves with inadequate analytical tools to assess the economic efficiency of particular governmental actions.

Many economists in search of free trade have urged provision of adjustment assistance to firms and workers applying or qualifying for increased protection, as a "bribe" or social payment to avoid disturbance to the general open market forces. In trying to design adjustment assistance programs, however, there has been very little success in defining the optimum time period for assistance, or the optimum payment. Jan Tumlir's paper for the MIT workshop goes into this question of time horizon in connection with determining social versus private costs and benefits.[6] It is a problem in intertemporal equilibrium which has plagued the debate of many years about structural adjustment and exchange rate adjustment policy in connection with balance-of-payments adjustments (and still is a subject of controversy in connection with deciding how much "management" of flexible exchange rates there should be). Defining what "fundamental disequilibrium" was under the regime of the 1950s and 1970s was not a simple matter, and in any other usage of this concept the same problems would arise: how long a period of persistent difficulty, at what rate of profit squeeze or reserve outflow, as compared with what asset or reserve structure, constitutes a set of circumstances which can be appropriately described as a structural disequilibrium situation?

This problem is even more complex than it appears when put that way, because the adjustment of different economic entities will take different time paths, and there will be continuously evolving pockets of disequilibria within any system, however stable it may appear in macroeconomic terms. Consequently, there is both an intertemporal interdependence among decisions taken in separate parts of the economy, and interdependence in the outcomes of simultaneous decisions taken at any one moment in time. Defining the scope of a decision module, the period for efficient assessment of what is happening, and the appropriate rules for redesigning a decision system are very complex, theoretically difficult questions. In such a complex system, as we have in our modern economies, there is an important economic incentive to maintain the status quo and to vary its structure only slowly, decision makers concentrating their attention on events that turn out significantly different from expectations. The overall (aggregative macro) stability of the system is important, because if there is a high degree of stability or regularity of movement among a large portion of the variables which affect the whole market, then unexpected outcomes in particular areas will not destabilize the whole system. The rules that provide the framework for economic decisions must be fairly stable, too. This means that stop-go policies and continual change in laws and regulations, at home or abroad, create a degree of uncertainty which tends to deter trade and investment.

Although governments may not consciously understand why they intervene to provide ground rules and incentives and disincentives to preserve orderly change, this may not be economically inefficient when account is taken of how we go about assessing and deciding in a market system.[7]

Governments, because they usually work on the basis of some form of bureaucratic and political consensus, take time to alter their policies. If the legislative process is involved, the time required can run a number of years.[8] On the other hand, within the boundaries of policy and law, the individual units affected can react in a volatile manner to current circumstances. Thus it takes a long time for governments to negotiate and implement basic changes in the rules of the game, and consequent changes in national policy, while in a short period substantial trade disruptions can occur in the day-to-day workings of the trading system as it exists at any particular moment.

The Outlook for Trade Policies

Other papers on trade for this volume go into specific aspects of safeguards, adjustment assistance, export controls, and commodity market management. Consequently I shall not dwell on these questions seriatum.

Let us look instead at the case of GSP, where the developed nations have taken specific action to assist the export opportunities of developing nations. The negotiation and implementation of the GSP scheme took more than a decade. The scheme has built into it various types of special safeguards, so that for example, nations that become highly competitive in certain products have their products moved back into the MFN category, the theory being that preferences should help those less competitive. In addition to the trigger mechanisms for reconsideration, there are other complicated criteria. One of these is the degree of value added in the developing country concerned. The U.S. criterion is fairly simple, but the administrative room for interpretation is considerable. In the EC case, the value-added rules vary among products and origins. In addition, especially in the EC case, the classification among tariff categories is highly uncertain (products which enter the EC through Italian ports may be differently classified from the same products entering through Rotterdam). The Japanese system is even more administratively complicated, with even more administrative discretion.

This complexity and uncertainty constitute a hostile environment for introduction of new products. Having liberalized with one hand, the developed countries created with the other new deterrents that minimized the benefits.

This example is given to highlight the continuing difficulty, even in areas where liberalization is ostensibly taking place, of improving the export climate for the developing nations.

The complexity and uncertainty of the nontariff distortions have already been noted. In addition, there are a number of other forces at work which tend to create further market uncertainty. For example, the Soviet Union and Eastern European nations buy very little from the developing nations, and provide very little development assistance. On the other hand, because of rising raw material, food, and technology costs, there is good reason to suppose that these nations will have strong incentives to expand their exports of products of higher value added, especially of manufactures and semimanufactures. Since the international trading rules do not fully apply to systems where the internal prices are administratively determined, a strong new force of international competition is likely to emerge that is more likely to affect the trading position of the developing nations than of the developed nations in competition in world markets.

As the developing nations diversify and move into higher value products and producers' goods, export financing will become a more significant factor in their competitive position as compared with alternative sellers in the industrialized nations. The international rules here are ambiguous and geared to the strong treasury and foreign policy interests of the industrialized nations.

In the pursuit of economic cooperation among the developing countries themselves, as called for at UNCTAD IV, intradeveloping country trade is impeded by an even more complex and administratively erratic array of border measures and procedures typically found in the developing nations themselves. A transnational enterprise is better able to penetrate and cope with market conditions in a developing country than an exporter from another developing country. Thus attempts at preferential liberalization of trade among LDCs, if not accompanied by other, more positive measures, will at least in the initial period tend to benefit mainly the multinationals already in possession of transnational marketing networks.

At the same time, since the political incentive in a developed country is to maintain as great a degree of freedom of action as its major trading partners will allow, the evolution of multilateral trade negotiations is in the direction of keeping if not enlarging the scope for international safeguard actions. It does not matter too much whether this freedom is actually exercised a little less or a little more, since already the threat of it affects potential investors.

The longer-term trend of developed country trade policies, and access to their markets, will also depend upon the evolution of the international institutional framework for commercial transactions, especially the evolution of the transnational enterprises. These enormous economic systems are not just conduits of capital and technology; they are important marketing and distribution systems. If the transnationals draw back from heavy involvement in the developing nations, because of an adverse political climate, a marketing and distribution vacuum will be left that has to be filled in other ways. Moreover, these enterprises have so far been a force favoring more liberal, freer trade policies in the industrialized nations. Thus, if they now concentrate expanded activity in the developed economies, they will tend to become more protectionist and more interested in building up bargaining power and ensuring stable supplies from a "friendly" base. Although such a trend would be costly to the developed countries, it would be even more disruptive to the economies of the developing nations. Breaking through the impediments to trade that already exist, without the help of the international enterprises, would be extremely difficult in many product areas. This is true for penetration of developing country markets as well as of the industrialized nations' markets.

An NIEO or a More Orderly Trading System?

It is my opinion that the developing countries are oversimplifying their problems in calling for declarations of intent to restructure the patterns of world trade and production. We do not know whether we can cope with the rate of restructuring already attained. The great emphasis placed by official negotiators of the developing nations on the principle of differential treatment leaves aside most of the issues that will be important to them in the long run. When reference is made to a *new international economic order*, the word order refers to a structure of relationships assumed to be stable, when the avoidance of disorderly market developments and disorder in policy management may be even more important.

To illustrate, consider the discussions taking place in Geneva in the Multilateral Trade Negotiations (MTN) in the mid-1970s. The Europeans, Japanese, and Canadians have called for a change in U.S. practice in the application of countervailing duties, which would result in introduction of an injury test (the U.S. practice and law predate the GATT, and the United States consequently does not have to determine injury when countervailing duties are under consideration). The United States in response has proposed that a code on subsidy practices be negotiated, covering indirect, internal aids as well as overt export subsidies. The United States has moreover urged that agriculture and industry both be covered by such a new set of rules, while the EC has argued vigorously against this. The developed countries as a group have agreed to handle export financing separately, in the OECD.

While the Geneva scenario is unfolding, the United States has itself been pressed by industry and other domestic complaints to take more vigorous action in the countervailing duty area. Among the nations affected by the new activism have been developing countries exporting such products as shoes and leather products and even cut flowers.

The representatives of the developing nations have concentrated their energies on the elaboration of principles of differential treatment in the area of subsidies, but have paid almost no attention to the basic concepts that they would like the developed country governments to abide by. What are the interests of the developing countries here? Clearly they should want to codify the rules and procedures for application of countervailing duties, so that the uncertainties are removed for exporters. They should also want to limit the freedom of developed countries to subsidize their exports to one another and to third markets where they are in competition with exports from developing nations. They should want to draw in agricultural aids and a matter such as export financing, and they should definitely want to limit and regularize the indirect aids which governments offer in the developed nations.

The industrialized nations can afford to fail to agree on the issue of aids and countervailing duties, and on balance the relative strength of their treasuries puts them in a favorable position with respect to potential competition from developing nations. The developing countries have more at stake in the details and in a successful negotiation. There is a mutual interest, not a conflict of interest in this area, and the question of differential treatment, which can subsequently be dealt with, is a matter of secondary importance.

In the area of quantitative restrictions, the developing nations have called for differential treatment, which is meaningless, since the important restrictions really apply only to developing countries (with the exception of restrictions on Japanese exports, which are fading in importance as Japan's economy comes into line with the structure and performance of the U.S., Canadian, and European economies). Instead, they should be deeply involved in an examination of the multilateral safeguard rules, so as to tie down the developed country governments and force them to follow specified criteria and procedures, and in particular constrain the developed country governments in their use of voluntary restraint agreements.

As regards such matters as standards, customs procedures, and valuation practices, and other administrative controls, both at the border and internally, an effort to introduce regularity would generate much greater benefits to smaller-scale exporters, especially those in developing countries. In the government purchasing area the developing countries also could benefit from enhanced visibility of the criteria for purchasing and the procedures for qualification. On the whole, in these problem areas, introduction of public procedures, published criteria, provision of reasonable adjustment time for foreign suppliers, acceptance of foreign certification, and other such administrative improvements should be of great importance to the developing nations.

A New Mutuality of Interests?

In all of these problem areas, there is a mutuality of interests that is greater than the conflicts of interest between the developed and developing nations.

Turning then to the treatment of primary products and raw materials, there would seem to be some common ground for new styles of negotiation between the developed and the developing countries. The doctrinal differences between those favoring intervention of governments to fix and index prices and those who believe the invisible hand should be left unfettered to work its will in the market have become arguments that are not only tiresome but irrelevant. Given the already existing influences of governments, and the political likelihood that governments will increasingly involve themselves in ownership, management, control, or intensified regulation of producing and trading activities, the real issues are whether (1) adequate investment will take place in a context of political uncertainty and (2) the policies of governments can be carried out in ways that can be considered economically efficient, ensuring stable flows of adequate supplies in relation to trends in demand.

The developing countries have focused on the desire to set and maintain prices at high levels for the primary products they export. There are many well-known arguments against this: nations that do not have exportable commodities will not be helped, and may even be harmed; the primary beneficiaries of higher primary product prices will be the largest exporters of such products which include Canada, Australia, South Africa, the United States, and the Soviet Union; high prices encourage overproduction and substitution; and so on.

On the other hand, the developing countries are interested in assured conditions of market access, and the opportunity economically to process their raw materials. They are interested in stabilization of market conditions, but they would not want prices held down in the face of unusually strong upward price pressures. The developed countries are interested in stability of supplies, and avoidance of inflationary price-ratcheting effects of "destabilizing" speculation. As the political environment gradually alters the role of vertical integration and puts exploration and capacity expansion in the hands of independent suppliers, the developed country governments and businesses are likely to find a change in their own perceptions of what constitute desirable market forces.

Again there is likely to be some growing mutuality of interest, in bargaining about the terms and conditions of supply on the one hand and the assurance of access to markets on the other. This can take place in many ways, bilaterally, regionally, multilaterally, in cartels or cartel-like operations, or independently. This is as true in agriculture as in extractive industries. The political ability to liberalize imports of agricultural products depends in part on the assurance that if a nation becomes more import-dependent, the security of its supplies increases in parallel fashion. Otherwise, self-sufficiency is politically more attractive, where possible. Now no single supplier nation can give a binding assurance, because that nation may suffer drought or pestilence or become caught up in extraordinary inflationary forces that bring about export limitations. The collectivity of all suppliers can, however, give assurances based on the insurance principle of risk pooling—assurances that may be backed by buffer stocks that could cover the shortfalls of individual suppliers.

Collective assurances do not require common stocks, but they might. A collective approach does not require price fixing, although it might. The real question is whether there is a will to work out common rules that apply to commercial activities in raw materials and primary products including farm products, rules that bind governments, government trading entities, and to a considerable extent set boundaries on the activities of private traders. Krause has argued that this is the right avenue, and that general principles governing all commodity trade are both negotiable and desirable.[9] Such a package could of course contain other logically related benefits for developing countries, such as reduction of the escalation of tariffs on processed products entering the industrialized nations. Fred Bergsten's paper in this volume suggests some conceptual packages in the same spirit.[10]

Whatever the approach, it would seem evident that bilateralism or selective collusion should be avoided; that governments will be active anyway and therefore their policies need to be channeled, to minimize intergovernmental conflicts and distortions; that the agreed policies must ensure that adequate long-term investment takes place in exploration and production of raw materials; and that market forces play a positive role only when the rules of the game, comprising all these considerations, are fixed.

Thus liberalization is by itself not an adequate policy for developed countries, nor is it all that the developing countries should want. Doctrinal pursuit of the virtues of free markets cannot be meaningful without establishing boundaries for legitimate government action, since governments must act for political reasons. Indeed, it could be said even more strongly that there is no virtue in the free market, indeed there is no free market, without fixed rules of all kinds, including those establishing boundaries for government action.

The trading system should provide opportunity for rearrangement of economic functions in some approximation of long-term comparative advantage, but the adjustment process must be sufficiently orderly to avoid major reassessments of trade policy and general economic policy that lead to economic insularity. The process of interdependence brings overall economic gain, but the market does not necessarily distribute the gains in an equitable way internationally any more than it does on a national basis, and this means that care has to be taken to manage the relationships of social and private costs and benefits. The distortions that can arise in international commercial relations may be intentional, or they may result from differences in economic and social policies and have accidental effects. The complexities and uncertainties implicit in trade policy and economic policy management constitute a deterrent to trade expansion of developing nations, both in their trade with the industrialized nations and in their trade with one another.

The Need for Orderly Trading Policies as well as an Orderly Trading System

This essay takes a slightly different perspective, then, from the traditional discussions of the need for more open trading policies combined with adequate adjustment assistance policies (particularly for labor). Emphasis here is put on policy interactions in a politically active world, and the need to reduce the complexities and uncertainties that are consequent to policy interactions. Liberalization is one of the tools to use in building a better system; but it is not in itself sufficient.

The developing countries need (1) orderly macroeconomic and microeconomic adjustment procedures that facilitate adjustment in the developed countries; and (2) an orderly multilateral trading system with rules and obligations that limit the freedom of action of all nations, so that the richer and stronger nations cannot act freely to limit or assist selected trade flows on the basis of power alone.

The developing countries need to depoliticize the microeconomic adjustment policies in the developed countries as much as possible, and to get the developed countries committed to common rules that can act as a restraint on the special interests of each economic sector. Putting the trading house in order may require that the developing nations themselves undertake commitments, but this is not a question of reciprocity. Rather, if all the parties to the system are following common rules, the stronger and richer are by that means brought into a more equal relationship with the weaker and poorer. From that basis one can talk about differential policies that bring about income redistribution and structural rearrangements. But if the trade policies and practices of the industrialized nations are left as they are now, with token exceptions being granted here and there in the form of preferences and tropical product concessions, the road to trade expansion for the developing countries will be long and difficult.

From the point of view of the developed countries, putting order in the trading house, and consequently limiting the boundaries of policy freedom, is desirable at a time when political activism is getting out of control, and policy inconsistencies and administrative complexities are causing increasing distortions and escalating budgetary expenditures.

Notes

1 The author is grateful to Jan Tumlir, Gardner Patterson, and Lawrence Krause for comments and suggestions.

2 A number of studies on nontariff trade distortions have been written by Robert Baldwin, Ingo Walter, Gerard and Victoria Curzons, and others. For an introduction to the current negotiating problems, taking into account legal and institutional matters, see Matthew J. Marks and Harald B. Malmgren, "Negotiating Nontariff Distortions to Trade," *Law and Policy in International Business*, Vol. 7, No. 2, 1975, pp. 327-411.

3 Mahbub ul Haq, "Industrialisation and Trade Policies in the 1970s: Developing Country Alternatives" in Paul Streeten, ed., *Trade Strategies for Development*, Macmillan, London, 1973, p. 95.

4 J. Bhagwati, "Market Disruption, Export Market Disruption, Compensation, and GATT Reform" in J. Bhagwati, ed., *The New International Economic Order*, The MIT Press, Cambridge, Mass., 1977.

5 Many of the intricacies of the law and the procedures under it relating to certain types of safeguard action are explained in Marks and Malmgren, "Negotiating Nontariff Distortions."

6 J. Tumlir, "Adjustment Cost and Policies to Reduce It," MIT Workshop paper.

7 See my argument about the nature of macroeconomic equilibrium in H. B. Malmgren, "Information and Period Analysis in Economic Decisions" in J. N. Wolfe, ed., *Value, Capital, and Growth: Papers in Honour of Sir John Hicks*, Edinburgh, 1968.

8 I have discussed the problem of inertia in connection with the history of the evolution of the Trade Act of 1974 in "Sources of Instability in the World Trading System," *Journal of International Affairs*, Spring 1976.

9 Lawrence Krause, statement before the Subcommittee on International Organization, Committee on International Relations, U.S. House of Representatives, May 19, 1975; and statement before the Subcommittee on International trade, Investment, and Monetary Policy of the Committee on Banking, Currency and Housing, U.S. House of Representatives, July 10, 1975. My own monograph, *The Raw Material and Commodity Controversy*, also goes into all these issues (International Economic Studies Institute, Contemporary Issues No. 1, Washington, October 1975).

10 C. Fred Bergsten, "Access to Supplies, Export Cartels, and Reform of the GATT" in *The New International Economic Order.*

References

Bergsten, C. Fred, 1977, "Access to Supplies and the New International Economic Order" in J. Bhagwati, ed, *The New International Economic Order* (The MIT Press, Cambridge, Mass.).

Bhagwati, J., 1977, "Market Disruption, Export Market Disruption, Compensation, and GATT Reform" in *The New International Economic Order.*

Malmgren, H. B., 1968, Information and Period Analysis in Economic Decisions in J. N. Wolfe, ed., *Value, Capital, and Growth: Papers in Honour of Sir John Hicks* (Edinburgh).

Malmgren, H. B., 1975, October, *The Raw Material and Commodity Controversy*, International Economic Studies Institute, Contemporary Issue No. 1, Washington, D.C.

Malmgren, H. B., 1976, Spring, "Sources of Instability in the World Trading System," *Journal of International Affairs.*

Marks, Matthew J., and Malmgren, Harald B., 1975, "Negotiating Nontariff Distortions to Trade," *Law and Policy in International Business*, Vol. 7, No. 2, 327-411.

Tumlir, J., "Adjustment Cost and Policies to Reduce It," MIT Workshop paper.

Ul Haq, Mahbub, 1973, "Industrialisation and Trade Policies in the 1970s: Developing Country Alternatives" in Paul Streeten, ed., *Trade Strategies for Development* (Macmillan, London) 95.

Comment
Gardner Patterson

I will limit my comments to emphasizing, and elaborating, the point Malmgren makes about the efforts in the current Multilateral Trade Negotiations (MTN) to provide special and differentiated treatment for the developing countries. My central point is that this is a very pervasive and deep-seated development and that it has great implications for the form and content of the new international economic order, a part of which is being hammered out in these trade negotiations.

As the world grappled with the many-faceted problem of economic development and, in particular, the problems of expanding the production and export of manufactured and processed goods from developing countries, a great many people, including some in this workshop, concluded that high on the list of obstacles were the old and established commercial policy rules and, notably, most-favored-nation (MFN) treatment. It became conventional wisdom that MFN treatment meant discriminatory treatment when applied to countries at unequal levels of development.

I think it can be said that, following the long debate which resulted in the institution of the Generalized System of Preferences (GSP), an accepted element in, if not indeed a major objective for, trade relations between developed and developing countries became discrimination in favor of the latter.

This development was strikingly shown in Tokyo in September 1973 when the trade ministers of over 100 countries launched the present MTN and unanimously adopted the Tokyo Declaration—a statement that had been laboriously negotiated, word by word, during the preceding summer. This states in paragraph 5:

... The Ministers recognize the need for special measures to be taken in the negotiations to assist the developing countries in their efforts to increase their export earnings and promote their economic development. ... They also recognize the importance of maintaining and improving the Generalized System of Preferences. They further recognize the importance of the application of differential measures to developing countries in ways which will provide special and more favourable treatment for them in areas of the negotiation where this is feasible and appropriate.

This ministerial declaration also apecifies that the situation and problems of the least developed among the developing countries are to be given special attention, and that such countries are to receive special treatment in the context of any measures taken in favor of developing countries generally.

Let there be no question about the importance of these words. They are a commitment. And a great deal of thought, time, and effort is being given these days in the MTN in Geneva, and in a great many capitals, as to the precise ways in which this obligation to devise differential measures to provide special and more favorable treatment to developing countries, and even more special and favorable treatment to the least developed among them, can be discharged.

It is no longer a question of whether there shall be differential and special treatment. It is now a question of how.

We now have in the MTN six major negotiating groups dealing, respectively, with: tariffs, agriculture (with subgroups dealing with the problems of trade in cereals, meat, and dairy products), sectors, safeguards, tropical products, and nontariff measures (with special negotiating subgroups on subsidies and countervailing duties, quantitative restrictions, standards, and customs matters).

In each one of these groups, specific and concrete efforts are being made both by representatives from the developing *and* the developed countries to find ways in which special and differentiated treatment can be provided. In the field of tariffs, for example, there are proposals for deeper cuts than a general formula will provide for products of special interest to developing countries that are not included in the various GSPs; shallower cuts for products that benefit from the GSP; establishment of new tariff subheadings to permit differential treatment for developing countries' exports; advance implementation of any agreed cuts for products coming primarily from developing countries; exclusion from any exceptions list products imported from developing countries; elimination of tariff escalation on products of interest to developing countries; and so forth.

In the field of agriculture, for some products the special treatment being sought for tariff and nontariff measures may be applicable. But the search does not end there. Thus, in preliminary discussions regarding the possibility of international commodity arrangements for certain major agricultural products, it has been proposed to give preferences to purchases in developing countries, should there be stockpiling arrangements; to possibly exempt developing exporting countries from any maximum prices that may be agreed upon; to exempt developing importing countries from commitments to import certain quantities at the minimum price when the world market is weak; and so on. This is not to say that such proposals will be accepted, or that some of them are not being violently opposed, but the point I wish to make is that they are being seriously put forward and seriously examined.

In the sectors negotiations, the possibility is being explored of selecting sectors of particular interest for developing countries for free trade treatment from the raw materials through the most finished products. This is one way of dealing with the problem of tariff escalation, but it is an approach that also covers all nontariff measures.

In the negotiating group on safeguards, several proposals are on the negotiating table as to ways in which differentiated treatment could be provided for developing countries. Among the possibilities put forward are a general commitment to exclude imports from developing countries from the application of safeguard measures by developed countries. Where such total exclusion is not feasible, it has been proposed, inter alia, that safeguard restrictions be applied to exports from developing countries only if it has been verified that imports from developing countries have caused serious injury in terms of employment and production levels in the importing countries and only if such restrictions are accompanied by adjustment measures in the importing country designed to move resources out of the competing industry. It has also been proposed that no safeguard measures may be applied if they cause serious injury to developing countries in terms of employment and production.

In the area of nontariff measures the search also goes on. In the field of quantitative restrictions one proposal is to eliminate forthwith those applying to imports from developing countries. Where this is not possible, an easing should be applied first to developing countries. Too complicated to go into here is the discussion of how to provide special and differential treatment in a possible code on standards. A major element in the trade negotiations is the effort to find solutions to the problem of subsidies and countervailing duties. Here too there is a major effort to negotiate rules favoring the developing countries. Thus, inter alia, it has been proposed that there be established a "positive list" of export subsidies authorized for developing countries and immune from countervailing action by others; that the injury criteria, when invoked against imports from developing countries, must be with reference to the industry as a whole in the developed country and not just to certain units; and that injury criteria in developing countries be less demanding than in developed countries.

The negotiations on tropical products are by their nature highly concentrated on products of interest to developing countries and here the special treatment primarily takes the form of this being recognized as a priority sector with an effort being made to reach agreement on opening markets in developed countries for tropical products at an early stage in the negotiations. I might note, parenthetically, that considerable concrete progress has already been made in fulfilling this commitment.

Perhaps it needs to be pointed out that the proposals I am citing here are not simply being mentioned casually in conversations but are positions that have been put in written form as concrete proposals, with supporting justification and defense.

Finally, I should mention that the Tokyo Declaration—mandate for these trade negotiations—also provides that consideration shall be given to improvements in the international framework for world trade, sometimes referred to as "reform of the international trading system." It is obvious that a great deal of reform of the trading system will be a direct consequence of the detailed negotiations in specific fields, whether they be sectors, safeguards, countervailing duties, subsidies, tariffs, commodity agreements, or whatever. However, not all questions of reform will be treated there, and it is to be noted that at the last meeting of the Trade Negotiations Committee, the top oversight committee of the trade negotiations, a proposal was made to establish a negotiating group with the following mandate: "To improve the international framework for the conduct of world trade, particularly with respect to trade between developed and developing countries and differentiated and more favourable measures to be adopted in such trade." Discussions on this are now underway, but the point I wish to make here is that on the most comprehensive level of reform, as well as in the specific details of the negotiations, great efforts are being made to provide, within the trade negotiations, for differentiated and special treatment for developing countries.

It needs to be stressed that while the initial drive for special rules and special treatment originated in the developing countries, the developed countries have accepted as legitimate that there shall be such differentiated treatment. The efforts to provide it pervade the entire negotiations.

In conclusion, note again that it is not my purpose here to defend or to argue with what is going on. It is only to emphasize that anyone seriously concerned with the subject of this conference—reform of the international trading system—must accept that powerful forces are at work creating a two-tier, or perhaps a many-tiered, international trading system.

9
Commodities: Less Developed Countries' Demands and Developed Countries' Responses
Harry G. Johnson

1. A Disobliging Introduction

Since trade in primary products—foodstuffs and raw materials—constitutes by far the preponderant part of the exports of the developing countries as a group, that part of the demands for a new international economic order that is concerned with a so-called integrated commodity policy is quantitatively by far the most important of these demands, and if implemented would involve the most far-reaching changes in the system not only of international trade but of domestic economic organization in both the developed and the developing countries. It would be more accurate to say, however, "if an attempt were made to implement it," since the integrated commodity policy is neither integrated nor a policy, but an attempt to paper over with semantic ambiguity a variety of inconsistent policies and policy objectives for particular commodities and their producers, policies whose presumed feasibility rests on the creation of a degree of comprehensive monopolistic organization of international trade in commodities that has never even remotely existed in the past and has no possibility of being achievable in the present.

Commodity agreements as a solution to the various problems of primary product exporters are neither a new idea, nor yet an idea that has not been tried in practice, in historical experience. Commodity agreements of one kind and another have on the contrary over a half century of experience behind them, all of it a history of failure: of the various commodity agreements that have been experimented with, only the latest tin agreement survives, and only in a truncated fashion—and tin has the peculiar advantage of involving fairly large-scale enterprises. Yet the faith in commodity agreements as a panacea survives, particularly (academically) at Oxford, the home of lost causes. And, as is usually the case, the faith rests either on ignorance of past history or the obstinate belief that what went wrong last time was attributable to lack of will or cleverness, or unwillingness to commit sufficient financial resources to the enterprise, but never to inherent difficulties that could be understood in terms of elementary economic analysis.

Nor is the concept of an integrated commodity policy a new concept, though it may appear so to those innocent of the history of UNCTAD. (For a survey of issues raised at the First United Nations Conference on Trade and Development, see Johnson, 1967.) In fact, Professor Bhagwati and I participated some eight years ago in an exercise conducted in preparation for the second UNCTAD, the purpose of which was to assist the secretariat to develop an integrated policy for commodities. In the course of that exercise it quickly became apparent that the task was impossible, because the objectives sought to be implemented were inconsistent at even the most elementary level of economic analysis. They included such objectives as stabilizing prices in the short run, raising prices in every run, achieving prices that would be fair and just to producers while not being unfair to consumers ("equitable to consumers and remunerative to producers," in the current phrase), maximizing profits from exports, maximizing foreign exchange earnings from exports, and achieving parity (though it was usually not called that) of real income for primary product and manufacturing goods producers (see Johnson, 1968).

The integration part of the integrated commodity policy was only too obviously a political integration, UNCTAD style—that is, the word integration applied not to the policy, but to the demand for something for nothing for anyone who thought he deserved it. The contemporary demand for an integrated commodity policy has exactly the same features of being integrated only in the sense of demanding the creation of a monopoly of the same general sort for a sufficient number of would-be monopolists to make the idea of organized exploitation of consumers by producers politically appealing to a majority of producers; it is integrated in fact only in the sense of seeking to establish a common fund to finance detailed schemes of an as yet to be worked out kind for individual commodities; and it attempts to enlist the support of the consumers whom it is intended to exploit as willing accomplices in their own exploitation by deliberate misapplication of concepts of fairness and justice derived from unconnected areas of economic discussion. (The most noteworthy example is the attempt to misapply the concept of indexing, as a means of providing automatic protection of income recipients against the windfall gains and losses inherent in an unanticipated inflationary increase in the *general* level of *money* prices, to the quite different and debatable proposal to fix the *relative real* prices of particular primary commodities in terms of industrial products.)

Before proceeding to detailed consideration of the proposed integrated commodity policy, it is relevant to call attention to the extent to which that policy, and the demand for a so-called new international economic order of which it is a part, is based on a fossilized piece of politico-economic analysis of the development problem whose inspiration was the economic phenomena of the Great Depression of the 1930s, and in particular the Prebisch world vision in which the terms of trade between commodities and manufactures inevitably turn trendwise against commodities, requiring policies on the one hand of forced industrialization and on the other of countervailing monopolization to counteract the presumed monopoly powers of the industrialized countries to force down commodity prices in terms of manufactures. The strength of this mythological view of the process of economic development, a view that UNCTAD's own so-called experts have been unable to document statistically, except by the intellectually shady process of taking each successive peak of commodity prices reached under world boom conditions as the floor from which to make subsequent measurements, can be accounted for only by a deep emotional and political need to find an external scapegoat for the condition of economic backwardness—a need whose strength has to be appreciated if rational consideration of proposed ostensibly economic policies is to be at all possible. One aspect of the Prebisch world view is especially worth mentioning, since its significance has come to be appreciated only recently, and still imperfectly. The historical experience of deep world depression from which the Prebisch vision originates was a phenomenon of the (Keynesian?) short run, during which population as well as technology can be safely assumed to be constant for practical purposes. Any longer-run proposition or policy proposal concentrating on the terms of trade as a strategic variable cannot hope to comprehend the economic forces at work without paying great attention to the role of population—and particularly to the classical Malthusian presumption that, unless checked, population tends to breed to the level of subsistence—in determining the international division of the gains from trade, including the possibility of altering this distribution by the organization of producer (or producer-country) monopoly power.

2. An Integrated Program for Commodities

The Integrated Program for Commodities (Secretary-General of UNCTAD, 1975)[1] has four general objectives:

(i) to encourage more orderly conditions in general in commodity trade, both with regard to prices and the volume of trade, in the interest of both producers and consumers; (ii) to ensure adequate growth in the real commodity export returns of individual developing countries; (iii) to reduce fluctuations in export earnings; and (iv) to improve access to markets of developed countries for developing country exports of primary and processed products.

These are restated in relation to commodity arrangements as follows:

(a) Reduction of excessive fluctuations in commodity prices and supplies, taking account of the special importance of this objective in the cases of essential foodstuffs and natural products facing competition from stable-priced substitutes;

(b) Establishment and maintenance of commodity prices at levels which, in real terms, are equitable to consumers and remunerative to producers . . .

(c) Assurance of access to supplies of primary commodities for importing countries, with particular attention to essential foodstuffs and raw materials;

(d) Assurance of access to markets, especially those of developed countries, for commodity exporting countries;

(e) Expansion of the processing of primary commodities in developing countries;

(f) Improvement of the competitiveness of natural products vis-à-vis synthetics;

(g) Improvement of the quantity and reliability of food aid to developing countries in need.

However, "to ensure that no developing country experiences an adverse net effect from commodity pricing policies pursued within the integrated programme, differential measures in favour of developing importing countries . . . should be an accepted feature of international commodity arrangements established within the programme," including "special measures for 'least developed' and 'most seriously affected' developing countries which are exporting or importing members" of arrangements within the integrated program. Specifically mentioned are exemption from sharing the financial costs and risks of stocks, and preferred treatment in the allocation of export quotas.

Priority is to be given to seventeen commodities of importance to developing countries in international trade, covering three quarters of their exports from their agricultural and mineral sectors (*excluding petroleum*), and particularly to ten "core commodities" (cocoa, coffee, tea, sugar, hard fibers, jute and manufactures, cotton, rubber, copper, tin).[2]

The specific proposals of the Secretary-General of UNCTAD for international action are as follows:

(a) The establishment of a common fund for the financing of international stocks;

(b) The setting up of a series of international commodity stocks;

(c) The negotiation of other measures necessary for the attainment of the objectives of the programme within the framework of international commodity agreements;

(d) Improved compensatory financing for the maintenance of stability in export earnings.

The common fund and the international stocking policies are regarded as the core of the program. The other measures essentially remove any integrative element of the program such as might be provided by a standard format for the individual stocking arrangements, leaving the common fund—described as "essential if impetus is to be given to the building up of international stocks of major storable commodities"—as the only integrative feature. The provision for improved compensatory financing for stabilizing export earnings is an indirect recognition of the fact that stabilizing, and even on average raising, the prices of commodities is an indirect and inefficient way of stabilizing and possibly increasing the flow of disposable income to the developing countries. Taken as a whole, the action program can without blatant unfairness be described as a demand for a massive investment of funds by the developed countries to underwrite experiments with and promotion of individual commodity-by-commodity agreements, experiments to the pursuit of which the UNCTAD Secretariat and its developing nation clientele are committed in spite of an uneasy half-recognition that international commodity agreements—aside from the difficulty of devising and operating them—

are an exceedingly doubtful instrument for promoting economic development.

The common fund is crucial to the whole policy, the main reason given for it being to encourage the development of stocking schemes by assuring finance. The total sum mentioned is $3 billion, $1 billion of capital and $2 billion of loans. The point is made that the common fund would need less finance than the aggregate of the individual stocking schemes. How significant this pooling effect would be is doubtful, for two main reasons. One reason is that the fund is envisaged, not as a common pool of finance, but as a source for finance of the individual commodity schemes; hence there is no assurance that surplus financial assets in one scheme will be available to finance stocks of commodities in other schemes. The other reason is that the economies of finance achievable by pooling finance are greater or less according to whether the financial needs of the pooling members vary inversely or directly with one another; and, as studies by Richard Cooper among others have shown (and as is evident from the empirical studies of business-cycle-related behavior of commodity prices in general), there is probably not that much scope for economies from pooling finance among commodity agreements (pooling of foreign exchange reserves might possibly offer more gains). Mention should also be made of two mysterious allusions to presumptive advantages—the increased "bargaining strength" of the common fund, and "redressing the balance between the developed and the developing countries."

Turning to stocking arrangements, the relevant paragraph reads as follows:

International stocking measures are proposed for export commodities subject to natural variation in supply (e.g., tropical beverages, sugar, cotton, jute and hard fibres). They are also advocated for commodities with a history of disruption in output or demand, and where international stock management would help to prevent temporary restriction of production, wastage and uneconomic investment (copper, tin and rubber). Furthermore, security of basic food grain supplies at reasonable prices, entailing the creation of international stocks of wheat and rice, is in the interest of developing countries as importers, among other measures for assistance with food trade problems of importing countries.

The problem of storage of food grains against famine or scarcity conditions will not be dealt with in this paper, since it is in principle a problem different from commodity price stabilization in general. It involves food distribution facilities as well as stocks, is dealt with by other writers, and in any case cereals are not included in the core of ten commodities. The first two sentences of the paragraph lump together two different economic problems— instability of supply, and instability of demand—requiring quite different solutions, in a manner that one has to learn to tolerate as measuring the economic illiteracy of the UNCTAD economic secretariat. The elementary economic analysis required to demonstrate that, apart from certain exceptional cases of constellation of demand and supply elasticities, stocking aimed at stabilizing prices will reduce the instability of producer incomes when the instability of prices is due to random or unforeseen cyclical demand shifts, but will increase that instability of incomes when the instability of prices originates on the supply side, is too familiar to need rehearsal to this conference, though obviously not so for UNCTAD's economists. The section on compensatory financing in fact recognizes that "more stable world prices may not always [sic] stabilize earnings for an individual country if its export supply is adversely affected by poor crop conditions."

The section on other measures for individual commodities stresses supply management (including export quotas and uniform export taxes) and concludes that while "By means of stocking, supply management or trade commitments, or by combinations of these measures, it should be possible, for some commodities at least, to achieve the objective of maintaining prices at adequate levels in real terms," and that "in some cases it might not be possible to prevent a deterioration in the trend of prices in real terms, especially if world inflation continues to be relatively rapid." Why commodity prices, whose volatility it is the objective of the program to counteract, should be stickier than other prices in adjusting to inflation, is not explained, especially given the emphasis often placed in Prebisch-style arguments on the rigid administered nature of the prices of manufactured goods. The main point, however, is that the argument of this section changes the intended purpose of commodity agreements from price stabilization to the maintenance or raising of the real price of the commodities covered by the agreements in terms of manufactured goods (or other goods in general). In other words, it becomes the maintenance of what in the history of American agricultural policy was described as parity between farm and industrial prices, though, as a later reference indicates, this objective is confused, either in ignorance or deliberately, with the notion of indexing of prices.

The section on compensatory financing refers generally to the inadequacy (undefined, except by implication) of existing provisions, and asks for more emphasis on a commodity orientation and on real export earnings, and more liberal terms, including a grant element for the poorest countries.

3. Critical Discussion

Contemplation of the Integrated Program for Commodities suggests any number of questions, of which only three general ones are raised here. The first is whether the developing countries group, in its own interests, is well advised to press for a new international economic order based on the effort to exploit monopoly power in particular commodities on a fair shares basis to be achieved somehow by agreement among exporting and importing nations with varying interests in particular commodities. The second, closely related, question is why it is that political figures (including in this term the staff of UNCTAD) are so tenacious in their insistence on formulating questions of exploitation or more neutrally of justice in terms of schemes for rigging prices and adjusting supplies and production, in spite of the virtually axiomatic elementary economic principle that prices neither define the true problem nor provide an effective way to its solution. With respect to both questions, one might well venture the judgment that the ideas of Raúl Prebisch, especially as institutionalized and vulgarized through UNCTAD, have become an increasingly powerful obstacle to cooperation in the promotion of the development of the developing countries, in the specific sense that sympathy with aspirations for development has to be demonstrated by the acceptance of economic nonsense and the endorsement of proposals that not only maximize the prospective costs and minimize the prospective return for the developed countries, but are certain to create dissension among the developing countries as well (witness the need to develop a new category of especially disadvantaged countries to reflect the differential impact among developing countries of the increase in the price of oil).

The third question is why so little attention has been paid to the means by which an integrated program for commodities might be implemented so as to achieve the objectives (or some of them) that it is intended to serve, as compared and contrasted with the effort put into argument for new institutional arrangements and discussion of their objectives. An apparently simple but in fact almost impossible to solve question is: What should the manager of a commodity stock actually do, in his day-to-day operations, in order to smooth out price fluctuations? As a protracted discussion of practical operating rules in *The Economic Journal* in the early 1950s showed, there is no easy answer, *even if* one vastly oversimplifies the problem by assuming that producers act in ignorance of the fact that the stockpile manager is operating to affect prices. One can, of course, assume that producer incomes do not matter, that the real purpose is to stabilize and increase the taxes that governments of developing countries can extract from their primary producers; but while that assumption is only too congenial to some varieties of economic development specialist, it both prejudges the issue of what development means and how it is best achieved, and makes nonsense of the moral rhetoric about the obligation of the rich to contribute resources to the poor. (There is nothing morally commanding about a presumed obligation of taxpayers and consumers in countries whose average citizen is well off to surrender resources to the governments and ruling elites of countries whose average citizen is poor—especially if the latter's poverty is maintained and increased by the policies of his government toward him.) To approach the point from a different angle, it is rather ironic that at the same time as central banks have been abandoning their conviction that they know how to intervene to stabilize exchange rates, and commercial banks their belief that they can outguess the private exchange speculators, the developing countries have been demanding changes in the organization of world trade in commodities that assume that international organizations can easily manage the very similar markets in commodities.

The purpose of this workshop, however, is not to raise broad issues about the politics and economics of development as currently conceived, at least by the group of developing countries in the framework of UNCTAD, but to consider and discuss specific proposals and desirable developed country responses to LDC demands regarding the new international economic order. In that context, it seems to me that acceptance of the proposition that what is most required is the organization of commodity trade in a series of stocking agreements reinforced by measures to restrict output and raise prices, or to fix real prices of commodities in terms of manufactures or import goods in general, and implementation of that acceptance in the concrete form of subscribing a large sum of investment capital to finance commodity schemes, would be a most undesirable response. It would certainly be a response that denied both the experience of history and the relevance of elementary economics (by which, to guard against waste of time in ideological polemics, is meant the economics of rational behavior by individuals and economic groups confronted with possibilities of substitution).

It would also be a response that disregarded what comes close to being a professional consensus among those who have looked carefully into the problems that are sought to be remedied by commodity policy. That consensus can be summarized briefly, in two general principles. First, insofar as stability is concerned, compensatory financing related to shortfalls of foreign exchange earnings (and possibly in some cases excesses of import expenditure) in relation to expected levels is the most effective approach. Second, insofar as resource transfers from richer to poorer nations are concerned, aid related to needs and capacities to pay is far superior to transfers related to exports and imports of particular commodities. Awareness of either principle is scarcely reflected in the assertion that existing compensatory financing arrangements are inadequate.

The only favorable partial response to this particular demand that could conceivably make sense would be the subscription of money to a common fund, subject to a firm maximum limit, and with no commitment to policing the commodity agreements so financed, as a means of educating the developing countries in the problems of defining and achieving stabilization of commodity prices, or possibly of establishing "prices that are equitable to consumers and remunerative to producers." Even that concession would be likely to result in the equivalent of what might be termed "the burden of debt financing syndrome," by which the advanced countries find it easier to throw good money after bad than to admit to themselves and force the developing countries to recognize that the initial investment was a bad idea in the first place. (Recall that contributions to the finance of food storage arrangements as insurance against the natural disasters of crop failures, earthquakes, and so forth, are regarded here as being a problem different from the general case of international commodity arrangements.)

If a constructive response to the demand for commodity arrangements—a response that makes some concession to the proposition that such arrangements could under favorable circumstances and with intelligent management ease the problems of the governments, perhaps even of the publics, of developing countries—is desired, one approach might be to contribute resources generously to further research on the management principles and operating rules required to achieve the objectives that commodity agreements are intended to achieve. What does a price stabilization stocking arrangement have to do, in terms of deciding when to buy or to sell and how much, to be successful in achieving its objective? How should it conduct its operations to minimize the destabilizing effects of its running out of cash, or out of commodity?[3] Another important question, raised by the prospective simultaneous existence of agreements covering a majority or all of the commodities most important in developing country trade, is the requirement of consistency among the actions of the different stocking schemes, for example those projected for coffee, tea, and cocoa (or even more seriously, among the seventeen major commodities, those for hard fiber, jute, and wool). This kind of question becomes far more serious if the objective of the commodity agreements is to raise and not stabilize prices. In that event, questions would also arise about the development effects of export quotas, taxes, and related arrangements for restricting exports and/or production, especially since the UNCTAD literature tends to ignore the effects of such adjuncts to price-raising schemes in creating instability in producer production planning and investment decisions, not to speak of reducing the income-earning opportunities of at least some groups of producers.

A more fundamental research approach, though one not likely to command much interest in the confrontational setting of the United Nations and the limited economic understanding of the UNCTAD staff, would be to concentrate on the issue of why commodity prices fluctuate as much as they do, how far and in what respects such fluctuations have the undeniable adverse development effects that UNCTAD lore—and earlier popular beliefs about the development problem—invariably and sweepingly attribute to them, and on what if anything can be done to mitigate the fluctuations by tackling the basic causes rather than the symptoms (in the form of price fluctuations themselves). One might suggest that both the instability and the low level (by comparison with aspirations or expectations) of the commodity export earnings of developing countries are associated with the limitation of access to alternative income-producing opportunities, in the exporting developing countries, a consequence partly of the low level of economic development itself, as reflected in relative current scarcity of industrial skills (including the skills required by modern agriculture), and partly of a rapid rate of growth of population which both inhibits the development of skills and creates an elastic supply of low-income-earning labor. This, in turn, would suggest a constructive response to less developed country demands in the indirect forms of substantial support for population control policies and for programs of mass elementary education with an emphasis on vocational training.

Notes

1 It is sometimes argued, with apparent seriousness, that the wording and argument of documents of this kind should be disregarded, as being politically constrained pronouncements, and that instead the economist should either concentrate his attention on the internal staff documents that are presumed to provide the scientific basis for the propaganda publications (but which unfortunately are generally not available for public scrutiny), or assume that such documentation exists and supports the propaganda publications. This argument is both disingenuous and inadmissible, quite apart from the published evidence that the UNCTAD directorate has deliberately suppressed expert scientific studies whose findings disagree with its published propaganda. The secretariat of an international institution must be held responsible for the scientific quality of the documents it puts into circulation, and it is certainly no part of a professional economist's responsibility to connive at that secretariat's efforts to pass propaganda off as scientific work.

2 The other seven are bananas, wheat, rice, and meat; wool; and iron ore and bauxite.

3 One point raised in subsequent conference discussion is worth drawing attention to. Some experts thought that the problem with commodities was that there is not enough speculation, in the sense that speculation takes a too short-run perspective and hence tends to produce destabilizing "bandwagon" effects on prices. An alternative way of putting this point is that markets function reasonably well in fair weather but go wild when disasters strike. If this proposition is accepted, it raises a very serious problem indeed with respect to the probable effectiveness of commodity stock arrangements, since such arrangements necessarily assume that a stock of finite size, related to normal trade volumes, is sufficient to provide the desired degree of stability, whereas the contention is that it is the cases of deviation *outside* the normal range of variation that cause the serious trouble—and would in turn require a capacity for market intervention far transcending that of a normally constituted buffer stock.

References

Johnson, H. G., 1967, "Economic Policies toward Less Developed Countries" (Brookings Institution, Washington, D.C., and George Allen & Unwin, London).

_____, 1968, "Alternative Maximization Policies for Developing Country Exports of Primary Commodities," *Journal of Political Economy*, 76, 489-493.

Secretary-General of UNCTAD, 1975, "An Integrated Programme for Commodities: Specific Proposals for Decision and Action by Governments," Report TD/B/C.1/193, October 28, 1975; supporting documents, TD/B/C.1/194-197.

Appendix:
The Elementary Algebra of Buffer Stocks

Choose units so that average price and quantity are each unity; x_d and x_s are shift parameters for the demand and supply curves, p the change in price, and a and b the demand and supply elasticities:

$$q_d = 1 + x_d - ap$$

$$q_s = 1 + x_s + bp.$$

In the absence of stocks and price stabilization,

$$q_d = q_s$$

$$p = \frac{x_d - x_s}{a + b}$$

and producer revenue $= (1 + p)q_s$

$$= 1 + x_s + \frac{x_d - x_s}{a + b}(1 + b + x_s) + \frac{b}{(a + b)^2}(x_d - x_s)^2.$$

For demand variations, set $x_s = 0$, and consider two shifts, x_d and $-x_d$. Two-period producer revenues are

$$1 + \frac{x_d(1 + b)}{a + b} + \frac{bx_d^2}{(a + b)^2}$$

$$1 - \frac{x_d(1 + b)}{a + b} + \frac{bx_d^2}{(a + b)^2}.$$

By comparison with stabilization (equal revenues of 1 per period each period) the average deviation is $x_d(1 + b)/a + b$ per period; and the increase in average revenue is $bx_d^2/(a + b)^2$ per period. Stabilization of price reduces variance of receipts at the cost of reducing average revenue.

For supply variations, set $x_d = 0$ and consider two shifts, x_s and $-x_s$. Two-period producer revenues are

$$1 + x_s - x_s\frac{1 + b + x_s}{a + b} + \frac{b}{(a + b)^2}x_s^2$$

$$1 - x_s + x_s\frac{1 + b - x_s}{a + b} + \frac{b}{(a + b)^2}x_s^2.$$

By comparison with price stabilization, which produces an average per period deviation of x_s, the average per period deviation is

$$x_s\frac{a - 1}{a + b}$$

which will be less than x_s unless $a, b < 1$ and $a < \frac{1 - b}{2}$. In other words, except for very low demand and supply elasticities, producer income will vary more with price stabilization (than in its absence).[1] On the other hand, in the absence of stabilization average income is reduced by

$$\frac{a\,x_s^2}{(a+b)^2}.$$

In summary, price stabilization through buffer stocks stabilizes producer income at the expense of reducing its average level, in the case of instability due to demand shifts; by contrast, in the case of instability due to supply shifts, it (normally) increases instability of producer income, while increasing its average level.

Turning to the question of combined instability on the demand and supply sides, special interest attaches to the "cobweb cycle" case, $x_d = -x_s$. In this case, two-period producer revenues in the absence of stabilization are

$$1 + x_s - \frac{2x_s}{a+b}\,(1+b+x_s) + \frac{b}{(a+b)^2}\,(-2x_s)^2$$

$$1 - x_s + \frac{2x_s}{a+b}\,(1+b-x_s) + \frac{b}{(a+b)^2}\,(+2x_s)^2.$$

The average deviation is $x_s\left[1 - \dfrac{2(1+b)}{a+b}\right]$ and will be greater (absolutely) than x_s if a (the elasticity of demand) is less than unity. In this case, average producer revenue is

$$1 + \frac{2x_s^2}{(a+b)^2}\,(b-a),$$

and will be higher or lower than the case with buffer-stock stabilization according as $b \gtrless a$ (the elasticity of supply is greater or less than the elasticity of demand).

Note

1 The implication that low demand and supply elasticities, rather than the reverse, are exceptional may be disputed, since the elasticities are typically assumed to be substantially less than unity for trade in primary commodities. However, while the first four of the core ten commodities may fit this stereotype, the facts are debatable with respect to the remainder of the ten core and seventeen total commodities mentioned. Moreover, the simple analysis presented here does not make the important distinction between short-run and long-run elasticities. Finally, note that the required condition is much stricter than simple less-than-unitary elasticity: in a very rough sense, it requires probable elasticities of one third or less.

Comment
I. M. D. Little

I think that buffer stocks are in the forefront of the NIEO partly because it is hoped that they will facilitate cartelization. For instance, in the case of tea, prices are rather stable but a buffer stock is nevertheless proposed. Despite this I shall confine myself to the stabilization issue, and here I share Harry Johnson's skepticism. Furthermore, even if some stabilization were achieved, it can be doubted whether the value of this to mankind would be worth the cost. Here I am talking about only the ten core commodities (coffee, tea, cocoa, sugar, cotton, jute, hard fibers, copper, tin, and rubber) not cereals, which are discussed in other papers and raise problems of greater welfare significance than the core commodities.

There are three supposed benefits. The first is that more stable prices may be analogous to an improvement in the quality of the product. This would benefit both producer and consumers. This argument applies only to materials. I cannot myself assess its importance, but some stress is laid on it for those commodities—rubber and the fibers—where there is most competition from manufactured substitutes.

The second potential benefit is that stabilization of GDP and exports makes macroeconomic management easier, and that this should promote growth. As against this one can argue that a country's government can itself do much to offset the effect of price fluctuations on private incomes, and to stabilize investment and employment by accumulating and decumulating reserves. However this is admittedly not easy, and a ratchet effect on money supply and inflation may be very hard to avoid:; also it is probably wrong to assume very good management.

However, the reason why I cannot judge the potential benefits to be very important is that rather few countries suffer from large fluctuations in GDP as a result of price changes. Zambia and Zaire together with some small sugar producing countries are the clearest examples—to which one can add Chile and Ghana if export instability is held to be particularly important. The proportion of the world's poorest people in these mostly middle-income countries is tiny.

The third potential benefit could be direct stabilization of poor producers' incomes, not only in the above countries, but where poor producers suffer from fluctuations even if the country does not. In considering this, one should distinguish cases where the profits of companies or plantations take the main part of the shock (and where output stability may be more important than price stability, for the poor), and cases where the bulk of production is from small holdings. In the latter case, governmental schemes, such as producers' boards or administered prices, are often operative. A casual impression would thus be that international price stability does not have a great deal to offer on this count for very large numbers of poor people—and I can find not even a casual analysis of this aspect in UNCTAD documents. The possible exceptions seem to be jute and sisal, in which many millions of the poorest people are involved.

I have been assuming that price and income stability go hand in hand. Harry Johnson makes much of the point that they may not. I found the algebra in his paper insufficiently illuminating, because it assumes perfect stabilization which would not be the aim of any buffer stock. With partial stabilization, and very low elasticities, I guess that there may not be too much risk of the partial price stabilization (which UNCTAD emphasizes) being income destabilizing.

If income stabilization were costlessly achieved (together with, possibly, some resultant improvement in the present value of future incomes), no one should be against buffer stocks, even if the welfare benefits could not be expected to be very large. The probability of such an achievement has to be assessed. The UNCTAD simply assumes that private speculation is destabilizing, and public speculation would be stabilizing. I find the former incredible (recent destabilizing stock movements were, surely, governmental—and private speculative stocks of say, copper, are now said to be large, and surely stabilizing).

The cost obviously depends on the success of the fund managers. If they make enough money, even ignoring the real welfare value of any transfer to poor countries, it is a good investment. If they bought in the initial stocks at very low prices, there would be an initial transfer to producing countries, but, if not, much of the transfer would be to private speculators. In the latter case, if the initial subscriptions and loans were treated as "aid," and were not additional so that other aid was reduced, then there would be an initial transfer from developing countries.

Tea and jute are the commodities that are almost entirely produced in the poorest countries and that affect most poor people. Ignoring politics, I guess that $3 billion spent on improving prospects for the producers of these two commodities would be a better use of public money than the UNCTAD scheme.

III
World Food Problems

10

Increased Stability of Grain Supplies in Developing Countries: Optimal Carryovers and Insurance
D. Gale Johnson

In recent years there has been considerable discussion of international grain reserves or buffer stocks for the major grains. In some instances the reserve objective has been to minimize fluctuations in the international market price of the grains. In other cases the reserve objective has been to provide for the particular food requirements of the developing countries. Thus far grain reserve proposals remain in the discussion stage. The problems involved and the conflicting interests are such that it appears virtually impossible to achieve broad international agreement on any reserve proposal. And it is not at all clear that if agreement could be reached with respect to some specific proposal for reserves, the proposal actually implemented would constitute an improvement compared to what would happen in the absence of such an agreement. A poorly designed proposal, resulting from the numerous conflicts in objectives and circumstances, could well result in a false sense of security that would prevent individuals and governments from taking appropriate actions in terms of their own interests.

The following proposal has the advantage that it is well within the capacity of the United States to carry it out for all developing countries. It also might attract the voluntary participation of other major exporting nations and even of some of the affluent importers.

Proposal for Grain Insurance

The proposal is a simple one, namely that the United States and any other industrial countries desiring to participate assure developing countries that any shortfall in grain production larger than a given percentage of the trend level of production would be made available. If a particular country's trend level of production were 50 million tons and the program were to meet a production shortfall in excess of 6 percent, a production level of 44 million tons would result in a payment of or the delivery of 3 million tons during the marketing year. Thus if the government of the developing country or its private sector did absolutely nothing to minimize consumption variability from year to year, the maximum reduction in grain supply would be 6 percent.

In fact, and this is an important advantage of the insurance program, a government could achieve a further reduction in consumption variability by a reserve program at a relatively modest cost. In other words, this insurance program would not entirely eliminate the advantages of stock holding in a developing country.

The selection of a 6 percent shortfall from trend production as the criterion for making payments or deliveries is arbitrary. Other percentages, specifically 5 and 4 percent, have been used in calculations and some results based on these criteria are presented later. In fact, though the details have not been worked out, it might be desirable to use different criteria for different countries. Countries with somewhat higher per capita incomes and more adequate grain marketing systems might have the 6 percent criterion applied while other countries with lower per capita incomes and/or a grain marketing system that results in relatively large and variable regional price differentials due to production fluctuations might have the 5 or 4 percent criterion applied.

The selection of the percentage criterion should reflect two considerations—the incentive for holding reserves in the developing country and the effect of the insurance payments on the output behavior of local producers. If the percentage is too low, say 1 or 2 percent, there would be no economic incentive for holding reserves and the magnitude of the grain transfers could be large enough to significantly reduce the average expected returns of the local producers and thus lower the rate of growth of domestic grain production.

I have not come to any conclusion with respect to the premiums that might be charged for the grain insurance. One possibility is a zero premium, with the grain insurance program representing economic aid. As will be seen from data presented below, the aid transfer implied by the 6 percent criterion is relatively small compared to past food aid transfers. A second possibility would be an insurance premium based upon a constant real price of grain. The advantage of this proposal for a developing country would be that if its short crop coincided with relatively high grain prices in the international market, grain would be available to that country at what, in fact, would amount to a fixed real price. In other words, the insurance premium would cover both the availability of the grain and the price of the grain.

My own preference is for a zero premium for all developing countries with less than a specified level of per capita income. This specified level might be set somewhat above the highest income level now achieved by any country classified as a developing country. As developing countries passed this level of real per capita income, a gradually increasing premium could be charged until at some level of per capita income the premium would be an actuarially sound one. It should be noted that the premium, when charged, would vary from country to country depending upon the probability distribution of production variations around the trend.

Objective of the Proposal

The primary objective of the proposal is to assist the developing nations to hold year-to-year variations in grain consumption to a reasonable or acceptable level. A secondary objective is to achieve the degree of stabilization of grain consumption with a minimum impact upon foreign exchange reserves or, alternatively, upon the exchange rate of the developing countries.

The proposal should constitute the primary form of food aid provided by the countries that participate in the provision of the grain insurance. A very strong case can be made that the large-scale food aid provided during the 1950s and 1960s contributed relatively little to economic growth or the improvement of the state of nutrition (Schultz, 1960). This is not to say that the insurance program should be the only form of food aid. There are natural disasters, such as the recent earthquake in Guatemala, that can be partially alleviated by food aid. And some food aid can be effectively utilized in particular development projects. By being "effectively utilized" I mean that the food aid would approximate the effectiveness of an unrestricted cash transfer.

But the proposal does rest on the conclusion that continuous transfers of significant quantities of food aid, such as the 10 million tons of grain envisaged by the World Food Conference would not represent an effective use of the world's resources. The grain insurance program would result in a net food transfer to the developing countries, but it would do so only during years of small crops. The program would not provide food aid during years when grain production was average or above trend or even when grain production was somewhat below the long-term trend.

The grain insurance proposal would not eliminate the economic feasibility of holding national grain reserves. However, a given degree of consumption stability could be achieved at much lower cost with the insurance program than without it. Some examples of the reduction in costs are provided later.

The generally accepted rationale for grain stocks or a world food reserve is that production variability makes such stocks or a reserve desirable. The arguments for such reserves àre frequently similar to that given by the Director-General of the Food and Agriculture Organization (FAO, p. 3):

The purpose of the proposal is to ensure that a minimum level of world security is maintained against serious food shortages in periods of crop failure or natural disaster. There are two aspects to this issue. There is the food production problem, which is the concern of a large segment of FAO's regular and field programmes. There is also the separate problem of maintaining a safe level of food stocks to maintain a steady expansion of consumption and to offset the year-to-year fluctuations in output which occur and which will continue to occur even when the world production problem is solved. It is this latter aspect—minimum food stocks—on which the present proposal is centered.

The director-general emphasizes the role of year-to-year fluctuations in food production as the reason for holding food stocks. Such fluctuations might be the reason for an individual nation having a food reserve; it is not an adequate reason for significant reserves for the world. Year-to-year fluctuations in world grain production are relatively small and would not, if there were free trade in grains, make the holding of grain reserves in excess of working stocks an economic investment more than one year out of five.

Our research indicates that year-to-year variations in world grain production would result in positive world grain reserves in approximately one year out of five and in only one year out of twenty would such reserves exceed 18 million tons (see Table 10.1). It was assumed that reserves were optimal when the expected gain equaled the expected cost of holding an additional ton of grain.

I should add that our analysis did not include the effects of demand variability nor did it take into account the effects of destruction of crop output due to floods, storms, and other natural disasters.[1] However, annual demand variations are small, especially for the food grains in the developing countries, and the amount of reserves required for postharvest disasters would be modest.

The basic reason why world grain or food reserves are required is that governmental policies prevent ready access to the available supplies of grain. Potential purchasers are prevented access by export controls or export monopolies, such as exist in many countries. In addition, many governments enter the international market to purchase grain at one price and then resell it into the domestic market at a lower price, as has been the practice in recent years in the European Community, the Soviet Union, and China. At other times governments maintain domestic prices at relatively high levels when grain is available in the international markets at much lower prices. Such policies, in one case, increase prices in the international markets and, in the other case, depress prices below what would prevail if there were either free trade or fixed tariffs. In other words, the price system is not permitted to function to allocate the world's available supply of grain and this is the primary reason for the need to hold reserves (Johnson, 1975).

The reason why the world needs to hold food reserves, in excess of normal working stocks, is not a natural, but a political, one. Although there is relatively little possibility that governmental policies affecting grain prices and supplies will change in the near future, it at least seems desirable to recognize the primary reason why most reserves that have been held and will be held have had a useful function.

This discussion on the rationale for world grain reserves is relevant to my proposal for assisting the developing countries to minimize the effects of grain production variability upon the welfare of their citizens. It is presented for two reasons. The first is to protect myself from the criticism that the proposal represents not even a second best solution to the problem, but an nth best one. I do not need to be told that is the case. If there were free trade in grains, there would be little need for any special arrangements to assist the developing countries to minimize the consequences of their grain production variability. The second reason is that the discussion serves as a brief description of the setting in which the proposal would operate. It is a setting in which in the absence of very substantial grain reserves large annual variations in the prices of grain in international markets can result in price changes in the opposite direction that may be fifteen or more times as great as the percentage change in production.

I might add, not entirely as an aside, that if the developing countries (excluding China) were willing to have free trade in grains among themselves the expected optimal level of grain reserves as of 1975 would be relatively small—approximately 5 million tons in excess of working stocks. Thus the developing countries would not need to trade extensively with the major industrial countries, but only among themselves in order to have relatively stable grain consumption. But restrictions to grain trade are generally greater among the developing countries than among the industrial countries.

Assumptions and Limitations of Analysis

The grain insurance proposal requires reasonably accurate data on annual grain production—for the current year and for enough prior years to permit the calculation of the trend level of production for the current year. The accuracy of data on grain production in many developing countries leaves something to be desired, to put it mildly. The existence of the insurance program could give an incentive to a government to minimize its estimates of grain production in a given year in order to increase the grain actually transferred. Over time this practice would be self-defeating since estimates of trend production for future years would be affected by such underestimates. However, since many governments may assume a relatively short life, this self-correcting feature may not be of much value in many cases. It might be necessary for the insurance agency to have the right to obtain grain production estimates from an agency that was independent of both the developing country and the countries providing the grain.

The estimates of trend production used in the analysis were based on log linear estimates of the production for all the years for which the Food and Agriculture Organization has provided data. In some cases we have "cheated" in that we have worked out the level of insurance payments and optimal carry-overs using production data for the entire period, 1948 to 1973. In other words, we have estimated insurance payments and carry-overs for a year such as 1960 as though we knew not only annual production from 1950 through 1960 but also from 1961 through 1973. Fortunately the correlation coefficients for the trend regressions are very large. Thus when the analysis was conducted properly—only data known at the time the payment or carry-over was calculated—it gave results very similar to those in which we made the seemingly unreasonable assumption that we knew the future. Data on grain production are now available for a sufficient number of years so that trend production can be estimated with a considerable degree of reliability and thus it should not now be necessary to resort to the techniques we used for some of our illustrative calculations.

Both our computational procedures and our estimation of the production time series have imposed independence of production probability distributions over time. This means that the probability of, say, a 5 percent shortfall in year t is unaffected by the realized production year $t - 1$. A number of analyses of the production time series have indicated that for most countries and regions the independence assumption could not be rejected. If we had reliable production data for fifty or 100 years instead of for about twenty-five years, it is possible that the independence assumption would be rejected for many countries. However, if nonindependence prevails in many of the developing countries, it is unlikely to be a strong effect. Obviously, even if independence does exist, there will be instances in which a poor crop follows a poor crop and a very good crop follows a very good crop. These events are expected in a random situation—some of the time. And, of course, our methods of calculation take this latter possibility into account.

In order to illustrate some of the economic effects of the insurance program, calculations of optimal grain reserves are made for several developing countries and regions in the absence of the program and with it. I will not present the formal model used to calculate optimal reserves since the model has been presented elsewhere (Johnson and Sumner, 1976). Using a dynamic programing model, estimates are generated that give the optimal carry-over amount for each year, given a supply level for that year. If the supply level for a given year is unknown, the model permits estimates of the probability distribution of optimal carry-overs for the given year. Both types of estimates are presented below.

Briefly, the optimal carry-over satisfies the criterion that the expected marginal cost of adding to the carry-over equals the expected marginal gain. Cost is assumed to be a linear function of the quantity stored and includes physical storage costs and an interest charge. The physical storage cost is assumed to be $7.50 per metric ton and a real interest rate of 5 percent is assumed. The marginal gain can be calculated either as the expected change in the area under the demand curve or as the expected difference in the price of grain at the time grain is added to stocks and when it will be removed from stocks.

Based on available estimates of the price elasticity of demand for grains in the developing countries (Rojko, Urban, and Naive, 1971), we have used demand curves with a constant elasticity of −0.1. We have not disaggregated the grains and have thus assumed that the elasticity of substitution among the grains is infinity.

The demand functions were assumed to change over time in a systematic manner without an error term. This assumption is not wholly realistic but for the developing countries it does not introduce a large error.

In the calculation of optimal grain carry-overs for the developing countries we made the quite restrictive assumption that net grain trade remained constant over time. In other words, the developing countries did not use changes in international trade as a means of stabilizing domestic supply availability. Obviously a country, whether it is a net importer or net exporter, can achieve a considerable degree of supply stability by varying net trade. However, this approach to supply stability may not be acceptable to all or most developing countries. Various national policies that result in overvalued currencies, exchange controls, import and export controls may make the trade response difficult and costly. But, I hasten to add, any country if it wished could have access to trade as a means of stabilizing grain supplies within reasonable limits and it is a limitation of our analysis of optimal grain reserves that we do not take this possibility into account.

When results are presented for a region or area other than a single country, it is assumed that there is free trade in grains within that region. While we have not yet made estimates of optimal carry-overs for each country or of the insurance payments that would be required if each country were considered as a separate unit, such estimates could be made with relatively little difficulty.

Some Illustrative Results

The remainder of this paper consists of several tables and a few comments about their results. Table 10.1 gives estimates of optimal carry-overs, for various levels of probability, for a number of individual countries and several regions.[2] In Table 10.1 it is assumed that each country or region is entirely responsible for holding carry-overs and neither trade nor outside aid is available to reduce fluctuations in consumption. Part B of Table 10.1 indicates the effect of a higher price elasticity of demand on the size of optimal carry-overs; the effect is quite significant. Table 10.1 includes data for high-income countries and regions and for the world as a whole. These estimates of optimal carry-overs are included for whatever interest they may have since they are only indirectly related to the topic of this paper.

The rows giving estimates of optimal carry-overs in millions of tons at various probability levels should be interpreted as follows: at each probability level, the optimal carry-over would be the amount indicated or less. Alternatively, a specific figure in the 0.95 probability level column indicates that 5 percent of the time one would expect an optimal carry-over equal to or greater than the indicated amount. Thus one would expect that one year out of four the optimal carry-over level for India, with no insurance program, would be 9.5 million tons or more while in three years out of four the optimal carry-over level would be less than 9.5 million tons.

Table 10.2 indicates the optimal carry-overs for developing countries and regions assuming various insurance programs—shortfalls in excess of 6 percent, 5 percent, and 4 percent, respectively, are covered by some outside

Table 10.1 Optimal Carry-overs for Selected Countries and Regions, 1975 (million tons)

Country or Region	1975 Trend Production	Cumulative Probability Levels		
		0.50	0.75	0.95
A. Demand elasticity $\eta = -.10$				
Burma	6	0.3	0.7	1.2
India	100	6.5	9.5	13.5
Indonesia	16	1.6	2.9	4.4
Pakistan-Bangladesh	23	1.4	2.4	4.2
Philippines	6	0.1	0.2	0.3
Thailand	13	3.5	4.7	6.2
Other Far East	19	1.4	2.1	3.1
Africa	46	1.5	3.0	5.0
Far East	184	3.0	7.5	12.5
Latin America	78	2.5	5.0	8.5
Near East	48	2.5	4.5	8.5
All Developing Regions	353	2.5	7.5	15.0
Europe	231	1.3	5.5	9.5
North America	270	10.0	18.0	33.0
Oceania	18	8.0	10.5	15.4
U.S.S.R.	199	28.0	41.0	49.0
World	1,304	0.0	2.0	18.0
B. Demand elasticity $\eta = -.20$				
India		2.0	4.0	7.5
Africa		0.0	0.5	2.5
Far East		0.0	1.0	7.0
Developing Regions		0.0	1.0	7.0
North America		1.5	8.5	22.0
U.S.S.R.		13.0	24.0	37.0
World		0.0	0.0	7.0

Table 10.2 Optimal Carry-over Levels for Selected Developing Countries and Regions, 1975, Alternative Insurance Programs in Effect[a]

Country or Region and Insurance Program	Probability Levels for Carry-overs		
	0.5	0.75	0.95
A. 6 Percent			
Burma	0.1	0.3	0.7
India	1.5	3.5	7.5
Indonesia	0.7	1.5	2.9
Pakistan-Bangladesh	0.3	1.5	2.7
Philippines	0.0	0.1	0.3
Thailand	0.6	1.2	2.1
Other Far East[b]	0.3	0.7	1.5
Africa	0.0	1.0	3.0
Far East[b]	2.0	5.0	10.0
Latin America	0.5	2.5	5.5
Near East	0.5	1.5	5.0
All Developing Regions[b]	2.0	6.0	14.0
B. 5 Percent			
Burma	0.0	0.2	0.7
India	1.0	2.5	7.0
Indonesia	0.5	1.3	2.7
Pakistan-Bangladesh	0.3	1.3	2.5
Philippines	0.0	0.1	0.3
Thailand	0.3	1.0	1.8
Other Far East[b]	0.2	0.6	1.5
Africa	0.0	1.0	3.0
Far East[b]	2.0	5.0	9.0
Latin America	0.5	2.5	5.0
Near East	0.5	1.5	5.0
All Developing Regions[b]	0.0	6.0	13.5
C. 4 Percent			
Burma	0.0	0.2	0.6
India	0.5	2.5	6.0
Indonesia	0.5	1.1	2.6
Pakistan-Bangladesh	0.2	1.0	2.2
Philippines	0.0	0.0	0.2
Thailand	0.3	0.8	1.8
Other Far East[b]	0.0	0.6	1.3
Africa	0.0	1.0	3.0
Far East[b]	1.0	4.0	8.0
Latin America	0.5	2.0	4.5
Near East	0.0	1.5	4.5
All Developing Regions[b]	0.0	3.5	12.0

[a]Price elasticity of demand equals −0.1.
[b]Excludes China.

country or agency. The reductions in optimal carry-over levels due to the three insurance proposals are quite substantial for India, Indonesia, Pakistan-Bangladesh, Thailand, and other Far East. However, an insurance program that covers shortfalls in excess of 4 percent has only a slight effect on optimal carry-overs compared to the insurance program covering shortfalls in excess of 6 percent.

Table 10.3 indicates the magnitude of the insurance payments that would have been made to the developing countries and regions (excluding China) for each year from 1954 through 1973 for each of the three insurance programs. I should note that in constructing this table it was assumed that during each year we knew as much about the trend of production and the probability distribution of production variability as we now know. This assumption of omniscience had relatively little effect upon the results.

Given the assumptions that were made, the maximum annual payment or transfer with the 6 percent program would have been 9.4 million tons in 1966; the next highest would have been 8.7 million tons in 1973. With the 4 percent program the highest payments would have been 12.1 million tons in 1966 and 10.4 million tons in 1973.

Table 10.3 Insurance Payments to Developing Countries and Regions, 1954-1973, for Different Programs[a]

Year	6 Percent	5 Percent	4 Percent
1954	1.0	1.0	1.1
1955	1.5	1.7	2.0
1956	0.0	0.0	0.1
1957	5.0	5.7	6.8
1958	2.2	2.5	2.9
1959	1.3	1.3	1.4
1960	1.8	2.3	2.8
1961	0.0	0.3	0.7
1962	0.2	0.4	0.5
1963	0.8	0.9	1.1
1964	0.0	0.0	0.1
1965	6.8	7.7	8.6
1966	9.4	10.7	12.1
1967	1.2	1.3	1.5
1968	0.0	0.0	0.0
1969	0.5	0.6	0.7
1970	1.0	1.5	1.9
1971	0.0	0.0	0.0
1972	5.5	6.5	8.3
1973	8.7	9.6	10.4
Total	46.9	54.0	63.0

[a]The Far East is disaggregated as in Table 10.1; other regions included as single units. The size of insurance payments is affected by the extent of disaggregation.

The columns in Table 10.3 have been totaled; these totals need to be interpreted with caution. If every developing country were considered as a separate entity, the payments in individual years and thus the totals would have been substantially greater. Based on the effects of the disaggregation of the Far East, I would estimate that if the analysis had been done for each of the several score developing countries, the aggregate payments would have been increased by perhaps 60 to 80 percent. Thus the total for the 6 percent insurance program might have been in the range of 75 to 85 million tons or an average of 4.0 to 4.5 million tons for the twenty years. For the 4 percent program the total payments might have been from 100 to 115 million or about an annual average of 5.5 million tons. During the 1960s the United States provided 142 million tons of food as aid and on concessional terms.

Tables 10.4, 10.5, and 10.6 provide estimates of optimal carry-overs for India and Africa with no insurance program, a 6 percent program, and a 4 percent program. In these tables we have used only the information that would be available at the time carry-over decisions were made. Thus the optimal carry-over for 1968 for India reflects the production variability

Table 10.4 Effects of Carry-over Program on Available Supply Based on Actual Production, India and Africa, 1968-1975 (million tons)

Year	Actual Production	Optimal Carry-over	Available Supply	Trend
India				
1968	81.6	3.0	78.6	80.7
1969	85.1	5.0	83.1	83.2
1970	91.7	10.0	86.7	85.8
1971	90.2	10.0	90.2	88.5
1972	86.6	5.5	91.1	91.2
1973	95.4	7.0	93.9	94.0
1974	86.7	1.0	92.7	96.9
1975				99.9

at probability level

$$\text{Carry-over} < \frac{0.5}{4.0} \quad \frac{0.75}{4.5} \quad \frac{0.95}{6.5}$$

Year	Actual Production	Optimal Carry-over	Available Supply	Trend
Africa				
1967		(1.0)		
1968	40.5	2.5	39.0	38.2
1969	41.3	3.0	40.8	39.3
1970	40.2	2.0	41.2	40.4
1971	40.9	1.0	41.9	41.5
1972	44.4	2.0	43.4	42.7
1973	37.1	0.0	39.1	43.9
1974	42.2	0.0	42.2	45.1
1975				46.4

at probability level

$$\text{Carry-over} < \frac{0.5}{1.0} \quad \frac{0.75}{1.5} \quad \frac{0.95}{3.0}$$

Table 10.5 Effects of Carry-over Program on Available Supply Based on Actual Production, 6 Percent Insurance Policy, India and Africa, 1968-1975 (million tons)

Year	Actual Production	Optimal Carry-over	Insurance Payment	Available Supply
India				
1968	81.6	0.5	0.0	81.1
1969	85.1	1.5	0.0	84.1
1970	91.7	5.0	0.0	88.2
1971	90.2	4.0	0.0	91.2
1972	86.6	0.0	0.0	90.2
1973	95.4	1.0	0.0	94.4
1974	86.7	0.0	4.3	92.0

1975
at probability levels

$$\text{Carry-over} < \frac{0.5}{1.0} \quad \frac{0.75}{2.0} \quad \frac{0.95}{4.0}$$

Year	Actual Production	Optimal Carry-over	Insurance Payment	Available Supply
Africa				
1968	40.5	2.5	0.0	39.5
1969	41.3	3.0	0.0	40.8
1970	40.2	2.0	0.0	41.2
1971	40.9	1.0	0.0	41.9
1972	44.4	2.0	0.0	43.4
1973	37.1	0.0	4.2	43.3
1974	42.2	0.0	1.2	43.4

1975
at probability level

$$\text{Carry-over} < \frac{0.5}{0.5} \quad \frac{0.75}{1.0} \quad \frac{0.95}{2.0}$$

experienced from 1948 through 1967. It was assumed for India that there was no carry-over at the end of the 1967 marketing year since 1965 and 1966 were poor crop years and 1967 grain production was somewhat below trend level. For Africa a beginning carry-over of 1.0 million tons was assumed.

Table 10.4, which assumes no insurance program, indicates that for India, with two relatively poor crop years since 1967 (1972 and 1974), an optimal carry-over program would have resulted in relatively small deviations of available supply around the trend. The available supply in 1972 would have been almost exactly at the trend level, while in 1974 with production approximately 11 percent below trend, consumption would have been 4.2 million tons or approximately 4.3 percent below trend. With a price elasticity of −0.1, grain prices in 1974 would have been approximately 40 percent above those in 1973. Added imports of 2 million tons of grain would have held the price increase to approximately 20 percent.

It may be somewhat surprising to discover that for India in 1974 the 6 percent insurance program would not have provided as high a level of grain availability as did the optimal grain carry-over without an insurance program.

Table 10.6 Effects of Carry-over Program on Available Supply Based on Actual Production, 4 Percent Insurance Policy, India and Africa, 1968-1975 (million tons)

Year	Actual Production	Optimal Carry-over	Insurance Payment	Available Supply
India				
1968	81.6	1.0	0.0	80.6
1969	85.1	1.0	0.0	85.1
1970	91.7	4.0	0.0	88.7
1971	90.2	3.0	0.0	91.2
1972	86.6	0.0	0.7	90.3
1973	95.4	0.0	0.0	95.4
1974	86.7	0.0	6.4	93.1
1975		at probability levels		
	Carry-over $< \dfrac{0.5}{1.0} \quad \dfrac{0.75}{2.0} \quad \dfrac{0.95}{4.0}$			
Africa				
1968	40.5	2.0	0.0	39.5
1969	41.3	2.0	0.0	41.3
1970	40.2	1.0	0.0	41.2
1971	40.9	0.0	0.0	41.9
1972	44.4	1.0	0.0	43.4
1973	37.1	0.0	5.0	43.1
1974	42.2	0.0	1.0	43.2
1975		at probability level		
	Carry-over $< \dfrac{0.5}{0.0} \quad \dfrac{0.75}{0.0} \quad \dfrac{0.95}{2.0}$			

The insurance program would have encouraged higher levels of consumption from 1969 through 1973 and very low levels of carry-over at the end of 1973. Obviously the results for 1974 are due to the "accidents" of the production levels in the years immediately before 1974. The 4 percent program would have provided for a somewhat higher level of available supply.

The bottom part of each table gives similar calculations for Africa. In this case there are no surprises—the insurance program would have provided increased stability of available supplies. The stability of available supply for Africa would have been greater with any one of the three insurance programs than with optimal carry-overs alone. The major difference would have been in 1973 when an optimal carry-over program alone would have resulted in available supply of 4.8 million tons below trend; this would have been a shortfall of 11 percent. With the 6 percent insurance program the shortfall below trend would have been only 0.6 million tons; with a 4 percent program the shortfall would have been 0.2 million tons.

For the seven-year period the 6 percent insurance program would have reduced carry-overs in India to 12 million ton-years from 42.5 million ton-years without the insurance program. The savings in interest and storage costs would have been approximately $450 million at a grain price of $150 per ton. This saving would have required the delivery of 4.3 million tons of grain with a value of $650 million. With the 5 and 4 percent insurance programs the savings on holding carry-overs would be increased, but not by as much as the increased value of the delivered grain. However, over the seven-year period grain consumption in India would have been increased by approximately the amount of the payment under the insurance program and this needs to be considered in any cost-benefit calculation.

For Africa the 6 percent insurance program would not have reduced the optimal carry-over by very much since production variability for the years prior to 1973 implied a very low probability of a production shortfall equal to or greater than 6 percent. Only if the 4 percent insurance program had been in effect would there have been any significant reduction in optimal carry-over levels.

The illustrations presented here, as well as others we have prepared, indicate that if the developing nations would provide for optimal carry-overs within the framework of an insurance program that covered all grain production shortfalls from trend in excess of 6 percent, grain consumption variability would be held to low and manageable levels. By low and manageable levels I mean that in most years (nine out of ten, approximately) and in almost all developing countries negative deviations of consumption from trend would be held to 3 percent or less. This could be achieved by holding relatively modest levels of carry-over stocks in the developing countries and by an expected annual insurance payment for all developing countries of the order of 4 million tons.

It might be noted that with the insurance program in effect some developing countries might well find it more economical to use trade to offset the remaining consumption variability than to hold grain carry-overs. This probably will be true when the costs of holding reserves in a developing country are substantially above such costs in the major exporting countries, though other factors such as probability distributions of international grain prices and freight rates need to be taken into account.

Concluding Comments

The grain insurance program represents a means by which a limited form of economic aid could be provided to the developing countries. With reasonable management of domestic supplies of grain by the developing countries, the insurance program should eliminate undernutrition and hardship associated with grain production variability. The program would contribute very little to long-run problems of inadequate food supplies for the poorer people of the developing countries. Nor would it provide much assistance for the small number of countries that import a major fraction of their cereal supplies. If such countries merited aid, it would have to be supplied in other forms and in accordance with other criteria.

The insurance program would not interfere significantly with efforts within the developing countries to expand their own food supplies. The negative incentive effects, both upon governments who have in the past relied upon massive food aid as an alternative to measures to expand domestic production and upon farmers who have been adversely affected by previous food aid programs, would be very small. In the long run, per capita food supplies in most developing countries will improve primarily through increasing food production in those countries and not as a consequence of food aid. The possibility exists that the insurance program would reduce the incentive for certain investments, for example, irrigation, that contribute to stability of grain production. This possible result is similar to the effects of most insurance programs that have some adverse effects upon the behavior of the insured.

I believe that the grain insurance program is responsive to an important problem that exists in many developing countries and that it would make the world a somewhat more secure place for millions of poor people.

Notes

Research for this paper was supported by grants from the National Science Foundation and the Rockefeller Foundation. I wish to acknowledge the important contributions made by Daniel Sumner and Yagil Danin. I am solely responsible for the views expressed and no attribution to the National Science Foundation or the Rockefeller Foundation should be made.

1 Two further simplifications should be noted. The analysis assumed zero transportation costs and that the elasticity of substitution among the major grains was infinite. However, the very low price of elasticity of demand that was assumed (-0.1) resulted in a probable overestimate of the optimum levels of stocks that would offset, at least in part, the underestimate of stocks resulting from ignoring demand variability, transportation costs, and relative small elasticities of substitution among the major grains.

2 It should be noted that China is included in the world total but not in the all developing regions one.

References

Food and Agriculture Organization, 1973, *World Food Security: Proposal of the Director-General* (FAO, Rome).

Johnson, D. Gale, 1975, "World Agriculture, Commodity Policy and Price Variability," *American Journal of Agricultural Economics*, 57, 823-828.

Johnson, D. Gale, and Daniel Sumner, 1976, "An Optimization Approach to Grain Reserves for Developing Countries" (Department of Economics, University of Chicago, Chicago).

Rojko, Anthony S., F. S. Urban, and J. S. Naive, 1971, *World Demand Prospects for*

Grain in 1980 with Emphasis on Trade by the Less Developed Countries (U.S. Department of Agriculture, Washington).

Schultz, Theodore W., 1960, "Value of U.S. Farm Surpluses to Underdeveloped Countries," *Journal of Farm Economics*, 42, 1019-1030.

11

Cereal Stocks, Food Aid, and Food Security for the Poor

Alexander H. Sarris and Lance Taylor

1. Introduction

In the midst of the events called the world food crisis, the Rome Conference of November 1974 arrived at a well-publicized International Undertaking on World Food Security. The Undertaking amounted to recognition by the diplomats that unless there is an increase in international coordination, additional food crises may not be avoided. The conference proposed that one way of assuring food availability is to organize a coordinated system of nationally held cereal reserves. Further, the conference accepted the point that any reserve scheme must be coupled with a substantial flow of food aid toward poor countries in the medium-term future—if they are to maintain even the precarious nutritional standards they now "enjoy."

Since the time of the conference, these brave resolves have led to very little. Progress toward establishing a cereal reserve has been minimal, and, in part because of good crops in some of the most severely affected (MSA) countries and bad ones in the Soviet Union, concessional aid flows have not increased. Our main goal in this paper is to put these failures in perspective—to assess why the Rome proposals have not materialized and to offer a few modest suggestions that may prove useful. Our recommendations are in fact very similar to those put forth by the World Food Council (1976). They at least have the benefit of two years' worth of thought about the economic and political problems of food reserves (information unavailable at the time of the Rome Conference).

We begin with a brief historical sketch of previous attempts to institute international grain reserves, and then pass on to the present politics and economics of the world cereal trade. This institutional analysis leads naturally into a discussion of the economic theory of reserve stocks. As it turns out, simple economic considerations explain a great part of the politics of international reserves, and show that even if the political will existed on the part of some to create a world food security scheme, they might well be thwarted by the economic interests of more powerful actors. We then close with our proposed set of reserve and aid policies—policies that make analytical sense and may even be credible in the present political situation as we see it.

To finish setting the stage, we should illuminate all the good things that reserve/aid policy is supposed to achieve. World Food Conference Resolution XVII says a security reserve should ". . . assure the availability at all times of adequate world supplies of basic foodstuffs, primarily cereals, so as to avoid acute food shortages in the event of widespread crop failures or natural disasters, sustain a steady expansion of production and reduce fluctuations in production and prices." All participating governments accepted these estimable goals with a conspicuous absence of clarity about exactly what they were agreeing to.

2. Historical Background and Current Discussion

The 1974-1975 *Commodity Review* from FAO (1975b) gives a useful discussion of past international approaches to food stocks. We summarize some of the highlights here.

In the late 1940s establishment of a worldwide famine reserve was recognized as one of the objectives of the proposed World Food Board (a successor to a U.S.-U.K. wartime agency). The board never saw the light of day, but the idea of using reserves for succor and stabilization lived on, with the proposal for an International Commodity Clearing House (ICCH) being its next and most concrete manifestation. The ICCH was to stabilize commodities markets in the interests of consumers, and also provide emergency food relief. Like the Food Board, the ICCH was never instituted, as the perceived need for cereal reserves became less urgent with the buildup of American agricultural surpluses in the 1950s. The FAO did produce two more studies (1956 and 1958), which did a good job of analyzing reserve problems but offered little by way of new solutions.

Throughout the 1960s, it looked as if the United States would happily continue keeping a substantial world food reserve all by itself. This unilateral "security system" broke down in 1972/1973 when large purchases by the Soviet Union suddenly reduced U.S. and Canadian stocks to very low levels. The year 1973/1974 saw grain prices doubling and tripling in periods of a few months. World food markets registered the accelerating panic, leading to scare buying and stock building by the wealthy countries and, inter alia, to the Rome Conference and other gestures toward international cooperation. The main statement of purpose was the Undertaking on World Food Security. According to it, the participating nations are to

recognize that world food security is a common responsibility of all nations;

sustain a steady expansion of production, reduce fluctuations in production and prices and assist developing countries;

adopt national cereal stock policies which take into account the policies of other countries and ensure a minimum safe level of basic cereal stocks for the world as a whole, establish stock targets and ensure that they are replenished when drawn down;

furnish information about their stock policies and levels; and
consult together (through an FAO World Food Security Committee) on
progress.

There are a number of reasons why such an agreement could be adopted in
the few days of the Rome Conference. First, the undertaking puts no a priori
limitations on choice among the manifold possible formulas for international
cooperation. Second, it includes no conditions on points to be settled
through commodity negotiations. Third, the reserves to be built up are
national ones rather than internationally owned (though some commitment
was made to international management of nationally owned stocks). Fourth,
governments can keep full control of their own stocks. Enthusiastic acceptance of an undertaking toward nothing much besides good intentions was
one of the triumphs of Rome.

Since the 1974 food crisis peak, prospects for an international security
scheme have not risen. As of April 1976, the undertaking had been endorsed
by sixty-six countries that account for 95 percent of world cereal exports,
but only half of imports and less than 60 percent of production. China and
the Soviet Union had not as yet endorsed it, claiming that it violates their
national sovereignty (and certainly their customary secrecy about production
and stock levels). Of twenty-five developed participating countries only ten
have formulated explicit national stock policies and five (mostly Nordic, as
one might expect) have announced specific stock targets. Of forty-six
participating underdeveloped countries, twenty-eight are reported to have an
explicit stock policy. Major exporters, like the United States, Canada, and
Australia, have not committed themselves publicly to any reserve policy.
Most countries having such policies had set them up well before the World
Food Conference.

Talk, as opposed to action, has been abundant at the international level.
Discussions about reserve schemes continue apace, in at least four international bodies. FAO established its World Food Security Committee (WFSC),
which first met in Rome in April 1976. To date, its role has been to exhort
countries to formulate stock policies as soon as possible; its success has been
modest. In its first meeting it failed to establish even target dates for
institution of national stock policies. If it survives, the main tasks of the
WFSC will be to monitor the supply-demand situation and review government
policies toward implementing the Undertaking. The International Wheat
Council (IWC), a producer-consumer bargaining forum, is taking up the
reserves issue as part of its discussions about a new international wheat
agreement. In the GATT, the issue has arisen in the context of the
multilateral trade negotiations. Finally, UNCTAD includes grains in its
Integrated Program for Commodities.

The IWC discussions concern trade—their aim is to share a modicum of
benefits among negotiating nations. Regrettably, there are sharp disagree-

ments among the participants. Before going into the details, it is helpful to summarize the positions that countries have adopted to date, as is done in Table 11.1, which was prepared by reviewing the IWC discussions for 1975 and early 1976.

The question mark on U.S. acceptance of the use of stocks as a stabilizing device hints at the perversity of the American stand on reserves. A U.S. proposal of September 1975 in the IWC negotiations calls for a stock of 30 million metric tons of wheat and rice to be used for "food security" purposes, although what this means exactly is not stated. The reserve is supposed not to interfere with the commercial market, though how it can avoid doing so is difficult to see—30 million tons of wheat and rice constitute about 40 percent of world exports of these commodities. The key point of the proposal is a trigger mechanism depending on production and stock levels, and *not* on prices.

The reasoning behind American insistence on quantity triggers is easy to fathom. There are both theoretical and empirical arguments in support of the proposition that demand for grains becomes quite inelastic at low levels of

Table 11.1 Viewpoints on Reserve Issues Expressed in the IWC[a]

	U.S.	Can-ada	Aus-tralia	EEC	U.S.S.R.	Argen-tina	India	Egypt	Japan
Stock Policies as a Stabilizing Device	Y(?)	Y	Y	Y	Y		Y		Y
Price bands (triggers)	N	Y	Y	Y			Y	Y	Y
Quantity triggers	Y	Y							
Special provisions for LDCs	N		Y			Y	Y	Y	N
More food information	Y	Y							
Permanent International body				Y					
Access-supply arrangements		Y							Y
Food aid		Y	Y		Y				N

[a]In the table, Y means that a country explicitly agrees with the corresponding provision in a new wheat agreement; N means that it explicitly disagrees. A blank means that it is not clear from the minutes whether a country agrees or disagrees.

stocks. The implication is that prices rise rapidly as stocks deplete after an unexpected crop failure or similar event, even abstracting from panic purchases due to fears about impending food shortages. On the other hand, the numbers actually describing the grain situation appear only after some months' delay, and for some countries they are quite inaccurate. Clearly, the world's largest grain producer and the half-dozen companies that handle its export trade can reap high gains from lagged quantitative triggers as prices shoot up in supply-short food markets. The depressing effect on export revenues of stock releases after the data come in and are suitably discussed and analyzed by international functionaries is much less than it would be under a prompt price-triggered buffer stock response.

Other exporters such as Canada and Australia in general favor price triggers, but they are not enthusiastic about international reserves, given the recent price increases in world markets and recollections of large unsold stocks in the late 1960s and early 1970s. In the past, the United States, Canada, and Australia have acted as cooperating oligopolists in grain exports (McCalla, 1967, suggests that Canada is the price leader as long as all three countries retain salable stocks), and one would expect convergence of their positions as negotiations continue.

Importing countries in the IWC discussions tend to lean toward price triggers, especially the European Economic Community which relates the amount of subsidies paid to farmers under its Common Agricultural Policy (CAP) directly to international prices. The EEC introduced a proposal in January 1976 in the GATT for a new international grains agreement to stabilize prices between maximum and minimum levels via reserve stock operations. Further discussion on this proposal is not expected until mid-1976. In UNCTAD the original proposal for an integrated program for commodities includes cereals, but they are not among the commodities to be financed through the Common Fund for buffer stock operations.

The two major forums in which grain reserves and food security are now considered are the FAO (and its WFSC) and the IWC. Evidently, the two bodies are operating at cross-purposes. The WFSC has followed the lead of the Rome Conference undertaking in stressing self-reliance, with international support for individual developing countries that purchase, store, and sell grain reserves internally. The IWC focuses on trade and market shares and pays scant heed to the problem of the LDCs. Neither approach is integrated into a consistent conceptual framework. Such a framework is proposed later in this paper.

3. Recent Developments in World Cereals Markets

The history of the food crisis has been frequently recounted, and there is no sense going through it again here.[1] But some facts should be borne in mind when world food security is discussed. Table 11.2 shows the levels

Table 11.2 World Carry-over Stocks of Cereals (excluding China and the Soviet Union), 1970-76

	1970	1971	1972	1973	1974	1975[a]	1976 Forecast
Wheat	80	64	67	44	39	46	48
Rice	25	24	21	13	13	13	15
Coarse grain	73	57	73	59	50	44	46-49
Total Cereal Stocks	178	145	161	116	103	103	109-112
As Percent of Consumption	23	17	19	13	12	12	12

Source: FAO *Food Information Bulletin*, March 23, 1976, updated as of April 1, 1976.
[a]Preliminary.

of world carry-over stocks of grain at the end of recent marketing years in various countries.

The sharp drop in carry-overs occurred during the 1972-1973 crop year, at the time of the famous Soviet-American grain deal. The usual rule of thumb regarding grains is that the level of world grain stocks at the end of a marketing year ought to be about 10 percent of consumption, or about 110 million metric tons currently. If the rule is correct, food stocks for the last three years have been near the danger line, with almost no reserves (quantities above working stocks) at year ends. New crises have been averted simply because world production was adequate to cover demand.

Table 11.3 from USDA sources shows world grain production and consumption for recent years.[2] Note that, according to the table, 1973/1974 was a record crop year, with production 14 million tons higher than "consumption" (or, more accurately speaking, "disappearance" of the crop after all other uses are accounted for). There are two mysteries in these data. First, the FAO numbers in Table 11.2 do not show any 1973/1974 stock building, which would be consistent with Table 11.3. However, this anomaly can be dismissed by noting the difficulties of gathering stock data, in particular about increasing on-farm storage in the United States. More importantly, the most rapid acceleration of grain prices was observed precisely during mid-1973, when a world record crop was already starting to come to the market.[3]

For 1974/1975, Table 11.3 shows that production fell below consumption and Table 11.2 indicates that the stock situation apparently remained tenuous. In addition, Table 11.4 on recent grain export figures demonstrates that international demand for cereals continued to be strong through 1975, although it tended to drop off late in the year as spot prices for grains fell in relation to futures.

All this evidence points to an increase in excess demand for grains in 1974/1975, yet throughout that year prices did not increase further and even

Table 11.3 World Grain Production and Consumption with Trend Estimates, 1970 through 1974 (million metric tons)

Year	Grain Production			Grain Consumption			Consumption Production
	Actual	Trend[a]	Devia-tion	Actual	Trend[a]	Devia-tion	
1960/61-1962/63	799	793	+6	810	798	+12	
1969/70-1971/72	1069	1070	−1	1084	1066	+18	15
1972/73	1101	1132	−31	1131	1126	+5	30
1973/74	1194	1163	+32	1180	1155	+25	−14
1974/75	1142	1194	−52	1148	1185	−37	6

Source: USDA, *World Agricultural Situation*, WAS-6, December 1974, p. 27; and WAS-7, June 1975, p. 23.

[a]Linear trend is for the years 1960/61 through 1973/74.

declined. This is another odd bit of price behavior that needs to be analyzed. An initial clue lies in calculations by D. G. Johnson (1975) and P.C. Abbott (1976) that point out that normal market responses to demand-supply shocks, such as the disappearance of the Peruvian *anchoveta*, dollar devaluation, the commodity boom, and the general inflation in 1973, cannot rationalize more than 60 to 80 percent of the grain price increases in 1973. The remaining price movements must be discussed in terms of another theory that, as we will see, has considerable bearing on food security for consumers worldwide.

4. Theories of Commodity Markets

Several lines of economic theorizing can be brought to bear on the food security problem. We have just seen that one cannot explain (simple Marshallian stories about demand and supply with a few macroeconomic qualifications) all that occurred during the crisis.

In its "normative" welfare guise, demand-supply analysis also says something about how different producer and consumer groups are likely to respond to food shortages. The cleanest approach to welfare analysis in general equilibrium is to assume that long-run prices and quantities are determined in two markets for "food" and everything else, but that equilibrium is now and then perturbed by unexpected fluctuations in food production. One can read out the following conclusions.[4]

1. Suppose that the food demand curve is linear and supply rather inelastic in the short run. Then if one averages the values of consumers' and producers' surpluses at general equilibrium while supply of food fluctuates randomly,

Table 11.4 World Exports of Grains, 1971-75 (average million tons)

	1966/67- 1970/71	1971/72	1972/73	1973/74	1974/75[a]
Wheat	53.3	55.8	72.6	68.1	69.5
Coarse Grain	43.1	54.8	62.7	76.0	67.5
Rice	6.9	7.8	7.5	7.5	7.4

Source: FAO *Commodity Review*, 1974-1975.
[a]Preliminary

consumers can be shown to benefit and producers to lose as a result of the instability. If the two kinds of surpluses are weighted equally, the economy overall loses welfare. A stabilizing buffer stock buying when prices fall and selling when they rise would increase welfare, and producers should bribe consumers to accede to its establishment.

2. The preceding case is not very realistic, since it ignores the observation that demand for grain tends to become more inelastic as stocks go down and prices up. On theoretical grounds, one expects decreases in already low levels of stocks to be accompanied by sharp increases in spot prices relative to futures, as marginal convenience yields to processors of current stocks increase and speculators assume short positions. Empirically, a group of consultants to the FAO (1975a) measured higher arc elasticities of corn demand in 1970 than in 1974, with stocks in the former year being high.[5] If this evidence is taken at face value, it means that consumers lose and producers may gain in large magnitude when there is a production shortfall. A price-stabilizing buffer stock will benefit consumers, especially if they have a relatively low rate of discount against future hunger. Producers on the other hand may oppose a buffer stock, since they stand to gain so much when crops are short. In a "just" world producers should be taxed to pay for any losses a buffer stock might accrue (they might actually be minimal in the situation being discussed). But who is to guarantee justice?

3. The foregoing arguments generalize, with few surprises but many complications, to several trading countries with many groups of producers and consumers. Evidently, producers in an exporting country may benefit at the cost of consumers both abroad and at home during a supply shortfall (as indeed occurred in the United States during the crisis). The main conclusion to be drawn is that many conflicts are implicit in the functioning of a market such as that for cereals, and that inelasticities make them sharper during crisis situations.[6]

Another strand of theory, not so enshrined in the postwar canon, also tells something about price increases during the crisis. In Ch. 12 of *The General*

Theory, Keynes talks about how confidence that the near future will be similar to the past shores up the spirits of investors and keeps them in the securities market despite the enticements of liquidity. When confidence fails, in "... abnormal times in particular, when the hypothesis of an indefinite continuance of the existing state of affairs is less plausible than usual even though there are no express grounds to anticipate a definite change, the market will be subject to waves of optimistic and pessimistic sentiment, which are unreasoning and yet in a sense legitimate where no solid basis exists for a reasonable calculation."[7]

Now grains are not the same thing as shares, in particular because in food terms "liquidity" means stocks in the elevator and not money in the hoard. Nonetheless, when confidence fails and there is a crisis, a scramble for "liquidity" ensues and spot prices skyrocket. Sharp deflation of confidence must have occurred in grain markets in 1973, leading to the inflationary tendencies far stronger than one would anticipate on the grounds of demand versus supply. Thereafter, prices stayed up, even during the record 1974 crop year. In effect, the market was in a liquidity trap!

The grain situation had been stable for a decade prior to 1973. Because of the vagaries of its own internal price support policies the United States held very large surplus stocks, and the world had come to regard the United States as a residual supplier able to meet any market demand. Anticipating stable prices, importers did not hold any carry-overs in excess of working stocks. With the 1972/1973 crop year, the Soviet grain deal, and much else, knowledge that the United States was no longer a reliable supplier spread fast. The result was panic buying by almost every importer, often much in excess of requirements. Even currency speculators who had never before dealt in grains seemed to enter the market in a major way. The fallacy of composition worked in full, with buyers *trying* to acquire more and more grain at higher prices than ever before. When the record crop of 1973/1974 was harvested, the losses had already been incurred, and they were substantial. Table 11.5 shows the excess import cost for underdeveloped countries during the three-year period from 1972 to 1975. Transfers from consumers to producers within a market-linked exporting country such as the United States must also have been huge. The crisis of confidence translated itself into major income transfers and redistribution toward producers as prices rose.

A necessary condition for the food price inflation was the absence of any sort of international cooperation—at the level of nations, fear led to hoarding and to every man for himself. If a food security system had existed at the time, in the form of an authority holding stocks and authorized to sell them in a period of shortage, in all likelihood the panic would not have occurred. The main justification for a security scheme is to avoid a replay of 1972/1973. Its goal should be to ensure against undue and excessive fluctuations caused not by normal economic forces but by abnormal market psychology.

Table 11.5 Excess Import Cost, 1972-75

	1972	1973	1974	1975 Estimated
Quantity of developing country cereal imports (million metric tons)	34.5	47.0	48.0	57
Average price per ton (US $)	88.4	129.0	211.6	160
Value (million US $)	3,050	6,061	10,156	9,120
Annual excess cost[a] (million US $)		1,900	5,900	4,100
Cumulative excess cost		1,900	7,800	11,900

Source: World Food Council (1976).
[a]The excess cost is calculated by multiplying the difference in price between 1972 and each subsequent year by the quantity imported in each year.

5. Conceptual Problems in the Current Negotiations

We have seen that producer-consumer conflict is bound to appear in the buffer stock negotiations. One concrete example is the U.S. quantity-trigger proposal, and there are strong reasons to expect similar problems in the future. Second, at least in exceptional cases such as the food crisis, the market by itself is incapable of behaving in an equitable way. The market functions so as to take into account events within a short horizon, say, one crop year. Under heroic assumptions, it may even be said to provide short-term storage arrangements that are socially desirable, at least in the economist's narrow interpretation of that term. However, the market does not hedge on improbable events like those of 1973. When they occur, consumers—especially poor consumers—are the losers.

Any reserve stock/food aid scheme should work to reduce these losses at small cost to producers. But discussion has been handicapped by gross misapprehensions about what any functioning food security agency can achieve. For instance, there is the notion that a level of stocks somehow divided among participants and held against "crop shortfall" will solve the problem. There are many computations of shortfalls resulting from *past* production fluctuations, which are supposed to indicate how large stocks required to offset future risk might be. Although this method does indicate what reserves would have been needed, it provides no guidance on *how* to accumulate stocks ex ante.[8]

Accumulation of stocks in excess of working inventories in anticipation of an unlikely set of events is a risky and costly endeavor, flying in the face of "the dark forces of time and ignorance which envelop our future." One major problem is that even if a buffer stock agency were to sell in times of crisis at prices higher than those at which it purchased its stocks, the irregular arrival of major food shortfalls and accumulating storage costs might lead it to lose money over the years. Not enough work has gone into attempts to quantify this and other aspects of buffer stock operation, and until it is done a reliable system is not likely to emerge.[9]

The second widespread misapprehension is that one and only one reserve operation will simultaneously solve the price stabilization problem, the emergency supply problem, and the increased food aid objective. Clearly, quantities allocated for emergencies or food aid are net drains on the resources of a reserve, while buffer stocks for price stabilization are released in shortage but replenished in surplus. At least conceptually, the emergency and food aid problems must be separated from price stabilization.

Even under the latter heading, there is confusion. A price stabilizing buffer stock is supposed to interfere in the market when prices fall to a preset minimum or go up to a preset maximum. If the price band is too narrow, the buffer will inhibit the functioning of the market system and substitute for it. Given the enormous number of participants in agricultural markets who rely on prices for economic signaling, near complete suppression of the price mechanism would lead to financial loss and disruption of private incentives to store. (Something similar occurred in the United States, when government stockpiling was in full swing.)

A wider price band retains market incentives, but can still protect the consuming public against improbable events—in this sense a buffer stock is best viewed as an insurance mechanism against sharp price increases (and real income losses) during crop shortfalls. For reasons already discussed, the market will not provide this kind of insurance but governments can. A reserve of this type might well run financial losses, and this should be clearly understood by those who feel that a good buffer stock is one that makes profits. If profits were to be made from ensuring against food catastrophe, the market could do it.

6. Proposal for an Approach to Food Security

Here, we outline a system for world food security that we feel is realistic, economically feasible, and has a reasonable chance of being accepted politically. The basic approach is to separate the elements of an international reserve stock into the three categories just discussed, and distinguish the objectives for each part.

The first component of a worldwide system of food security should be comprised of provisions for national emergencies. Such emergencies occur infrequently and in different parts of the world, so it is impossible to predict them. An international reserve on the order of 500,000 tons of grain, as proposed by Sweden at the World Food Conference, would be drained after a few emergencies and an effort to replenish stocks would be required. The system we have in mind would be more permanent, based on fixed yearly commitments by rich donor countries, totaling perhaps 500,000 tons of grain or other foodstuffs. The committed stores would be held in these countries, and owned by them, but would be at the disposal of a multilateral relief agency such as the World Food Program and could be drawn on rapidly by *local* officials of the WFP in afflicted areas as the need arose. If the stores were not drawn during a given year, they would simply revert to the governments committing them in the first place.

The second component should assure a continuous flow of food aid to needy countries. By a standard accounting identity which holds in any country,

Net cereal imports = cereal consumption − production
+ consumed part of aid inflows,

where we abstract from domestic stock operations. Other things equal, the accounting suggests an inverse relationship between imports and production— if there is a crop shortfall it will be made up from international trade. Belt-tightening, domestic price increases, and similar responses to scarcity could be expected to move the import coefficient with respect to production away from minus one and toward zero, but a priori one would still expect trade to compensate at least in part for a bad crop.

Figure 11.1 shows the relationship over time between cereal imports and production for MSA countries. Apparently, when food production falls off in these countries, so also do their agricultural export potential, foreign exchange availability, and capacity to import—the simple regression coefficient of net cereal imports on cereal production is +1.15! Belts are tightened desperately as crops fail and imports decline in the MSA part of the world.

Not too much should be made of this result, since it depends on aggregate data and the simplest possible regression equation. But the far more careful studies of Abbott (1976) and Sarris (1976) point in the same direction as Figure 11.1. In a fully specified trade model estimated separately for a number of underdeveloped countries, Abbott observes import coefficients with respect to production clustering around −0.50, with some values exceeding zero. Using a similar model but a different data base, Sarris finds statistically significant import coefficients with respect to production ranging from −0.3 to −0.9, with developing countries having coefficients closer to zero than developed ones.

As shown in Figure 11.1, net cereal imports of MSA countries now run around 15 million tons per year; the standard deviation over the 1961-1974 period is 3.5 million. Since trade among these countries is not extensive and they hold few reserves, an annual food aid commitment of, say, 5 million tons would at least help to maintain their nutritional standards and provide modest room for improvement. An annual flow of 10 million tons of untied aid would be more realistic. If such a commitment is made, it should be in

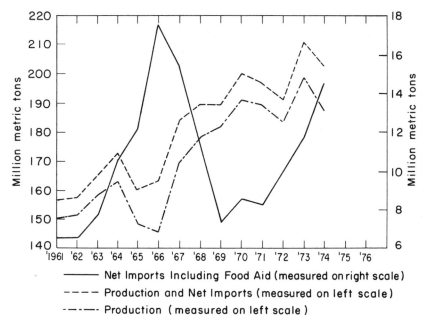

Figure 11.1 Cereal production and net imports of MSA developing countries. Source: Computed from FAO data.

physical and not value terms, to guarantee real consumption levels. In such a program the amounts received by recipient countries would vary from year to year to assure that only those with short crops would receive aid, and that the donated foods would not be reexported. In addition, were the food aid not "free," it should at least be on concessional terms. Some countries, for instance, are now financing food purchases on the world market with bankers' facilities at interest rates ranging upward of eighteen percent! Any rational food distribution scheme would avoid such usury.

The third and final component of a world food security system should be a buffer stock operated as an insurance scheme to benefit consumers of all countries. The basic.formula would be for the buffer stock agency to buy at slightly below long-term equilibrium prices and hold reserves against any well-defined contingency such as a major world crop shortfall or indication of very sharp international price rises (the price-trigger system would probably be preferable).

There is a trade-off between the quantity of reserves held and the price band around which the reserve agency would come into operation. The larger is the band, the lower is the required level of reserves and the longer on average is the period between interventions. Total storage cost may therefore increase as the price band widens. Better quantification of some of these trade-offs is necessary before details of a reserve scheme could be proposed. Producers are likely to lose if an insurance reserve is instituted, but by how much is a matter for analysis. Before it is decided who bears insurance costs, their probable magnitude has to be ascertained.

The effects of currently restricted domestic markets for most countries will also distort conclusions drawn from free trade theorizing. Sarris (1976) has computed the effects of various reserve schemes on producers and consumers under free and restricted markets and they can be quite different depending on the assumptions.

The approach suggested here clearly distinguishes between emergency relief and food aid as annual flows on the one hand, and the insurance reserve on the other. The quantities required would be different for the three functions. Half a million metric tons yearly for emergencies, together with 10 million tons for food aid, add up to an *annual* minimum grain flow of 10.5 million tons. For the reserve stock, a price band of 50 percent around the equilibrium price for an insurance reserve would require stocks of some 15-20 million tons of all grains, or 10 million tons of wheat only. This last figure should be compared with previously quoted figures of 60 million tons for all grains (at the World Food Conference) or 30 million tons for wheat and rice (U.S. proposal). If supplying countries are willing to forego the delights of food price hyperinflation in the midst of possible future crises, they may not find their share of the other costs of world food security to be unduly onerous.

Notes

The authors are grateful to the conference participants and discussants, and to Harry Walters, Roger Gray, Sartaj Aziz, and Philip Abbott for many of the ideas appearing here.

1 See, for example, Abbott (1976), Hathaway (1974), D. G. Johnson (1975), Schertz (1974).

2 The numbers in Tables 11.2 and 11.3 are not directly comparable, since USDA and FAO estimates of grain statistics differ in concept and coverage.

3 For both spring and winter wheat, prices approximately doubled during the third quarter of 1973, and leveled off thereafter. Coarse grain prices rose by 50 percent in the same quarter, and another 20-30 percent over the subsequent four quarters. Rice is not heavily traded internationally, but its price rose steadily over the period between early 1973 and mid-1974, somewhat more than doubling. For more detail, see FAO (1975b).

4 For the analytical details, see Sarris (1976). In a slightly different institutional context, the reasoning of H. G. Johnson (1976) parallels that here, particularly in its conclusion that some groups in the economy *can* benefit from price fluctuations in general equilibrium, whether they result from acts of God or just destabilizing speculators.

5 For the theoretical arguments phrased in terms of the "supply of storage," see Weymar (1968). The FAO calculation depends on corn crop forecasts to get the arc in its elasticity, and can be criticized for doing so. There may be some downward bias in elasticities derived in this fashion because sensitive speculative markets tend to overreact to sudden changes. However, it is difficult to see how one can do more to improve the calculation than note the probable direction of its error.

6 Some food experts argue that private storage firms setting expected marginal costs equal to expected returns for storage will abet the invisible hand's maximization of some sort of dynamic social welfare function. Even abstracting from benefit-cost evaluations of starvation or increased infant mortality from malnutrition, this argument is wrong in principle. A welfare optimum under uncertainty cannot be achieved by the simple certainty equivalence calculations they propose, except under very special circumstances. In general, a full dynamic programing solution for reserve stocks is required, which a market, even without impediments such as future contracts of twelve-month maximum length, cannot duplicate.

7 Keynes (1936), p. 154.

8 Examples of the type of mechanical calculation we have in mind appear in FAO (1974), Simaika (1974), and USDA (1974).

9 See Reutlinger (1976), D. G. Johnson and D. Sumner (1976), and D. G. Johnson (1977) for some beginnings. Reutlinger was perhaps the first to point out that a realistic international buffer stock will probably run losses on average.

References

Abbott, P. C. (1976), *Developing Countries and International Grain Trade*, unpublished Ph.D. dissertation, Massachusetts Institute of Technology.

FAO (1956), *Functions of a World Food Reserve—Scope and Limitations*, Commodity Policy Studies No. 10, Rome 1956.

FAO (1958), *National Food Reserve Policies in Underdeveloped Countries*, Commodity Policy Studies No. 11, Rome 1958.

_____ (1974), *World Food Security: Draft Evaluation of World Cereals Stock Situation*, CCP: GR 74/11, July.

_____ (1975a), "Food Reserve Policies for World Food Security: A Consultant Study on Alternative Approaches," ESC:CSP/72/2, January.

_____ (1975b), *Commodity Review and Outlook*, 1974/1975, Rome.

Hathaway, D. E. (1974), "Food Prices and Inflation," *Brookings Papers on Economic Activity*, No. 1, 1974.

Johnson, D. G. (1975), *World Food Problems and Prospects*, American Enterprise Institute for Public Policy Research, Washington, D.C., June.

_____ (1977), "Increased Stability of Grain Supplies in Developing Countries," in J. Bhagwati, ed., *The New International Economic Order*, MIT Press, Cambridge, Mass.

Johnson, D. G., and D. Sumner (1976), "An Optimization Approach to Grain Reserves for Developing Countries" (mimeo), University of Chicago, April.

Johnson, H. G. (1976), "Destabilizing Speculation: A General Equilibrium Approach," *Journal of Political Economy*, Vol. 84, No. 1.

Keynes, J. M. (1936), *The General Theory of Employment, Interest and Money*, Harcourt, Brace, New York.

McCalla, A. F. (1967), "Pricing in the World Feed Grain Market," *Agricultural Economics Research*, Vol. 19, October.

Reutlinger, S. (1976), "A Simulation Model for Evaluating Worldwide Buffer Stocks of Wheat," *American Journal of Agricultural Economics*, 58, 1-12.

Sarris, A. H. (1976), *The Economics of International Grain Reserve Systems*, unpublished Ph.D. dissertation, Massachusetts Institute of Technology.

Schertz, L. P. (1974), "World Food Prices and the Poor," *Foreign Affairs*, Vol. 52, No. 3, April.

Simaika, J. G. (1974), "Probability of Success of a 'Stock and Allocation' Policy," FAO, ESS/MISC/74-1, September 1974.

United Nations (1974), *Report of the World Food Conference*, E/CONF.65/20, Rome, November 5-16.

USDA (1974), *The World Food Situation and Prospects to 1985*, ERS, FAER, No. 98, December.

Weymar, F. H. (1968), *The Dynamics of the World Cocoa Market*, MIT Press, Cambridge, Mass.

World Food Council (1976), *International System of Food Security*, Report of the Executive Director to the Second Session, WFC/22, Rome, June 14-16.

Comment
Robert M. Solow

Lacking any special knowledge about LDCs or the world grain trade or foreign aid, I can only make some outsider's general remarks about these two papers. This may serve the useful purpose of helping to focus the discussion.

The two papers have a certain amount in common, and a couple of differences of opinion. One useful thing they try to do is to distinguish among various reasons for giving food aid. These can be grouped under three headings.

1. The delivery of food may be a response to single localized emergencies, like natural disasters. There seems to be no real problem here. Johnson agrees that it is sensible to give food to earthquake areas; and Sarris and Taylor suggest a special reserve of 500,000 tons to be set aside every year, used when necessary, at the instance of some outside agency, and replenished annually. No further discussion is called for.

2. Food can be thought of as just one form of foreign aid: continuing gifts simply to raise food consumption in LDCs above the level they could otherwise sustain. Here there is a sharp difference of opinion. Sarris and Taylor propose, as part of their "realistic" program, an annual flow of 10 million tons of grain to poor countries for the purpose of raising nutritional standards. Johnson, on the other hand, says that his insurance proposal *presupposes* that continuous transfers of grain—like 10 million tons a year—would not represent an effective use of the world's resources. This could mean several things. It could mean that such a transfer would not actually raise nutritional standards in poor countries, or that it would do so but they should not be raised, or that it would do so but have bad incentive effects on local grain production; or it could simply mean that equivalent transfers of cash or of something other than grain would be better. If, as I think, it means this last, then I understand. But I think one should ask seriously if the equivalent cash or other transfer would actually be made. Ten million tons of grain a year that *would* be transferred could be a less effective use of resources than an equivalent cash transfer actually carried out, but a more effective use of resources than an equivalent cash transfer not actually carried out. Since the time of the Irish famine, economists have distinguished themselves by preaching that people should not be relieved of starvation, *for their own good*. It seems to me that in practice one must recognize that food aid evokes a special response in the public mind, perhaps for reasons

Levi-Strauss has already analyzed, or for reasons Gary Becker may yet analyze. There is also an important distributional question: in practice, food transfers and cash transfers may tend to go to different people.

In any event, I must leave further discussion of this aspect of food aid to others who know more than I do about the issues and possibilities.

3. The third aspect of food aid is the one that concerns Johnson, and also appears in different form in Sarris and Taylor. It involves permitting the time series of consumption of grain in LDCs to be smoother than the time series of production. Johnson proposes a scheme in which rich countries would guarantee to ship to poor countries, individually, the difference between actual production and 94 or 95 or (1-x)100 percent of calculated *trend* production in any year. That would obviously put a lower limit under the annual consumption of grain in each LDC in any year; and, as Johnson points out, it would permit each country, by carrying its own stocks, to limit the allowable consumption shortfall to an even smaller amount. It is an important part of Johnson's scheme that this additional insurance would be relatively cheap, since it is not hard to self-insure against small losses, so long as the big losses are covered by someone else. It is exactly like the deductible on an automobile collision insurance policy, and performs the same function.

Sarris and Taylor propose a different system to accomplish more or less the same thing, namely a buffer stock to buy grain when its price is more than y percent below some normal, and to sell whenever the price is more than z percent above normal. If the relevant price-elasticity of demand is about one to ten, then a 50 percent price band would correspond roughly to a 5 percent quantity band, and both papers are at least in the same ball park.

There is an element of complementarity between the two analyses. If Sarris and Taylor are right that the world grain market is characterized by a tendency for a speculative scramble for grain stocks to take place when the price rises sharply, then the Johnson scheme would tend to prevent that happening, just as the buffer stock scheme would do. If that is the main object of world food security, then I guess either scheme would do the trick.

By the way, I wonder if the notion of a speculative rush for stocks may not be the source of those astoundingly low estimates of the elasticity of demand for grain. (Remember that anyone who spends *all* of a given income on grain must have a unit-elastic demand for grain, courtesy of algebra, not econometrics.) One can imagine how the slope of the underlying consumption-demand curve might be masked by speculative buying for inventory as the price rises.

I have two small questions about the Johnson scheme. One has to do with the way it rests on simple trend curves of grain production in individual LDCs. It appears to assume that there is no significant supply response to price, because otherwise those simple trend lines would not seem to have a clear meaning. Maybe that is the case, but I think experts should be clear about it.

The other question may simply betray my own ignorance. What about poor countries that have no substantial domestic grain production? Perhaps there are no such countries. Even if there are, it might not matter much, except for the "fact" that the elasticity of demand seems to be so small. If it is as small as one to ten, then even a 6 percent shortfall of supply in the market will push the price up by 60 percent, and that could be a drastic blow to the standard of living in a poor country that must import essentially all its grain. If there are such countries, then maybe they should be considered to have suffered an honorary earthquake.

This small elasticity of demand—Johnson uses one to ten and Sarris and Taylor suggest that the elasticity is even smaller at points on the demand curve with high prices—creates a lot of intellectual problems. I set myself the task of figuring out how much good the Johnson scheme might do in the abstract. One turns first to consumers' surplus calculations, but of course when the elasticity of demand is less than one, the area under the demand curve is infinite. One can do "utility" calculations under the assumption that grain is an "independent" good, that is, that social welfare is a function of consumption of all other goods plus a function of grain consumption alone, with the latter function having the form necessary to generate a constant-elasticity demand curve. Then it is not hard to calculate the expected utility when grain consumption is uniformly distributed. The Johnson scheme, seen from an LDC, amounts to chopping off the lower tail of the distribution, say, all below 94 percent of the mean, and piling up the corresponding tail probability at exactly 94 percent of the mean.

I have to confess that I have not actually carried out that calculation, for lack of time, but it is only arithmetic. I did make a related, simpler, calculation that I will not bother to describe, and convinced myself that the utility gain from the Johnson scheme could, in principle, be quite substantial. It is, unsurprisingly, rather sensitive to the assumed elasticity of demand, at least for small elasticities. The percentage utility gain might be three times as large for an elasticity of one to ten as for an elasticity of one to five—after all, the lower the elasticity, the more an extreme shortfall hurts.

Despite the uncertainty, I would conclude that either the Johnson insurance scheme or the Sarris and Taylor buffer stock scheme could be a very useful way of improving the standard of living in poor countries.

IV
Technology Transfer and Diffusion

12

International Technology Issues: Southern Needs and Northern Responses

G. K. Helleiner

Introduction

Although no one minimizes the importance of foreign exchange earnings, capital inflows, or domestic savings, there has recently been a relative shift in emphasis in the less developed countries toward the role of technology in development efforts. In many less developed countries, the possibilities of raising capital either at home or abroad now look less daunting than the problems associated with technological progress. There has emerged, in consequence of these new perceptions, a new set of issues for international debate and resolution—issues that, unlike those of commodity policy, market access, monetary reform, or aid, were scarcely heard of only a decade or so ago.

Technology "gaps" exist everywhere. In few sectors of the world economy would it be reasonable to assert or assume that the same technology everywhere governs production possibilities, that is, that all producers operate on the same production function. It is the fact of divergences in the state of the arts, as between countries or segments of the same country, that has bred the whole discussion of the "transfer of technology." (That is not to say, however, that observed differences in production technique—as measured by such indicators as the capital-labor ratio—necessarily reflect differences in access to technology; they may simply reflect different relative factor and input prices.)

The known technology even within the developed countries is far from uniform everywhere. Since the frontiers of knowledge are constantly being pushed back in all sectors, in consequence of ongoing research and development both in the public and private sectors, everyone everywhere must run quickly to stay abreast of the most recent technological breakthroughs. The process of diffusion of technology is thus by no means a matter purely of transferring "shelf" knowledge from rich countries to poor. Indeed, in this as in most other aspects of Third World economic relations in the world economy the importance of the developing countries is small. The process of diffusion or transfer of technology to poor countries is of relatively little overall consequence to most developed country technology owners. Because of this, the institutions, legal arrangements, and so forth, that affect or govern technological matters in the developed countries have been constructed by and large with the interests of only the developed countries in mind. Moreover, in the market economies of the West, there may well have been more attention paid to private property rights in their historical development than to the social interest, whereas in the developing countries *social* development objectives are today universally espoused.

Technological development and diffusion in the industrialized countries is primarily, then, a matter of "intra-northern" experience. The techniques developed and diffused are those that reflect the effective demands, the relative prices, and the physical environment of the developed countries. Only where there are firms or institutions *specializing in the concerns of the less developed countries* might one expect to find arrangements and techniques that cater to these countries' special needs. This is not to say that the technology (or its supporting legal and institutional infrastructure) of the developed countries is *necessarily* "inappropriate" for serving the interests of the less developed countries or for overcoming poverty problems; the point is simply that less developed country possibilities were not significant considerations in the developed countries' historical development.

This background has led those most concerned with the interests of the less developed countries to assess (1) the size and nature of the efforts to transfer technologies that *are* specialized in the problems of the less developed countries; (2) whether and where the technological "system" of the developed countries, and its reflection in the international economic order, is harmful or beneficial to the less developed countries.

It is difficult to construct *general* assessments of these issues but it is worth noting immediately that the expressed general views of the less developed countries on these issues are that: (1) existing efforts to transfer technology to them are far too small and severely flawed; (2) the present technological "system" of the industrialized countries is biased and fraught with imperfections that reduce the gains there from what might otherwise accrue to the less developed countries. These perceptions underlie all policy positions.

Market incentives have not, by themselves, generated much effort on the part of commercially motivated firms, which develop and sell technology, to devote special attention to the needs of the less developed countries. Rather, such firms have tended simply to sell technologies as they employ them— offering those already "on their shelf." Both their production and their consumption technologies[1] have therefore frequently been judged "inappropriate" in the sense that they are not adapted, or insufficiently so, to the peculiar physical, economic, and social environments of the less developed countries. Such efforts as there have been to transfer suitable technologies to the less developed countries have frequently been undertaken by agencies not geared to the profit motive—notably, charitable foundations and governments.

As far as the present system of technology development and diffusion is concerned, the principal point is that most technology that is made available to the less developed countries is not so much "transferred" as sold. The market for technology is a highly imperfect one in which information is limited, and monopoly, while sometimes mitigated by intertechnology substitution possibilities, is usual. Such international legal conventions as there are grant wide-ranging rights to the owners of intellectual property while imposing few developmental obligations upon them. As net purchasers of imported technology, the less developed countries understandably seek to increase competition, limit restrictive business practices, and alter the international conventions that govern technology trade and development. The search is therefore on for new institutions and means for producing and supplying technology, involving specialized firms prepared to deal at arm's length, governments, and the less developed countries.

The debate about international technology trade has, to a considerable extent, moved forward as a subcomponent of the general debate about multinational firms and the possibility of international antitrust action. Indeed, some, both on the left and on the right, see the technology questions as indivisible from the overall issues of international business and lament the "excessive theorizing" that has led to their separation. This interrelationship between technology and multinational firm problems stems from the fact that much of the recent technology transfer to the less developed countries has been effected through the medium of direct investment by multinational firms (Helleiner, 1975). Yet there is now increasing experimentation with the "unpackaging" not only of what direct investment has traditionally supplied (capital, technology, management, marketing) but also, notably in the Andean Pact, of the technological packages themselves. (One reflection of this fact is the recent precipitous change in the nature of disputes involving U.S. firms abroad. In the 1960-1971 period, over 71 percent of such disputes had to do with formal nationalization or expropriation; between 1971 and 1973, this proportion had fallen to only 22 percent, the bulk of the disputes having to do with contractual and managerial disagreements. See U.S., 1971, and U.S., 1974.) As this unpackaging has proceeded, it has become evident that the principal contribution of private multinational firms to host countries, and the main source of their market power, is their technology. Technology, in the words of one study, is the multinational firm's "trump card" (Stopford and Wells, 1972, p. 177). It may also constitute an important element in the national advantage of the countries in which its owners are based (Rodriguez, 1975).

There is nevertheless a lot to be said for the maintenance of the direct investment system for the transfer of much technology to developing countries. Wholly owned subsidiaries of multinational firms undoubtedly do have smoother, more automatic, and sometimes even (socially) cheaper access to technology—in the form of ongoing advice, information, and personnel—

than do licensees or one-shot, arm's-length purchasers of "shelf" technology (Behrman and Wallender, 1976). But the policy bias toward this form of private technology transfer to the less developed countries, which is engendered by most present investment guarantee programs of the developed countries, probably stems more from inertia than from a careful assessment of the alternative institutional forms which this trade now takes. Nor is there any developmental rationale for the restrictions frequently placed upon projects qualifying for such guarantees, say, those in the U.S. program that forbid support for government majority-owned firms.

There is, in any case, no mistaking the recent trends and therefore no escaping the technology issues now on the international agenda. As consumers of imported technology, the less developed countries are engaged in a vigorous international effort at "consumerism," the object of which is to raise the quality and lower the price of their purchases. Their individual shopping efforts are directed to more careful screening and harder bargaining. At the international level they seek to stimulate competition among the sellers of technology and cooperation among the buyers while increasing the flow of information all round.

No one expects or requests owners of industrial property to give up their income therefrom. They have invested in the production of technology and are acknowledged to deserve a fair return on the investment. Private firms are engaged in the pursuit of profit, not in charitable activities, and it would be misleading to expect them to do otherwise.[2] Although private profit is frequently consistent with social objectives, for example, in training and in some local subcontracting, this will not always be the case.

Many governments of less developed countries therefore now employ official screening mechanisms for the assessment of contracts involving the importation of technology. The screening of imported technology has so far been a rather imperfect process. Although the economic and legal aspects of new technology contracts have been relatively easy to assess, the analysis of the technological merits of particular products and processes relative to possible alternatives typically remains beyond the limited capacities of the screening agencies. Efforts to control technology imports rather than simply direct investments can nevertheless be expected to continue in those countries which already make them and to spread quickly to other countries as their expertise and administrative capacity expand.

All things considered, these and other domestic policies of the governments of the less developed countries are likely to have a greater impact upon the use and development of appropriate technologies than developed country policy and international convention. In the realm of international technology trade, terms will be very much influenced by the policies of the importing countries. The technology issues now placed by the developing countries upon the international agenda are nevertheless important and require responses from the developed countries.

Commercialized Technology: The Paris Convention, the Code of Conduct, and Improved Information

At the international level, the two principle nonaid issues in the field of technology are the revision of the Paris Convention governing patents, trademarks, and other industrial property, and the introduction of a code of conduct regulating the international transfer of technology.

Patents, Trademarks, and Other Industrial Property: The Paris Convention

Many of the issues surrounding the international debate concerning patents, trademarks, and other industrial property have to do with national level policy formation rather than international agreement. The facts that over 90 percent of the patents granted by developing countries are foreign owned and that a similar percentage of them are never employed in the developing countries that have granted them suggest that the patent system's role is more to preclude the employment of technologies in developing countries than to encourage their local development and use (Penrose, 1973). Moreover, in the absence of alternative advice, many developing countries have adopted a Model Law on Inventions, created for them by the WIPO (World Intellectual Property Organization),[3] which contains elements that when inspected by the expert eye seem to be injurious to them (Vaitsos, 1976). Industrial property legislation and conventions in developing countries are therefore matters for early reform.

Such reforms do not necessarily, and should not, involve the total repudiation of conventional industrial property rights. On the contrary, recognition of such rights—at least in selected areas—may be crucial to the development of technologies that are tailored to developing country needs. Such recognition is also likely to be of greatest importance to newer and smaller foreign firms (as distinct from the established transnational enterprises that have their own systems of knowledge protection), from which, other things being equal, less developed countries can hope to extract better terms.

The details of local reforms are matters on which the less advanced developing countries could use informed technical assistance. Among the principles that they ought certainly to incorporate are: developmental criteria for patentability; limitation of patent privileges to local production rather than, as at present, to imports as well; identification of key sectors or areas where patents will not be granted; simplified administrative procedures for the granting and enforcement of industrial property rights and shortened duration of patent privileges (Vaitsos, 1976). Appropriate changes in the Paris Convention would ease the introduction of such domestic reforms. They could also achieve systemic change great enough to induce greater numbers of less developed countries to join the Paris Union. (At present the union has only forty-five less developed country members and, in the absence of reform, their number might well decline; though many more do recognize international patent conventions.)

The basic objectives in the revision of the Paris Convention seem already to have been agreed upon. In the UNCTAD and the WIPO, the discussions that have been under way for some time have led to agreement on the preamble to a revised convention. It contains recognition of the need to balance the objectives of development against the rights of the owners of industrial property rights, to promote the use of inventions in each less developed country in which rights are granted, to facilitate the transfer of technology from industrialized to less developed countries on "fair and reasonable" terms, and to improve the institutional infrastructure in developing countries to permit them effectively to assess industrial property questions. At the same time, there is agreement that more technical assistance in this area should be provided for developing countries. There is therefore room for some optimism with respect to the prospects of a serious revision of this convention over the course of the next few years.

A Code of Conduct on the Transfer of Technology

There has been extensive discussion at the international level of the possibility or desirability of a code of conduct governing the transfer of technology to developing countries. The overlap of technology issues with the multinational corporation issue has already been noted. Codes of conduct for multinationals, and international antitrust efforts, are under discussion at the international level, *without* specific reference to the transfer of technology. But the technology code has, under UNCTAD pressure, made more progress than the broader objectives. Rival drafts have been prepared by the Group of 77 and by the developed countries. These drafts contain substantial areas of agreement. The question now, therefore, does not seem to be whether there is to *be* a code so much as what is to be its specific content and the modalities of its operation. The main points still at issue between the developed and the developing countries are the following:

(1) what precisely are to be regarded as "restrictive business practices" to be prohibited by the code (the latest draft from the Group of 77 lists forty items under this heading);

(2) whether the code should be legally binding in some way and backed by national laws, or merely offered in the form of voluntary "guidelines";

(3) whether it should incorporate the principle of special preferences for the less developed countries;

(4) whether such legal problems as arise in technology contracts should be subject to international arbitration or to resolution by the courts of the host or home country;

(5) whether it should include a number of guarantees that supplying firms are to offer to purchasers (say, that the technology supplied is "complete");

(6) whether it should include a number of general prohibitions and restric-

tions as to the terms of technology contracts (limits on royalty payments to parent firms, time limits on licensing agreements, and so forth).

What is the purpose of such a code? Individual governments, after all, possess the power to regulate and control technology imports and to prohibit related restrictive practices if they choose to exercise it, with or without a code; and many less developed countries already do so. Less developed countries can also set up joint rules for negotiations and contracts with foreign technology suppliers, without a universal code and without the compliance of the developed countries; and some, notably the members of the Andean Pact, have done so. In recent years, there has been considerable exchange of experience and information with respect to technology import policies among the less developed countries, and some modeling on the part of relative "late-comers" to this scene of the practice of the "veterans." Why then the intense pressure from the developing countries for an internationally accepted code of conduct for the transfer of technology? And why the vigorous resistance to the idea on the part of international business?

There undoubtedly *is* a case for jointly imposed rules to govern technology imports to the less developed countries—to raise their share of the rent accruing to technology owners (that is, reduce its price), and particularly to assist the weakest developing countries. What is the case for involving the developed countries in the enforcement of a code? The developing countries' desire for developed country involvement can, I think, be ascribed to three factors: (1) a desire for a formalized legitimation of policies that will in any case be pursued, (2) a desire for assistance in data collection and enforcement with respect to provisions of technology contracts (which would be more likely if there were agreement at the international level as to the "appropriateness" of their contents), and (3) a genuine concern to develop international controls over transnational enterprises, and, in particular, to extend to the international arena the provisions of the developed countries' own domestic antitrust provisions.

Opposition to the idea of a code (which is not obviously just self-interested special pleading) rests upon two basic (and mutually inconsistent) premises: (1) it will be unenforceable, and (2) it will reduce the volume, or increase the cost, of technology transfers to the developing countries.[4]

The problem of enforcement derives both from disagreement at the international level as to whether it could even in principle be legally binding, and from the practical problem of enforcement machinery. The problem is a difficult but hardly unfamiliar one. Few of those who make this case have urged the winding up of the GATT or the Paris Union. It is also noteworthy that the United States now favors a firm international agreement, backed by national legislation, governing certain other activities of multinational firms (relating to bribery and political influence). Whether individual countries would collaborate in breaches of the code or whether it would be totally enforceable would depend upon the same set of imponderables as affect all other such efforts at international regulation.

If the code is unenforceable, it is unlikely to affect significantly the scale or terms of technology sales to developing countries. If it has some "teeth," however, it may not be in the interests of the developing countries that are pressing for it, or so it is argued by business economists and spokesmen for the developed countries (Council for the Americas, no date, and de Cubas, 1974).

Too much limitation upon the rights and return of technology owners, it is argued, will lead them either to forego sales in the Third World entirely, or to demand higher prices (perhaps indirectly) for technology that is still sold in now less attractive conditions. It may also be that firms that have, in effect, supplied technology on an ongoing basis to subsidiary or related firms abroad will now identify such transactions as deserving of reimbursement when, before the technology transfer code, they never had done so.

These are, of course, arguments against more stringent technology policies rather than against a code qua code. Similar arguments have consistently (and incorrectly) been made with respect to attempts to extract higher resource rents from mineral exporting foreign firms, and attempts to bargain more effectively with foreign sources of direct investment in other sectors. Undoubtedly, some investment and some technology are lost through harder bargaining efforts, and, undoubtedly, larger proportions of rent accrue to host countries and increased development impacts are realized in consequence of those investment and technology flows that continue. At issue is the true shape of the supply schedule for the technology that is of greatest interest to the developing countries. There are strong grounds for the view that it is highly inelastic in the present range of prices since they far exceed the marginal cost of supplying (Vaitsos, 1970). Whether, on balance, the tightening of controls increases the welfare of the host countries concerned remains to be seen but, in any case, seems best left for them to judge. A learning process is likely to be required in order for host countries to employ their regulatory and tax powers most effectively. A certain amount of time must be permitted to elapse before final judgments can be offered. There is no a priori reason to take the gloomy forecasts of businessmen and spokesmen for developed countries too seriously, since they are so obviously interested parties.[5]

Whatever the eventual outcome, it is more likely to be favorable to the less developed countries if they coordinate their policies and adopt common positions than if they remain divided. Hence the importance of a common and generalized code. In the view of the international business community, it is the attempt to implement a *general* code that is so potentially damaging. A case-by-case approach, in which the screening agency considers each case entirely on its particular merits, is less likely, they argue, to produce rigidities, delays, and inefficiencies. Wherever there is a willing buyer and a willing seller, they argue, those should generally be allowed to get on with their bargain without regard to preestablished norms and without the necessity of dealing with another level of bureaucracy. But case-by-case, as opposed to general, approaches carry implications for the relative bargaining strengths of technology suppliers and importing countries (whether governments or firms). In particular, case-by-case approaches are likely to favor the more powerful parties to these bargains. Bargaining strength depends primarily upon knowledge, experience, and political power. In the less developed countries, these are often limited when compared to those of the multinational firm. The weakest developing countries clearly stand to gain the most from generalized approaches and common codes. Even businessmen from relatively strong importing countries, however, have noted the increased bargaining power vis-à-vis foreign firms that they derive from a set of minimum legal requirements in their contracts.

The reservations concerning the code found in some of the less developed countries—in ones that are relatively experienced and knowledgeable in the technology sphere—stem from the risks some of them see of establishing international norms less attractive to them than the policies they would otherwise pursue (or those they are already implementing). (See Vaitsos, 1975, pp. 87-88.) In order for a code to be made acceptable to the developed countries, they foresee the preparation of codes that imply undesirable and unnecessary limitations upon the policies of technology importing countries. As far as the obligations of supplying firms are concerned, they fear that what are imposed as minimum conditions will rapidly be taken as maximum ones. Whatever is in the code, it is unlikely that such countries as India, Mexico, Argentina, Brazil, or the members of the Andean Pact would turn back from their own recently introduced technology screening procedures or feel constrained in their application by terms designed with weaker technology importing countries in mind.

On the other hand, anxiety is also expressed on behalf of the weaker developing countries whose freedom of maneuver in attempting to offset their relative unattractiveness to foreign business may be inhibited by too rigid a code. In their case, however, they retain the possibility of influencing the many other dimensions (taxes, disclosure, local procurement, training, and so forth) of their relations with foreign firms—relations that are, in any case, more likely to involve capital as well as technology.

Even with the code, conditions for investment and technology sales by multinational corporations can thus be expected to vary from country to country. Tax treatment of fees and royalties, foreign exchange controls, and the strictness with which the international rules are applied, all still leave room for considerable competition among developing countries in technology and capital markets.

It seems safe to conclude that any code that could at present gain the agreement of both rich countries and of poor would be rife with escape clauses, and would almost certainly not be legally binding. If these conclusions are correct, one might wonder whether such a code's establishment might not simply generate a new international bureaucracy with imprecise functions and limited power. Whether such a bureaucracy is likely to be a "good" or a "bad" thing must inevitably remain a matter for judgment, over which reasonable men may legitimately disagree. Clearly, however, it *could* form the core and increase the pressure for a future GATT for the multinationals, internationalized antitrust action, and a center for objective data on international business. (Alternatively, existing institutions, such as the UN Centre for Transnational Corporations, WIPO, UNCTAD, GATT, and so on, could monitor the code's applications.)

Perhaps a more realistic view regards the discussion of the code as essentially educative in purpose. The more advanced host countries have technology contract assessment procedures firmly in place and are already busily learning by doing. The international discussion of the code, whether or not it ever generates an agreed upon code, will certainly inform the less advanced of the less developed countries as to the issues and create legitimacy for those who have developed or are developing policies in this sphere.[6] The "process" is more important than the end product (Perlmutter and Saghafinejad, 1976). From this standpoint, there is no urgency about reaching agreement. The object is to keep the discussion going.

Information Services

The greatest source of imperfection in technology markets is the limited information of the buyers. In part, the problem is inherent in the nature of knowledge markets. If one had sufficient knowledge to be able to assess the value of the knowledge one was purchasing, one would frequently not require the purchase. But, in larger part, the limited information of the buyers in the less developed countries is remediable. Their present sources of information are highly biased, coming as they do from technology and equipment salesmen, or from aid agencies and consultants—all consciously or unwittingly biased toward the particular technologies of the developed countries they know the best.

It is never easy for decision makers in developing countries to obtain a general impression of the entire range of technological possibilities with respect to any particular new undertaking, or to learn of new processes, techniques, and products relevant to existing ones. It is usually especially difficult, ·because of the North-South orientation of traditional communications flows, to learn of technologies developed or employed in other less developed countries (unless they are owned by multinational corporations that serve as transmission belts for some). Only for major projects can the costs of a systematic canvassing of the possibilities usually be contemplated. Even then, the sheer volume of printed material is so great that, without the hire of specialized expertise, the costs may be not feasible. There is therefore a strong case for international (perhaps regional) institutions that could avail themselves of scale economies and service the informational needs of many less developed countries that could not otherwise afford such services.

Consulting, information, or referral services, and exchanges of experience, are much discussed means of increasing consumer power in technology markets. Legal, technical, and economic information concerning the terms of contracts, the reputations of firms and consultants, and so on, might be centrally screened, organized, stored, and made available to individual less developed countries on request. It is clear that there might be disclosure difficulties stemming from the unwillingness or legal inability of individual governments to release to outsiders the full terms of their agreements. Moreover, formal institutional arrangements, libraries, and so forth, may involve rigidities and too great a distance from "the action." Perhaps more effective would be advisory services through which individuals experienced in particular sectors could be supplied on request; rather than drawing upon a bank of information, governments would employ expertise. Such service agencies might also be able to draw up model technology contracts on a sector-by-sector basis for use by a wide range of government or private clients in the less developed world.

Technology data banks have also been suggested, wherein information as to available technologies and their sources would be stored. This seems a little difficult to envisage since the diversity of activities is so vast and so changeable. It might be best to store information as to where to go for relevant information, while relying on trade associations, consultants, and traditional channels for the specifics in their own particular areas of specialization. Joint "shopping services" and referral services nevertheless might be established in particular priority sectors and/or among particular cooperating countries. Among the sectors deserving priority are certainly pharmaceuticals, food processing, and agricultural inputs.

UNIDO and FAO already have services of this sort in their respective fields of interest; and UNCTAD (1975) and the ILO (1976) have proposed the establishment of new institutions for developing appropriate technology, exchanging information, and improving the terms of technology trade. To the extent that these various measures and institutions would tend to perfect international technology markets and to assist the developing countries, they must be counted as beneficial. If new institutions are primarily financed by the developed countries—in addition to present levels of development assistance—they would, of course, be especially attractive to the developing countries.

Appropriate Technology: Choice and Development

Choice of Technique
Apart from the prices paid by the developing countries for technology imports, the other principal technology issue is the "appropriateness" of im-

ported technologies to local physical, economic, and social environments. These two issues of price and quality are interrelated since the lowering of the relative price of unsuitable technology may, through undesirable substitution effects, generate socially perverse effects.[7]

The vast bulk of the technology supplied to the developing countries was not designed with their particular problems in mind. Although technical progress is generally assumed to be beneficial in its economic effects, it is easy to demonstrate that technological change (for example, that which is labor saving in a labor-surplus economy) can lower the importing country's total welfare (Cohen, 1975, pp. 32-43). Thus, inappropriateness may be not merely a cause for regret as to the absence of alternatives, but the cause of absolute damage. Distortions in local factor and product prices frequently can render imported technologies privately profitable even though they are socially undesirable. Governments can also be induced by "marketing" efforts of private firms and aid donors to adopt inefficient or socially undesirable technologies. There can therefore be no presumption of benign national economic effects from technology importing.

The most frequently discussed aspect of inappropriate imported production technology (and by no means all new technologies are inappropriate) is its capital-intensity in circumstances of severe unemployment or underemployment of labor. It is by now agreed that capital-intensity is not undesirable per se in any particular activity; in many instances, it is socially efficient. But, in the developing countries' employment circumstances, there is by now virtually unanimous agreement that labor-intensive technologies should be employed in those instances where there *is* a potential choice of technique without sacrifice of efficiency.

Efficient adaptations in the direction of greater labor use are now seen as possible in virtually every productive process—even in the relatively short run. These can be achieved through alterations in the conduct of ancillary activities, physical alterations in equipment, increased work speeds, increased shifts, and so forth. Even if all activities were characterized by fixed coefficients that did not change over time, there would still, in the longer run, be an infinite number of product mixes from which a society could "select." If the use of overly capital-intensive technology persists in the developing countries, one must presume that the incentive systems there have generated it and that local decision makers prefer it that way.[8]

Similarly, the inappropriateness of consumption technology (the characteristics and degree of differentiation of products) is, in principle, controllable. Although it too can be, and often is, altered in what most would agree to be socially deleterious fashion (Helleiner, 1975), such alterations presumably reflect decision-makers' preferences.

Adaptation of imported technology is possible in dimensions other than that of factor-intensity. Indeed the economics profession has probably overdone this component of the "inappropriateness" issue. There are all manner of adaptations and innovations in products and processes that are potentially highly productive in the special circumstances of the less developed countries. These involve such matters as efficient small-scale techniques, uses for by-products, modifications associated with locally available inputs, tropical storage facilities, ultracheap mass consumer goods, and so on. The case of agricultural technology is especially instructive in this regard.

Physical conditions (soil, availability of water, temperature) and socioeconomic conditions (for instance, factor prices, tenurial arrangements, customs, tastes) are so different and so variable, and tropical crops so many, that direct transfers of agricultural technology from the primarily temperate regions of the developed world may be impossible or even harmful. The techniques developed for the growing of a particular crop are specific to a particular biological, climatological, and economic setting. Some techniques may be better than anything else available in less developed countries, and will therefore be transferred. In some instances, in agriculture as in industry, distorted local factor prices will make new techniques privately profitable to Third World farmers when their social profitability is limited; in others, their adoption may throw off undesirable social effects, notably displacement of small holders or tenant farmers. In general, however, as Evenson (1975) has argued persuasively, agricultural technology transfer makes its greatest positive impact when it is transferred *indirectly*—when, that is, there is sufficient local research capacity to permit adaptation of the imported technology so as to suit the local environment. Adaptive research capacity seems, in this sector, to be crucially important to technology transfer.

Development of Appropriate Technology

According to a much quoted estimate of a few years ago, only 2 percent of the world's research and development expenditure is devoted to the particular problems of the less developed countries.[9] This would not necessarily imply relative inattention to their needs if they could easily borrow from a shelf of universally applicable technologies. But their physical, economic, and social environments are sufficiently different from those of the developed countries that direct unadapted transfer of existing technology from the developed countries frequently may be of limited assistance or even do positive harm.

If more appropriate technologies and products are to be developed, incentives will have to be created for their production. To a substantial degree these incentives can be the automatic outgrowth of development in the poor countries. International communication will improve for the poor countries. Their demands grow. It will be increasingly profitable for someone to meet them. All in all, the opportunities in and demands emanating from the poor countries can be expected to differ from those generated in the developed countries. Some multinational firms—in electronics, agricultural machinery, automobiles—are already responding (Stewart, 1975, pp. 38-40; Helleiner, 1973). To a considerable degree, however, such incentives are the product of conscious political choice on the part of governments of the less developed countries—choice as to income distribution, public expenditures, and a variety of exchange rate, trade barrier, factor pricing policies.[10] Technology policies and the structure of local incentives for technological use and development are ultimately matters for the governments of the developing countries themselves. If incentives do not exist in the developing countries for the use of more appropriate technologies, there can be little point in developing them.

One can nevertheless ask whether there are policy instruments that might be employed by the governments of developed countries to encourage the development of more suitable technologies and products. Clearly, one option is simply to support research on technology for developing countries in the same way government supports research on space exploration, nuclear power, and defense.

If developed country governments were to finance (wholly or in part) research and development on technological problems of particular concern to the less developed countries and make the resulting knowledge freely available to them, the gains could be considerable. This is the approach adopted in the UN World Plan of Action (1971) which not only recommended such governmental support, but also identified a long list of priority areas for research, and for the application of existing knowledge.[11] Many of these priority areas are in the "social" sphere, where the structure of local incentives does not affect the likelihood of their adoption.

Some increased governmental support for such research—especially in the spheres of population and food production—is already evident. (See also Stewart, 1974, p. 41.) Such support can take the form of incentives and subsidy schemes rather than full funding.

One is entitled to question the social opportunity cost of such efforts. If the funds to be expended for such research and development efforts were to be freely available for alternative purposes, could they be put to more productive use in the interests of development or poverty alleviation? If they were made available directly to the governments of the less developed countries, would these countries spend them on research and development? Neither question can be confidently answered one way or the other, and neither is usually addressed. Recommendations in this sphere are therefore best regarded as requests for further government-supported assistance to developing countries, rather than as the product of an economic analysis of the optimal allocation of such assistance. It seems safe to say that expanded governmental expenditures of this type are more likely to be "additional" to aid budgets than those involving direct transfers to foreign governments or international institutions.

Scale economies are typical of many research and development efforts. Whether such efforts are organized and financed in developed countries or in less developed ones, there is therefore a strong case for multinational cooperation in one form or another, as opposed to each country pursuing its own independent path. Hence the various international agricultural research institutes (such as IRRI, CIAT, CIMMYT, IITA, ICRISAT) and the proposals for international industrialization or appropriate technology institutes by the United States (Kissinger, 1975) and the ILO (1976, pp. 150-154), respectively. National efforts that are not coordinated with other countries' efforts are probably best oriented to adaptive research designed to fit shelf technology to the particular local environment.

Noncommercialized Technology and the Role of Aid

Technology transfer problems differ greatly from sector to sector. Most of the international discussion under this heading relates to industrial technology, indeed to industrial technology of a sophisticated nature. One must not lose sight, however, of the issues surrounding the transfer of technology in agriculture, health sciences, services, and also in more basic industrial technology. In these sectors, knowledge is relatively free from private claims on intellectual property, and the institutions for technological development and diffusion are therefore less often commercially motivated. Further, in these sectors, the importance of the reform of the Paris Convention and of the development of a code of conduct for the transfer of technology are relatively slight. Apart from their intrinsic interest, these sectors may also offer some indication of the problems that would remain if major reforms in intellectual property systems were achieved.

Agricultural research and extension efforts have brought about dramatic changes in the technology employed in developed countries' farms. Progress in medicine and health has been no less dramatic. Much of the organization and financing of these efforts has been undertaken by the state. The knowledge developed in these efforts can, if conscious decisions are taken, be transferred to other countries in nonmarket transactions; and much of it has been transferred to less developed countries.

In these spheres, particular responsibility rests with governmental authorities and international agencies, since the crucial importing decisions are usually nonmarket determined and uninfluenced by commercial considerations. The developed countries cannot expect to have much influence over the decisions of the less developed countries' governments. But their own aid and related programs and those of the international institutions to which they belong should incorporate policies that encourage the "correct" sorts of decisions, or at least not encourage the "incorrect" ones. Not infrequently, the latter tendency can be found along with pious declarations concerning the need for more appropriate technology, more attention to poverty, and wiser decision making. In particular, procurement restrictions, which limit the use of local goods and services, and "project fixation" have tended to bias the character of technology transferred under the aegis of official development assistance toward import-using and large-scale techniques. Given the paucity of efficient labor-intensive techniques employed in the aid supplying countries, the restrictive conditions in these flows have probably also produced a bias away from labor-intensive technologies. As technological capacity increases within the Third World, it will become increasingly important to retain and expand the provisions in aid contracts that permit procurement locally and in other less developed countries. The international discussions as to the possibility of unifying and otherwise loosening the conditions surrounding official development assistance, abandoned in 1971, might now be resumed under the banner of improving the price and appropriateness of imported technology.

Technology transfers also occur under the heading of "technical assistance." Although much of this assistance has been invaluable, particularly in the least developed countries, it has often carried technological biases into local demand structures and decision making. Familiarity with developed countries' production techniques and consumption standards has, not surprisingly, influenced the technical assistants' advice, with the result that inappropriate consumption and production technologies have been brought by them to less developed countries. Technical assistance, even in the best of circumstances, may thus improperly influence the demand side of technology policy and choice as well.

Apart from these impediments to the free flow of technology under aid auspices—all of which influence what is available—aid also, of course, affects the relative price of different techniques. Those that are offered on concessional terms, other things being equal, are more likely to be purchased. Export credit and/or investment guarantee programs in the developed countries similarly distort incentives in the less developed countries in such a way as to reduce the likelihood of the adoption of more labor-intensive, small-scale, local input-intensive techniques. In some instances, the relevant laws of developed countries are explicitly protectionist in their intent and are designed to deflect activity in foreign countries away from the use of technologies that would improve their comparative advantage in appropriate sectors. For example, the U.S. Investment Insurance program (OPIC) will not ensure technology contracts or investments in the case of "runaway" industries or textile undertakings engaged in exporting to the United States.

Although there may be fewer imperfections in knowledge markets in those sectors that seem to be free from commercial secrecy, there may still be imperfections in the markets for the inputs required for a particular technology's employment. The channels through which information as to new medical or agricultural technologies flows are not totally frictionless and neutral. Producers of inputs associated with different techniques will be active in efforts to "sell" their own, by both fair means and the illegitimate purchase of influence, to potential users in the Third World and to technology transmitters in aid agencies and international bodies. Many of the resulting transactions in equipment and inputs are far from "pure" market transactions in which consumers express their preferences in textbook fashion. Rather, they are frequently the result of administrative decisions on the part of government or research institutions—agencies that do not face market tests and are therefore susceptible, especially in the weak administrative systems typical in developing countries, to "marketing" efforts of the more dubious sort. Tractors and mechanical equipment for government schemes and research stations at least must face some sort of market test when they are offered to farmers for adoption (albeit sometimes with subsidies). In the case of medical equipment and pharmaceuticals, decisions of the relevant authorities are unlikely to be influenced by efficiency criteria. In the fields in which technology is not wholly commercialized, the need for improved information services is thus every bit as great as in others.

The Development of Technological Capacity in the Third World

Even if developed country governments and private firms were to turn their activities toward the development of suitable technologies for use in the less developed countries, these countries would remain dependent on imports that might well be expensive and uncertain. Ultimately the long-run development of indigenous technological capacity is more important than the negotiation of a more suitable price for the short-run imports of technology.

Let us turn to a variety of domestic issues that regard educational and scientific policy. They are relevant to the developed countries only insofar as such countries have the capacity to advise or assist.

Most of the proposals offered at the international level concerning technological development in the less developed countries involve the expenditure of increased amounts by the governments of developed countries. Only in cases of gross ineptitude would such *increased* expenditures, ostensibly in the interests of developing countries, not actually be beneficial to them. A much more difficult question is whether, with fixed total expenditures available for use in various forms of development assistance, expenditures on the various technological development proposals now before the international community can be viewed as likely to be more productive than alternative possible expenditures. Are some efforts to build local technological capacity more productive than others? Are some imported technologies or modes of technology transfer more "nutritious," in the sense that they stimulate the development of indigenous technological capacity, than others? The answers are by no means clear.

As Nelson (1974) has emphasized, we really know very little about the relationship between science and development. We presume that science enables the production of new technologies that, as they are diffused, alter production functions. But we cannot even explain with much confidence the role of basic research, as against applied research, in this process. The uncertainties are such that economic analysis cannot always carry one far in giving advice to science policy makers as to how much to spend or on what. (Evenson, 1975a, would disagree with so bald a statement.) It does not follow, however, that the market should therefore be left to handle the problem. The role of government in the less developed countries is too great for this, in any case, to be an option.

Adaptive and *applied* research capacity would seem to be the first priority, in an economic sense, for developing countries. On the other hand, there is at least some evidence that such research may be relatively ineffective in the absence of some local buildup of basic research capacity (Evenson, 1975a and 1975b). According to Evenson, the greatest gains from the so-called Green Revolution occurred in areas where there was sufficient local research capacity to screen the available varieties, determine the optimal regions for them, and develop more suitable local varieties through further breeding efforts. The capacity for such activities appears to be correlated with the capacity for basic research. The conduct of relatively "pure" research in the developing countries, although frequently the product of self-seeking pressures from local scientific communities, may therefore be not *all* bad.

It is evident that every country would do well to have some basic minimum of technological capacity and capacity for independent decision making in the technology sphere. Without that, it is unlikely that the less developed countries will ever gain self-perception, or the possibility of independence, or, therefore, the potential for stable relations with other countries. Assistance in this realm would be welcome and wise—if only we knew more about how best to offer it!

Conclusions

The following recommendations for developed countries' policy flow from the above discussion:

1. Developed countries' governmental encouragements to the export of technology to the less developed countries should not be structured so as to favor particularly the direct investment form. Existing restrictions upon support measures should be removed, that is, those on textile exporting firms and government majority owned firms in the U.S. OPIC scheme.

2. Private multinational firms based in the developed countries are not the only potential developers of new technologies. Efforts should be made to encourage new efforts by small firms in the developed countries and by less developed countries' firms, both private and public.

3. Assistance should be offered to individual developing countries seeking to reform their industrial property laws and procedures, and the Paris Convention should be revised, so as to raise the social productivity of patents, trademarks, and other industrial property conventions.

4. The proposed code of conduct on technology transfer would particularly

serve the interest of the poorer countries, and, while probably not of crucial significance to them, should be sympathetically considered.

5. Improved information systems, shopping services, and information exchange concerning international technology markets would be very helpful to the less developed countries, and would deserve support. It may be best to begin with focused effort on a few priority sectors.

6. There are limits to what developed countries can do about choosing from existing techniques in the less developed countries, in the face of the great influence of local incentive structures. Developed countries can, however, remove obstacles that limit appropriate choices in their development assistance programs, notably restrictions in procurement.

7. Support can be offered to private firms and public institutions for the development of new technologies for use in the less developed countries through incentive schemes or direct subsidies.

8. The building of indigenous technological capacity in the less developed countries is ultimately of the greatest importance, and deserves international support.

Where these measures require increased governmental budget support, one must inquire as to the opportunity cost from the standpoint of the less developed countries' own interests. One can be categorical about the desirability of such cost only if one is confident that support for it is not obtained at the expense of other forms of development assistance. (Presumably, all the proposals for new international support measures are conditioned by the assumption that increased aggregate support will be forthcoming.)

In the multidimensional bargaining now under way between North and South, concessions on one front are bound to be related to developments on all the others. Whether the issues and proposals discussed in this paper are more "important" than others is impossible to say outside of the overall context of the bargaining. But one can confidently say that the discussion of international conventions with respect to patents, trademarks, and restrictive practices in technology trade has reached a stage of legitimacy such that reform in this sphere is now basic to progress in the resolution of North-South disagreements. One can also hazard a guess that technology issues will retain their place at the center of the stage on which international and domestic discussions of development questions take place.

Notes

I am grateful to Jagdish Bhagwati, Robert Dohner, Richard Eckaus, Surendra Patel, Carlos Rodriguez, Hans Singer, and Jan Tumlir for comments on an earlier draft. None are to be implicated in any way in the contents of the present version.

1 Consumption technology relates to the characteristics of products, as analyzed by Lancaster, 1966. For further elaboration of the need for distinguishing between

production and consumption technologies, see Helleiner, 1975.

2 Harry Johnson has recently summarized the behavior of private business in this sphere:

Its capacity to make profits derives essentially from its possession of productive knowledge, which includes management methods and marketing skills, as well as production technology. It has no commercial interest in diffusing its knowledge to potential native competitors. Nor has it any interest in investing more than it has to in acquiring knowledge of local conditions and investigating ways of adapting its own productive knowledge to local factor/price ratios and market conditions. Its purpose is not to transform the economy by exploiting its potentialities (especially its human potentialities) for development, but to exploit the existing situation to its own profit by utilization of the knowledge it already possesses, at minimum cost to itself of adaptation and adjustment . . . Hence, it will invest in technological research on the adaptation of its technology and in the development of local labour skills only to the extent that such investment holds a clear prospect of profit (1975, pp. 79-80).

3 The World Intellectual Property Organization (formerly the United International Bureau for the Protection of Intellectual Property) is a nongovernmental body based in Geneva that concerns itself with laws on patents, trademarks, and the trade in proprietary technology.

4 To the extent that avoidance of enforcement involves real costs that can be passed on to the developing countries, these premises may not be wholly inconsistent.

5 There is already some evidence of substantial gains to technology importing countries following the introduction of technology vetting procedures. It has been estimated that Mexico saved $80 million in payments for foreign technology for the duration of contracts that were revised in direct consequence of the application of its new technology law in 1973 (Wionczek, 1976, pp. 152-153). The Japanese experience is, of course, a better known historical example of success with such policies.

6 Jagdish Bhagwati has commented that there is no reason to assume that those in the forefront in this sphere are doing sensible things. (No doubt views on this differ.) If they are not, however, their experience should be as instructive to late-comers as if they were.

7 It is possible, of course, for the positive income effects of price reductions to offset the effects of undesirable substitution effects.

8 Much of the policy that would encourage the use of more appropriate technology "is in many ways in direct conflict with the interests of the political and economic elites" (Cooper, 1973, pp. 300-301). See also Helleiner (1975), pp. 181-182.

9 Even some of this 2 percent is probably misdirected in consequence of the influence of inappropriate developed country research models.

10 At a microlevel, there may also be intense political opposition to the introduction of new technologies that threaten the interests of entrenched suppliers of inputs to the old techniques.

11 Priority research areas included high-yielding varieties of staple foods, edible protein, fishing, pest and vector control, tropical hardwoods and fibers, groundwater, desalination, arid land, natural disaster warning systems, indigenous building materials, industrial research and design, schistosomiasis, and human fertility. Priority areas for the application of existing knowledge included storage and preservation of agricultural products, control of livestock diseases, human disease control, housing construction methods, and secondary school teaching of science.

References

Behrman, Jack N., and Harvey Wallender 1976, "Technology Transfers to Wholly-Owned Affiliates: An Illustration of the Obstacles to Controls." Paper presented to International Studies Association, Toronto (mimeo.).

Cohen, Benjamin, I., 1975. *Multinational Firms and Asian Exports* (Yale University Press, New Haven and London).

Cooper, Charles, 1973. "Choice of Techniques and Technological Change as Problems in Political Economy," *International Social Science Journal*, Vol. 25, 3.

Council of the Americas and Fund for Multinational Management Education, no date, *Codes of Conduct for the Transfer of Technology: A Critique*, New York (mimeo.).

de Cubas, Jose, 1974, *Technology Transfer and the Developing Nations* (Council of the Americas and Fund for Multinational Management Education, New York).

Evenson, Robert, 1975a, "Technology Generation in Agriculture" in Lloyd Reynolds (ed.), *Agriculture in Development Theory* (Yale University Press, New Haven and London), 192-223.

_____ , 1975b, "Agricultural Trade and Shifting Comparative Advantage" in George S. Tolley and Peter A. Zadrozny (eds.), *Trade, Agriculture and Development* (Ballinger Publishing Co., Cambridge, Mass.), 181-200.

Helleiner, G. K., 1973, "Manufactured Exports from Less Developed Countries and Multinational Firms." *Economic Journal*, Vol. 83, 329, March, 21-47.

_____ , 1975, "The Role of Multinational Corporations in the Less Developed Countries' Trade in Technology," *World Development*, Vol. 3, 4, April, 161-189.

ILO, 1976, *Employment, Growth and Basic Needs: A One-World Problem* (Geneva).

Johnson, Harry, 1975, *Technology and Economic Independence* (Trade Policy Research Center, MacMillan, London).

Kissinger, Henry, 1975, Address before the Seventh Special Session of the United Nations General Assembly, September 1.

Lancaster, Kelvin J., 1966, "Change and Innovation in the Technology of Consumption," *American Economic Review*, Vol. 56, 2, May, 14-23.

Nelson, Richard R., 1974, "Less Developed Countries–Technology Transfer and Adaptation: The Role of the Indigenous Science Community," *Economic Development and Cultural Change*, Vol. 23, 1, October, 61-78.

Penrose, Edith, 1973, "International Patenting and the Less Developed Countries," *Economic Journal*, 83, 331, 768-786.

Perlmutter, Howard V., and Taghi Saghafi-nejad, 1976, "Process or Product?: A Social Architectural Perspective of Codes of Conduct for Technology Transfer and Development." Paper presented to International Studies Association, Toronto.

Rodriques, Carlos Alfredo, 1975, "Trade in Technological Knowledge and the National Advantage," *Journal of Political Economy*, 83, 1, 121-135.

Stewart, Frances, 1974, "Technology and Employment in LDCs," *World Development*, Vol. 2, 3, March, 17-46.

Stopford, John M., and Louis T. Wells, Jr., 1972, *Managing the Multinational Enterprise* (Basic Books, New York).

United Nations, 1971, *World Plan of Action for the Application of Science and Technology to Development* (New York).

UNCTAD, 1976, "Technological Dependence: Its Nature, Consequences and Policy Implications," TD/190, prepared for Fourth Session, Nairobi, May 3.

United States, 1971, "Nationalization, Expropriation, and Other Takings of United States and Certain Foreign Property since 1960," Department of State, Bureau of Intelligence and Research, November 30.

_____, 1974, "Disputes Involving US Foreign Direct Investment, 1st July, 1971 through 31st July, 1975," Department of State, Bureau of Intelligence and Research, February 28.

Vaitsos, Constantine V., 1975, "Foreign Investment and Productive Knowledge" in Guy F. Erb and Valeriana Kallab (eds.), *Beyond Dependency: The Developing World Speaks Out* (Overseas Development Council, Washington, D.C.), 75-94.

_____, 1976, "The Revision of the International Patent System: Legal Considerations for a Third World Position," *World Development*, 4, 2, 85-102.

_____, 1970, "Bargaining and the Distribution of Returns in the Purchase of Technology by Developing Countries," *Bulletin of the Institute of Development Studies, Sussex*, October.

Wionczek, Miguel, 1976, "Notes on Technology Transfer through Multinational Enterprises in Latin America," *Development and Change*, Vol. 7, 135-155.

13

Information and the Multinational Corporation: An Appropriability Theory of Direct Foreign Investment

Stephen P. Magee

Here, we analyze private market creation of "information" (technology), relate it to the observed behavior of multinational corporations, and draw policy implications for the purchase of information by the less developed countries (LDCs). The theory proposed is a natural evolution of the views of Hymer (1960), Vernon (1966), and Caves (1971) on foreign direct investment and of Arrow (1962), Demsetz (1969), and Johnson (1970) on the creation and appropriability[1] of the private returns from investments in information. Such a consolidation of views is necessary for systematic consideration of policy proposals aimed at inducing greater "transfers of technology" through multinational corporations. The formulation adopted is based on six ideas.

1. Industries in which the demand for new products is high have a high derived demand for new information.

2. For these industries, investments must be made to create five distinct types of information; specifically, information is required for product

   a. creation;

   b. development;

   c. production functions;

   d. markets; and

   e. appropriability.

Thus, the term "technology transfer" by private firms is ambiguous until the type of information being transferred is specified.

3. There are decreasing marginal returns on the stock of information applied to a given product and information-saving growth in production in the long run (that is, information flows as a factor of production become relatively less important after some point). Thus, investments in new information will be high early in a product's life and will decrease as it ages. Vernon (1966) developed a technology cycle for individual *products* that is consistent with these statements; we shall build here upon a technology cycle developed elsewhere for entire *industries*.[2]

4. The public-goods aspect of information and the attendant calculations by firms of the appropriability of the private returns from creation of information is one of the most important considerations determining both the type of technology created and the sectoral allocation of private research effort. Private markets bias their information investments toward sophisticated infor-

mation because appropriability is higher for complicated ideas than for simple ideas.

5. The cost of trading each type of information dictates whether it is transmitted most efficiently intrafirm or extrafirm. Optimum firm size for 2a is small (many products are discovered by lone inventors). Optimum firm size is increased by 2b through 2e because of lower costs of intrafirm movements of new information, economies of scale in the use of new information across many products, greater intrafirm appropriability of the private returns to investments in new information, and greater managerial skill in industries creating new information (the sophistication required to successfully coordinate 2b, 2c, 2d, and 2e dictates that managers in "new product industries" be more highly skilled than the norm; hence, the managerial constraint on firm size will be less in these industries). These considerations explain the correlation (though not necessarily the causation) between the tendency of multinational corporations to be large and their tendency to produce sophisticated, information-intensive products.

6. The legal, political, and economic systems of the LDCs differ significantly from those in the DCs. These and other considerations indicate that their welfare would be increased by modifying their adherence to the Paris Convention (the code of international patent behavior).

We consider only finished manufactured products, as examined in Vernon's (1966) product cycle and in Caves' (1971) "horizontal" type of direct investment; raw materials are excluded in this analysis. There is a long and rich literature on the multinational corporations as conveyors of new products and technologies to the world. The pioneering study by Hymer (1960) on the monopoly advantage held by multinationals in technology and Vernon's (1966) product cycle developed this theme. However, no paper to date has dealt simultaneously with the five different types of information created by firms and their "transfer" to developing countries, with the appropriability question, with optimum firm size, and with the international policy issues that these points raise vis-à-vis the LDCs for information created by multinational corporations.

We apply these six ideas to the multinational corporations and generate the following hypotheses. Multinational corporations are specialists in the production of information that is less efficient to transmit through markets than within firms. Multinational corporations produce sophisticated technologies because appropriability is higher for these than for simple technologies. The appropriability of the returns from these public goods (information) and complementarities among the five types of information dictate large optimum firm size. The large proportion of skilled labor employed by multinationals is an outgrowth of the skilled-labor intensity of the production process for both the *creation* of information and *appropriability* of the returns from information. The relative abundance of skilled labor in the developed countries dictates that they have a comparative advantage in creating and exporting new information. There are diminishing returns to information in the short run. Output growth of new products ultimately has an information-saving bias in production. And all of these considerations generate a technology cycle at the *industry* level.

In Section 1 we develop the hypothesis and discuss the effects of the different types of information on the firm. In Section 2, we discuss some of the conventional wisdoms with respect to the behavior of the multinational corporation and how the theory proposed here provides a convenient framework for organizing and explaining some of the stylized facts of foreign direct investment. In Section 3, we evaluate policy proposals for the transfer of information between developed countries and developing countries and suggest a modified adherence by the LDCs to the Paris Convention.

The Hypothesis

Let us consider the generation of economically useful information. Information is a durable good, in that present resources must be devoted to its creation and its existence results in a stream of future benefits. Information is also a public good, in that once it is created, its use by second parties does not preclude its continued use by the party who discovers it. However, use by second parties does reduce the private return on information created by the first party. This is the "appropriability problem" (see Arrow, 1962).

We should expect that for information of all types, economic actors will invest resources in the generation of information until the expected private returns will be equated to the returns on other investments of equal risk. Four traditional types of information are created by private markets in the generation of new products: information required for (1) discovery of new products, (2) development of the products, (3) development of their production functions, and (4) creation of their markets.

An important fifth type of information affects each of the previous four, namely, (5) knowledge of the degree to which creators of information can appropriate to themselves the returns on the new information. It is a near tautology that the greater the public-goods aspect of new information, the lower its private market appropriability and the more reason for private markets to underinvest in it. Johnson (1970) noted the two ways historically in which society has dealt with this problem of the public-goods nature of information: either the *government* creates the information and provides it freely to private markets or the legal system permits *private* firms to internalize the returns by either creating temporary monopolies through the patent system or allowing restrictions on free trade in information through trade secrets.[3] Is welfare higher with government or private market creation of information?

1.1 Government versus Private Market Creation of Information

Consider a technological breakthrough resulting in the creation of a new product or service whose demand, marginal revenue, and marginal cost curves are represented by D, MR and MC in Figure 13.1 If private markets develop the ideas and if the rights to the breakthrough are fully protected legally by patents or trade secrets, output of the product will be Q_m, the price will be P_m, monopoly profits will be B, and the gain to society will equal the sum of B and the consumer's surplus triangle A. If the government develops the same product and distributes the information freely, absence of the legally sanctioned monopoly and the presence of many competitive firms will drive market output to the competitive level Q_c, the price to P_c, and the gain to society will equal the consumer's surplus areas, $A + B + C$. With a government's free dissemination of the information, welfare is higher than under patent protected creation of the information by area C. These points are developed in some detail in Johnson (1970).

However, the issue of public versus private creation of information is more complicated than this. If welfare is always higher with government distribution of information, why are patents and trade secrets permitted as incentives for creative activity? The previous analysis indicates that there are two

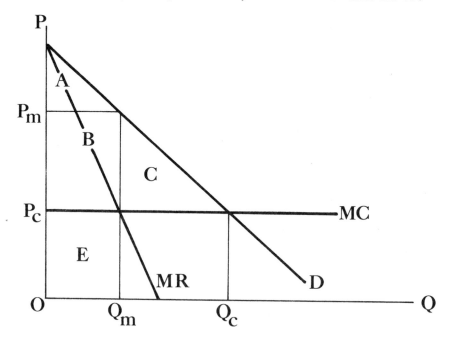

Fig. 1

Figure 13.1

alternative ways in which society could be made better off by government intervention. The first would be for the government to let private firms create information through the patent system. Once an important discovery had been made, the government could purchase the discovery from the inventor, pay him the present value of the monopoly profit stream (the current flow equals area B in Figure 13.1), and provide the information freely to private producers. In this way, welfare would increase by area C. Three difficulties with this solution are that markets in information are not "efficient" (in the way in which some securities are "efficient") so that establishing the present value of new information might be more costly than the social gains from its free provision; sellers of information would attempt to extract the entire social value of the patent, equal to the monopoly profits plus $A + C$, and this would create redistribution problems that would be costly politically; and sellers of patents would waste real resources attempting to influence politicians and bureaucrats equal to, at most, $A + B + C$. Sales of new military technologies to the U.S. Department of Defense are good examples of these problems.

The second solution is for the government to do the research and development itself and make the results freely available. The problem with this solution is that the selection of the research and development projects would be determined as much by political investments and bureaucratic idiosyncracies as by social rates of return. Since organizational costs for political groups in society are far from identical, there is no reason to believe that political investments in pork-barrel lobbying would be proportional to expected social returns on new information. (See Brock and Magee, 1975, for an analysis of investments in politicians.) Thus, the *allocation* of government research and development may be less correlated with social returns in many product areas than the monopoly profits conferred by the patent system. In cases in which the welfare losses from *underprovision* of new products by patent holders is more than offset by the superior private *allocation* of research and development, then private rather than public creation of knowledge is justified. Casual empiricism suggests that private research and development is probably superior for toasters, hand-held hair driers, and radial ply tires, while government research and development is better for some types of agricultural research. An important argument against privately patentable research hinges on varying private appropriability of the returns from such research, given even the protection of the law. The more uncorrelated are private appropriabilities of new information and their social returns, the less efficient is private market allocation of research and development. We examine next the types of information required during the product and industry technology cycle.

1.2 Five Types of Information

New Product Discovery The technology cycle developed here differs from

Vernon's (1966) product cycle in that we deal here with a cycle for both the product and the entire industry.[4] In spite of some notable exceptions, five papers in the NBER Study (1962) of inventions indicated that a simple maximization model is a good first approximation in explaining inventive effort (see Nelson, 1962, p. 11). Nevertheless, the discovery of major new products (locomotives, autos, aircraft) is difficult to explain if it is not random. The same is true in explaining why some industries have a high demand for new products. We shall sidestep these problems by assuming that inventions of major new products occur randomly.

The investments in innovation can be described more systematically. This approach is taken because *innovation* rather than *invention* is the focus of multinational corporation activity. Once a major invention has occurred, the expected return on new technology for the components of the new product is high. The development of the automobile increased the returns on improved technologies for carburetors, electrical assemblies, clutches, gears, and even tires (the demand for rubber and rubber substitutes was greatly increased, although synthetic rubber was not commercially successful until the 1940s). Thus many minor inventions follow a major discovery rapidly, until the returns on new information start to decline.

Nelson (1962) has observed that patents for a given *industry* follow an S-curve over a long period of time, reflecting an eventual retardation in new investments in information for creation, development, production, and appropriation of the industry's products (see Figure 13.2). The steeply rising part of the curve reflects the derived demand for components, economies of scale inherent in the production of information, and the complementary applicability of new information to other products in the same industry. At some point in time, the marginal returns decline on the flow of additional information, as the transferability to other products declines and as the market demand for standardization is reached. As industries mature, all of these considerations lead to decreases in the share of industry value added going to investments in information. In effect, growth becomes "information saving in production." Throughout the industry technology cycle, "technological change," "factor productivity," and the effects of "learning by doing" are all endogenous and determined by the existing stock of information and rational investments in new information. As a result, research and development investments and changes in factor productivity should be high early in an industry's life cycle and low late in the cycle. This prediction is supported by the data: the simple correlation between research and development investments as a percent of sales and the average industry age for twenty-nine U.S. three-digit SIC industries in 1967 is $-.34$.[5] Vernon's cycle dealt only with individual products so that he had no theory of the eventual decline in research and development by entire industries. Here, we have provided a rationale and evidence for industry-wide declines in research and development with maturity of the industry.

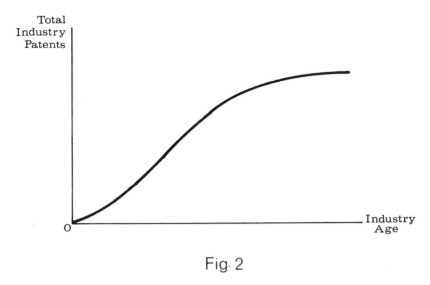

Fig. 2

Figure 13.2

Another important empirical regularity is that investments by each industry in the *creation* of new products is not necessarily done by the firm that develops the products commercially. For example, Mansfield (1974, p. 151) points out that many industrial innovations are based on relatively "old science." Many inventors and small firms make breakthroughs that result in the creation of new products. Although an increasing proportion of patents has been granted to corporations, private inventors still play an important role (Nelson, 1962, p. 5). Thus, we expect that optimum firm size may be smaller in young industries than in older industries.[6] One reason is that the low appropriability of the private returns on information generated in industries with small optimum firm size is well protected in this stage by the patent system. The patent system is more effective in protecting new products than in protecting the next three types of information.

Product Development Research and development expenditures by large firms are primarily for the development rather than the creation of new products. Mansfield (1974, p. 150) has outlined the stages for which information is important in the development process: "applied research, preparation of product specification, prototype or pilot plant construction, tooling and construction of manufacturing facilities, and manufacturing and marketing start up," with the entire process frequently taking five to ten years. Large amounts of information are required to estimate the costs of each step and high managerial capabilities are needed to coordinate their undertaking.

Certain firms, such as multinational corporations, develop comparative advantages in creating information for controlling product development. The information generated by creating one product becomes applicable, through learning by doing, to other new products. Since this information is usually transmitted more efficiently intrafirm than through the market, optimum firm sizes increase in the development stage. Another characteristic of the industry cycle, which parallels Vernon's product cycle, is that product differentiation is high for new industries and low for older industries. The correlation in 1967 between product differentiation and the average industry age for 101 U.S. three-digit SIC industries is −.29, indicating that older industries have less product differentiation and more standardized products. Finally, the appropriability problem for this type of information is particularly serious.[7] The patent system does not provide full protection for the early prototypes of many new products. Rivals can free ride on the development process of innovating firms if they can make apparently major though inexpensive changes in the characteristics of the product.

Three important steps remain that are information-intensive: the firm must develop the production function, generate market demand, and appropriate the returns.

Creation of the Production Function The most important source of derived demand for information on the supply side is for the development of the production function for the new product. Although economists frequently assume that engineers or technicians provide such functions, actually large and costly investments in information must be made to create the most efficient methods of production. Vernon stresses how the production function shifts from being skilled-labor-intensive early in a *product's* life cycle to unskilled-labor-intensive and capital-intensive late in the cycle. This is consistent with a framework that includes the stock of information along with the other physical inputs in the production function. As that stock increases, diminishing returns and "information saving" growth help explain what Vernon calls "standardized production" processes in stage 3 of his product cycle. With standardized production processes, new investments in information are low, including in information implicit in the human capital employed by the industry (in both production and nonproduction labor). This implies that production wages will be lower for old industries than for new ones. The data are ambiguous on this point: for ninety-three U.S. three-digit SIC industries in 1967 there was no relationship between production wages and the average age of the industry. However, when the same data are aggregated to seventeen two-digit SIC categories, the correlation between the two variables equals −.30, as expected.

An important structural factor also explains the eventual standardization of the production process for an entire industry. As patents begin to lapse, monopoly and oligopoly structures characteristic of the early life of some new industries begin to crumble. Increased competition erodes the private market appropriability of the returns from new production technologies so that the production function is "frozen" or becomes standardized at the most efficient process extant. Although processes are protected by patents, patents provide less appropriability to processes (especially simple ones) than to products. As a result, industry structure is relatively more important in protecting production technologies. If industry structure does not change, then the existing structure plus the normal economic process already discussed (diminishing returns on information and so forth) will eventually standardize the production process.

Market Creation The firm introducing new products must invest in information to discover the market *and* to determine the most efficient method of communicating information to consumers on the existence of a new product or technique. In this section, we discuss only the second type: communication investments or advertising. Since the amount of information conveyed must be higher for new industries, we expect a negative correlation between the age of the industry and the amount of advertising done. At the three-digit SIC level in the United States for 1967, we had only thirteen observations on these two variables and they were uncorrelated. The only supporting empirical evidence is indirect: the correlation between advertising as a percent of sales and research and development as a percentage of sales for sixteen four-digit SIC industries in the United States in 1967 is .37. Of course, the causation in this relationship may be determined by the joint dependence of both variables on another variable, such as market structure.

Nelson (1970) has drawn a distinction in the advertising literature between "search" goods and "experience" goods. With experience goods, it is impossible to determine from physical examination whether the goods actually live up to the advertisements for them. With a search good, on the other hand, the qualities advertised can be tested by visual inspection before purchase. Advertising by search-good firms must communicate information (because it can be easily disproved) while that conveyed by experience-good firms creates only brand loyalty. But there is an economic logic to firms specializing in the marketing of many experience goods (see Telser, 1976), establishing brand recognition, and becoming large in the process. The reputations of these firms convey market information and are established by firms' consistency in selling goods of a predictable quality. This reduces the costs of search and uncertainty about product quality for purchasers. For example, in retailing, consumers frequently use firm names rather than product names in selecting the quality and prices of products that they are going to sample before purchase. There is a natural hierarchy of retail stores whose ranking from low to high quality products goes from a discount store to a Zayre to a J. C. Penney to a Sears and finally to a Saks Fifth Avenue.

A similar process is at work with the multinational corporations. They specialize in the development, production, marketing, and appropriation of an experience good, new information. The quality of the technology they produce and the price at which it is sold is determined partly by the accumulated experience of the market as to the reliability of past information sold by each firm. Multinational corporations provide an important screening device for the retailing of new information. However, in the development of markets, they differ somewhat from the Nelson (1970) dichotomy since they are selling experience goods and yet their advertising must convey verifiable search information, namely, on *existence* of a new product.

The appropriability problem for returns to advertising will be more severe for search goods and homogeneous goods than for experience goods and differentiated products since returns on advertising for the latter are more firm specific. The positive correlation noted earlier between industry research and development and advertising is consistent with this observation. For all industries, including older search-goods type industries whose products contain little new technology, appropriability of the returns on firm advertising should increase with industry concentration.

Appropriability We have discussed the appropriability problem for each of four types of information created by multinationals. We consider here a final investment in information, namely, the determination of how much must be invested to stop interlopers from copying these types of information. As noted earlier, society attempts to remedy free riding caused by the public-goods nature of information—through patents, trade secrets, and legal means—but the protection is never complete. If a firm develops a new product with a one-shot next period stream of $1 million in monopoly profits, then an interloper wishing to copy the idea (who feels that the probability equals p that he could win an infringement suit brought by the innovating firm) would be willing to invest up to $p/(1 + r)$ times $1 million in legal fees in this period to protect his infringement (r is the return on a risk-equivalent investment). The knowledge of this possibility will certainly affect the amounts invested in information by the innovating firm.

Lack of appropriability is analogous to depreciation of the information investments. In the development stage, the multinational corporation must estimate the anticipated depreciation rates on each of the expected information investments in product creation, product development, production function development, and market development. Higher expected depreciation rates result in smaller investments in information. Thus, the firm must invest in information to determine the probability of leakage of new ideas, the reduction in revenues if information is lost, the cost of legal and extralegal remedies to prevent leakage, and the cost of punishing interlopers. The firm will invest in private appropriation schemes until the marginal dollar spent equals the marginal dollar of the expected present value of revenue saved.

It should be pointed out that generation and implementation of this information, as well as of the previous four types, is skilled-labor-intensive. For example, computer firms invest to camouflage the technology in new models of their computers to prevent copying by rival firms. The rational firm will create artificial and sophisticated masking devices, artificial product differentiation, and expend resources to appropriate the returns on earlier investments. These are more efficiently done intrafirm than through the market. Although these appear to be wasteful from a social point of view, they are an inherent by-product, and in some cases a sine qua non for the creation of information by private markets. The current success of a firm in its appropriability investments affects its expectations about the future appropriability of returns on present investments and, hence, the supply of future information.

The two most important variables affecting appropriability are the efficiency of the legal system in preserving appropriability and the industry structure. For a given legal system, the more "potentially" competitive the industry, the more likely that investments by one firm in information will be copied by rival firms. A monopolist has no appropriability problem unless there are "potential" entrants who can enter to emulate innovations made by the monopolist (for expositional ease, the term "potential entrant" is ignored in succeeding discussions of market structure).

One irony is that private expenditures by individuals and firms to prevent loss of appropriability are also public goods. The first firm in an industry may expend large sums to establish proprietary rights and precedents for technologies appropriate to the industry. Since subsequent innovators do not share in these investments, but benefit from the appropriability protection they provide, such innovators take a free ride and private investments in appropriability will be too low. Monopolistic or cartelized industries are less plagued by this problem than competitive industries since their collusion on other matters provides a useful framework in which to share the costs of private enforcement of appropriability. The less developed countries are at a disadvantage on this score since they specialize in products with competitive market structures. This is *one* explanation of the low level of research and development by the LDCs.

A more important question is why so little research and development is devoted to the creation of simple, unskilled-labor technologies, which are in high demand in LDCs. There are good economic reasons why production technologies developed by the multinationals are "inappropriate" for developing countries. One reason multinationals do not develop simple technologies is that their appropriability is so low that they are not profitable. It is impossible, even with patents, to prevent the rapid depreciation of returns on ideas that have high social returns but low private returns. Multinationals, for example, generally cannot capture the return on discovery of a superior rearrangement of unskilled laborers. As a result, they cannot be expected to create unskilled-labor technologies. The gap between the private and social rate of return on this information for LDC firms is also high. Developing countries do not possess skilled labor forces, they specialize in industries that are highly competitive and they produce old and standardized products with no experience-goods characteristics. On the other hand, it is possible that for some industries, the social return is also low so that the existing technology is the optimum.

Vernon (1966) gave some convincing reasons why production will occur early in the product cycle in developed countries and late in the cycle in developing countries. These arguments carry over to the industry technology cycle. In order for the production functions to match different factor markets, production functions should be skilled-labor-intensive early in the cycle and unskilled-labor-intensive late in the cycle. But variation in technology is costly so that the firm creates initially a technology that lies between the two extremes. During the cycle, modification costs prohibit the technology from having as much variance as factor markets. The average factor-intensity of the production function created early in the cycle is thus biased away from techniques using unskilled labor for two reasons: unskilled-labor-intensive production occurs much later in the technology cycle so that it gets a lower weight because of *discounting* and returns on the development of unskilled-labor-intensive and simple technologies are *less appropriable.*

Finally, the appropriability theory provides a compelling argument for the fact that multinational corporations have biased their research away from simple, unskilled-labor-intensive technologies. The appropriability of these types of information is lower than for sophisticated technologies. We have already established that concentrated industry structures are more favorable than competitive ones to the private creation of information. A rational monopolist or collusive oligopoly will prevent or delay the introduction of a randomly discovered new unskilled-labor-intensive technology with *low* appropriability if it is highly substitutable for an existing technology that has a higher *private* present value because of its *higher* appropriability.

1.3 Optimum Firm Size

There is a problem of determining the direction of causation in relating the creation of information to the structure of industry. We know one reason why monopolists will be more likely than perfect competitors to invest in information: they will be more successful in appropriating the returns (the naive counterargument is that because of sloth, they will underinvest in information). But causation can run the other way. Firms creating information may expand to internalize the externality that new information creates. Let us summarize the arguments as to why firms that create information will be larger.

First, though the relationship is far from perfect, there is a tendency for new products to be "experience" goods and for standardized products to be "search" goods. Optimum firm size will be larger, ceteris paribus, for retailers of experience goods. For multinationals, subsidiaries are more likely than licensing for experience goods.

A second point is that sales of many high technology products must be accompanied by sales of service information. The firm's optimum size is expanded because of service subsidiaries in the information creating industry. IBM's servicing is a case in point.

Third, the average number of products produced by information creating firms should be greater than the number produced by other firms because of complementarities in the use of new information across products. Fourth, complementarities among the last four types of information (development, production, marketing, and appropriability) and their more effective intra-firm rather than extrafirm transmission increase firm size.

Fifth, there is risk associated with the creation of new products. Negative covariation in the returns to creating different products suggests that multiproduct developments will reduce both risk and costs to the firm. For example, mistakes made in developing one product can be avoided in subsequent ones. In many cases, this information (regarding minor failures) cannot be transmitted through markets as efficiently as intrafirm. For this reason larger firms will be more efficient in minimizing the costs of duplication of errors.

Sixth, as products become older and the technology diffuses, the spread narrows between the buyer's and the seller's evaluations of the information created by the firm. This reduces the cost of market transactions, since less search is required, so that licensing is likely late in the cycle and subsidiaries are important early in the cycle.

In summary, what do we expect to happen to optimum firm and plant size through the technology cycle? We know that small firms and inventors create many new products. Optimum firm size should then be smaller for new product industries. However, optimum firm size grows rapidly as the product ages, that is, as the firm exploits the patent in the information-intensive stage of development, production, marketing, and appropriation. The market shares of the largest firms will then decline slowly as the appropriability of the returns on information falls because of entry and increased competition from other firms. Vernon's (1966) product cycle did not deal with this question of optimum *firm* size. He did suggest that optimum *plant* size might rise through his cycle as mechanization and assembly-line production accompanied the standardization of production. All of these considerations suggest the relationship between optimum firm size and optimum plant size through the technology cycle shown in Figure 13.3.

The evidence on the hypothesized relationship between optimum firm size (or industry structure) and industry age is mixed. Figure 13.4 shows a scatter diagram of the four-firm concentration ratio and the average product age for 137 four-digit SIC industries in the United States in 1967. The

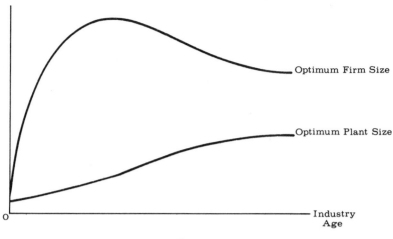

Fig. 3

Figure 13.3

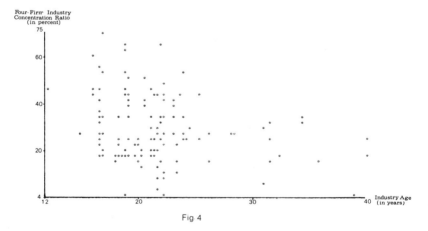

Fig 4

Figure 13.4

correlation between the two variables is low. However, it is clear that the older industries are less concentrated than the rest. The youngest industry was 11.7 years old and the oldest was 39.3 years old: 25.5 years is the midpoint of this range.

We divide the industries into two groups: there are 119 industries with ages below, and eighteen with ages above, 25.5 years. The average four-firm concentration ratio was 34 percent for the younger group (with a standard deviation of 15 percent), and 26 percent for the older group (with a standard deviation of 9 percent). A Behrens-Fisher t-test of the difference in the means indicates that they are significantly different at the .01 level. An F-test of the difference in the variances shows them to be significantly different at the .025 level. Although we find no evidence for increasing concentration with age for the very youngest industries, the very oldest industries are less concentrated than the rest, as hypothesized.

One variable we have not discussed is industry size. If it increases sufficiently with age, then firm size might be unrelated to age. However, a plot of average sales for the largest four firms in each industry looks quite similar to Figure 13.4. The use of the four-firm concentration ratio as a proxy for optimum firm size should also be defended. Since multinational corporations are, almost by definition, statistical outliers in terms of size, we should be concerned most with explaining the largest firms in each industry. On the other hand, most of the other empirical results reported in Section 1 are based on domestic U.S. data. Thus the hypotheses developed here are general and not exclusively international.

2. Appropriability, the Technology Cycle, and the Stylized Facts

The previous discussion provides a framework within which to interpret recent discussions of the multinational corporation, direct investment, and technology transfers. The framework here emphasizes that multinational corporations generate new products requiring large investments in five complementary types of information. It is fruitful to treat information like any other tangible good and to think of the international operations of the multinational corporations as international trade in this commodity (see Helleiner, 1975). The revenue from trade in information is the present value of the monopoly profit streams permitted by international patent agreements and trade secrets. The price of the information is the present value of the monopoly profit streams permitted by international patent agreements and trade secrets. The price of the information is the monopoly element in the price of the new product. What implications follow from this approach?

Since *international trade* in information is analogous to international trade generally, both exporters and importers will play optimum tariff games (see Rodriguez, 1975). Importers will tax it and exporters will restrict its flow (for example the opposition of the U.S. government to General Electric's sale of jet engines to France in 1972). Importing regions mistakenly equate the monopoly profits on new products with export taxes by exporting countries. Monopoly profits are consistent with competitive rates of return on investments in information ex ante.

Information importers should realize that levying optimum tariffs on information can increase their welfare but will *reduce* the quantity of information imported below free trade levels and hence reduce the "transfer of technology." In the same context, some discussions of "technology gaps" get very sloppy. If we think of technology transfer as international trade in information, then the phrase "technology gap" is a misunderstood catchword equivalent to other equally misdirected phrases such as "fuel gaps," "wine gaps," and "cloth gaps"—any situation in which a country is a net importer of a product. Some regions have comparative advantages in creating information and others comparative disadvantages. The theory of comparative advantages applies to trade in information just as it applies to steel, autos, and textiles: countries that do not have a comparative advantage in creating it should import it.[8]

It is clear why horizontal direct investment and product *differentiation* are correlated. Caves (1974, p. 136) has said: "... the multinational making horizontal investments tends to flourish in just those industries afflicted with strong product differentiation, and perhaps other sources of high entry barriers as well." This association is more than affliction: in fact, a cornerstone of the appropriability theory is the important behavioral link between the creation of information and concentrated market structures. Brand loyalty in the marketing of experience goods, information, and product differentiation are important instruments used by private firms in appropriating the returns on new information. If product differentiation and barriers to entry were eliminated, investments in privately created information would fall, and Caves' own industrial organization theory of direct investment would be weakened.

New products are exported to *foreign markets* long before the originating firm sets up production facilities abroad. Vernon (1966) cited several important reasons for this; however, another is suggested by appropriability. Appropriability suggests that depreciation of new information increases with the number and the geographical dispersion of plants, since both the probability of leakage and the costs of preventing leakage increase.

The U.S. data are consistent with this hypothesis. The correlation in 1967 between industry age and the U.S. geographical concentration of industry employment for thirty-two three-digit SIC industries is $-.35$, indicating that production for young industries is concentrated in a few locations while production for older industries is widely dispersed. If developing countries wished to speed up production relocation for new products within their national borders, guarantees of greater appropriability of returns would increase transfers of technology by private firms.

The term *defensive investment* may be a misnomer for the normal process of increased competition as entrants erode the rents to innovating firms (as appropriability is being lost). Rather than "following each other around," multinationals may be simply increasing industry competition (for industries well into the cycle). Another explanation is that multinationals are free riding on the information investments of their rivals. If one firm succeeds in marketing a new product in a given country, its multinational competitors will follow.

Take-overs of host country production facilities and *mergers* of multinationals with host country firms are normal consequences of the expansion in optimum firm size early in an industry's technology cycle. They may be aimed at slowing the depreciation of the stock of information by absorbing the most likely interlopers. This is another example of expansion to internalize an externality. Limits to take-overs by host country governments, through forced joint ventures or forced licensing, redistribute current income to the host country but reduce optimum firm size, appropriability, and future information flows. Since these policies are equivalent to taxation, they should be evaluated by host governments in an optimum tariff framework.

The phrase *transfer of technology* must be refined. First, the connotation of a costless gift should be discarded: all information transfers entail some cost. There are many ways in which information is transmitted: intrafirm transmission through the multinational corporations, market transfer through licensing, and government transfer through aid. Second, for the multinationals, we have already emphasized that several types of information are created and transferable, and the type of information transferred should be specified. Third, the fact that existing information is a public good does not mean that speeding up its transmission is a welfare improvement. For example, a policy imposed speedup in the transfer of sophisticated production technology may cause its premature introduction into unskilled-labor-abundant countries.

As indicated in Figure 13.3, optimum firm size should fall after the innovation stage in the technology cycle. This suggests that *licensing* should increase relative to direct investment after some point. These market, rather than intrafirm, transactions will increase since increased market information about the technology possessed by the multinational corporation reduces the variance in the valuation of the technology and thereby reduces market search costs.

Finally, since multinationals can practice price discrimination across markets, there is the question of whether LDCs pay more or less than DCs for identical technology imports. Johnson (1970, p. 41) speculates that the price elasticities of import demand for high-technology goods are higher in LDCs than DCs. If the marginal delivered costs of the products are similar worldwide, then the elasticities indicate that discriminating monopolists would charge the LDCs less than the DCs for new technology. However, the Vaitsos (1974) study shows that Johnson's (1970) speculation does not apply to Colombia: prices paid by Colombia for its imports are much higher than the world average. If this is true generally, then the view that international *price discrimination* permits LDCs to pay less than their pro rata share of the worldwide costs of generating new information may be false.[9] (Such assertions must be tempered by the realization that the LDCs will not import the new technology until later in the technology cycle. This consideration will lower their pro rata share.)

How much more than the world price do the LDCs pay for their information-intensive goods? The only evidence presented here comes from the Vaitsos (1974) study. Matching a sample of $5 million in pharmaceutical imports into Colombia with Vaitsos' price estimates indicates that $3 million of the $5 million in imports (60 percent) are payments in excess of the world price.

If international price discrimination in these high technology products could be costlessly eliminated, Colombia's welfare would increase by $4.5 million at current world prices, or by almost the value of existing imports. These calculations can be illustrated in Figure 13.1. Let P_c be the world price and P_m the price now paid for the sample of pharmaceutical imports. Area E, $2 million, corresponds to the cost of the imports at world prices, and area B, $3 million, is the excess Colombia pays because of international price discrimination. If Colombia purchased the pharmaceuticals at world prices, Colombia's consumer's surplus and welfare would increase by the current discriminatory monopoly profit paid to foreign exporters, area B ($3 million), and the eliminated deadweight loss from discrimination, area C ($1.5 million). (With linear demand curves, area C is always one half of area B.)

3. Conclusions and Policy Implications

We examine here the role of the multinational corporations as international traders in information. We stress the ambiguity and possible meaninglessness of the traditional use of the term "technology gap," suggest a redefinition, and enumerate five types of information generated by the multinational corporations: information for product creation, for product development, for development of production functions, for market creation, and for appropriability. We review for entire industries a technology life cycle that parallels Vernon's (1966) cycle for individual products. We note that private market generation of new information and new techniques may require concentrated industry structures and large optimum firm size. Thus, any policy proposal aimed at "increasing private market technology transfer" through reducing the market power of the multinationals via increased intraindustry competition is close to a contradiction in terms. Multinational corporations are successful in transferring technology either because they have expanded to internalize the externality created by the public-goods aspect of new information or because they have been in industries with high concentration initially. These and other implications follow directly from the "appropriability theory" of foreign direct investment.

Two types of information may be seriously underprovided by existing private means: simple product technologies; and unskilled-labor-using production technologies. Multinational corporations and private markets undersupply this information because they cannot appropriate the returns. They will delay introduction of simple technologies (with *low* appropriability) if their introduction lowers sufficiently the returns on existing sophisticated technologies (with *high* appropriability). LDC firms also will not undertake these projects because small optimum firm size, free entry, and standardized products and processes reduce the private appropriability of returns. This leaves an excess of the social return over the private return. Solutions to these problems could come from government financed research or from government tax-subsidy incentives. The evidence suggests that the creation of information is responsive to such economic incentives. Governments could increase the supply of both types of technologies if they were willing to purchase these new technologies at their social rather than private value. The multinationals are probably not suited to create these types of information, given existing incentive structures. Even if incentives were provided, I suspect that they would largely continue to specialize in the more sophisticated technologies demanded in the DCs.

An economic criterion was suggested here for whether governments or private firms were more efficient at creating new information. Both institutions suffer from inefficient social *allocations* of investments in the types of information created: governments because of differential organization costs of lobbies advocating alternative research projects and firms because of differential appropriability of the private returns across information investments. If the government is more efficient on this allocation question, it should create the information. If private firms are more efficient on the allocation question, then the decision hinges on the trade-off between superior private allocation but suboptimal private supply due to patent-induced monopoly practices versus inferior government allocation but superior supply of the information if the government distributes it freely.

We emphasize that information is not a free good and that even though existing information has nearly a zero marginal cost, the LDCs would not want to "steal" it if this would cut their future information imports below the optimum levels. This issue of price hinges on the empirical question of the importance of LDC markets in calculations by technology creators of the profit maximizing levels of future technology to be supplied to the world: if LDC markets are unimportant, then LDCs should push the effective prices they pay for existing technologies as low as possible since this will not affect the supply of future information to themselves or to the world.

To the extent the multinationals are important sources of current information flows to the LDCs, neither the impression of strict codes of conduct nor revisions of the Paris Convention in favor of technology importers will encourage them to increase their real flows of information to the LDCs. Applying greater political pressure to the multinationals (equivalent to increased taxation of their information creation in the LDCs) pushes back their target date for movement of production facilities to the LDCs in the technology cycle. This reduces the weight of the LDC relative factor-price structure in the present value calculations for the type of production function to create for new products and thereby accentuates the "inappropriate technology" problem. LDCs should evaluate all technology policies in an optimum tariff framework since the price as well as the amount of "technology transferred" is critical for welfare calculations. LDC "codes of conduct for technology" should be carefully formulated so as not to restrict future information flows below optimum levels. I suspect that a number of the current policy proposals will be beneficial to the LDCs (the welfare gain from cutting the price on existing technologies will more than offset the welfare loss from reduced flows of future information). These proposals include limitations on all of the following: restricting package licensing, tied purchases, contract durations, quality control, and territorial constraints.[10]

Two of these proposals deserve special attention. The first is aimed at the current practice of sellers of technology restricting exports of new products from the purchaser's country. Creators of information gain from this ability to engage in price discrimination across countries. But the higher variance that this causes in the world price of information is an important welfare cost to technology purchasers. There is no social rationale for the cost of computers to differ between Colombia and Peru because of political boundaries.

The second proposal is for the LDCs to modify their adherence to the International Convention for the Protection of Industrial Property (the Paris Convention). This treaty was first signed in Paris in 1883, has been revised half a dozen times, and has grown from including eleven countries in 1884 to seventy-eight in 1970. The terms of the convention are largely devised by technology exporting countries and so they cannot be expected to be optimal for technology importers. Since the legal systems and the types of technology demanded in LDCs differ from those in the DCs, we should expect the socially optimal legal instruments protecting rights to privately created information to differ. Differences have evolved naturally. For example, the average duration for patents in forty-five LDCs is only eleven years while it is seventeen years in fourteen DCs.[11] Because of the simplicity of the types of information demanded in the LDCs, it is appropriate for them to have patents that are easier to obtain and of shorter duration. Such a legal instrument is the "utility model."[12] It is much easier to obtain than a patent and of shorter duration, generally of three to six years. It has been used with great success in Japan and Germany, two countries with rapid technical change in the last two decades. Utility model patents were 52 percent of new patent applications (and patents granted) published in Japan in 1972.[13] (Japan and Germany accounted for 440,000 of the 770,000 new patents published by ten major developed countries in 1972; the United States was a poor third with only 75,000 published new patents.)[14] The LDCs would gain by shifting their laws away from the longer duration patents (favored by technology *exporters* in the Paris Convention) toward the simpler and shorter utility models.

Multinational corporations have received strong criticisms in recent years; some were justified and some not. Critics should remember that the patent system and trademark laws stimulate the private creation of new ideas by explicitly guaranteeing that successful innovators can behave outrageously for, say, seventeen years. The appropriability theory indicates that limitations on particularly onerous types of outrageous behavior should be dictated by the optimal supply of information, and not by mindless cuts in firm size.

Notes

The author is indebted to Doug Van Ness, Fran Finnegan, Stephen Thompson, and David Caprera for research assistance; to Robert Z. Aliber, Jagdish Bhagwati, and Ken Clements for comments; and to the National Science Foundation for financial support.

1 By "appropriability" we mean the ability of private originators of ideas to obtain for themselves the pecuniary value of the ideas to society.

2 See Magee (1977).

3 Alternatively, the government could auction the right to produce each unit of the new information and its utilization would be the same as under free provision. For expositional ease, use of the term "free provision by the government" hereafter includes the possibility of auction.

4 See Magee (1977) for greater detail on the industry technology cycle. The three stages are similar to Vernon's (1966): invention, innovation, and standardization.

5 See the appendix for a description of the data used in all of the empirical results reported in the text.

6 Enos (1962, p. 304) reports that almost all of the nine major inventions for thermal cracking and catalytic cracking in the petroleum industry were made by men who were close to the oil industry but who were not attached to the major firms. Mueller (1962) found that fifteen out of twenty-five of DuPont's major new products and processes were not discovered by DuPont scientists. They were "on-the-shelf" or existing technologies that DuPont purchased from individuals or smaller firms.

7 For this reason, process patents, utility models, and patents for the "mechanical arts" are frequently shorter than other patents (see United Nations Conference on Trade and Development, 1975a).

8 About 6 percent of world patents granted in 1970 were made by LDCs and only 1 percent were held by nationals of LDCs (United Nations Conference on Trade and Development, 1975b).

9 Table 14 in the United Nations Conference on Trade and Development (1975a, p. 53) also provides evidence in this area. It indicates that, for all four of the major product

areas considered, the proportion of DCs who excluded patentability *exceeded* the proportion of LDCs excluding patentability. The hypothesis that the DCs are "stealing" more technology than the LDCs should be investigated, since both the Vaitsos (1974) and UNCTAD (1975a) results are consistent with it.

10 See the United Nations Conference on Trade and Development (UNCTAD), 1975c, pp. 20-28, for descriptions of these proposals, and UNCTAD, 1975a, pp. 20-29 for abuses.

11 These averages were calculated from UNCTAD (1975a, Table 15, p. 54).

12 Utility models are discussed in UNCTAD (1975a, p. 4) and UNCTAD (1975b, p. 37).

13 See UNCTAD (1975a, p. 19).

14 Ibid.

References

Aliber, R. 1970, "A Theory of Direct Foreign Investment" in C. P. Kindleberger, ed., *The International Corporation* (The MIT Press, Cambridge, Mass.).

Arrow, K. J., 1962, "Economic Welfare and the Allocation of Resources for Invention" in *The Rate and Direction of Inventive Activity: Economic and Social Factors*, a report of the National Bureau of Economic Research (Princeton University Press, Princeton).

Bhagwati, J., 1972, "R. Vernon's *Sovereignty at Bay: The Multinational Spread of U.S. Enterprises,*" *Journal of International Economics*, 2, 455-459.

Brock, W.A., and S. P. Magee, 1975, *The Economics of Pork-Barrel Politics*, Center for Mathematical Studies in Business and Economics, University of Chicago, Report 7511, February.

Caves, R., 1971, "International Corporations: The Industrial Economics of Foreign Investment," *Economica*, 38, 1-27.

_____ , 1974, "Industrial Organization" in J. H. Dunning, ed., *Economic Analysis and the Multinational Enterprise* (Praeger, New York).

Demsetz, H., 1969, "Information and Efficiency: Another Viewpoint," *Journal of Law and Economics*, 12, 1-22.

Enos, J. L., 1962, "Invention and Innovation in the Petroleum Refining Industry" in *The Rate and Direction of Inventive Activity: Economic and Social Factors* (Princeton University Press, Princeton), 299-321.

Helleiner, G. K., 1975, "The Role of Multinational Corporations in the Less Developed Countries' Trade in Technology," *World Development*, 3, 161-189.

Hufbauer, G., 1970, "The Impact of National Characteristics and Technology on the Commodity Composition of Trade in Manufactured Goods" in R. Vernon, ed., *The Technology Factor in International Trade*, Universities-National Bureau Conference Series (Columbia University Press, New York).

Hymer, S. H., 1966, *The International Operation of National Firms: A Study of Direct Foreign Investment* (MIT Press, Cambridge, Mass.).

Johnson, H. G., 1970, "Multinational Corporations and International Oligopoly: The Non-American Challenge" in C. P. Kindleberger, ed., *The International Corporation* (MIT Press, Cambridge, Mass.).

Kindleberger, C. P., 1974, "Size of Firm and Size of Nation" in J. H. Dunning, ed. *Economic Analysis and the Multinational Enterprise* (Praeger, New York).

Magee, S. P., 1977, "Multinational Corporations, the Industry Cycle and Development," *Journal of World Trade Law.*

Mansfield, E., 1974, "Technology and Technological Change" in J. H. Dunning, ed., *Economic Analysis and the Multinational Enterprise* (Praeger, New York).

Mueller, W. F., 1962, "The Origins of the Basic Inventions Underlying DuPont's Major Product and Process Innovations, 1920 to 1950" in National Bureau of Economic Research, *The Rate and Direction of Inventive Activity: Economic and Social Factors* (Princeton University Press, Princeton).

National Bureau of Economic Research, 1962, *The Rate and Direction of Inventive Activity: Economic and Social Factors* (Princeton University Press, Princeton).

Nelson, P., 1970, "Information and Consumer Behavior," *Journal of Political Economy*, 78, 311-329.

Nelson, R., 1962, "Introduction" to National Bureau of Economic Research, *The Rate and Direction of Inventive Activity: Economic and Social Factors* (Princeton University Press, Princeton).

Rodriguez, C., 1975, "Trade in Technological Knowledge and the National Advantage," *Journal of Political Economy*, 83, 121-135.

Telser, L., 1976, "Comments on Political Information," *Journal of Law and Economics*, 19, August.

United Nations Conference on Trade and Development, 1975a, *The Role of the Patent System in the Transfer of Technology to Developing Countries* (United Nations, New York), TD/B/AC, 11/19/Rev. 1.

_____ , 1975b, *Major Issues Arising from the Transfer of Technology to Developing Countries* (United Nations, New York), TD/B/AC, 11/10/Rev. 2.

_____ , 1975c, *An International Code of Conduct on Transfer of Technology* (United Nations, New York), TD/B/C, 6/AC, 1/2/Supp., 1/Rev. 1.

Vaitsos, C., 1974, *Intercountry Income Distribution and Transnational Enterprises* (Clarendon, Oxford).

Vernon, R., 1966, "International Investment and International Trade in the Product Cycle," *Quarterly Journal of Economics*, 80, 190-207.

Appendix

The age of each industry in 1967 was calculated by subtracting the average "first-trade date" (see Hufbauer, 1970) of the products in the industry from 1967. The product differentiation variable also came from Hufbauer (1970). Research and development as a percent of sales and advertising as a percent of sales in 1967 were obtained from averages of firms in 4 digit SIC industries from the COMPUSTAT tapes. Production wages were obtained from the U.S. Department of Commerce, Bureau of Domestic Commerce, *Industry Profiles, 1958-1969*, U.S. Government Printing Office, October 1971. The four-firm concentration ratio at the 4-digit SIC level came from the Federal Trade

Commission, *Industry Classification and Concentration*. The geographical concentration of employment is the Herfindahl index of the share of employment in each of nine geographical regions in the United States in 1967 and comes from the U.S. *Census of Manufactures*, 1967. If s_i represents the share of employment in region i, then the Herfindahl index, H, equals the sum of the shares squared: $H = \Sigma_i s_i^2$.

The varying sample sizes for the results reported in the text were caused by different industry coverage for each variable. For all correlations, all of the observations available for both variables were used. The only excluded observations were two outlier industries (one from each of the two groups) in the data used for Figure 13.4 (SIC 3121 and SIC 3421). This reduced the sample from 139 to 137 industries.

The import data matching the Vaitsos (1974) price data for Colombia was obtained by Frank Reid from the National Department of Statistics, Bogota, Colombia.

Comment
Charles P. Kindleberger

Stephen Magee has produced an elegant and imaginative paper that extends the discussion of technology transfer from developed to developing countries a considerable distance. It is closely reasoned, related to the limited empirical material available, and a distinct advance on the rhetorical and legalistic discussions of the new international economic order. The few comments I have to offer are in the form of trivial qualifications to an overall analysis and derived policy recommendations with which I largely agree. A word or two might usefully perhaps be added on the diffusion of existing as contrasted with newly produced knowledge, on the Japanese experience in licensing as contrasted with admitting multinational corporations, and finally on the applicability of history rather than theory to further investigation of the topic.

Magee's emphasis on the creation of knowledge disturbed me as I started his paper, because so much of the problem historically, and in the policy debates in developing countries, deals with the diffusion of existing knowledge. The topics are of course joined. If no new information were to be produced, the problem would be solely one of diffusion. If on the other hand, as is the case, new information of economic value is produced, the character of diffusion of existing knowledge has an impact back on the production of information. During the industrial revolution, new industrial processes in Britain were developed for a variety of reasons—ranging from profitability to pure creativity. A few inventors, such as Bertholet who developed chlorine for bleaching, had no interest in restricting utilization. For the most part, however, British investor-producers tried to safeguard their industrial secrets, and the Continent tried to beg, borrow, buy, or steal them. There were restrictions on the export of machinery and the emigration of artisans of the sort that were briefly contemplated by the United States government under the Nixon administration—and not for the optimum tariff reason that Magee, looking at the problem from the LDC viewpoint, states is the only valid basis for taxing or otherwise restricting technology inflows into developing countries. Without vertical integration, however, machinery makers in, say, cotton textiles had an interest that was different from the producers of cotton cloth, and ultimately achieved the removal of restrictions on machinery exports. Rents on existing knowledge can be distinguished from returns on research and development as an activity. A great deal of the difficulty between multinational corporations and developing countries arises from the fact that the former looks at information creation as a continuous process, whereas the latter is concerned mainly with the diffusion of existing knowledge under which past research and development expenditures are appropriately regarded as sunk costs. The difference in perspective is not of course unique. When company and trade union debate the establishment of an overseas subsidiary to manufacture for the local market, each has a different counterfactual in mind. To the company, exports are drying up, and investment is necessary to hold the market in the long run. To the trade union, if the investment were not made, the market would continue to be served by exports in the short run. There is no easy way that I can see to focus both parties on an identical model when they have different shadow rates of interest.

In the discussion of pure diffusion, moreover, the Japanese case, not discussed by Magee, is highly instructive. Rather than admit the multinational corporation, the Japanese have preferred to hire the capital, license the technology, and provide their own management, limiting the rents on foreign technology from creating markets. It is not always open even to the Japanese to do so, when a foreign owner of technology for which they have an imperative demand, say IBM, is interested only in an investment opportunity and is unwilling to license at rates the Japanese customarily pay. Other countries, however, lack the Japanese capacity to follow this practice of disassembling the multinational corporation package. As a recent paper by Sune Carlson notes ("Company Policies for International Expansion," presented to a conference at MIT, January 9, 1976), an important element in trade in modern products is software, and software in the form of instruction is particularly important in the purchase of technology. The Japanese have a higher capacity than most countries to work out in practice how technological principles can be applied to the conditions of their country. Like the Germans in the nineteenth century, who took over foreign enterprise once after the mining investments of the 1850s and a second time after the electrical investments of the 1890s, and who moved from importing locomotives in 1840 to intensive import competition five years later and exporting on balance in 1853, an aptitude for application of the technology of others to local circumstances makes a difference in the extent to which a country needs to depend on multinational corporations. Unhappily, many developing countries lack the qualities that the Japanese, Germans, and doubtless other countries such as Israel and Taiwan bring to this problem. What these qualities are and how amenable they are to cultivation remains a topic for research.

My small points are trivial and I should apologize for taking the time of this assembly for mentioning them.

First, the a priori appeal of Magee's technological cycle is strong. Its reality, however, might well be tested historically. I am impressed, for example, that British locomotive design made enormous strides in the 1830s and 1840s, and again, after a fifty-year period of quiescence, in the period from 1891 to 1906 when Churchward of the Great Western Railway brought out a new improved design every third year. The float process in plate glass would appear to be another example of a belated renewed spurt in process, as opposed to product innovation.

Second, Magee's identification of innovation and size of firm strikes one as cogent. His distinction between firm and government as innovators, however, leaves out the industry, which has been tried in Britain, with how much success I do not know, but that matter may be worth evaluation. In this case innovation may be made a collective, midway between the private and the public good. There may be a question as to whether this would benefit the developing countries, however, since the trade association might be as jealous of its monopoly (cartel) rents as a large private firm would be.

Third, in response to a lecture I gave at Harvard, Stephen Marglin suggested that the patent system might be scrapped in favor of a system of governmental prizes, followed by free public use of knowledge, plus perhaps a market that would spontaneously develop in the software. The practicality of this suggestion should be investigated. In his *Capital and Steam Power*, John Lord asserts that prizes failed to stimulate invention when the capital requirements of industrial research and development became so large that they posed too great risks for capital markets. This has a plausible ring to it, but I would like to see the subject investigated at greater depth. There are, in economic history, some harrowing stories of inventors who spent a large part of their lives appealing to parliament for an ex post subvention. Ex ante stipulation of the prize money poses risk that costs may outrun reward. This is also true of course of patents. Ex post awarding of prizes will surely tempt legislatures, in the same way that developing countries are tempted today, to focus on the character of the prize as rent on old knowledge rather than as an incentive to the production of new.

V
**Panel Discussion on the
New International Economic Order**

Panel Discussion

1. C. Fred Bergsten

The calls for a new international economic order (NIEO) derive from two contemporary developments. One is the continued poverty of the countries of the Fourth World, which comprises mainly South Asia and most of Sub-Saharan Africa. This problem has been the focus of most of the discussion at this conference. The explicit or implicit purpose of most of the policy proposals has been to help the poorest countries. Thus the bulk of the analysis and suggestions for change have been economic. This is natural for a group composed primarily of economists, and desirable because of the continued urgency of finding new means to help alleviate global poverty.

But the emergence of the NIEO as a serious international issue derives primarily from the rapidly growing strength of the countries of the Third World, which comprises virtually all of Latin America and the Middle East and most of East and Southeast Asia. Their interests in seeking a NIEO are at least as much political as economic. The Third World wants a greater participatory role in managing the world economy, both for reasons of status and because it believes that only through such a larger decision-making role can its interests be protected on an ongoing basis. It is demonstrably willing to link its rising economic power to political objectives to promote its demands. Hence political factors are central to any serious effort to develop a constructive response.

The political and economic issues interact in two very important ways. First, the Third World wants more political power partly in order to promote its economic objectives. But the immediate targets of its international efforts differ importantly from the targets of the Fourth World. Third World countries focus largely on acquiring new economic opportunities: access to the markets of the industrialized countries for their exports of manufactured goods, access to international capital markets, access to modern technology. The Fourth World, on the other hand, continues to stress its need for resource transfers through the traditional medium of foreign aid.

This important difference between the goals of the Third and Fourth Worlds, however, is reconciled by the second interaction between the politics and economics of the debate over a NIEO: the importance to the Third World of championing the aspirations of the Fourth World. This objective is particulary important to the OPEC countries, which wish desperately to avoid political isolation and universal condemnation for disrupting the world economy with their massive increase in the price of oil.[1] To achieve that end, they must retain the support of the other developing countries—no mean task, since those countries have suffered severely from that event.

The importance to OPEC of championing the causes of its allies, to preserve the alliance, has been heightened by the rapid diminution of its ability to provide them with direct financial aid. By 1976, only the third year of expensive oil, only three OPEC countries—Saudi Arabia, the United Arab Emirates, and Kuwait—are running substantial current account surpluses, and even they are talking publicly of reducing their aid programs. In such a milieu, OPEC is virtually forced to use its oil leverage on behalf of the policy targets of the other developing countries if it wishes to head off rapidly growing disillusionment and hence growing political isolation.[2]

Nor is OPEC alone among Third World countries in seeking to use its economic power to promote its political standing with its poorer colleagues. Several countries that aspire to regional dominance increasingly seek to position themselves as interlocutors between their regions, including the poorest members thereof, and the industrialized world. Examples include Brazil's far-reaching proposals for reforming the GATT and Indonesia's pioneering of new forms of contract relationships with the multinational oil companies. Such steps promote the economic interests of the countries undertaking them, but are also viewed as enhancing their leadership vis-à-vis the Fourth World.

This double fusion—of economic and politics, of Third World and Fourth—has major implications for all efforts to resolve the NIEO debate. On the economic side, there emerged from our discussion three alternative approaches for transferring resources from richer to poorer countries. One is the traditional means of contributing budgetary funds. This can be done directly, through foreign assistance programs (including debt relief). Or it can be done indirectly through providing adjustment assistance to *domestic* workers and others in the donor countries who are displaced by increased imports from, and perhaps direct investment in, recipient countries.

The second alternative is for consumers in richer countries to finance the transfer directly, by permitting the prices of LDC exports to rise above market levels. For commodity trade, this can be done through successful unilateral action by "producers' associations" à la OPEC or through international commodity agreements, comprising consuming as well as producing nations, which either aim consciously at setting prices above market levels or do so inadvertently. (Some commodity agreements aim simply to stabilize prices, though they may also "transfer resources" in the sense that reduced price instability has real economic value for producing countries.) For manufactured goods, it can be done through monopoly pricing practices of local firms with the power to do so, including the local subsidiaries of multinational enterprises. All such efforts, even when successful in the short run, may of course be counterproductive for the developing countries involved over the long run because of the inherent risk of triggering the production of more competitive alternatives.

A third approach is to increase the developing countries' share of the rents generated by a variety of economic activities. They can take from producing companies a bigger share of the profits resulting from commodity or manufacturing output—"expropriating the profit" rather than the property.[3] In practice, this approach may be hard to distinguish from the previous alternative: a redistribution of rents is involved if there is no increase in final consumer prices, a charge to consumers if the companies involved succeed in passing on the larger LDC take in their own pricing.[4]

There are numerous other ways in which the Third and Fourth Worlds can also increase their share of world economic rents. In cases where their exports are limited by import controls in developed countries, they can at least seize the resulting scarcity rents by effectively organizing the remaining market.[5] A number of the proposals made at this conference, such as the "brain drain" tax and taxes on various uses of the oceans, seek to enhance the share of the developing countries in the rents generated by those activities. A special case is the proposal for linking Special Drawing Rights to development assistance, which seeks to promote the LDC share of the seigniorage created by international money.

The choice among these methods, assuming a basic decision to increase resource transfers, depends on three factors: their relative economic effectiveness, their international political impact (particularly along the North-South axis itself, but also in terms of relations among the industrialized countries and among the developing countries), and their domestic political impact in donor countries. There may be sharp clashes among these criteria. For example, northern acceptance of price-propping commodity agreements or producers' associations would go far toward easing North-South political tensions, because the South has chosen to place priority emphasis on the issue. But such an approach would almost certainly be economically counterproductive over the longer run (by triggering the production of alternative goods) and could be disastrous in terms of domestic politics (as when the U.S. Congress reacted to OPEC by excluding its members from the U.S. system of generalized tariff preferences and initially rejecting the entire fourth replenishment of the International Development Association).

On the other hand, there may be important congruences among the three criteria. Adjustment assistance for workers in industrialized countries displaced by imports from developing countries, for example, supports consumer and anti-inflation objectives in "donor" countries. It promotes industrialization, the most important component of the economic strategy of most developing (especially Third World) countries. Hence it should rank high on both economic and international political grounds.

The following table arrays the three alternative means of resource transfer against the three criteria just cited, and ranks each method in terms of these criteria. For example, reallocating rents is probably the most efficient (least inefficient) of the three methods because, at least initially, it does not disturb existing patterns of production. "Consumers pay" methods are most inefficient, because they consciously violate market signals. Budgetary transfers *may* prove highly efficient, particularly when implemented indirectly through devices such as domestic adjustment assistance or when promoting the creation of "infant industries" that eventually become competitive on their own, but demonstrably can also lead to uneconomic projects and development programs.

Resource Transfer Methods and Selection Criteria
(ranked down each column)

Resource Transfer Methods	Selection Criteria		
	Economic Efficiency	International Politics	Domestic Politics in Donor Countries
Budgetary Transfers	2	3	2
Consumers Pay	3	1	3
Reallocate Rents	1	2	1

The rankings by no means purport to provide definitive answers to which approach is "best," a choice that in any event will differ from country to country and from specific program to specific program. Its main objective is to suggest a framework for thinking about the trade-offs involved. In general, however, the economic needs and *direct* political concerns of Third World countries—as opposed to their indirect political concerns for programs to help their Fourth World allies—can best be met by steps to improve their economic opportunities, particularly regarding trade in manufactured goods. Traditional budgetary transfers, on the other hand, will remain a more central component of policy responses to the Fourth World.

Implementation of some mix of these economic measures is a necessary condition for dealing constructively with the demands for a NIEO. Even implementation of all of them would be insufficient to restore stable North-South relations, however, because of the more explicitly political component of those demands. A comprehensive northern response must therefore include enhancing the role of the South in the decision-making machinery of the international economic system.

Two steps are probably required. First, the developing countries *as a group* must heretofore be adequately represented in all important decision-making arenas. Indeed, the Conference on International Economic Cooperation (CIEC) was created in Paris for precisely this purpose. To some extent, this is why the Committee of 20 (and its successors) supplanted the Group of 10, whose membership came solely from the First World, to negotiate international monetary arrangements. And UNCTAD has tried to seize control of international trade policy partly because many LDCs are not members of the GATT. The reforms that are needed in a whole array of international institutions must encompass adequate representation for the Third and Fourth Worlds.[6]

In addition, selected *individual* countries from the Third World should participate directly in the smaller decision-making groups that lie at the center of the international machinery. For example, the most advanced of the developing countries—perhaps Brazil, Iran, and Mexico—should be invited to join the OECD. Saudi Arabia should be invited to join the Group of 10. The most relevant historical precedent is the emergence of Japan as a major economic power around 1960, and the accommodation of that power via its accession to membership in these same institutions. In addition to accommodating directly the strength of the new economic powers, membership in such bodies would enhance their ability to promote the interests of other developing countries and hence support their broader political goals.

Such increased involvement in the decision-making process would of course carry responsibilities as well as rights for the new entrants from the Third World. Two particular responsibilities stand out: support for economic progress in the poorest countries, and recognition of the impact of their own actions on the functioning of the entire international economic system. It is urgent to begin promoting such an acceptance of global responsibilities, on the part of at least the most advanced countries in the Third World, because there is strong evidence that their major focus now—in the IMF, GATT, and elsewhere—is a search for new exemptions from such responsibilities at just the time when their increased economic capabilities require them to accept more instead.

Nevertheless, these countries cannot—and should not—be expected to accept responsibilities as far-reaching as those which must be (though are not always) accepted by the more mature industrialized countries. Hence it becomes necessary to create a third group of countries for purposes of international rights and obligations, in recognition of the emergence of a true international "middle class"—the Third World. The traditional bifurcation of the globe into "haves" and "have-nots," "rich" and "poor," "developed" and "less developed," no longer fits the facts.

The new middle class (NMCs) would have more rights and fewer responsibilities than the developed countries (DCs), and fewer rights and more responsibilities than the less developed countries (LDCs). For example, they need not give concessional aid—but neither should they receive any. They need not extend tariff preferences—but neither should they receive any. They would face more lenient rules than the DCs regarding the use of such trade measures as import quotas and export quotas, but would not enjoy the full exceptions from the usual rules accorded the LDCs.

Careful analysis and tough negotiations would be required to determine the place of individual countries in the three new categories. Some countries might be treated as DCs for one policy purpose, and as NMCs (or even LDCs) for another. For example, Saudi Arabia as the world's second largest holder of monetary reserves should accept the highest order of responsibility in the international financial area (placing its holdings of reserve currencies in the country of issue rather than in the Eurocurrency markets, with the resulting "carousel" effect on credit creation), but as a totally nonindustrialized society might still receive tariff preferences.

Equally important to the original placement of countries would be subsequent shifts in their position. Just as Japan "graduated" from the ranks of the developing countries around 1960, and as members of the Third World are doing so today, there will in the future be constant alterations—usually in an upward direction, but occasionally downward as well. Shifts in international rights and responsibilities should be made concomitantly with these changes in underlying power positions.

It is clear that a NIEO, or at least significant change in the old order, is already emerging. Numerous economic concessions have already been made. New institutions have been created, and many more proposed. The underlying realities of economic and, hence, political power among the nations of the world assure that this evolution will continue to the point where a new equilibrium, and a method for further evolution to maintain that equilibrium, are found.

To reach that point, it will be necessary to distinguish clearly between the Third and Fourth Worlds, and between the economic and political objectives of each. It will be necessary to look at the three alternative means of transfering resources—budgetary appropriations, higher prices for consumers, and reallocation of economic rents—against the three criteria of economic efficiency, international politics, and domestic politics in donor countries. The Third World must be integrated into the international decision-making structure. The emergence of a new international middle class, with newly defined sets of rights and responsibilities, must be accommodated through changes in international institutional arrangements. On such bases, it should be possible for North and South to work together toward a NIEO.

Notes

1 See Fried and Schultze (1976) for empirical evidence on the extent of this disruption, including to the developing countries.

2 The OPEC countries have been remarkably successful in this effort so far. They forced commodity trade and broad developmental issues onto the international agenda by abandoning the first ministerial session of the "energy dialogue" in Paris in April 1975. In terms of more concrete payoffs, they won sizable liberalization of IMF credits at Kingston in January 1976 by linking the usability of their currencies directly to liberalization of the credit tranches and by prompting the liberalization of the compensatory finance facility through their tactics in Paris.

3 As they are now doing successfully across a wide range of industries. For details, see Bergsten (1974) and Bergsten, Horst, and Moran.

4 Both elements appear to be present in the case of bauxite. See Bergsten (1976).

5 This is done most easily if the importing country either allocates its quotas on a country basis or implements its controls via negotiating "voluntary export restraints," which leave the market organization wholly to the producing country. See Bergsten (1975).

6 See Bergsten, Berthoin, and Mushakoji (1976) for a detailed agenda of such reform needs and suggestions for actively engaging the developing countries at all stages.

References

Bergsten, C. F., 1974, "Coming Investment Wars?," *Foreign Affairs*, October 1974.

_____ , 1975, "On the Non-Equivalence of Import Quotas and 'Voluntary' Export Restraints" in *Toward A New International Economic Order: Selected Papers of C. Fred Bergsten, 1972-1974* (D.C. Heath and Co., Lexington, Mass.), especially pp. 163-170.

_____ , 1976, "A New OPEC in Bauxite," *Challenge*, July/August 1976, pp. 12-20.

_____ , G. Berthoin, and K. Mushakoji, 1976, *The Reform of International Institutions*, a report of the Trilateral Task Force on International Institutions, Triangle Papers, 11.

_____ , T. Horst, and T. Moran, *American Multinationals and American Interests* (Brookings Institution, Washington, D.C., forthcoming), especially Chs. 5 and 10.

Fried, E. R., and C. L. Schultze, eds., 1975, *Higher Oil Prices and the World Economy* (Brookings Institution, Washington, D.C.), especially pp. 169-195.

2. Richard N. Cooper

Why should foreign assistance be given? Why should one group of countries voluntarily transfer resources to another? The various possible answers to this question will properly influence the form of assistance, of transfers of resources, and thus have an important bearing on the proposals for a new international economic order.

Although many of us have come to take the desirability of foreign assistance for granted, it is not in fact self-evident that communities, or nations, should voluntarily relinquish some part of their incomes, or of their claims on wealth, to provide transfers to other communities. Although enormously high both by historical standards and in comparison with incomes in many parts of the world today, incomes in industrial countries have not yet reached the point of psychological satiation. We know from the perennial battle over wage claims and from the often agonizing decisions that have to be made over the size of government expenditures that industrial countries can quite comfortably absorb higher incomes than they now have.

The arguments for extracting some (usually tiny) fraction of this insufficient income for transfers to other, poorer countries have rested partly on ethical or moral grounds, partly on grounds of prudence and political expediency. There has often been a good deal of tension between the ethical arguments and the prudential arguments, for they often require both the character and the direction of foreign assistance to be quite different. There has been a second tension, which is likely to become even more pronounced in the years to come, between the ethical arguments for foreign assistance and the exaggerated sense of national sovereignty that all nations, but especially in this context developing nations, have acquired. I want to say something about each of these tensions, but particularly the second one.

The Western industrial nations have a long tradition, both of religion and of rationalism, favoring a distributive justice that pushes toward greater equality. The Christian tradition of charity is deeply rooted. Economists have perhaps been more influenced by the rationalistic utilitarian tradition, which early attempted to show that a more equal distribution of income would lead to greater overall welfare. More recently we have John Rawls' attempt to show, through original social contract reasoning, that society should organize itself to maximize the net income of those of its members that are worst off. There are intellectual difficulties with all these various attempts to rationalize some measure of redistribution toward greater equality, from Bentham's sum-of-utilities to Rawls' maximin criterion. But it is significant that the effort persists; and there is little doubt that the sentiment for some form of distributive justice—if not in circumstance, then at least in opportunity to better one's circumstance—is very strong. And there is widespread recognition that adequate nutrition, health, and (in today's world) education are necessary conditions for creating and taking advantage of opportunities for individual betterment.

This is not the occasion to dissect the various ethical frameworks that have been put forward. But it is important to note that all of the main lines of ethical thought apply to individuals (or families), not to collectivities such as nations. Much recent discussion on transfer óf resources falls uncritically into the practice of what I would call anthropomorphizing nations, of treating nations as though they are individuals and extrapolating to them on the basis of average per capita income the various ethical arguments that have been developed to apply to individuals. This is not legitimate. If ethical arguments are to be used as a rationale for transferring resources, either a new set of ethical principles applicable to nations must be developed, or the link between resource transfers must be made back to the individuals who are the ultimate subjects of standard ethical reasoning. We need therefore to ask explicitly about the connections between any given proposed transfer of resources and the ultimate ethical objectives to be served.

Not to ask questions about these linkages would be morally obtuse. Yet to ask them involves peering inside the national shell, an activity that many developing countries view as a gross and unwarranted infringement of their national sovereignty. The current mood among developing countries resists strongly the notion that donor nations have a legitimate interest, much less (on the above argument) a moral obligation, to inquire closely into the use of resource transfers to be sure that their ethically based objectives are being served.

A clear impasse thus results. Ethical arguments, based on the welfare of individuals, cannot be used to support resource transfers that do not serve the ethical aims; but attempts to assure the service of ethical aims leads to rejection by recipient countries as an affront to national sovereignty.

One logical way out of the impasse is possible: a claim or a belief that resource transfers to countries with low per capita incomes from countries with high per capita incomes will always somehow lead to betterment of the relatively disadvantaged persons in the former country, no matter what policies that nation may actually be pursuing and no matter how the resource transfers are used in the first instance. It is a new version of the trickle-down theory, operating through the state rather than through the marketplace. But if trickle-down theories are admissible, it is difficult to find one that competes favorably with that of international trade economists: liberal trade will lead, under conditions that are not likely to be grossly violated in practice, to an improvement in the factor earnings of the resource that each country holds in relative abundance. And for resource-poor developing countries this means unskilled labor, generally the least well-off members of the labor force. Indeed, one could argue that it would be hard to rival a policy of liberal trade by developed and less developed countries alike as a mechanism for assuring steady improvement in the real earnings of the poorest (healthy) residents of less developed countries over a period of time long enough for the structure of economic activity to adjust to the policy—and assuming also that population growth is somehow kept under control, an assumption that is also necessary for resource transfers to be effective in improving welfare of the poorest. (Liberal trade does not assure improvement for the poorest residents of resource-rich developing countries, since it does not create a demand for much labor; some internal transfer of the resource rents would be necessary.)

If we are to justify resource transfers on ethical grounds, then, it must be on the basis of knowledge that via one mechanism or another the transferred resources will benefit those residents of the recipient countries who are clearly worse off than the worst-off "taxed" (including taxes levied implicitly through commodity prices) residents of the donor countries. That is, general transfers must be based on some kind of performance criterion satisfied by the recipient country, or else transfers should be made only in a form that benefits directly those who, according to the ethical arguments, should be benefited. But this proposition has profound implications for the acceptability of a number of proposals made at this conference, for it implies that no completely general transfer of resources from country to country can be supported on ethical grounds. This restriction would encompass the direct SDR link, general debt relief, actions to improve (not merely stabilize) the terms of trade of developing countries, and a brain drain tax that automatically remitted the tax to the country of emigration. Ethically based transfers should discriminate among recipient countries on the basis of performance in improving, directly or indirectly, the well-being of their general population, and/or they should discriminate among uses of the transfers to maximize the flow of benefits to those who are the intended beneficiaries, which generally means concentration on general nutrition, health care, and education in the recipient countries.

The standard objection to such categorical assistance is that it distorts preferences and that in any case funds are fungible and so categorical assistance does not really achieve its purpose. These arguments are of course in opposition: to the extent that funds are fully fungible, categorical assistance does not distort preferences; and to the extent that funds are not fully fungible, it does achieve its objective, even though some funds may be siphoned off into other uses. In this instance "distorting preferences" is precisely what is wanted on ethical grounds, and since categorical assistance involves substitution as well as income effects, any fungibility is likely to be far from complete: resource transfers directed toward improvements in agriculture, in health care, and in education are likely to be diverted only in part into other uses.

Pursuit of distributive justice is not the only reason for giving foreign assistance. There are "prudential" reasons as well; foreign assistance can play a role, occasionally (but not usually) even a decisive role, in maintaining good relations between donor and recipient countries and more generally in giving recipient countries enough of a stake in ongoing international arrangements to behave according to conventions acceptable to the donor nations. Here it is governments, not individuals, that are the relevant units for examination, and the appropriateness of assistance is not necessarily related to economic performance and is certainly not related to relative poverty. On the contrary, it will tend to be the better-off developing nations that could, if so minded, create the greatest difficulty for the developed nations both in the short and in the long run, in terms of such issues as making atomic weapons, supporting radical political activities in other countries, or withholding cooperation from issues of global concern that require their cooperation. Therefore, these middle-range countries, not the poorest ones, are the most likely recipients of assistance. Moreover, prudential considerations often (though not always) dictate that assistance should flow bilaterally, from individual donor to individual recipient, rather than through multilateral channels. Thus it is unlikely that completely general transfers of resources, such as the direct SDR link or general debt relief, would be supportable by prudential considerations either; indeed, several of the most important developing countries have specifically rejected the suggestion of across-the-board debt relief, presumably on grounds they can do better without it.

In general, "transfer of resources" is an unfortunate choice for emphasis in discussions of the new international economic order, for it suggests taking from one group and giving to another, a process that is rarely harmonious and is especially unlikely to be so when the developing countries insist that the transfers be made with a minimum of scrutiny and guidance, for that undermines the one basis on which transfers are likely to be agreeable to those making them, namely, satisfying general sentiments in favor of distributive justice.

There are, happily, a number of areas where *mutual* gain can be had by close cooperation between developed and developing nations, and where therefore the knotty questions raised by "transfers" arise if at all only in muted form. Let me close by suggesting four areas for concentration in discussion for improvements in the international economic order, where I believe there are ample grounds for cooperation among governments and avoidance of adversary relations (constraints on space prevent elaboration).

First, cooperation in management of the "global commons." At the present time this includes most notably efficient management of the living resources of the oceans, of the oceans and atmosphere as media for waste disposal (but common standards throughout the world will in general be neither necessary nor desirable), of radio frequencies and civil air and merchant shipping routes, and of world monetary conditions. Revenue may be raised as a by-product of such efficient management, for example, from fisheries, permitting the beginnings of transfers through a world fiscal system. But, as is the case within nations, the nature of the resulting expenditures is of interest to all parties to the revenue raising.

Second, reduction in the volatility of commodity prices. Wild price movements of the magnitude experienced from 1972 to 1975 are disadvantageous both to producers and consumers. Attempts to rig the terms of trade in favor of primary producers, apart from being quite capricious in the net resource transfers that would result, will probably succeed only in torpedoing price stabilization schemes that would be to mutual advantage.

Third, deescalation of the tariff structures of industrial countries by stage of processing would improve market incentives to locate early-stage processing of primary products in the primary producing countries, to the ultimate economic benefit of both groups of countries. Relatively small tariffs can lead to very substantial effective protection of some processing activities, which from an efficiency point of view should not be located in the industrial countries. Relocation in primary producing countries would generate a number of the externalities that industrial activity is alleged to generate, including activities to service the processing sector and activities to use the cheap waste materials, which in industrial countries it is sometimes more economical to discard.

Fourth, the global activities of multinational corporations should be subject to at least as much concern from the home countries as from the host countries, and both groups of governments have ample reason to cooperate in their approach to MNCs. This is true for example of illegal bribes. It is also true of maintaining global competition. Too often antitrust policy stops at national borders. Yet the American government, for example, should be just as much concerned in today's interdependent world if only one or two firms dominate several European economies as the European governments are (when they are foreign firms!). Foreign take-overs by American firms reduce potential competition in the American market, and Americans have every reason to be concerned about the long-run consequences of that.

In all these areas there would be much gain from shifting away from the adversary relationship that has prevailed in the past, and that seems all too frequently to arise when the activities of different nations are involved, the instinct being to "defend one's own," to a cooperative relationship that is justified by a careful inspection of the underlying issues.

3. Harry G. Johnson

The discussion of the new international economic order at this conference, and elsewhere, has convinced me that there is one extremely important, indeed fundamental, point that the economist must always be aware of in his thinking, analysis, and policy prescription in the development area. This is that there is a very sharp distinction to be drawn between the economic welfare of *people*, and the welfare economics of distributional policies as the economist professionally analyzes and recommends them (as redistributions among *people*), and the welfare (in political and social as well as economic terms) of *national governments*, and the normative and positive economics of income and other redistributions among *national governments*. It is one thing to call into play the ascientific but generally accepted ethical norm according to which redistributions from rich to poor people are regarded as desirable (unless their economic cost becomes in some sense "too large"), and to believe that the people of "the Third World" deserve assistance from those of "the developed countries." It is quite another thing to argue that there is some sort of moral imperative about redistributions from governments of rich countries to governments of poor countries. Not only may the actual payers at the one end and payees at the other not conform in any way to the implied characteristics of affronting affluence sharing with pitiful poverty, but the support thereby afforded to governments in poor countries may well represent reinforcement of political and social systems that worsen the lot of the typical poor-country citizen not only economically but more seriously (from a human dignity and decency point of view) in terms of personal opportunity and liberty. (I should perhaps make explicit the point that personal freedom is not at all necessarily dependent on there being a free enterprise or capitalist economic system, though in the absence of the latter there is little defense for the individual against the encroachments of the state.)

This particular point is made all too often by radicals and socialists, in criticism of what they assume to be the standard behavior of "imperialist" advanced capitalist economies in policies toward the less developed countries. What needs to be recognized, however, is that the whole thrust of the demand for a new international economic order involves an exactly similar process of entrenching government, regardless of its nature and the restraints on the freedom of its citizens that it imposes, on the basis of an outside source of income whose delivery the new international economic order seeks to guarantee, without political strings, by a "moral" commitment of the developed countries to enforce the arrangements of the new international economic order at the cost to their own consumers of paying a sort of tax over the spending of whose proceeds those consumers will have no political control whatever. In fact, the new international economic order in the large, as well as in the small (as many of us have noted in commenting on aspects of it, for example, the integrated program for commodities), seeks to invert a largely mythological view of past relations between advanced and less developed countries as "imperialism" into a reverse imperialism for the benefit of the governments of the poor countries. All the elements of imperialism are there, from the collection of imperial tribute, regarded as a matter of right, to the freedom of the imperial rulers to waste the tribute in lavish and wasteful consumption and grandiose unproductive construction of monumental buildings; the only real difference, though it is a crucial one, is that whereas the ancient empires were built and held by military conquest and force, the new empires of the poor nations are hoped to be built by political majority in the United Nations and kept by moral blackmail on the one hand and the extension of the power of an international ruling class of international officials and experts on the other.

It is, in fact, no accident, but a matter of self-interested logic on the part of the international administrators, the national political leaders and their civil servants, and the vast majority of the intellectual elites of both less developed and developed countries, that the demand for a new international economic order is essentially a demand to replace the market system by a vast bureaucratic system (requiring lots of political figureheads to sanctify decisions and seal compromises of principle on politics, and masses of intellectuals to explain what is going on to the public, and to provide the rhetoric of moral obligation to accept transfers of both control and use of private resources from private individuals to inflated and overpaid governmental bureaucracies). The replacement of the market by the bureaucratic process inevitably creates a new power elite qualified either by formal education or political skill. Neither of these means of qualification constitutes either a moral claim for social and economic preferment or a demonstration of the ability to promote economic development more efficiently and humanly than the anonymous market does. Moreover, both types of qualification have two side-characteristics that militate against a broadly based and democracy promoting style of economic development: first, both types of career are more difficult to enter (and, perhaps more important, more difficult to be dislodged from, once status has been acquired) than the career of finding something one can do efficiently and to mutual producer and consumer gain, and doing it as well as one can. Second, the political career, the bureaucratic career, and the intellectual career all involve continued demonstration (at least in the careerist's own judgment) of individual superiority over other men, particularly in the sense of manipulating or controlling them for one's own career ends; and this confidence in one's superiority over other men easily leads to treatment of them with covert or overt contempt for their humanity, expressed particularly in willingness to deprive them arbitrarily of their economic, political, and human rights.

It is for this sort of reason that I think it extremely important for professional economists to be very wary of discussing proposals of the kind embodied in the demand for a new international economic order purely in terms of their economic aspects, and above all to be wary of the facile assumption that the international transfers asked for will accrue to the benefit of the peoples rather than the governing elites of the poor countries. I could illustrate that point with reference to the topic of my own paper (Ch. 10, "Commodities"), where it is easily shown that an internationally enforced price-raising agreement could easily result either in an expansion of the government bureaucracy or in the creation of a class of wealthy landowners, while reducing the real incomes and farming opportunities of the ordinary peasant and farm worker. But I will instead illustrate it by the possibility that the proposal to impose a special tax on emigrant educated people trained partly at least at public expense, which can be (and has been) presented quite ably and convincingly as a logical application of "second-best" international economic welfare theory, could become a means of partially closing one of the few defenses the educated citizen (as contrasted with the uneducated citizen) still has against the tyranny of his own (by no means necessarily either elected or supported by majority opinion) government, namely, emigration to another country. It would be scant comfort indeed to know, if one were a political refugee obliged to pay special taxes to the government from whose tyranny one had fled, out of the earnings that were all you had to live on, that the obligation to pay is justified by the best economic theory analysis of which the international profession of economists is capable.

4. Charles P. Kindleberger

I am deeply skeptical about the possibilities of developed and developing countries sitting down in a grand negotiation like the Congress of Vienna and putting together an elaborate bargain, with something for every country, covering commodity stabilization, access to commodities, foreign aid, rescheduling of debts, developing country access to technology, including the patent system, the multinational corporation, the link of aid to the Special Drawing Right (SDR), and so on and on. It seems to me a simple fallacy to suggest that if two countries cannot agree on one subject, they are more likely to agree if they deal simultaneously on two—though I recognize the possibility of quids being exchanged for quos. Nor do I think the extension of two countries, two topics to N countries and N topics brightens the chances of reaching effective understandings. There is, to be sure, a precedent in the General Agreements on Tariffs and Trade where tariff bargaining takes place simultaneously among many countries on many commodities, and, with some difficulty, bargains are struck. The analogy seems to me overdrawn. In tariffs it is possible to evoke escape clauses and withdraw concessions without the whole arrangement unraveling—although other countries frequently withdraw their concessions when the escape clause is invoked. Trade concessions are commensurable, more or less, and do not involve the welter of disparate gains and losses involved in the range of issues raised by UNCTAD (the United Nations Conference on Trade and Development).

Moreover, I doubt that there is a meeting of minds. When minds do not meet, it is a mistake to agree on a form of words that papers the cracks, since the paper bargain struck will not be kept. The developing countries have many times asserted their right to cancel unilaterally contracts or agreements made with developing countries. There is no possibility, much less assurance, that they would adhere to commitments made under an overall big-package bargain, on those aspects of the agreements that proved painful to them, although they would insist with vehemence that developed countries should adhere to their side of the bargain. The world has a long record of agreements without a fundamental meeting of minds. They are not worth the trouble.

I have heard proposals put forward that are regarded as unsatisfactory in themselves, but somehow valuable in their totality, because of their by-products, or as a symbol of sympathy for the plight of the developing countries. Mahbub Haq, for example, notes that the Pakistan tax on its nationals abroad, which at most would have produced $10 millions the first year, brought to a halt the flow of immigrant remittances that yielded $300 million annually, and also led to a sharp decline in the return flights by emigrants to Pakistan on which Pakistani Airlines depends, but he is for it. Charles Frank thought that while the integrated commodity scheme would not work it would produce information on commodity production, stocks and disappearance, and the like, that would be useful; he did not say why it would be impossible to get the information without adopting a scheme regarded as unworkable. Gerald Helleiner wanted to change the world patent system, albeit noting that many of the developing countries do not belong to it and get along without it, and to institute a code for the transfer of technology to the developing countries from the developed, albeit recognizing that "any code that could be agreed upon would be rife with escape clauses and would almost certainly not be legally binding." For each scheme for transferring resources from developed to developing countries, a serious question has been raised as to whether it would add to the total of resources made available or merely lead to a reduction of aid in some other form. It is on this point, to be sure, that an overall agreement covering all forms of economic relationships might contribute, since it could be said to resolve the "additionality" problem.

I regard the exercise of a big-package bargain as thoroughly dysfunctional. It would quickly collapse, and the blame for its collapse would not be put upon unworkability ab initio but on sabotage by the "imperialist powers." In a world where interpretations of events and relationships differ as widely as those of developed and developing countries, it seems to me futile for the developed countries to agree to deliver on promises on which delivery is impossible. I go further: the conventional wisdom has it that commodity agreements are acceptable when consuming countries have been consulted and have agreed to the design of the scheme and the numbers chosen. This is asking the chicken to choose the method and to help carry out his plucking, preparatory to blaming him if the operation fails. I would rather tell the developing countries to raise prices by whatever means and in whatever amount they deem suitable, given the elasticities of demand in the market, and the developed countries to promise not to retaliate. In such a setting as the Cocoyoc Declaration, the developing countries have asserted that they must be self-reliant. Let them be. Let them levy the optimum tariff on commodities they sell to the developed countries, without fear of retaliation, albeit noting that a tax higher than the optimum will rebound on them, as Magee suggests has already been done in taxes on the multinational corporation.

Many of the wiser among the economists from developed countries have told me that the promise of developed countries not to retaliate cannot be kept. In the United States, for example, even if the administration could be induced to show forbearance in exchange for escaping the necessity to agree to a big package, the Congress would refuse to be bound. If other countries levied the optimum tariff on us in copper, bauxite, bananas, nickel, and so forth, we would find difficulty in holding off levying an optimum or supraoptimum tariff on them in wheat. Perhaps more knowledge of the political realities than I possess counsels big package rather than optimum tariff without retaliation. On the basis of my casual political insight, however, I fail to see that it is easier to agree to do something than to agree to do nothing.

One of our deeper divisions at the conference has been between those like Mr. Onitiri who thinks that the reliance on the market is "laughable," and Harry Johnson who states that while the market is by no means perfect, it has been impossible historically to find a mechanism which performs better. As Winston Churchill said about democracy, and some of us feel about honesty, marriage, well-behaved children, free trade, and other old-fashioned institutions, the market does not work very well but it is superior to the available alternatives.

It is difficult to replace the market; it does not follow that it cannot be improved. Two polar cases may be envisaged when it behooves governments, in my judgment, to supplement the action of the market. One is when goods are in very long supply, and prices are collapsing; the other is in periods of great shortage and panic, with a rush for goods (or liquidity) described by Sarris and Taylor in food, with a most apposite quotation from Keynes. The market is a fair-weather friend, and while the weather is mostly or perhaps only frequently fair, we should be prepared to contend with an occasional storm. In periods of shortage the governments of the world should allocate goods in short supply, rather than separately cut off exports or buy up imports on a sauve qui peut basis as happened in 1973. When distress goods come on the market, or new goods enter as did Japanese exports in the 1950s and 1960s, and manufactured exports from the developing countries will do in the decades ahead, we must find a place in the market for them on some sharing basis, rather than each country separately fencing them out. But the need to plan for extreme conditions should not lead us to substitute planning for the market under ordinary and usual circumstances, any more than we should wear oilskins and boots and carry umbrellas when the sun is shining. The schemes of Gale Johnson and of Sarris and Taylor appeal to me, without going into the differences between them, to the extent that they stabilize the market in extreme conditions, without throwing it out unnecessarily. By analogy between market breakdown and liquidity crisis in extremis I should like to disassociate myself from the Chicago school which believes in letting markets in money and capital handle liquidity crises without discounting in a crisis. It seems to me that Walter Bagehot had it right: in ordinary times liquidity should grow along a trend; in crisis, the system should be flooded with liquidity in the interest of preventing unnecessary collapse. We must recognize the dilemma, of course, that if the market can anticipate certain rescue it tends to lose discipline leading to more frequent breakdown.

The doctrine of "benign neglect" should extend from commodities to questions of patents, technology, multinational corporations. It is futile to try to work out a code of rights and duties for the multinational corporation in the absence of a meeting of minds. Let the LDCs do what they like, but accept the consequences, which may well be a decline in the flow of technology. I would not cut off foreign aid for countries that nationalize foreign properties with no or only derisory compensation, but I would do nothing to urge enterprises in the developed world to continue to invest in such countries. In particular, I would cancel schemes of insurance of foreign investment in LDCs, for instance, OPIC. No country or group of countries has to encourage capital inflows; any country that wants such inflows, however, has to create the conditions that make it attractive for individual enterprises.

A few more firmly held but possibly wrong-headed opinions can be expressed pithily. I doubt that the access problem that worries Bergsten is serious. Worldwide renegotiation of debts in an effort to provide more aid to LDCs by this route, as suggested by Kenen, seems to me misguided, and likely to rock the boat so much as to endanger it, although I believe that the World Bank has been too fearful of individual defaults in the past, notably after the collapses of Nkrumah and Sukarno. Foreign aid for economic purposes, both bilateral and multilateral, seems to me the moral duty of the developed countries: the market for resource allocation, but the market buttressed by devices to prevent both collapse and explosion, and foreign aid for income redistribution. If the developed countries want to use the optimum tariff for further redistribution, however, I am content to have them try without retaliation and without reducing foreign aid available through budgetary channels.

Let me close in making a distinction between national (private) and international (public) goods. Within countries using the market system, government provides the public goods of money, macroeconomic stability, and the solvent of tempering the extreme conditions of poverty and unseemly riches that hold the community together and make it possible to accept the dictates of the market when they are not too outrageous. In the international field there is no government, and international organizations are too weak, and too subject to the quiet sabotage of the free rider to function effectively in all times and under all conditions. At a minimum, the world economic system needs the public goods of stable international money, a market for distress goods, a system of allocation in periods of great scarcity, counter-cyclical capital movements, stable exchange rates, and coordinated macroeconomic policies and rediscounting in a crisis. Countries such as Canada and Sweden that set an example in altruistic behavior help enormously, but another requirement is leadership to enforce a public-spirited mode of behavior on the ordinary run of country. In the nineteenth century that leadership came from Britain; between 1945 and about 1968, from the United States. Before the new international economic order can function effectively, we need to build stronger and independent international institutions, which seems utopian at this conjuncture, or to find new or renewed leadership that will police the free riders, accept a disproportionate share of the cost of public goods, act as an enforcer, and in all these ways make the system work.

5. I. M. D. Little

Coming on top of, as it were, the successful realization of power by the OPEC countries, I think the NIEO is primarily about independence, not about development or poverty. The OPEC success has created a greater feeling of confidence and independence among developing countries than before: it has made it obvious that many developed countries are more dependent on others than many developing countries. This is to be welcomed. The high tension generated in great international conferences and confrontations must owe much to this feeling of powerlessness and dependence. Anything, including greater participation in international decision making, and even cartelization, that reduces the feeling (whatever the reality) is useful.

Earlier I cast some doubt on buffer stocks. I am against most new initiatives. But I suggest (in line with Charles Kindleberger) that a very relaxed attitude be taken to commodity cartelization. This is not because I believe it would do good in terms of welfare (it would hurt many of the poorest countries) but because richer countries have cartelized some commodities, and have no right to oppose, and because the successful exercise of economic power by some developing countries may be politically beneficial in the long run. On rather similar grounds, I think that one should support regional investment and trade groupings, despite the risk that they would reduce interest in exporting to the enormously bigger markets of developed countries.

I believe UNCTAD should concentrate on the old chestnuts of more aid and freer trade. Concerning aid, although there is something in some of the arguments against it, I feel that on balance it does good, despite the grave imperfections of many developing country governments, and that there is a moral obligation for the rich to help the poor. Where trade is in question, the reduction of tariffs and nontariff barriers is something that LDCs can most legitimately demand, given the philosophy of the developed market economies. But I think their demands would be strengthened if they gave so-called concessions themselves (most of us economists believe that many of these concessions would benefit them anyway), for they could then elicit support from developed country exporters. I certainly do not think that securing let-outs from international rules, with the fantastic complications involved, is a good approach. If one takes into account that generalized special preferences, with their own let-outs for developed countries, probably excused the latter from removing nontariff barriers, it is possible to doubt whether even that initiative was a good idea. In summary, I suggest that the principle of nonreciprocity may not work in the best interests of developing countries.

Finally, I agree with Sir Arthur Lewis' castigation of the pessimists. For the aggregate of LDCs, the past quarter of a century has shown remarkable development—and the increased worry about income distribution does not negate this. Nevertheless, the prospects are gloomy and disturbing in some regions, and most particularly for India and Bangladesh; where the population problem, in relation to land and other resources is most acute. One must hope that other parts of the world soon realize that slowing population growth takes a very long time: and that a doubling or even trebling of numbers may still be built into the situation when it comes to be realized that there is a problem.

6. Erik Lundberg

Having no special competence and research experience in this field, I need very much such a confidence-creating reference. Here it is—a visit to Red China in October 1975. I was invited to the great celebration of the day of revolution, October 1, in Peking. The high point of the speech by the Acting Prime Minister Teng Hsiao-Ping in the Congress Hall was: "There is great international disorder and we in China like it!"

We here have indeed also realized that there is international disorder and in our way—however very different from that of Mr. Teng—we also like it, from the point of view of problem creation. But we have been very selective in our choice of problems, choosing and emphasizing those which seem fruitful for scientific analysis. In fact I find that we have been too pure and scientific by keeping to marginal issues in some areas of importance.

In particular, I wish to draw attention to certain difficulties in regard to the vision of a more integrated world with a radically improved division of labor between the North and the South. Most of us believe that rapidly increasing trade in manufactured goods is the most effective way of promoting growth in the LDCs. And I agree completely with Jan Tumlir when he maintains that there is no adaptation cost *in the long run,* only gains on both sides.

But, I am afraid, *in the shorter run* there are and will be serious adaptation problems. There are risks that short-term reactions from the side of governments in developed countries will often be so negative and restrictive that the theoretical possibilities of big long-term gains from increased division of labor will only in a very imperfect way be permitted to influence development.

I shall therefore raise some questions as to the possible future responses of developed countries when the demands of the LDCs for export markets of manufactured goods are not just marginal as at present. Some structural tendencies in the developed part of the world may imply serious obstacles to a steady and progressive adaptation process.

In our discussions we have heard much about the reactions of the U.S. economy, administration, and Congress. Of course the United States plays a dominant role in regard to many of the matters discussed. But it is time we considered also the reactions and adaptation problems of other countries. I shall look in particular at the risks of negative response from the point of view of a small country like Sweden. I do this because the trends in Sweden are surely not unique.

Of course, Sweden is in several respects a privileged small country, having attained affluence, full employment, as well as social goals. Sweden has so far been relatively liberal as to import policies toward developing countries. But new tendencies are appearing. Having "solved" many of the standard policy aims, it seems as if the Swedes are creating new serious problems that may block desired adaptation processes. Of course I do not mean that it is important for LDCs what little Sweden does. When lecturing abroad about

Swedish policy questions I find—although Sweden's importance as such is insignificant—that people like to hear about Sweden's ways either as a warning example or as a picture of other countries' probable future. It is in the latter sense that I now give you three types of structural trends that have rather an unfortunate bearing on our problems and also may be generalized to other countries.

1. There is the problem of *weak and big government*. This combination is quite bad. Governments in the Western democracies are weak, uncertain as to their longevity in face of coming elections. This makes them shortsighted, looking for quick results from their policies. At the same time, the impact of central government on the economy is big and rising. In Sweden 50 to 60 percent of the total gross incomes flows through government channels. What is especially dangerous from the point of view of an adaptation process is the increasing government intervention in private business, with direct and indirect subsidies to capital and labor. The modern neomercantilist state means a complicated mix of government and business for rather short-term stability aims and that mix mostly seems to lead away from market flexibility.

2. There is in Sweden a *new trend in full employment policy*. The old flexibility norm of the 1950s and 1960s is losing ground rapidly. The Swedish full employment and labor market policies that worked so well from the adaptation point of view are being radically transformed. In the 1960s the structural adaptation to rapidly rising imports and changing demand was supported by means of active labor market policies (reeducation, training programs, compensation for migration, and so forth). A large part of the rapid rise in industrial productivity was in fact due to the effective shift of labor and capital resources from less to more productive plants and industries.

During the 1970s, attitudes have changed rather radically. The social costs of structural shifts and high mobility of labor are now considered too high. Full employment has now got a new dimension, implying *security of the job,* implying a minimum of movement to other plants and regions, combined with sharply increased difficulties and costs in dismissing employees. Labor is thus becoming more of a fixed cost for each firm than earlier. This tendency has, from the flexibility point of view, become aggravated by the rising ambition of labor to participate in decision making at all levels of plant and corporation management. All this will mean much more rigidity in the structure of production and employment and less of the type of flexibility that the adaptation to rapidly multiplying manufacturing imports from LDCs would demand.

3. *Slower growth of GNP* will also tend to make a positive response to LDC demands still more problematic. Such retardation of growth that has already occurred and is built into the five-year forecasts follows from the rising obstacles to labor mobility and the continued shift of resources to services and to the public sector. These tendencies are strengthened by various kinds

of efforts to equalize incomes—the squeezing of profit margins and the countering of market forces that tend to widen the low wage differentials between skilled and unskilled labor.

These observations regarding developments in Sweden are put forward in order to point out rising obstacles to a desired generous and liberal response from the side of developed countries to the needs of rapidly rising exports of manufactured goods from the ˙LDCs. The possibilities of attaining an improved international order very much depend on how well the market functions *within* the developed countries; and my analysis of the factors at work in Sweden is an unhappy one from this viewpoint.

Since the establishment of improved international division of work with rapidly increasing trade is therefore likely to meet serious obstacles because of slow policy response from the side of the DCs, *official aid* over a long period would appear to be a necessary complement to trade. We have discussed the need for increased direct aid to LDCs far too little at this conference. I would like to end by raising the question of why the supply of official aid from the various DC governments is generally so weak and varies so much with regard both to size and trend (in relation to GNP). The big variability of political responses to the tremendous aid needs of especially the poorest developing countries is an interesting question that should be examined. Why is the share of official aid so relatively high in a small country such as Sweden—approaching one percent of GNP—and so small in a big country like the United States? There should be no difference between the DCs as to knowledge of poor results, frustrations with performance, apprehensions that aid funds do not reach the poor in the poor countries, and so forth. In Sweden there is, in spite of all such worries, a general acceptance of the necessity of granting a rising share of aid. All political parties agree on this; there are only some differences as to the selection of countries for bilateral aid. I cannot find any other "explanation" for this than the "egalitarian spirit" that, for good and bad, has been established *inside* a country like Sweden and that seems in a very half-hearted way to extend beyond its boundaries. I consider that this problem of the varying DC response to aid demand merits serious scrutiny—as it doubtless has an important bearing on the outcome of any efforts at constructing a new international economic order.

7. Ali A. Mazrui

Why should the workers of Detroit be taxed in order to subsidize the ruling elite of Zaire? Why is the French government to be congratulated for forcing the dockworkers of Marseille to help subsidize the petty bourgeoisie of the Ivory Coast? In short, why should the poor of the industrialized North transfer resources to the seemingly self-indulgent rulers of the Third World?

These are important moral questions. The debate on these issues has not, however, distinguished sufficiently among alternative concepts. When we ask the affluent countries to transfer resources to the developing countries, are we confusing the interests of Third World *governments* with the interests of their *societies*? Or are we confusing the interests of *societies* with the interests of *individuals*? Or are we mistaking aid to governments for aid to individuals? Or are we equating countries with people? These are different levels of confusion. Yet some participants in this workshop have not always recognized that in the concepts of *people, country, society,* and *individual* we have four categories and not merely two.

Another confusion is between charity and economic justice. Charity is indeed praiseworthy—but logically it implies going beyond the call of duty. When giving money to the poor becomes an enforced obligation, it is no longer charity. Some influential participants at this workshop have assumed that the demand for a new international economic order is a demand for new forms of charity. We have been reminded that "the Christian tradition of charity runs deep in the Western industrial nations."

The old school of foreign aid was to some extent a charitable impulse. Within that context, aid totally without strings should have been regarded as an insult to human dignity. For such aid, were it indeed given without strings, would have been unmitigated charity. And charity is not a relationship between equals, however virtuous it may be. Aid without strings never occurs among genuine equals. Any transfer of resources from, say, Britain to France, must always be conditional on some kind of a quid pro quo. *Equality implies exchange.*

What the new international economic order demands is a new basis of exchange in an interdependent world. Questions concerning commodity stabilization, indexation, monetary reforms, and even foreign aid as a form of international compensation, now go beyond "alms for the love of Allah"! Such demands have now been translated into "justice for the love of man." One need not be an atheist to affirm—with Karl Marx—that in this world of the here and now "the supreme being for man is man."

If I had left this meeting before the final day I would have been very depressed. The tone of many discussions during much of the meeting was characterized by skepticism on the part of several participants about almost all of the demands of those who ask for a new international economic order. In particular, Richard Cooper posed as a moral philosopher, suggesting that people owe distributive duties only to individuals and not to collectivities. If this were Dick's own position, it would be astonishing enough. But in addition Dick claims that he has been through the literature and has found that all of the main lines of ethical thought apply to individuals (or families), not to collectivities such as nations. Why then should rich countries (collectivities) transfer resources to poor countries (other collectivities)?

Dick must either have been very selective in the literature he consulted or very selective in how he interpreted the philosophical literature as a whole. He certainly seems to have ignored the whole collectivist school of morality from Plato to contemporary Marxian ethics. The literature is full of the rights and duties of classes, nations, races, castes, societies, and other collectivities. Plato discusses his Republic virtually as an individual writ large. He assigns duties and rights to guardians and auxiliaries in collectivist terms. Rousseau's General Will as the yardstick of public morality could hardly be more collectivist. And even the Benthamite calculus—to the extent to which it is predicated on the principle of "the greatest happiness of the *greatest number*"—has to rely on the idea of *gross* justice. The principle of utility carried the seeds of a collectivist approach to social justice. It is no wonder that toward the end of his life John Stuart Mill found himself increasingly attracted to socialism.

As for Marxism, it is surely the most influential and most obvious collectivist school of morality in history. I am surprised Dick Cooper did not notice it as he consulted ethical literature. In the words of Robert Tucker (1961, p. 233):

Marx . . . was essentially something other than an economist. He was a moralist who came to speak in the idiom of political economy, and *Capital* is basically a work of German philosophy in its post-Hegelian development into myth.

Even if Dick Cooper is right that *charity* is between individuals, he would still be wrong in assuming that *justice* is never between collectivities.

If Karl Marx anthropomorphically treated "the people" or "the proletariat," contemporary international law anthropomorphizes nation-states. Nation-states and their governments have a number of *international* economic duties already that an analyst like Dick Cooper presumably would insist upon. Among governmental duties Cooper would presumably recognize are duties to treat foreign firms as persons with corporate rights and entitlements. Would this not be an anthropomorphic treatment of transnational corporations? Those who oppose a moratorium on debt payment assume that poor *countries* have obligations to pay debts incurred by their governments—even when those governments have already been overthrown as "tyrants." This again is to anthropomorphize countries—forcing them to bear the burden of debts incurred and conceivably spent by some *individuals* in power at a given moment in time in the past. Why should we force poor *countries* to pay back what was borrowed by specific *individuals* two coups before the last one?

It looks as if people such as Cooper and Johnson want to have their rich "northern" cake and eat it too. When it comes to aid, poor countries should not be treated as persons; but when it comes to paying back debts, those same poor countries should be held accountable, regardless of which persons are currently in power or which persons received the loans in the first place.

Champions of the new international economic order, on the other hand, are not saying that countries should not be treated as moral agents. They are simply saying that international moral duties need to be redefined. International law—which grew out of the European state system and Western diplomatic history—needs to be amended now that the diplomatic arena has expanded and international actors have become diverse.

Paul Streeten has pointed out that our discussions so far have been singularly *ahistorical.* I agree. We should put the demand for a new international economic order more firmly in an international context.

The Western world evolved a new international *religious* order in the sixteenth and seventeenth centuries. The Peace of Augsburg of 1555 formalized the doctrine of *cuius regio eius religio.* The Holy Roman Empire came to be divided between Catholic and Lutheran princes, who in turn determined the religion of their countries. This was basically a doctrine of religious sovereignty—a doctrine of noninterference of one kingdom with the religious affairs of another.

But in fact the consequence was to give each prince the power to force his own religion down the throats of his subjects. A classic dilemma between collective sovereignty and personal privacy had come into being. How was this dilemma to be resolved? In order to secure the privacy of conscience for individuals should the collective sovereignty of the kingdom be violated? We are back to Dick Cooper's moral problem, but in an older and less secular version. Europe's new international religious order from the Treaty of Augsburg lacked an adequate legal infrastructure.

The stage was set for the Thirty Years' War in the following century. With the Treaty of Westphalia of 1648, Europe not only consolidated a new international religious order but also inaugurated a new international *legal* order. In the words of Hans Morgenthau (1963, p. 277):

These rules of international law were securely established in 1648, when the Treaty of Westphalia brought the religious wars to an end and made the territorial state the cornerstone of the modern state system.... On its foundation, the eighteenth and, more particularly, the nineteenth and twentieth centuries built an imposing edifice....

The "edifice" Morgenthau is referring to is precisely that of a new international legal order, which has continued to the present day.

But meanwhile two world wars shook the twentieth century. And Europe experienced the horrors of the Third Reich, Japan the agony of nuclear destruction, and the rest of the world the deprivations and dislocations of global conflict. The Nuremberg trials helped to redefine aspects of morality and gave coherence to the idea of "crimes against humanity." The formation of the United Nations signified that new global institutions were needed. The anticolonial movements in Asia and Africa heralded new triumphs for the principle of self-determination. And racism based on color all over the world found itself increasingly on the defensive. We were witnessing the birth pangs of a new international *moral* order.

It is partly on the basis of that new moral order that we now hear demands for a new international economic order. Indeed, the latter hardly makes sense without a redefinition of international morality itself. The demand for a new international order is a culmination of a quest for appropriate norms to govern relations among collectivities—a quest that goes back to the Treaty of Augsburg of 1555 and far beyond.

Those who accuse the Third World of being "economically illiterate" may sometimes be political simpletons themselves. They may also be steeped in ahistorical naiveté.

Those who claim that the workers of Detroit should not be forced to subsidize the ruling elite of Kenya or Zaire are, unfortunately, the same ones who would be alarmed by the ruling elites of Kenya and Zaire going socialist. Salvador Allende paid with his life not because he was getting too elitist but because he was trying to transcend economic elitism in Chile.

When Third world leaders are elitist and corrupt, we are told that no dock-worker of Marseille should be forced to subsidize them. When Third World leaders are earnest and socialistic, and seek to end elitism and corruption, we are told that they are recklessly interfering with the market—and the dock-worker of Marseille must not subsidize them either.

It looks as if Third World leaders get it either way. They are either guilty of elitism or of socialism. They are either condemned as corrupt or as interfering with the market.

For the time being they are at best caught between the indignity of charity and the ambition of economic justice. Is it surprising that they long for some new international economic order?

References

Morgenthau, H., 1963, *Politics Among Nations: The Struggle for Power and Peace*, New York: Alfred A. Knopf, Third Edition.

Tucker, R., 1961, *Philosophy and Myth in Karl Marx*, Cambridge: Cambridge University Press.

8. Paul Streeten

Some of us had good fun exposing the elementary analytical errors of the commodity agreements advocated by UNCTAD. I should like to begin by putting these demands into their historical setting and helping us to understand the underlying reasons.

I believe that the call for an integrated commodity programme and the Common Fund (and the link, and preferences for manufactures) is the result of three phenomena: the disappointment with aid, the disappointment with political independence, and the success of OPEC.

Development aid, on which so many hopes were pinned in the 1950s and 1960s, was inadequate in amount and poor in quality. Intergovernmental aid negotiations led to pressures, frictions, and acrimony. Performance criteria and political, as well as economic, strings poisoned the atmosphere. It was this that led I. G. Patel to call for a "quiet style in aid." By this was meant a transfer of resources that was automatic or semiautomatic, hidden, or at least unconditional. We all know the proposition in welfare economics that it is best to allocate resources through competitive prices and to redistribute income through nondistorting lump sum taxes and subsidies. But we also know that all is for second-best in this best of all feasible worlds and that we may have to swallow the inefficiencies and some of the inequities of commodity agreements and cartels if we want any transfer at all.

The second cause of the call for automatic transfers is the disappointment with political independence that has not produced the hoped-for economic independence. True, most Latin American countries have been independent for a long time, but it is precisely from there that the doctrine of *dependencia* has emerged. It explains the demand for "sovereignty over resources" and the opposition to transnational companies and to the international rules of the game as they evolved after the war.

The third cause is the success of OPEC and a few other mineral producers. This success was accompanied by a change to a sellers' market and to world shortages of food and raw materials (temporary or permanent?). This encouraged developing countries to explore the scope for similar actions on other fronts.

In the controversy of stabilization *versus* jacking up prices, one is reminded of the well-known distinction between scholars and "practical men" (politicians and officials). Scholars reach agreement by sharpening distinctions and definitions; practical men reach agreement on action by blurring distinctions. As scholars, we wish to draw a sharp line between agreements that stabilize prices round an average trend, but when Third World practical men talk about "stabilization" they mean a combined operation of stabilizing and jacking up prices. Stabilization in the strict sense should be profitable. Like Joseph in Egypt, who, as a result of his fortunate dreams correctly foresaw the future, speculators should "do well by doing good" (in the words of Tom Lehrer's dope peddler). And any proposed stabilization scheme would have to take into account that it may, to some extent, simply replace private buffer stock holding and stabilization through futures markets. (It will also reduce consumers' surpluses, if linear supply fluctuates randomly, and reduce producers' surpluses if linear demand fluctuates randomly.)

The invisible and automatic nature of commodity agreements and producers' cartels that attempt to jack up prices has drawbacks for both efficiency and fairness. And one may ask two questions: Are they feasible?, Are they desirable? Even if, as I shall argue, they are not entirely desirable, one may wish to strengthen their stability: to paraphrase Harry Johnson's hucksters: "If something is not worth doing, it *is* worth doing well."

The feasibility and stability of an agreement will depend on the creation of a structure of incentives and penalties to prevent defection from the agreement and the growth of competition and substitution outside the agreement. The relative lack of success, in the past, is not necessarily a clue to the future.

Solidarity among developing countries is an important condition for their joint exercise of bargaining power. But solidarity is difficult to achieve. The reason for this is best illustrated by the case of a restrictive, price-raising cartel of primary product exporters, but it applies with equal force to other exercises of joint bargaining power.

Solidarity is difficult to achieve because the more effective a cartel or a cartel-like agreement, the greater is the reward for any one member who breaks it. But the fear that anyone may break the agreement will induce those who would otherwise be willing to adhere to prepare for the breakup. For, sticking to an agreement while others abandon it makes the loyal members worse off than they would have been without any agreement. The potential defectors cherish the *hope* of operating *outside* the agreement. But this encourages in the conformers the *fear* of a situation *without* the agreement. This fear is ever present, even if there are no actual or potential defectors. The fear itself leads to actions that undermine the agreement. Action outside the agreement is an ever-present hope and action without the agreement an ever-present threat.

Those emphasizing solidarity, joint actions, common fronts, that give rise to such unstable situations *should, therefore, pay attention to instituting a system of rewards and penalties that shifts the incentives so as to make the unstable solution stable.*

Important sources of rewards in commodity agreements are diversification funds and technical assistance to diversification. These have a double virtue. First, they compensate countries for restricting supplies and, second, where opportunity costs are positive, they absorb resources in alternative uses, thereby reducing the danger of erosion of the cartel. Through geographical and commodity diversification, countries previously dependent on one or a few markets and one or a few crops or minerals or services can thereby be made more self-reliant and their loyalty to the cartel can be increased.

Another factor that will enhance the stability of the cartel is the ability of a supplier to do without any earnings, or with substantially reduced earnings, for a period. (This is one of the forces that strengthens OPEC.) Withholding supplies is a powerful weapon of the cartel. If a supplying country is not able to withhold supplies because it depends on earnings, the cartel can be strengthened by other members (of this cartel or of some other agreement), thus compensating the country for withholding supplies.

I suggest that more thought be given to the provision of powerful incentives, both rewards and penalties, that would make defection less attractive and therefore reduce the fear of defection by others. Relevant considerations in devising such a system of incentives will be: fair sharing with due regard for the needs of the poorest; reconciling differences in preferences for the distribution of net gains over time; differences in current and future costs of production and in the ability to hold reserves.

Even if commodity agreements can be made to work, they may be criticized on grounds of desirability. From the point of view of accelerating development in the Third World and of promoting a more equal income distribution, they have certain drawbacks.

First, there is the question of the internal and international distribution of gains from price increases. The beneficiaries of these cartels may be large farmers, plantation owners, or mine owners, who belong to the rich in poor countries, and the consumers hit by price increases may be the poor in rich countries. If these plantations or mines are owned by rich foreigners, say, by transnational companies, the benefits, or part of the benefits, take the form of aid or redistribution to the rich countries.

Second, many poor countries, and the largest ones among them, have few commodities that lend themselves to successful cartelization (tea and jute are poor commodities, produced by very poor countries) and rely heavily on imports of commodities more readily cartelized or on imports of manufactures that incorporate these materials and that are exported by relatively better-off countries. Unless compensatory development aid is concentrated on these importers or unless safeguards are built into the commodity agreements, divisions within the so-called Third World will be aggravated. In addition, some rich countries are exporters of commodities that would benefit from cartels. Developing countries account for only 30 percent of world exports in nonfuel commodities, though they would benefit, unevenly, from agreements on the commodities proposed for the Common Fund.

The World Bank has calculated that developing countries containing about 300 million people are likely to benefit substantially from the rise in the price of oil, as a result of improved terms of trade in 1980, another 100 million mineral producers are unaffected, and 1,600 million in developing countries are likely to suffer a serious deterioration. The poorest countries will be the most seriously affected.

Third, the developing countries most likely to benefit from commodity agreements will tend to be small countries in whose economy foreign trade plays a relatively important part. But it is precisely these countries that already get more aid per head than large countries. The so-called small-country effect of development aid would be reinforced by commodity agreements, unless the rise in import prices due to the cartelization of imported commodities wiped out any benefits they derived from rises in their export prices.

Fourth, where commodity agreements require quota arrangements (rather than buffer stocks) both between producing countries and within each country, high-cost producers are favored over low-cost producers and the latter find it more difficult to expand their production. While the forces of competition continue to operate through a cartel (a cartel is the continuation of competition by other means, as Clausewitz nearly said), and to that extent to make it less stable, insofar as it succeeds in achieving stability, it discriminates against low-cost producers and adaptation to technical change.

Fifth, such restrictions are not only inefficient but are also inequitable, when they fall more severely on the supply of the poorer producers within member countries (small farmers) and of poorer countries.

Sixth, while jacking up export receipts increases the *means* to diversification, industrialization, and general development, it simultaneously reduces the *incentive* to do so. Successful cartelization may therefore delay or impede the growth of industrial exports in which the countries may have a long-term comparative advantage.

Not all commodity agreements aiming at higher average export prices (contrasted with those aiming merely at stabilization of prices) need take the form of a confrontation between exporting and importing countries. The United States used the threat of a grain cartel in an attempt to beat OPEC. But producers and consumers have cooperated on a sugar agreement, a coffee agreement, and others. The main interest of consumers in remunerative prices for producers is that these ensure higher levels of investment and therefore continuing supplies. Very low prices, on the other hand, tend to discourage investment and to lead to excessive dependence on imports. They carry the seeds of future shortages and deprivation of supplies. Short-term restrictions, leading to very high prices, tend to encourage the growth of substitutes and economies in the use of the product, and thereby carry the seeds of future surpluses. There is, therefore, an area in which producers' and consumers' interests coincide. Both will want to avoid setting a price that, though in their short-term interest, is self-defeating in the long run. A higher average level of prices, combined with a larger volume of production, can therefore be in the interest of both consumers and producers.

In the light of all this, you will see that, like an inverted Voltaire, I agree with everything Harry Johnson says, but I will fight his right to say it (especially in his particular way).

Name Index

This index does not include note and reference citations.

Subject Index

"Abnormal competition," 162
Abu Dhabi, 204
"Additionality," question of, 92
Adjustment costs, 186-190
Administrative controls, for international
  trading system, 230
Africa
 drought in, 18
 effects of carry-over program on, 267-
  268, 269
Agencies. *See also* Aid programs; Foreign
  aid
 international aid, 28-29
Agreements
 commodity, 240, 348, 375-378
 international, 220
 on textiles, 169, 170, 193, 212
Agriculture
 and government intervention, 225-226,
  229
 and GSPs, 237
Aid programs, 2. *See also* Development
  assistance; Foreign aid
 allocation of, 27, 30-40
 attitudes toward, 4-5
 budgetary requirements for, 80
 and income distribution, 91-93
 link, 101 (*see also* Link)
 and population size, 32, 33
 purposes of, 371
 technology and, 309
 for transferring food, 19
Algeria
 ICOR for, 45
 and increase in oil prices, 40
"Algerian-style" rhetoric, 14
Alliance for Progress, 93
Allocation
 in periods of great scarcity, 365
 of research and development, 321
Andean Pact, 297, 301
Anticolonialism, 374
Anti-inflationary policy, 174
Anti-trust policies, 358
Appropriability, of information, 326-328,
  332, 337
"Appropriability problem," 319
Argentina
 debt-relief proposals for, 65-66
 grain policy of, 276

technology screening procedures of, 303
Arrangement Regarding International
  Trade, in Textiles, 169, 170, 193, 212
Article XIX, of GATT, 160-161, 165, 170,
  171, 172, 174-175, 192, 193
Associations, producers, 203, 204, 348
Australia
 export controls of, 206
 grain policy of, 276
 primary products of, 209

Balance of payment crisis, 79
Bananas, tariffs on, 363
Bangladesh
 economic problems of, 367
 grain insurance programs for, 266
Bank credits, developing countries' bonds
  as, 59
Banks, and commodity trade, 246
Bargaining
 multidimensional, 313
 tariffs, 362
Bauxite
 international association for, 199, 203
 tariffs on, 363
"Benign intent," 3
"Benign neglect," 2, 364
Benthamite calculus, 372
Bhagwati-Ramaswami-Srinivasan proposition, 190
Bhagwati tax proposal, 126, 127-128,
  131-133. *See also* Tax, emigration
Bilateralism, 232
Bonds, issued by developing countries, 59
Borrowing
 after debt relief, 59
 by developing countries, 69-70, 96
 growth of, 51
 sanctions against, 59
Brain drain. *See also* Tax, emigration
 gains from, 125
 tax on, 17, 134-135
Brazil
 aid programs for, 45
 export controls of, 206
 and Fourth World, 348
 international role of, 351
 price leadership of, 204
 technology screening procedures of, 303